T0391021

THE BELT AND ROAD INITIATIVE AND THE WORLD'S LARGEST SMALL COMMODITY MARKET

Yiwu Business Circle

WSPC-ZJUP Series on China's Regional Development

Print ISSN: 2661-3883
Online ISSN: 2661-3891

Series Editor
SHI Jinchuan *(School of Economics, Zhejiang University, China)*

Advisory Board Members
GU Yikang *(China Academy for Rural Development, Zhejiang University, China)*
MAO Dan *(School of Public Affairs, Zhejiang University, China)*
LU Lijun *(Zhejiang Institute of Administration, China)*
CHEN Lixu *(Zhejiang Institute of Administration, China)*
CHEN Shengyong *(School of Public Administration, Zhejiang Gongshang University, China)*

Since China's reform and opening-up in 1978, the world's most populous country has enjoyed rapid economic development. This book series sheds new light on China's phenomenal success by examining its regional development and disparity. The series starts from first few volumes focusing on Zhejiang province, one of the country's forerunners in economic, social and political transformation. These volumes analyse Zhejiang's local governance innovation, regional economic development, and social and cultural changes over the past few decades.

Published:

WSPC-ZJUP Series on China's Regional Development – Vol. 4

THE BELT AND ROAD INITIATIVE AND THE WORLD'S LARGEST SMALL COMMODITY MARKET

Yiwu Business Circle

LU Lijun

Zhejiang Institute of Administration, China

et al.

Translated by

SHEN Xuhua, ZHOU Yiyu

ZHEJIANG UNIVERSITY PRESS
浙江大学出版社

World Scientific

NEW JERSEY · LONDON · SINGAPORE · BEIJING · SHANGHAI · HONG KONG · TAIPEI · CHENNAI · TOKYO

Published by

World Scientific Publishing Co. Pte. Ltd.

5 Toh Tuck Link, Singapore 596224

USA office: 27 Warren Street, Suite 401-402, Hackensack, NJ 07601

UK office: 57 Shelton Street, Covent Garden, London WC2H 9HE

and

Zhejiang University Press
No. 148, Tianmushan Road
Xixi Campus of Zhejiang University
Hangzhou 310028, China

Library of Congress Cataloging-in-Publication Data
Names: Lu, Lijun, 1944– author.
Title: The Belt and Road Initiative and the world's largest small commodity market :
    Yiwu Business Circle / Lijun Lu.
Description: Hangzhou : Zhejiang University Press ; New Jersey : World Scientific, [2020] |
    Series: WSPC-ZJUP series on China's regional development, 2661-3883 ; vol. 4 |
    Includes bibliographical references and index.
Identifiers: LCCN 2019049583 | ISBN 9789813279599 (hardcover)
Subjects: LCSH: Yi dai yi lu (Initiative : China) | Economic development--China--Yiwu Shi. |
    Market towns--China--Yiwu Shi. | Yiwu Shi (China)--Commerce. |
    Yiwu Shi (China)--Economic conditions.
Classification: LCC HF3840.Y588 L84 2020 | DDC 381.095124/2--dc23
LC record available at https://lccn.loc.gov/2019049583

British Library Cataloguing-in-Publication Data
A catalogue record for this book is available from the British Library.

For any available supplementary material, please visit
https://www.worldscientific.com/worldscibooks/10.1142/11256#t=suppl

Desk Editors: Anthony Alexander/Lixi Dong

Typeset by Stallion Press
Email: enquiries@stallionpress.com

About the Author

**Lu Lijun**, former director of the Institute of Theoretical Studies of Zhejiang Administration College, the first dean of the School of Economics of Zhejiang Gongshang University and of the School of Economics and Management of Zhejiang Normal University, is currently a Distinguished Professor of Zhejiang Normal University, Chief Expert of Hangzhou International Urban Studies Research Center and of Zhejiang Urban Governance Research Center. Since 1993, he has served as an advisor to the Yiwu Municipal People's Government and director of the Yiwu Market Economic Research Institute. His main research interests are political economy, regional economy, professional market, and circulation modernization.

Contents

Conclusion Expansion of "Yiwu Business Circle", Innovation of "Yiwu Development Experience"

Bibliography

Introduction to
2019 Edition

The first author of this book has proposed the concept of originality of "Yiwu Business Circle" so as to sum up the cross-region division of labor collaboration network established by the relevant regions and economic subjects in Yiwu, where the largest global small commodity market locates those at home and abroad. The good news is that 10 years later "Yiwu Business Circle" has achieved further expansion and has withstood the test of time in the unpredictable international and domestic economic environment. It has a strong business flow, logistics, capital flow, and information flow platform established and shared by global production, trade enterprises, and general merchants, which highly fits the concept orientation and construction mechanism of "The Silk Road Economic Belt" and "The 21st-Century Maritime Silk Road" (hereinafter referred to as the Belt and Road). The relevant regions and economic subjects associated with "Yiwu Business Circle" have brought positive influence over the economic and social development of Yiwu and formed a good relationship of mutual benefits and harmonious symbiosis while making contributions to the construction of the cross-region division of labor collaboration network, evolving towards the value of community.

I New Development of "Yiwu Business Circle" between 2006 and 2016

1. The reform and development of the core area of the business circle leaps into a new stage

1.1 Small commodity market innovations and integration have attained great development

Since 2006, Yiwu has made great efforts to develop e-commerce and modern logistics in order to adapt to the trend of modern information technology, especially following the big outbreak of the Internet economy and the intrinsic requirements of reform and innovation of the business mode. The market of simple commodity suppliers is transforming into one of the integrated service providers. The market function further expands towards commodity exhibitions, information distribution, price formation, tourism services, product innovation, technology exchanges, standard development, rule output, and other complex directions.

The trading mode transforms from the traditional cash, spot goods, and spot transactions to negotiating orders, e-commerce, logistics, and other modern trading modes. It has taken the lead in establishing online-offline integrated, format structure-diversified, trading means-electronized and service functions-combined modern new specialized markets in the country. It has also made efforts to enlarge the import and re-export markets, and speed up the "going-out" pace of the market to push it to be a real international trade center of "Buying from the World and Selling to the World". Since October 2006, the "Yiwu–China Commodity Index", which was compiled by the Ministry of Commerce, has been regularly published globally and has become the "weather vane" and "barometer" of global commodity production trade price changes; in October 2008, Yiwu released and implemented the first domestic industry standard of *Specific Commodity Classification and Codes*, providing the global commodity with a "Yiwu Classification" which has opened up broader space for China's consumer goods to go forward to the international mainstream market.

In recent years, in order to promote benign interaction and integrative development of the online and offline market, Yiwu has vigorously developed e-commerce and committed to building a global net goods marketing center, a national e-trader cluster center, and a cross-border e-commerce highland so as to create an international e-commerce capital. To this end, Yiwu relies on the real market, renovates the traditional purchase and sale mode, and makes full use of professional e-commerce platforms, APP mobile information platforms, Weibo, WeChat, and other marketing tools. Its purpose is to vigorously cultivate and develop the online intangible market and focus on promoting integrative development of the intangible market and the real market, showing a situation of organic online-offline interaction and cooperative development. At present, Yiwu, with its domestic trade and foreign trade net traders density respectively ranking the first and second among all cities in the country, has ranked top of "100 Excellent E-Commerce Counties in China" for three consecutive years, has released the world's first regional e-commerce development index "Yiwu E-commerce Development Index" and has become the only county-level city approved to create the national e-commerce demonstration city and carry out a county area e-commerce big data application statistics pilot. In recent years, it has implemented a large number of e-commerce projects including the Alibaba "Yiwu Industrial Belt", DHgate "Global Net Goods Center", IZP "Yiwu Global Sales" and import platform www.haixuan.com. Moreover, it has succeeded in holding seven consecutive China International Electronic Commerce Expos since 2011 and four consecutive World E-Commerce Conferences since 2014. In 2016, the city achieved an e-commerce turnover of 177 billion Yuan, which was 10.29 times that of 2009 (17.2 billion Yuan; the city started the statistics of the annual turnover of e-commerce in 2009), where the average annual growth rate reached 39.52%. At present, the number of e-commerce accounts registered in Yiwu has exceeded 250,000, and there have been more than 105,000 Taobao active sellers in the city (accounting for about 1.1% of the national total), 3,500 Tmall active shops (accounting for about 3% of the national total), 36,000 AliExpress sellers, 35,000 eBay sellers, 6,000 Amazon sellers and 4,500 Chinese supplier sellers. On October 21, 2012, Yiwu "China Commodity City" market's official website "Yiwugou" was launched and has gained rapid development in the past few years. The platform provides the market operators and global buyers with e-commerce services with tangible market characteristics. The operators can carry out shop management, product display, online transactions, foreign trade early warning, business communication, and other operations through the platform; the buyers can browse 3D panoramic shops, publish procurement demands, complaint about shop credit, as well as enjoy price credit, quality credit, service credit and other procurement protection through the platform. The unique shopping mode of "Yiwugou", i.e., the buyers click on the product in the panoramic shop to launch online purchase, restores the purchase in an offline real shop with the aid of information technology simulation, and provides a shopping experience that is not available on many online trading platforms. It can be said that the development of e-commerce has become a strong power source for the transformation and innovation of Yiwu commodity market.

The prosperity of the market has brought a great flow of people, information, and capital for the exhibition tourism industry of Yiwu; the booming of the exhibition tourism industry has further become an important impetus for functional innovation and level promotion of the market. The organic interaction and integrative development of the market and exhibition tourism have given birth to new formats and modes, but have also injected new momentum and vitality for the transformation and upgrading of the Yiwu manufacturing industry. Now, Yiwu has formed an exhibition economy system led by "China Yiwu International Commodities Fair (Yiwu Fair)", "China Yiwu Cultural Products Trade Fair", "China International Tourism Commodities Fair", "China Yiwu International Forest Products Fair", "China Yiwu International Manufacturing Equipment Expo", "China International Electronic Commerce Expo", "Yiwu Spring Fair: Imported Commodities Fair", and other national, large-scale brand exhibitions, and has been rated one of the top 10 exhibition cities in China. Driven by the huge market merchants flow, Yiwu's tourism industry, especially business travel, has attained rapid development. In December 2005, Yiwu International Trade City was approved as a national 4A level shopping tourism area, becoming the first shopping tourist attraction to receive the honor. In May 2016, Yiwu was successfully created as the first "China International Business Travel Destination" city. The "Silk Road No. 1" pedestrian street, located at District 5 of Yiwu International Trade City with an operating area of 5,000 square meters, integrates shopping, tourism, and leisure; it is committed to be built into a comprehensive scenic shopping location. Table 0.1 shows the statistical table of turnover of real market and e-commerce in Yiwu (2006–2016).

Table 0.1: **Statistical table of turnover of real market and e-commerce in Yiwu (2006–2016)**

Year	Annual turnover of real market (100 million Yuan)	Annual turnover of e-commerce (100 million Yuan)
2006	415.0	—
2007	460.1	—
2008	492.3	—
2009	556.1	172
2010	621.1	250
2011	677.9	347
2012	758.8	520
2013	879.5	856
2014	1,073.9	1,153
2015	1,244.5	1,511
2016	1,371.7	1,770

Source: Statistical Bulletin of National Economic and Social Development in Yiwu City (2006–2016), Yiwu E-Commerce Work Leading Group Office.

1.2 Industrial transformation and upgrading strides forward

Since 2006, Yiwu has rigorously implemented the "Four-Replacement and Three-Fame" project for the purpose of enhancing quality, brand, and efficiency. The transformation and upgrading of the traditional competitive industries was vigorously promoted, focusing on the development of new materials, electronics & electrical appliances, biology, auto parts, and other emerging industries. Yiwu has actively cultivated and developed daily fashion consumer goods, information network economy, advanced equipment manufacturing, and food & medicine. These four strategic industries pushed industrial development to transform from being investment-driven to being innovation-driven and from resource dependence to technological support, striving to build a modern industrial

system driven by both the modern service industry and advanced manufacturing industry. At present, the city has established 14 national industrial bases, and has become the world's second largest seamless underwear industry base, forming an industrial chain with both scale advantage and cost performance advantage as well as increasingly prominent features of industrial development agglomeration, industrial structure upgrading, and high-end trend of industrial competition. Over the past 10 years, the city has fostered seven main board listed companies, 11 new OTC listed enterprises, and 66 regional stock exchange center listed enterprises, and a number of well-known enterprises, e.g. Neoglory Jewelry, Soton Drinking Straws, Easy Open Lid, Diyuan Instrument, etc., have emerged.

In order to enhance the level of industrial development, in recent years, Yiwu has set up intensive green ideas in the industrial development, adhered to "Yield Per Mu Base", and constantly deepened the market-oriented reform of resource elements to create a good environment for industrial economic development. Since 2013, it has carried out several comprehensive evaluations of yield benefit per mu. In 2015, it has revised the comprehensive evaluation method of the yield benefit per mu, dividing enterprises into A, B, C, D types. The city has implemented policies of differentiated allocation of resource elements including an urban land use tax, differentiated water and electricity prices and environmental resources, etc., and strived to allocate more limited resource elements to the high-quality enterprises in good financial health, with a high yield benefit per mu, and great social contribution. At the same time, it has deeply promoted the "Four-Replacement and Three-Fame" project[1] and introduced

---

[1] "Four-Replacement and Three-Fame" is a policy of Zhejiang Province to promote economic transformation. "Four-Replacement" refers to "replacing old industries with new industries", "replacing labor with machines", "replacing land with high rate of output" and "replacing real market with e-commerce"; "Three-Fame" refers to famous enterprises, famous products and famous figures.

a number of Fortune Global 500 enterprises and domestically well-known foreign enterprises such as SK from the R. O. Korea, Chia Tai from the Thailand, Geely Group, ProLogis, Wuchan Zhongda Group, etc. The project has also implemented a large number of high-end industrial ventures, such as the Hualu BUPT (Yiwu) information culture maker space project with a total planned investment of 2 billion Yuan, Refond LED expansion and new energy project with a total planned investment of 2 billion Yuan, Z&L special vehicle project with a total planned investment of 2.2 billion Yuan, ProLogis (Yiwu) logistics park project with a total planned investment of USD 1.65 billion, Chia Tai Continental central kitchen, meat products deep processing, and supporting project with a total planned investment of 2.44 billion Yuan, HC SemiTek (Zhejiang) Co., Ltd. project with a total planned investment of 6 billion Yuan, Yiwu Forest Lighting LED lamps base project with a total planned investment of 5.5 billion Yuan, Zhejiang Aixu efficient solar cell project with a total planned investment of 6 billion Yuan, Sageset Networks Communications technology project with a total planned investment of 2.01 billion Yuan, etc. In the framework of strategic docking between the Belt and Road construction, "Made-in-China 2025", and German "Industrial 4.0", Yiwu relies on the Geely automobile project (including the Geely Fengrui engine project with a total planned investment of 2.065 billion Yuan, Geely Yili power assembly project with a total planned investment of 7.5 billion Yuan, Geely Yiwu new energy commercial vehicle project with a total planned investment of 7.2 billion Yuan, and Geely engine project with a total planned investment of 6.3 billion Yuan) and green power town construction that actively builds the Sino-European (Yiwu) Intelligent Park. With a planning area of 6.92 square kilometers and a total planned investment of 40 billion Yuan, the park focuses on introducing industrial technologies, development concepts and management experience of the European developed countries to vigorously develop the key automotive parts, high-end intelligent equipment, energy saving and environmental protection industries, and creating an innovation-driven "intelligent" highland.

In order to optimize and enhance the product structure and level, in recent years Yiwu has vigorously promoted scientific and technological innovation, implemented "Five Projects" of scientific and technological innovation, and has given full play to the leading role of modern technologies in industrial transformation and upgrading. It has introduced and built the National Daily-used Commodity Quality Supervision and Inspection Center, the National Commodity Quality and Safety Testing Key Laboratory, the National Tourism Commodity R&D Center and other national research and testing institutions and R&D bases. Yiwu has also established a large number of innovative and creative platforms including China Yiwu Industrial Design Center, Beijing Zhongguancun Off-site Incubator, Zhejiang "Recruitment Program of Global Experts" Yiwu Industrial Park, Chinese Academy of Sciences Shenyang Institute of Automation Yiwu Center, Chinese Academy of Sciences Guangzhou Institute of Electronic Technology Yiwu 3D Printing Engineering Application Center, Yiwu Korea Design Center, Yitai Creative Design Center, Virtual Research Institute of Research Institutes, Yiwu–Zhejiang University Incubator Center, Yiwu Innovation Park, Yiwu–UIBE Collaborative Innovation Center, China Academy of Art Zhejiang Modern Intelligent Manufacturing Promotion Center Yiwu Sub-center, etc., and set up government venture capital funds of 500 million Yuan to guide more society capital and corporate funds to open up financial and innovative channels and push the development of Yiwu's industry to transfer from being element-driven to innovation-driven. Meanwhile, Yiwu has also vigorously promoted the quality and brand system construction, and established the "Strong Quality City" development strategy in 2011 to strive to create a "National Strong Quality City–Demonstration City". In addition, it has attached great importance to brand creation and protection work. In 2016, its three indexes (effective trademark volume, the number of domestic trademark applications, and the number of domestic trademark registrations) ranked first among all counties in the country. Currently the city has a total of 22 well-known trademarks with administrative

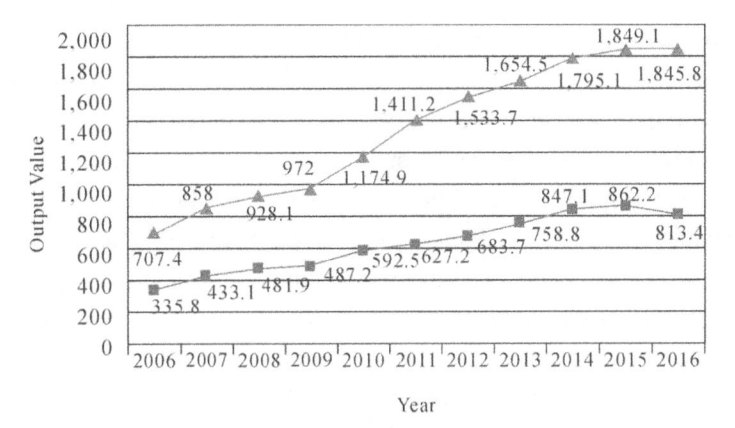

Year

— Industrial Output Value above the Designated Scale (100 million Yuan)

— Total Industrial Output Value (100 million Yuan)

Figure 0.1: Statistical diagram of Yiwu's industrial output value and total industrial output value above the designated scale (2006–2016)

Source: Statistical Bulletin of National Economic and Social Development in Yiwu City (2006–2016).

recognition, 144 provincial well-known trademarks, 46 provincial brand-name products, and five provincial trademark and brand bases (shirts, hosiery, zipper, jewelry and seamless underwear manufacturing); its comprehensive trademark and brand strength has ranked at the forefront of the counties in the country for many consecutive years. In May 2016, Yiwu became the first county-level city in Zhejiang Province to be awarded the "National Intellectual Property Demonstration City". Figure 0.1 shows the statistical diagram of Yiwu's industrial output value and total industrial output value above the designated scale (2006–2016).

1.3 Urban functional level and international recognition are dramatically enhanced

Since 2006, by adapting to the international trend, Yiwu has integrated its development with the new round of China's opening-up pattern, and made arrangements in consideration of the global

economic cooperation, industrial division, and construction of a world-class urban agglomeration in the Yangtze River Delta. It has endeavored to improve its internationally-oriented functions and service level, put great energy in molding itself into a world-renowned trade city and modern metropolitan area benefiting business, tourism, and residence, and has kept enhancing its international recognition. In recent years especially, Yiwu has been highly acclaimed by President Xi Jinping on six major international occasions successively. It has also experienced a rapid increase in urban size between 2006 and 2016, with the urban area expanding from 56 to 103 square kilometers, urban population growing from 540,000 to 980,000, and the urban road area growing from 10.9 million square meters to 15.162 million square meters. In 2014, it was selected as a comprehensive pilot city for the new urbanization program of China. From 2006 to 2016, Yiwu underwent a significant rise in its overall development level and comprehensive strength, while its regional GDP rose from 35.206 billion Yuan to 111.81 billion Yuan, showing a 2.18-fold increase and an annual growth rate of 12.25%; its per capita GDP calculated based on the registered household population has risen from 50,148 Yuan (about USD 6,300 after conversion as per the average exchange rate in 2006) to 143,972 Yuan (about USD 21,675 after conversion as per the average exchange rate in 2016), showing a 1.87-fold increase and an annual growth rate of 11.12%; the per capita disposable incomes of the urban and rural residents rose from 21,576 Yuan and 8,810 Yuan to 60,773 Yuan and 30,570 Yuan, respectively, showing a 1.82-fold and a 2.47-fold increase, and an annual growth rate of 10.91% and 13.25% (as shown in Table 0.2).

To follow the path of new urbanization, improve the urban functional level and internationalized level, further the upgrading of international trade, and promote its position in the international division of labor, in 2014, Yiwu has decided to construct three new zones: Silk Road New Zone, Land-Port New Zone, and Science and

Table 0.2: **Statistical table of key economic and social indicators of Yiwu (2006–2016)**

Year	2006	2007	2008	2009	2010	2011	2012	2013	2014	2015	2016
Regional GDP (100 million Yuan)	352.1	420.9	493.3	519.5	614.0	726.1	802.9	882.9	968.6	1,046	1,118.1
Per capita GDP (Yuan)	50,148	59,144	68,508	71,457	83,539	97,642	107,009	116,688	127,468	136,003	143,972
Urban per capita disposable income (Yuan)	21,576	25,007	28,708	30,841	35,220	40,078	44,509	48,962	51,899	56,586	60,773
Rural per capita disposable income (Yuan)	8,810	10,255	11,885	12,899	14,775	17,121	19,147	21,273	25,963	28,433	30,570
Built-up area (sq km)	56	73	78	83	90	96	100.1	100.5	102	103	105

Source: Yiwu Statistical Yearbook (2007–2017).

Innovation New Zone. Silk Road New Zone is planned and built with focuses on "global trade and international services". It has put great energy into cultivating industries concerning data information, international business, international convention and exhibition, trade finance, cultural services, cross-border e-commerce, etc., and consists of several blocks such as the international forum, international community, international services, and international culture, aiming to make Yiwu more adaptable to the international situation, and promote the foreign trade and economic cooperation, as well as the cultural and educational exchanges. Land-Port New Zone is planned and built with focuses on "providing convenient logistics and port services".

It consists of functional blocks such as domestic logistics, intelligent storage, express logistics, railway logistics, airport logistics, and comprehensive bonding. It has attached key attention to the cultivation of the modern logistics service, as well as auxiliary service industries including finance, insurance, and information, aiming to create a transportation platform integrating the railway, seaway, highway, and airline, as well as a "Sino-Euro" international railway container transport platform, and construct a number of airports and railway ports. Science and Innovation New Zone is planned and built with focuses on "forming a talent pool and pursuing growth driven by innovation". It has put great energy into cultivating and introducing institutions of higher learning and scientific and research institutes from home and abroad, and has gathered a crowd of high-level innovative talents of science and technology. This aims to provide more scientific and innovative elements for the Yangtze River Delta and other regions, create an urban platform integrating higher education, technical R&D, innovative designs, innovative services, scientific incubation and other functions, and form an atmosphere that attracts more innovative ideas for the city in the future.

To adapt to the developmental trend and requirements of modern information technology and advance the urban sustainable development, Yiwu has made efforts in recent years to promote the innovative application of new-generation information technologies such as Internet of Things, cloud computing, and big data, aiming to build itself into a smart city relying on those technologies. More endeavors have been made to promote information-based urban planning and management, provide intelligent infrastructure and convenient public services, further the modern industrial development, and refine social governance. In this connection, Yiwu has proactively promoted 10 key projects for the smart city, including the construction of a province-level pilot "smart mall", "smart governmental service", "smart sanitation", "citizen card" program, "smart education", "smart public transportation", "smart grid administration", a network management platform concerning the "smart water service, smart environmental protection and smart treatment of the sewage, prevention of the flood, drainage of the waterlog, protection of water supply and water conservation (or called "five-water treatment"[2] for short)", construction of the "smart logistics" system, as well as a geographical space framework built for the "digital Yiwu" program. By the end of 2016, Yiwu's Internet coverage reached 75%, higher than the average of the nation and Zhejiang Province (47.9% and 68.9%, respectively); almost the entire city has access to 4G network, and 99% of citizens have access to optical cables, making Yiwu meet the standards for an all-optical network city. It has a total of 9,000 free wireless APs; the free public wireless network in key public areas has been completed and put into operation. A data exchange platform and three fundamental databases (providing data related to the population, legal persons and spatial geography) have been completed lately, which enables the data exchanges among 12 government sectors respectively in charge of market supervision, construction, public security, land tax, national tax, administrative services, administrative enforcement of law, floating population management, human resource & social insurance, territory, civil administration, and sanitation. There are 20 demonstration digital schools, 20 demonstration digital labs, and 15 demonstration digital libraries built in Yiwu, making the "One-Card" services, including social medical care, available in the entire city.

To advance the new urbanization program, promote the organic integration of the "industry, city and citizens", and balance the urban and rural development in both economy and society, Yiwu has promoted the construction of several special towns in an orderly manner,

---

[2] It refers to sewage treatment, flood control, drainage, water supply and water saving.

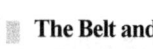

and made them the new highlights of urban economic and social development. By the end of 2016, a big pattern has taken shape in Yiwu, which is headed by the Silk Road Town (a province-level special town), followed by the Silk Road Charming Town, Land-Port Town, and Green Power Town (three city-level special towns in Jinhua), and backed by a number of special towns such as Light Source Science & Technology Town, Senshen Health Town, Cloud Express Town, Lemeng Town, Paradise Town, Beidou Town, Navigation Town, Education (National Science) Town, etc. To improve the taste of the city and harmonize the relations among humans and nature, economic and social development, and ecological environmental protection, Yiwu has endeavored to advance the "Beautiful Yiwu" program, and has meticulously implemented the "large-scale rural environment improvement and demonstration" project,[3] beautiful village program, "811" special actions (for three times),[4] "three renovations and one demolition",[5]

---

[3] It refers to taking village planning as the leading role, starting from the governance of "dirty, chaotic, poor and scattered" phenomena, to intensify the environmental improvement of villages and improve rural infrastructure, strengthen grass-root organizations and build democracy in rural areas, accelerate the development of social programs in rural areas, make a significant change in the appearance of rural areas, and accelerate the modernization of agriculture and rural areas.

[4] In October 2004, the "811" campaign against environmental pollution was launched for pollution control in Zhejiang Province. "8" refers to the eight major river systems in Zhejiang Province; "11" refers to the 11 cities in Zhejiang Province and 11 province-level key environmental protection administrative zones designated by the Zhejiang Provincial Government for outstanding regional and structural pollution control.

[5] It refers to the decision made by the Zhejiang Provincial Government to carry out in-depth renovation and demolition of illegal buildings in old residential areas, old factory areas and urban villages from 2013 to 2015 across the province.

"four-area three-aspect improvement",[6] "five-water treatment", and other environmental improvement measures. Thanks to those efforts, the urban environment quality keeps improving, and the quality of the water from all seven sections under provincial and municipal control and all three sections at the river boundary remain stable enough to meet the standards of Class III surface water. In 2016, Yiwu enjoyed 72.6% of days with good ambient air quality, 14 percentage points more than that of 2013 (it began to monitor the ambient air quality according to new national standards since 2013); its yearly average concentration of PM 2.5 in the atmosphere was 51 μg/m^3, a 22.7% decrease from 2013.

1.4 International trade comprehensive reform pilot project strides forward

Since 2006, as "Yiwu Business Circle" continues with its outward expansion and keeps strengthening the radiation power, the Yiwu wholesale market has played an increasingly significant role in the international small-commodity trade network. However, restricted by several factors, the current foreign trade management mechanism fails to meet the requirements proposed by Yiwu wholesale market (as a part of the "world market") for the international trade environment and services. For example, through years of development, a unique mode of foreign trade has taken shape in Yiwu wholesale market, in which the buyers purchase goods exported from a professional market instead of the manufacturers (also called the market-oriented trade). This mode, benefiting from features such as low unit price, a wide variety of products, rapid updating, small trading volume of an order,

---

[6] It refers to the project proposed by Zhejiang Provincial Party Committee and Provincial Government to carry out cleaning, greening and beautification operations in areas such as road side, railway side, river side and mountain side (referred to as "four-sided area").

a great many trading entities, LCL service, etc., cannot be compatible with the traditional monitoring and service system aimed at mass export trade. Therefore, it is urgent to build a complete set of policy systems, monitoring rules, and a uniform operation platform applying to the market-oriented trade in order to facilitate the clearance of exported goods purchased from the market. A well-developed "traceable" mechanism and monitoring system can ensure the clearance to be completed quickly and controlled easily, and achieve the convenient process, normalized regulation, and long-lasting effect in the meantime. In this connection, on March 4, 2011, the State Council has approved the launch of "Zhejiang Yiwu International Trade Comprehensive Reform Pilot Project" ("Yiwu Pilot Project" for short).

The proposal and launch of the "Yiwu Pilot Project" has an in-depth theoretical and practical foundation. As a process of change to a marketing system mainly relying on reductions in trade cost, it reflects the rules of institutional reform that the productive relations should meet the needs of development of the productive force, and the superstructure must go on with a good economic foundation. By launching this project, we mean to exploit and bring out the unique functions of the Yiwu wholesale market in the international trade network and division system; through bold explorations and trials, we aim to create an environment with looser and more convenient international trade policies, set up a normalized and efficient international trade monitoring system, and provide all-round services to ensure that international trade advances towards a convenient, normalized and high-end path. All those efforts are made to build Yiwu into an international center for the circulation, exhibitions, trades, information exchanges, and pricing of small commodities with low trade costs, good faith, convenient information communication, new means and good services. These efforts are also made to demonstrate China's transformation of a foreign trade development path, a significant base driving the industrial transformation and upgrading, a world-leading small commodity trade center, and a world-renowned trade city benefiting business, tourism and residence.

The launch of "Yiwu Pilot Project" is of special strategic significance to enhance our ability to reconstruct the global small-commodity value chain and the competitive strength of the medium, small, and micro-sized enterprises, transform China's foreign trade development mode, reform and innovate the administration mechanism, promote and balance the urban and rural development, etc. Particularly, it will dramatically promote the power of "Yiwu Business Circle" to reconstruct the global small-commodity value chain, further consolidate and enhance the Yiwu market's well-developed trade channels, control force, and right of speech in the world, and lead the professional markets and medium, small, and micro-sized enterprises in Zhejiang and all over China to transform their foreign trade development mode, facilitate the transformation and upgrading, expand their shares in the global market, and participate in the global labor-division and coordination network. All those efforts will help Chinese professional markets and medium, small and micro-sized enterprises gain new strengths in the international economic cooperation and competition under globalization.

Since the State Council approved the launch of "Yiwu Pilot Project" in March 2011, under the support of Provincial Party Committee and Government, the Party Committee and the Government of Yiwu carried forward the spirit conveyed by the approval, performed the tasks of the pilot project, and made breakthroughs in various fields successively. In face of small-commodity trade, which covers a wide variety of products and batches to be exported in small amounts and by means of LCL service (thus involving several parties), the government came up with the market-oriented trade mode. In April 2013, eight ministries and commissions, including the Ministry of Commerce, established the market-oriented trade mode by jointly issuing the official

document, and decided to put it into trial use in Yiwu. They also created a customs control code "1039", and carried out the reform by clearing customs based on classification, innovating the inspection & quarantine mechanism, promoting the convenient cross-border settlement, simplifying the tax control mechanism, innovating the control over business entities, and setting up a local comprehensive management mechanism. Those measures have fundamentally solved problems faced by the professional market while advancing foreign trade, such as the absence of targeted systems, and paved a new path for ease of the medium, small, and micro-sized enterprises to participate in international trade. With over 4 years of practice, this institutional innovation has played an increasingly notable role in advancing the international small-commodity trade: in 2016, the export volume achieved by applying the market-oriented trade mode accounted for 84.1% of the total export volume of Yiwu; the experience of Yiwu in practicing this mode has been gradually popularized all over the country. In September 2015, according to the Several Comments of the General Office of the State Council on Maintaining the Stable Growth of Export and Import Volume (GBF [2015] No. 55), the market-oriented trade mode has been further applied to Dieshiqiao International Home Textile Mall in Haimen, Jiangsu Province, and Haining Leather Mall in Zhejiang Province; in September 2016, subject to approval by eight ministries and commissions including the Ministry of Commerce, the mode has been applied to Jiangsu Changshu Garment Mall, Huadu Leather & Leatherware Mall in Guangzhou of Guangdong Province, Linyi Mall Engineering Material Market in Shandong Province, Hankoubei International Commodity Exchange Center in Wuhan of Hubei Province, and Baigou Bags & Suitcases Market in Hebei Province.

In addition, in March 2012, the State Council officially approved the Yiwu Economic Development Zone to be upgraded into a national economic development zone, making it the first national economic development zone established in a county region of the central and western part of Zhejiang Province; in November 2012, the Ministry of

Land and Resources approved the Special Scheme of Yiwu on Reform of the Land Management System for its International Trade Comprehensive Reform Pilot Project; in December 2012, the head office of the Bank of China officially approved Yiwu to launch the personal cross-border trade RMB settlement pilot project, making Yiwu the first pilot region in China; in August 2013, nine ministries and commissions including the Central Bank jointly issued the Special Financial Program for Yiwu International Trade Comprehensive Reform Pilot Project; on July 1, 2014, Yiwu became the first in China to launch the personal-trade foreign exchange control pilot project, and officially implemented the Rules on Control over Foreign Exchange from Personal Trade. To adapt to the economic globalization and further promote the open economic development of Yiwu, the Party Committee and Government of Yiwu also made great efforts and strived to build up several big platforms for open development, e.g., in February 2014, four ministries and commissions including the General Administration of Customs jointly approved the establishment of Yiwu's bonded logistics center (Type B), which started operation in November 2014; in December 2014, Yiwu's aviation port was officially opened to the public, while a cross-border e-commerce monitoring center was built up and put into operation; in December 2015, the State Port Management Office officially approved Yiwu West Railway Station to be opened as a temporary port, which made the Station the only temporary railway port of Zhejiang Province opened to the public; in May 2015, General Administration of Customs, State Post Bureau, and China Post approved the establishment of Yiwu International Mail Exchange Bureau and Station, which was completed and put into operation on December 31, 2015.

1.5 Become a key foothold of the Belt and Road Initiative

Since President Xi Jinping proposed the Belt and Road Initiative in 2013, Yiwu has fully involved itself in the cause. The city has put great energy into promoting the planning and construction of the Silk Road New Zone, Land-Port New Zone, etc., cultivating, expanding, and strengthening the African Product Exhibition & Sale Center, China–

ASEAN Commodity Trade Center, Central and Eastern European Product Exhibition & Sale Center, and other important trade exchange platforms aimed at countries and regions along the Belt and Road. Yiwu has opened Yiwu–Xinjiang–Europe railway line ("YXE line" for short), and proceeded with the establishment of new stations, line expansion, and efficiency improvements. It also has taken active part in the construction of Yiwu–Ningbo–Zhoushan Grand Open Channel, and dedicated to molding itself into a two-way "bridgehead", also a key foothold of the Belt and Road Initiative.

As early as the end of 1990s, merchants from Pakistan, Afghanistan, India, Iran, Iraq, UAE, Yemen, Jordan, Syria, Egypt and other countries and regions along the Belt and Road had settled in and set up purchase points in Yiwu successively. Through long-term trading, investment, and labor, they have built up close ties with Yiwu through cooperation in personnel, trade, culture, and science and education. Yiwu has made trade contacts with 64 countries along the Belt and Road, and achieved an export-import volume up to 114.54 billion Yuan in 2016 through trading with those countries, accounting for 51.38% of the total export-import volume of Yiwu; the export volume totaled 113.99 billion Yuan, showing a year-on-year growth of 4.86%, accounted for 51.78% of the total export volume of Yiwu.

On September 26, 2014, when meeting with Spain's Prime Minister Mariano Rajoy, President Xi Jinping said: "As planned, the YXE railway line will start from Yiwu, Zhejiang, and end at Madrid (terminus). We warmly welcome the Occident to participate in the construction and operation of the railway." On November 18, the YXE line, which begins from Yiwu, runs through Alataw Pass of Xinjiang, and ends in Madrid, the capital of Spain, was officially opened. It then grew into a safe, efficient, and convenient Sino-Euro international trade channel, and dramatically strengthened the aggregation and radiation effect of "Yiwu Business Circle" on countries and regions along the Belt and Road. By the end of 2016, eight new lines have been built to connect the five countries in Central Asia (Alam-Ata), Iran (Teheran), Afghanistan (Mazar-i-Sharif), Russia (Chelyabinsk), Latvia (Riga), the Republic of Belarus (Minsk), and UK (London), making YXE line rank first among all China–Europe lines in overseas cities it can reach, and categories of goods it has carried. Yiwu became the city with the most China–Europe lines opened in China. By the end of 2016, YXE trains had run for 139 round trips, and carried a total of 10,566 TEUs. On the 118 onward trips, a total of 9,966 TEUs had been delivered; the trains from Yiwu to Madrid had run for 97 trips, carrying a total of 8,074 TEUs; the trains from Yiwu to Russia had run for 6 trips, carrying 580 TEUs; the trains from Yiwu to the Republic of Belarus had run for 1 trip, carrying 92 TEUs; the trains from Yiwu to Afghanistan had run for 11 trips, carrying 984 TEUs; the trains from Yiwu to Iran had run for 1 trip, carrying 64 TEUs; the trains from Yiwu to Latvia had run for 1 trip, carrying 84 TEUs; and the trains from Yiwu to London had run for 1 trip, carrying 88 TEUs in total. On the 21 return trips, a total of 600 TEUs had been delivered. At the very beginning, only small commodities from Yiwu were exported via YXE international container trains; now roughly 2,000 kinds of products "Made in China" from eight provinces and municipalities such as Zhejiang, Anhui, Fujian, and Shanghai have been involved. Those trains also have carried goods imported from UK, Germany, Spain, etc., including milk powder, products for babies, electronic products, electric tools, red wine, olive oil, soda water, furniture, ceramic ornaments, agricultural and sideline products which are "Made in Europe", building up a two-way trade pattern. On May 13, 2017, when meeting with Spain's Prime Minister Mariano Rajoy who came to China to attend the Belt and Road Forum for International Cooperation, President Xi Jinping highly affirmed the development of YXE railway lines. He said: "The railway line from Yiwu to Madrid, once put into operation, will become a crucial bridge connecting the Eurasia, and an early outcome achieved by the Belt and Road. We should leverage our own strengths, and launch pragmatic cooperation in a great deal of fields."

In recent years, Yiwu has taken active part in the construction of Yiwu–Ningbo–Zhoushan Grand Open Channel, a major project established by the Zhejiang Provincial Party Committee and Government to support the Belt and Road Initiative. By developing intermodal freight transport, such as sea-railway transportation and highway-railway transportation, Yiwu has gradually achieved synergetic development between Yiwu Land Port and Nongbo Zhoushan Seaport. In November 2014, Yiwu, as the port of departure, dispatched its first sea-railway intermodal freight train from Yiwu to the Beilun Port of Ningbo. The seaport is now dispatching five trains a week under routine operation. In 2016, the sea-railway intermodal freight trains from Yiwu to Beilun Port carried a total of 24,600 TEUs, showing a 50% increase from the previous year, accounting for roughly 10% of the year-round sea-railway intermodal transport volume of Ningbo Zhoushan Port. Yiwu has been closely cooperating with Ningbo and Zhoushan in customs, inspection, and quarantine, making part of the functions of Ningbo Zhoushan Port available in Yiwu (allowing people to pick up and return containers to the port just in Yiwu). Thanks to those efforts, Yiwu Land Port can deal with export & import activities far away from surrounding provinces and municipalities, and the range of aggregation and radiation of "Yiwu Business Circle" has been greatly expanded, making Yiwu an "international land-port city", and a key node to connect the maritime silk road with the land silk road.

2. Radiation range and capacity of the business circle has increased significantly

2.1 Domestic and foreign trade aggregation and radiation level has been significantly improved

Since 2006, Yiwu has established a close relationship with more and more domestic and foreign regions and economic entities. More manufacturers and dealers have sold their products globally through the Yiwu market; more traders and retailers have also purchased goods worldwide through the Yiwu market, which has made it grow substantially in many aspects such as the transaction size, space scale, commodity size, the main scale, and so on. The gathering level of "Yiwu Business Circle" has improved continuously and the scope of radiation has been expanded day by day. From 2006 to 2016, the turnover of the whole Yiwu market increased from 41.5 billion Yuan to 137.17 billion Yuan, an increase of 2.31 times the average annual growth rate of 12.7%; the total market area rose from 2.6 million square meters to 6.4 million square meters, an increase of 1.46 times; business shops increased from 50,000 to more than 75,000, an increase of 50%; goods for trading from more than 400,000 single products to more than 1.80 million single products, an increase of 3.5 times. Finally, the number of market entities increased from 93,700 to 326,000, an increase of 2.48 times.

Since 2006, with the improving gathering level and rising radiation scope of "Yiwu Business Circle", more and more domestic regions have established close production and marketing relationships with Yiwu. At present, the market has connected more than 200,000 small, medium, and micro-sized domestic enterprises, which has directly created more than 10 million jobs for industrial workers. In particular, the radiation range of the processing industry has been expanded, involving over 3.5 million rural surplus laborers (mostly left-behind women and old people with working ability) from 31 provinces (municipalities and autonomous regions) in China. Connecting with the Yiwu market facilitates the medium, small, and micro-sized enterprises to participate in international trade, which also provides a solid industrial support for the development of the market, including foreign trade. For example, on October 22, 2016, the Reservoir Resettlement Authority of Xianju (Zhejiang Province) signed a strategic agreement with Yiwu City Federation of Processing Technology, where in the coming 5 years, the city will provide a material processing business valuing at least 200 million Yuan to Xianju County, and train 1,500 qualified processing brokers. On March 23, 2017, cadres of Women's Federation of Guixi City of Jiangxi Province along with processing brokers visited Zhejiang Province's Women Processing and Promotion Center and Women Innovation Park in turn, eager to establish a business relationship within the Yiwu market so as to help more women be employed. On April 26, 2017, Luoyang City (Henan Province) and Yiwu's Federation of Processing Technology signed a strategic cooperation agreement, which planned that from 2017 to 2020, Yiwu will provide a material processing business with a valuation of at least 2.6 billion Yuan to the poor people in Luoyang so as to take targeted measures to help people lift themselves out of poverty.

Since 2006, as the business circle's aggregation level and radiation range kept promoting, the city's foreign trade development made a big leap (as shown in Figure 0.2). From 2006 to 2016, Yiwu's import and export volume increased from USD 1.466 billion to USD 33.565 billion,

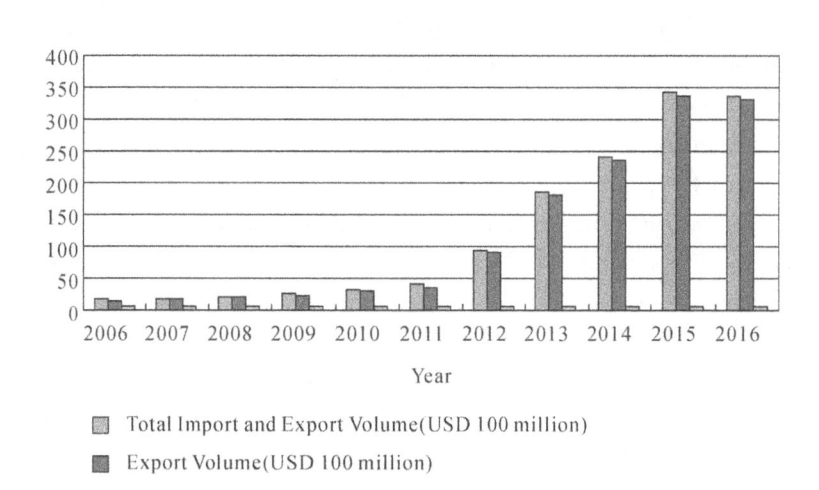

Figure 0.2: Yiwu City, import and export data statistical diagram (2006–2016)

Source: Yiwu Statistical Yearbook (2007–2017).

an increase of 21.90 times, with an average annual growth rate of 36.77%, among which the export volume has increased from USD 1.341 billion to USD 33.145 billion, a 23.72-fold increase, the average annual growth rate of 37.82% and the import volume from USD 125 million to USD 420 million, an increase of 2.36 times, with average annual growth rate of 12.88%. The countries and regions that Yiwu commodities has been exported to increased from 178 to 221. "Yiwu Business Circle" gathering level and increasing scope of radiation has continuously enhanced the contribution of Yiwu's foreign trade to the province and our country from 1.05% and 0.08% to 10.04% and 0.92%, an increase of 8.53 times and 10.00 time, respectively. The proportion of the city's foreign trade export volume to the province and our country increased from 1.33% and 0.14% to 12.46% and 1.59%, an increase of 8.38 times and 10.49 times. Especially in 2012, after the implementation of the Yiwu pilot market procurement trade program, the growth of foreign trade in Zhejiang has been greatly promoted. From 2012 to 2014, Yiwu's export volume had contributed to the foreign trade growth of Zhejiang by 65.8%, 41.3%, and 22.3% for each respective year; in 2015, when our country's exports declined, Yiwu's exports still maintained a high-speed year-on-year growth rate of 42.8%, driving the province's export growth rate by 3.7 percentage points; in 2016, the contribution Yiwu's foreign trade exports made to Zhejiang's total foreign trade was 19.52%.

The improvement of the gathering level and radiation range made "Yiwu Business Circle" increasingly become a bridgehead for global consumer goods to enter into China. Since 2008, Yiwu has established an import commodity museum, covering an area of 100,000 square meters, which has introduced more than 100,000 kinds of specialty products from more than 100 countries and regions. Since 2012, Yiwu also has hosted a yearly imported goods exhibition, which was eventually upgraded to a fair for import commodities. It ranked No.1 in terms of its current scale among exhibitions of the same kind nationwide and the first brand among China's imports of consumer goods exhibitions. The third Yiwu Import Commodities Fair held from

May 6th to May 9, 2017, attracted 1,518 organizations from more than 100 countries and regions, and set up 2006 international standard booths, with a total business volume of 1.276 billion Yuan. The number of attendees and/or buyers totaled 151,300, visiting from India, Malaysia, Pakistan, UK, Italy, and more, with a total of 69 countries and regions as well as 28 domestic provinces and cities such as Guangdong, Shanghai, and Jiangsu. Among them, there were 42 countries and regions along the Belt and Road such as Russia, Kazakhstan, Georgia, Malaysia, India, Turkey, Iran, the United Arab Emirates, Poland and others who came to the exhibition for promotion.

2.2 Commercial flow and logistics gathering capacity has been significantly enhanced

Since 2006, more and more domestic and foreign producers, trade enterprises, and merchants have participated in the construction and development of Yiwu businesses. The gathering and radiation capacity of "Yiwu Business Circle" has continuously increased in commercial flow, logistics, and information flow. The core area of the commercial flow of "Yiwu Business Circle", both domestic and overseas, has been enhanced day by day; from 2006 to 2016, the number of foreigners registered in the city had increased from 850,000 to 1.24 million, an increase of 46.24% and an average annual increase of 3.87%, and the number of foreign businessmen registered in the Entry and Exit Management Bureau had increased from 131,600 to 469,700, an increase of 2.57 times (13.57%); permanent residents of foreign visitors and businessmen in Yiwu had increased from 8,000 to 13,000, an increase of 62.50%, or average annual growth of 4.97%; the number of foreign-related institutions had increased from 921 to more than 5,300, an increase of 4.75 times (19.12%). At present, the city has more than 2,650 Chinese foreign joint venture enterprises, accounting for 75% of the country; annual road passenger traffic increased from 189.01 million to 228.99 million, an increase of 21.15%; civil aviation passenger traffic increased from 328,000 to 1,227,000, an increase of 2.74 times (14.10%); annual flights of Yiwu Airport increased from

Table 0.3: **Statistical table of Yiwu Airport operation and domestic and foreign tourists received by the city (2006–2016)**

Year	2006	2007	2008	2009	2010	2011	2012	2013	2014	2015	2016
Yiwu Airport Flight (sorties)	3,466	5,091	5,312	5,319	6,143	6,740	8,330	10,632	10,749	11,272	11,302
Civil aviation passenger traffic volume (10,000 person)	32.8	50.3	50.5	55.3	69.5	76.2	93.7	116.1	120.5	119.7	122.7
Number of tourists (10,000 person)	437.3	515.6	595.2	684.8	810.8	959.2	1,081.4	1,169.4	1,313.2	1,536.2	1,773.2
Number of foreign tourists (10,000 person)	26	31.2	34.8	37.5	45.0	53.2	59.0	62.2	65.7	77.8	92.7

Source: Yiwu Statistical Yearbook (2007–2017), Yiwu National Economic and Social Development Bulletin (2006–2016).

3466 to 11,302, an increase of 2.26 times (12.55%). With the increase in the degree of contact between Yiwu and places at home and abroad, the number of merchants, and the number of tourists (including travel and shopping tourists) also showed rapid growth. From 2006 to 2016, the number of tourists received by Yiwu City increased from 4.373 million to 17.732 million, an increase of 3.05 times (15.03%); the number of foreign tourists increased from 260,000 to 927,000, an increase of 2.57 times (13.56%) (as shown in Table 0.3).

Yiwu's business exchanges with domestic and foreign economies have been increasing, specifically with a significant increase in the volume of logistics, logistics gathering, and dispersing level. From 2006 to 2016, the annual usage of road transportation in Yiwu had increased

from 30.87 million tons to 64.116 million tons, an increase of 1.08 times (7.58%); annual export container volume from 350,000 standard containers to 886,000, an increase of 1.53 times (9.73%). In May 2013, Yiwu was identified as one of the first 17 international port cities by the United Nations Economic and Social Commission for Asia and Africa. Yiwu has also been selected as one of the first batch of innovation and development of modern logistics pilot cities in the country, the country's largest retail cargo loading center, second grade logistics park layout city, and one of the three pilot cities to simplify customs clearance procedures approved by the Zhejiang Provincial Government. In 2016, the city's express delivery volume reached 1.03 billion, a year-on-year increase of 78%, accounting for 20% of Zhejiang's volume and 3.3% of the country's volume; international parcel business volume reached a new high of up to 58.3294 million units, a substantial year-on-year increase of 62.1%; after more than one year's operation of the International Mail Exchange Bureau and Bonded Area Logistics Center (Type B), its business volume ranked fourth and tenth, respectively, in the province and country. At present, the city has 1,639 domestic logistics, 1,056 international freight forwarding, more than 100 air freight forwarding, 134 express delivery, and more than 100 cross-border e-commerce logistics enterprises, forming a big multi-mode co-development pattern of road logistics, railway logistics, aviation logistics, bonded area logistics, multi-mode transportation, smart logistics, and other logistics. Express giants such as DHL, FedEx, UPS, TNT, and other international renowned shipping corporations such as China Shipping COSCO, Maersk, France Dafei, and Pacific have set up branches in Yiwu. In order to enhance its external logistics distribution ability and efficiency, since 2006 and especially in recent years, Yiwu has been vigorously promoting logistics infrastructure construction, as well as implementing the express logistics hub, YXE Line Transport Center, Global Logistics Properties, the domestic highway port logistics center, the railway port, and other major logistics projects. The city has also planned the construction of 43.67 square kilometers of an international port logistics park (Land Port New Area) covering ten large functional blocks that

specialize in domestic logistics, international logistics, express logistics, electricity business warehousing, and logistics business gathering. The city's logistics industry's technical level has also achieved a large leap, and the Shentong courier and SF Express companies have been using advanced automated sorting equipment, which has realized the amount of delivery handled per hour up to 16,000 and 20,000, respectively, and greatly improved logistics efficiency. On October 21, 2016, the country's first express data real-time analysis system was officially launched in Yiwu, which could demonstrate Yiwu Express's accuracy of real-time data vividly and directly.

3. Significant day-by-day improvements of internal business circle cooperation and communication

3.1 The new relationship between supply chain and industrial chain is deepening under the environment of electricity business

With the continuous expansion of "Yiwu Business Circle", the cooperation between regions and economic entities within the circle has displayed a more diversified trend, and the grade and level also has been improved since 2006. Especially with the big outbreak of the Internet economy and in recent years with the rapid development of e-commerce at home and abroad, Yiwu Small Commodity Market has gradually built up a new relationship between supply chain and industrial chain under the environment of the electricity business with many domestic and overseas regions and economic entities. For e-businessmen, the core of business is to find a spot source with distinctive features and competitive advantage, which could take a favorable position in the fierce market competition. The small commodity market in Yiwu, in the process of development, has gradually accumulated a strong advantage in supplying and organizing goods, coupled with the characteristics of cheap and necessary commodities that are easy to package and transport, making Yiwu's entity market fertile for the e-businessman to grow. We conducted a survey showing that about 50% Yiwu's local mixed batch

of e-businessmen and about 70% retail e-businessmen are purchasing from the Yiwu entity market; other domestic and foreign e-businessmen have also purchased commodities from Yiwu's commodities market in large quantities and then carried out Online wholesale or retail. At present, Yiwu Small Commodity Market has become the country's largest network of goods supply base and the national micro-supply center.

Yiwugou, Yiwu's official commodity market website has also carried out a positive exploration in the construction of an industrial chain and supply chain collaboration system under the electricity business environment. In early 2014, it started the implementation of the global "Cooperation Plan", which is based on Yiwu mother market, through self-built, joint and commissioned management, to build domestic and overseas sub-markets and provide guidance for website construction, operation and docking of the Yiwu market, and other integrated services for the cooperation markets. The plan has also integrated sub-markets at home and abroad to Yiwu Purchase platform by means of information technology, constructing a global market platform with integrity as the basis, having the Yiwu mother market as the core, massive commodities as support, and an interactive integration online and offline. In May 2016, Yiwu Purchase has launched Cooperation Plan 2.0 Overall Solution of B2B2R model. The first B is the main warehouse on Yiwu Purchase cloud platform, mainly for the integration of cooperation market and quality merchant commodities; the second B is the sub-warehouse on the cooperation market cloud platform, mainly for docking main warehouse commodities for the cooperation market; R is the cloud platform radiation in the surrounding area, with the cloud sub-warehouse as the center, radiating the commodities source to the surrounding area. The core of Plan 2.0 is the homologous data which makes efforts to achieve full platform marketing including PC site, business version APP, micro-mall, micro-shop, mobile WAP, market management APP, etc., striving to settle the series of problems that many domestic and foreign cooperative markets confronted in the promotion of online and offline integration development, including the lack of experience in the operation of the real e-commerce, difficulties in changing modes within the market for e-commerce, and training the operational personnel. At present, Yiwu Purchase implemented the global "Cooperation Plan" and has signed agreements with nearly 100 partners at home and abroad. At the same time, Yiwu Purchase is also actively building an online import platform to promote the two-way development of foreign trade in import and export. On May 6, 2017, the Yiwu Purchase national museum project was officially launched online, where users can buy import products from around the world. Entities from USA, Japan, Australia, India, Malaysia, and other countries have become signed partners of the Yiwu Purchase International Pavilion. In the future, it is expected to become the online bridgehead of the Yiwu market's online version overseas commodity distribution center, overseas enterprises and commodities' entry into the Yiwu market so as to build a more closely managed production and marketing collaboration, logistics cooperation, and an information sharing relationship within the electricity business environment.

3.2 Many investments in two-way interactive projects have been made

With the sublimation of the business district's internal cooperation and exchanges, since 2006, the relevant economic entities have carried out more and more investment projects in addition to selling or purchasing commodities through the Yiwu market. As mentioned above, the world's top 500 enterprises from around the world including SK of R. O. Korea, CP Group of Thailand, Geely Group, GLP, and Wuchan Zhongda Group, have set up production, sales, warehousing, logistics, and research & development departments in Yiwu and have implemented a large number of high-end industrial projects. At the same time, Yiwu enterprises have also implemented

Table 0.4:   Overseas investment situation of Yiwu enterprises (2010–2016)

Year	Amount of investment (10,000 USD)	Number of investment enterprises
2010	2,166	14
2011	3,180	10
2012	4,611	5
2013	2,475	6
2014	3,285	15
2015	3,270	16
2016	28,004	11
Total	46,991	77

Source: Foreign Affairs and Overseas Chinese Affairs Office of Yiwu Municipal People's Government.

"going-out", especially since 2010, when overseas investment in Yiwu enterprises entered a new rapid growth stage (as shown in Table 0.4). By the end of 2016, the city had 100 offshore companies and offices approved (excluding written-off companies), and up to USD 769 million overseas investment in 34 countries and regions.

Yiwu enterprises' "going-out" approaches include overseas mergers and acquisitions, the establishment of overseas sub-markets, capacity cooperation, the establishment of overseas warehouses, etc., among cases with relatively significant influence. Some cases are as follows: Hexie Xinguang and Hexie Mingxin, which was established by Yiwu Industrial Park, and IDG capital, respectively, acquired the US MEMS semiconductor and Germany OSRAM lighting projects so as to build a complete LED industry chain pattern; China Merchants

Logistics Group Co., Ltd., Zhejiang China Commodities City Group Co., Ltd. and Yiwu Shi Tianmeng Industrial Investment Co., Ltd. reached a tripartite cooperation and settled in the China–Belarus industrial park in Minsk, the capital of Belarus, providing enterprises with goods display, sales, logistics, customs clearance, and other services to enhance the development in areas such as commodity trade, cargo transport, capital settlement, etc. among China, Belarus, and other European countries; Yiwu local enterprises such as Zhejiang Neoglory Jewelry Co., Ltd. and other Japanese companies carried out design cooperation and acquired US Dennis Wood Design Co., Ltd.; Zhejiang China Commodity City Group Co., Ltd. and Warsaw China Mall market signed a framework agreement in Warsaw, the capital city of Poland, becoming the first overseas sub-market of "China Commodity City"; Yiwu City Kaituo Hardware Co., Ltd. made the German factory OEM third categories, with more than 20 kinds of products such as the screwdriver and hexagonal pliers; Zhejiang Etina Knitting Co., Ltd. set up a seamless garment factory in South Africa, and shipped part of the domestic machinery and equipment abroad for second use. Finally, Yiwu Yanping Textile Co., Ltd. shipped the old production line to Ethiopia, and introduced the latest production line to realize the second development for the enterprise. In recent years, in order to crack the warehousing logistics problems in the development of cross-border e-commerce and enhance the terminal consumption experience, Yiwu enterprises have been going out to set up overseas warehouses. Currently, there are 22 that have been approved by the government, which have been located in areas such as the USA, the UK, Germany, Poland, Spain, Russia, Belarus, Australia, Malaysia, and other places.

3.3 Multi-laterally connected international exchanges begin to foster

Since 2006, with the sublimation of internal cooperation and exchanges in "Yiwu Business Circle", the regional exchanges with the rest of the world have become more and more frequent, and it continues to expand from its main field, economics and trade, to culture, science

and technology, education, health, environmental protection, and other fields. From 2006 to 2016, Yiwu City received overseas (territory) delegations of more than 2,600 batches of more than 15,000 people, including delegations above vice ministerial level—more than 160 batches of more than 800 people, cumulative reception of overseas (territory) media of more than 300 batches of more than 500 people, and invited more than 33,000 foreign businessmen to China. During this period, there were heads of state and government from over ten countries that visited Yiwu. On September 21, 2008, Nigerian Prime Minister Omar Lu visited the Yiwu commodity market and met with more than 40 long-term Nigerian businessmen in China; on May 2, 2010, Micronesian President Emmanuel Morrie visited Yiwu Langsha Hosiery and International Trade City; on July 8, 2011, a government delegation led by the President of the Republic of Mauritius, Anelod Jagnett, visited Yiwu China Commodity City; on February 10, 2012, Mozambique's Prime Minister Aires Ali visited Yiwu; on June 10, 2012, the Prime Minister of the Republic of Fiji Josaia Warren Geim Banez together with his wife visited Yiwu China Commodities City. Over the past 10 years, the number of international cities friendly to Yiwu increased from 3 to 26, which are New York City Brooklyn District (USA), San Antonio (USA), Oubai Heirier (France), Brescia (Italy), Barcelona (Spain), Leganas (Spain), Fuen Lavrada (Spain), La Penglanta (Finland), Avon (Poland), Budapest (Hungary), Minsk (Belarus), Awaji (Japan), Seoul Central (R. O. Korea), Jeju (R. O. Korea), Pyeongtaek City (R. O. Korea), Great Wall County (R. O. Korea), Ararat (Australia), Paramata City (Australia), Horse (Turkey), Bucharest City (Romania), Hebron (Palestine), Klang City (Malaysia), Lang Son (Vietnam), Montego Bay (Jamaica), Dar es Salaam (Tanzania), and Flacq District (Mauritius).

Since 2006, with the sublimation of "Yiwu Business Circle" expansion and internal cooperation and exchanges, especially Yiwu's international influence, continue to be enhanced with more and more international conferences being held in Yiwu; domestic and overseas people from foreign political, enterprises, and academics fields have discussed issues such as economic development, trade, international investment, non-government exchanges and environmental protection, which has significantly promoted issues such as the concept of exchange, policy communication, and industry collaboration in "Yiwu Business Circle" within the regions and economic entities. For example, in 2013, the China–West Asia and North Africa Sustainable Development Forum, New Silk Road Strategic Development International Forum, and China–ASEAN Free Trade Area Joint Committee Third Meeting was held in Yiwu; in 2014, the China–West Asia and North Africa Vision for Future Development Dialogue Conference, and the second session of China–Central Asia Cooperation Forum was held in Yiwu; in 2015, forums and conferences such as the fourth China–Africa non-governmental forum, 2015 Silk Road Economic Belt City International Forum, China–Nordic Youth Leaders Forum, and the Seventeenth China–Japan–Korea Friendship City Exchange Conference were held in Yiwu; in 2016, forums such as the fifth session of the China–Africa Think Tanks Forum, and 2016 China (Yiwu) Silk Road Economic Belt International Forum were held in Yiwu.

During the outward expansion of "Yiwu Business Circle", Yiwu, as the core of "Yiwu Business Circle", taking culture exchanges and cultural products as a carrier, launched two projects: "Bang the Drum and Realize Chinese Dream Together" and "I Am Lucky Because of My Integrity" in March, 2014. At present, there are more than 200 enterprises that have acquired production licenses for theme products, and Chinese Dream series goods have been exported to more than 30 countries and regions such as the USA, the UK, Germany, France, Italy, Portugal, Russia, and others, with up to 45 million in cumulative sales. In addition, in order to improve the services for foreign businessmen in Yiwu and promote international cooperation and exchanges, many measures to optimize foreign-related management services have been adopted. For example, a special Yiwu International Trade Service Center has been established to provide one-stop services through a window and supermarket service model for foreign investors acquiring an entry visa to obtain the company's business license, consulting investment firms to obtain rental information, and translation services for legal aid and other matters. The service center also issues friendly foreign businessman cards to foreigners of integrity so as to manage them by the law and at the same time provide them with convenience services such as bus travel, small consumption payments, and other functions. The International Service Center actively improves the city's international functions and builds a number of functional blocks such as international hospitals, international schools, and so on. Among these, the fourth Affiliated Hospital of Zhejiang University Medical College has been completed and put into use. International service facilities have been introduced such as Shanghai Yueyang Hospital, Fudan Fuhua School, Dalian Maple Leaf International School and the service center is actively exploring a new foreign-related police mechanism and looking to establish foreign affairs officers and a foreign affairs liaison system. The first county-level foreign-related Disputes Committee and more than 10 foreign affairs mediators from more than 10 countries have been employed.

II Reconsideration on the Formation Mechanism of "Yiwu Business Circle"

1. The coupling of "Yiwu Business Circle" and the Belt and Road construction

1.1 A high degree of fit between "Yiwu Business Circle" development mechanism and the Belt and Road construction

The Belt and Road construction has been implemented following the open and fair market economy laws and regulations, but also in response to the Chinese government's strong initiative and promotion, principles it initiated, co-construction and co-sharing, as well as proposals of open cooperation, harmonious inclusion, market operation, mutual benefits and win–win cooperation (which is also the mechanism that "Yiwu Business Circle" has demonstrated during its formation, development, and extension). The formation and development of "Yiwu Business Circle" is the result of domestic and foreign-related areas and economic

entities carrying out the supply chain and industrial chain cooperation based on division of labor, which is attributed to related service institutions, government, market managers, industry associations, and other subjects that were involved such as the producers, wholesalers, traders, and others. Of course, many of its economic and value creation effects produced also have been shared by domestic- and foreign-related areas and the main subjects. From a comprehensive view of the formation, development, and extension of "Yiwu Business Circle", its power source and core competitiveness lie in the high efficiency of resource allocation. This is a typical and vivid interpretation of making the market play a decisive role in resource allocation and the government play an important role. On the one hand, the formation and expansion of "Yiwu Business Circle" is based on the objective economic laws where the market is the driving force. For a long time, as a core area of "Yiwu Business Circle", Yiwu's main export market has been along the Belt and Road, which includes South Asia, Central Asia, West Asia, the Middle East, North Africa, Eastern Europe and other places. This is because of the above areas' high demand for industrial consumer goods and weak supply capacity; Yiwu Small Commodity Market mainly sells daily industrial products, enjoying special industry advantages. These products include ornaments, knitwear, toys, and so on, which makes the region have a good complementarity in supply and demand compared to the abovementioned areas. It is under this supply and demand coupling mechanism, not coastal, not along the borders, that Yiwu has gradually grown into the International Commodity Trade Center where "Yiwu Business Circle" has been expanding, radiating to the above areas, and becoming an open, inclusive, co-sponsored, sharing, co-prospering, and cooperative system. On the other hand, Yiwu Municipal Party Committee and Government have played an important role in the formation and expansion process of "Yiwu Business Circle" where all previous party committees and governments adhered to the overall development strategy of "Flourish Business and Build City". At the same time, based on the actual changing situation, they are good at putting forward specific development strategies in

line with the objective situation of various historical periods, such as when in the mid-1990s of 20th century they started to promote the introduction of commerce and making changes in the industry; at the beginning of the 21st century, they had a clear vision about the international development orientation, and then in recent years, they have gradually established the development goal of becoming the World Commodity Capital. In particular, after the State Council approved the "Yiwu Pilot Project" in March, 2011, all previous and current party committees and governments have been playing the Visible Hand role, and vigorously promoting the implementation of "Yiwu Pilot Project" reform tasks. They made breakthrough results in many areas such as the foreign trades supervision system, financial system, logistics system, factors supply system, foreign-related management system, and others, having formed distinctive institutional mechanisms and policy environment advantages. They have also been approved for the top national reform pilot in ten areas such as the domestic comprehensive reform of trade circulation system, rural land reform, new urbanization, and so on. Therefore, they have created a good policy and development environment, which has enhanced the external radiation and gathering capacity of "Yiwu Business Circle" .

The key to the Belt and Road Initiative is policy communication, facility connection, smooth trade and finance operation, and a good understanding among our people, which is also the core of the formation, development and expansion of the business circle. In the process of its external expansion, policy communication has been playing an important role because of various economic entities from around the world having different business backgrounds and business habits. In the process of the extension and international radiation trade rules of "Yiwu Business Circle", supervision policies of different regions involved differ. Therefore, relevant regional and economic entities at home and abroad, through communication, negotiation, and collision, and after long-term mutual acknowledging, understanding, tolerance, docking, and integration have formed an open, cooperative,

inclusive, mutually beneficial, win–win business consensus, business rules, and business practices. In the external expansion process of "Yiwu Business Circle", facility connection is an important foundation and support. This includes the expansion of external roads, railways, aviation, and other lines, especially the mutual connection, joint construction, and sharing of warehousing and logistics facilities. The radiation range of "Yiwu Business Circle" has been extended from the formation of Yiwu to surrounding cities and around the world at present; Yiwu's domestic logistics network has covered more than 1,500 cities in the Chinese mainland, connecting to Ningbo Zhoushan Port, Shanghai Port, and other domestic ports and the world's major hub ports, with airlines to more than 10 large and medium-sized cities in the country as well as Dubai (the United Arab Emirates), Seoul (R. O. Korea), Bangkok (Thailand), and other places in the world. In particular, YXE Line has been running faster with more and more widely commodities suppliers, higher valued commodities, greater influences, and more stations abroad. It has also set up four overseas warehouses and five logistics distribution centers in Europe, becoming an important bridge for Asia–Europe interconnection and the early results of one Belt and Road construction. In the process of the expansion of "Yiwu Business Circle", smooth trade cooperation is the core; the business circle is a cross-regional division of labor collaboration network, and its formation is based on internal demand of domestic and foreign-related areas and economic entities to carry out commodity trading and industrial cooperation with Yiwu Small Commodity Market as a hub. This accelerates the expansion of "Yiwu Business Circle" trade network from the initial surrounding areas gradually to 220 countries and regions today. In this process, in order to promote trade facilitation and enhance the level of trade, Yiwu vigorously strives for the support of the General Administration of Customs, and makes the export of goods suitable for the Tourism Shopping Commodity supervision model. There is no need to submit the Foreign Exchange Receipt Verification Sheet and issue Customs Declaration Foreign Exchange Receipts or a Customs Declaration Tax Rebate Receipt, and

commodity categories have been simplified from more than 8,000 to 98; in accordance with the requirements of approved documents on "Yiwu Pilot Project" by State Council (National Letter [2011] No. 22), through active declaration and deep implementation, Yiwu strives to build an advanced display trading platform and convenient international trade channel so as to achieve world-class advanced trade efficiency and form a relatively modern trade system, facilitating the international trading system. In the process of the external expansion, capital financing is equivalent to the flesh and blood of the cross-regional division of labor network; in order to better serve domestic and international economic and trade exchanges with Yiwu Small Commodities Market as a hub, Yiwu is committed to building more levels and a diversified and open modern financial organization system, and has vigorously supported and promoted the financial institutions to provide more personalized, targeted financial innovation products and services for various subjects such as suppliers, operators, and buyers so as to solve large payment, long-term settlement, and installment problems. A financial business center covering an area of 1.7 square kilometers has been planned. The "Yiwu Pilot Project" approved in August, 2013, put forward requirements such as focusing on the development of trade finance, speeding up the formation of a comprehensive international financial system, and providing strong support and protection for trade, investment, and financing, which includes seven major tasks: to encourage financial institutions to actively innovate constructive trade financing businesses and overseas financing and loans, to explore the establishment of Yiwu non-resident personal transaction database, to allow qualified natural persons from abroad to open personal foreign exchange settlement accounts after the acquisition of individual and commercial business licenses, to deepen personal cross-border trade RMB settlement business pilot, and to explore qualified individuals directly making settlement by RMB in import and export. In the expansion process of "Yiwu Business Circle", understanding between our people is the foundation for the solid operation of this cross-regional division of labor and cooperation network; following the concept of

people-oriented services regardless of national boundaries, Yiwu has created good investments, entrepreneurship opportunities, and living environments for foreign investors from around the world. This is an invitation to foreign investors to participate in community management, auditing NPC, and CPPCC (two sessions). The entrepreneurial environment has made many foreign investors regard Yiwu as a second home, where they buy a car, a house, get married, settle down, and have children. A variety of folk culture, food culture, and religious culture has been blended, and different regional style restaurants, hotels, and bars are everywhere on the streets, such as in styles of the Arabs, Southeast Asia, South Asia, Africa, and others. New and old, domestic and overseas, Yiwu people have been coexisting here harmoniously, with many even starting businesses together. In the opening ceremony of the Sixth Ministerial Conference of the China–Arab Cooperation Forum held on June 5, 2014, President Xi Jinping mentioned: "In Yiwu, a place where Arab businessmen have been gathering, a man named Muhammad, a Jordanian businessman, opened a typical Arabian restaurant. He brought the original Arab food culture to Yiwu and made success in his career from Yiwu's prosperity. He ultimately married a Chinese woman and settled in China." Today, Muhammad's restaurant has doubled in area. In addition to operating the restaurant, he also carried out a foreign trade business, with annual turnover increasing by 60% compared with that of 2014.

1.2 The construction of the Belt and Road has been guiding the development of "Yiwu Business Circle"

The goal of construction of the Belt and Road is to work together to build a community with broad interests, sharing both joys, sorrows, and destiny, walking towards the direction of a community with a shared future, which is the common value of relevant regional and economic entities of "Yiwu Business Circle". In the future, the above objectives will be regarded as a guide to promote the extension and development of "Yiwu Business Circle". It is known from the previous content that "Yiwu Business Circle" is an open, mutually beneficial, and sharing system based on the market mechanism and rules, which originated from the improvement of external radiation scope and level of Yiwu Small Commodity Market. During the process that domestic and overseas relevant regions and economic entities carry out businesses in fields such as product sales, industrial collaboration, logistics and distribution, brands display, financial services, information sharing, labor cooperation, technology transfer, government exchanges and others, "Yiwu Business Circle" has gradually become a big exchange platform for domestic and overseas commodities, industry, humanity, information, capital, and others, a large benefits sharing platform transcending time, space, and borders, so as to promote the optimization of resources globally. In the future, according to President Xi Jinping's requirements put forward in his speech in the opening ceremony of the Belt and Road International Cooperation Summit Forum, we will build the Belt and Road into a road of peace, a road of prosperity, a road of opening, a road of innovation, and a road of civilization. Focusing on the development of this theme, it will adhere to the principle of openness and inclusivity, win–win cooperation, and industry cooperation as the core. The Belt and Road will further promote the business district mutual exchanges by integrating the four approaches within the land, the sea, the sky, and online into one orderly flow of production factors, efficient allocation of resources, deep integration of the market, and completely improve trade and investment liberalization and convenience, facilitate the new market system advantage with online and offline integration to enhance the construction of online Silk Road, and promote the relevant areas and the main body within the business circle to realize big integration, development connecting, and results sharing in the economy so as to jointly build an open, inclusive, beneficial, and balanced "Yiwu Business Circle".

On the plan and road map of the Belt and Road construction, President Xi Jinping clearly pointed out: from dots to the surface, from lines to the area, we will gradually form wide cooperation of regions. This is because the Belt and Road construction is a grand, long-term, systematic, and transnational project involving many aspects such as cross-border cooperation and exchange systems confronting many unknown situations and difficulties, having an extremely high demand on communication and coordination with relevant countries and regions. Therefore, we must fully estimate its complexity and arduous nature, cultivate and build a number of Belt and Road node cities selectively in regions with good basis and conditions regarding trading, personnel interaction, and culture exchanges, focusing on the layout of cooperation and exchange platforms, projects and carriers, and making a first attempt in commodity trade, personnel exchanges, capital access, and other convenience and liberalization so as to accumulate experience, gradually promote it, and give full play to the leading and promotion function through dots to surface and from lines to area. Therefore, as the core of "Yiwu Business Circle", Yiwu is willing to further make good use of its advantages such as the world's largest and best small commodity market, most convenient logistics network advantages, international trade reform policy advantages and environmental advantages of Chinese and foreign cultural integration. Yiwu must bravely take responsibilities as the supporter of the Belt and Road, so as to build itself into the node of a Silk Road on land, in the sea, and on the Internet. Specifically, the following aspects can be started with:

First, vigorously promote the Belt and Road cross-border trade and circulation cooperation. With the Silk Road New Area and Lugang New Area as the core platform, we will focus on building the city's international service functions and international trade services, such as cross-border settlement, cross-border e-commerce, international freight forwarding, international credit assessment, foreign-related administration and services. We will strive to build it into a central platform to undertake and serve big cross-border cooperation and exchange projects and carriers along the Belt and Road. We will also further make full use of the existing African products exhibition center, China–ASEAN Commodity Trading Center, Central and Eastern European Product Exhibition Center, and a number of national exhibitions, so as to make greater contributions to the construction of China's foreign trade platform and international marketing network. In line with China's strategy of promoting the exchange and settlement with local currency with countries and regions along the Belt and Road, with "Yiwu Pilot Project" financial special reform as the breakthrough point, we will vigorously promote RMB cross-border business with countries and regions such as Central Asia, West Asia, the Middle East, Southeast Asia and other countries and regions. Through the above efforts, we will strive to construct the Belt and Road market cooperation and commodity circulation chain, and build Yiwu into a daily industrial production and marketing platform between China and countries and regions along the Belt and Road.

Secondly, vigorously promote the Belt and Road cross-border transport logistics cooperation. We will speed up the construction of international port city, try to achieve the official opening of the railway port as soon as possible, strive for approval of designated ports for fruit, car, and other import commodities, vigorously develop sea and railway multi-modal transport and other multi-modal transport, speed up the construction of airports, actively cultivate an international air cargo market, add more international routes, and enhance traffic and logistics functions along the Belt and Road. We will further improve YXE Line by adding more stations, extending lines, encrypting and improving efficiency, explore the international transfer, international mail (express mail) transport and international business services, strengthen communication and coordination with countries and regions along the Belt and Road, sign closer cooperation agreements, and strive to create a YXE Line international trade channel. We will copy and promote the cooperation experience of YXE Line and Hangzhou cross-border e-commerce airport park, and build YXE Line cross-border e-commerce business model so as to help the development of the online Silk Road. Through the above efforts, we will build YXE Line into a demonstration project for the Belt and Road. Based on the Yiwu inland container yard, International Logistics Center, Yiwu Chengxi Logistics

Center, Yiwu Airport Logistics Center, Yiwu Railway Logistics Center, we will create a modern logistics service platform to provide modern logistics services support for carrying out businesses such as export, import, entrepot trade, and cross-border e-commerce and so on between countries and regions along the Belt and Road. We will further promote seamless docking with Ningbo Zhoushan Port, Shanghai Port, and other major ports at home and abroad (border ports in particular), especially strengthen the coupling linkage with Zhoushan Free Trade Port area and Ningbo Meishan New Area, promote Ningbo Zhoushan port function and port supervision functions so as to extend to the comprehensive international land port of Yiwu, promote the integration of dual-core port management operations and port supervision seamless docking, and jointly expand the harbor and land port hinterland, thus speed up the construction of Yiwu–Ningbo–Zhoushan Grand Open Channel. Through the above efforts, we will build Yiwu into one of the major transport logistics hubs connecting countries and regions along the Belt and Road in our country.

Thirdly, vigorously promote the Belt and Road cross-border cooperation in culture, science, and education. We will give full play to Yiwu's unique advantages that permanent foreign businessmen are mostly from countries and regions along the Belt and Road and have a long-term close relationship with Yiwu local enterprises, business households, and based on the already established contacts, business network; we will further strengthen the cooperation and exchanges in culture, science, and education with countries and regions along the Belt and Road. With "Bang the Drum and Realize Chinese Dream" as core carriers, we will focus on promoting the cultural connotation of the market goods, spread the value and function with the Chinese goods carrying the spirit of China, spreading Chinese culture and displaying Chinese concepts. We will make Yiwu into an important platform to display and spread the Chinese dream, Chinese culture, and Chinese spirit. Giving full play to platforms such as the fair and the tourism expo, we will vigorously introduce cultural projects of civilization and health, distinctive features, and the profoundness from countries and regions along the Belt and Road. We will build a number of international cultural exchange facilities in order to study cultures from regions such as Central Asia, West Asia, South Asia, Southeast Asia, and Middle East, and so on. With the leadership and support of relevant state ministries, provincial party committees, and the Provincial Government, we will strengthen cooperation and exchanges with cultural and technological institutions of countries and regions along the Belt and Road and make joint efforts in organizing activities such as science and technology week, cultural festivals, and so on. We will make full use of the advantages of the large quantity of practical commercial and trade talents in Yiwu, which accounts for a high proportion of the city's 400,000 youth, and strengthen talent exchanges with major cities along the Belt and Road with regards to commerce, culture, science and education. We will encourage and support Yiwu enterprises, businessmen, and ordinary people, to go to countries and regions along the Belt and Road for business, investment, entrepreneurship, study, and cultural and educational exchanges. Through the above efforts, we will strive to build Yiwu into a high-energy level open platform blending culture with countries and regions along the Belt and Road in China.

2. The expansion of "Yiwu Business Circle" based on the trade theory of regional division of labor

Published in 2006, "Yiwu Business Circle" Chinese version made a theoretical analysis from aspects of the market system, support industry, business groups, logistics network, and others, and revealed the state of the characteristics of "Yiwu Business Circle" and the forming mechanism. Ten years since then, based on "Yiwu Business Circle", we have been continuously practicing expansion, and formed research results based on the original basis. The following part focuses on our new understanding and new results.

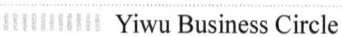

2.1 The internationalization of division of labor network and the expansion of "Yiwu Business Circle"

In order to solve the dilemma between the division of labor and the transaction costs due to the expansion of space and promote the evolution of the division of labor so as to bring about greater positive effects of the division of labor network and increase the gathering effect, we must find an organizational form. This can not only reduce the transaction costs, but avoid the organization cost of a transaction, and this organizational form is the division of labor network. A well-known American economist, A. M. Spence, defines the network as a special type of relationship that links a particular group of people, objects, or events. The people, things, or events that make up the network could be called Actors or Nodes. As an organizational form between the market and the management hierarchy, the important feature of the network is cooperation of mutual trust, long-term vision, and codes of conduct to be followed. The interconnection and infiltration between different subjects will ultimately construct a complex network structure between them and a variety of institutional arrangements. The network reduces the transaction cost when the contract is incomplete, which represents the development direction of the market organization and enterprise organization in the information era. In terms of its main function, "Yiwu Business Circle" is a division of labor network organization, also a highly developed cross-region and cross-border division of labor network.

In "Yiwu Business Circle" core—Yiwu Small Commodity Market, at the early days of its establishment, had a division of labor that mainly radiated the surrounding areas, then gradually expanded outwards, then tended to the nation and the globe so as to promote the expansion of "Yiwu Business Circle". Its internal mechanism is mainly reflected in the following aspects: (1) Increase the number of division of labor network participants. Yiwu Small Commodity Market has provided a low-cost, shared trading platform to attract a large number of domestic and overseas operators and commercial capital to enter into the market transactions, making the manufacturers, wholesalers, and others establish close contact with the market. With the expansion of the transaction scale, the increasing effect of scale returns has been becoming more and more obvious, attracting more operators to enter the division of labor and cooperation network, further deepening the division of labor relations, so as to promote the external expansion of "Yiwu Business Circle". (2) Reduce the cost of each transaction for the participated parties of division of labor and cooperation network. In Yiwu Small Commodity Market, due to the concentration of commodity price information, buyers and sellers can find the transaction object in a short period of time, thus the transaction cost is reduced; the increase in the number of transaction subjects makes the choice of trading objects have more room; after many games, activities against the market trading rules will be punished, thereby the additional transaction costs caused by the uncertainty factors have been reduced; gradually improved support services such as warehousing, logistics, finance, information, and so on have played a role of lubrication to reduce the cost of friction in a transaction. Because of this, Yiwu Small Commodity Market has attracted more and more relevant domestic and overseas entities to enter the market for transactions, or to carry out commodity distribution with its logistic network that connects China and the globe. Therefore, "Yiwu Business Circle" has achieved a substantial expansion. (3) Reduce the cost of maintaining business relations between the parties of the division of labor collaboration network. With the expansion of Yiwu Small Commodity Market and the continuous deepening and expansion of the division of labor collaboration network with the core of market, the level of specialized production and sales of economic entities has increased day by day, and so is the dependence on each other, thus, the intention of cooperation is getting stronger. Especially after the increase in the number of transactions between the parties, mutual understanding and trust have been improved, therefore, the risk of protection expenses originally used to maintain a business-to-business relationship between the cross-regional and even cross-border division of labor collaboration network of the parties has been greatly reduced, and an increasing

number of domestic and overseas economic entities and regions have participated in this cross-region division of labor collaboration network. "Yiwu Business Circle" has achieved the expansion from various regions to the whole country and the globe.

With the professional market as a link to carry out cross-regional division of labor, it could bring increasing benefits to the parties to increase and ultimately reflect and demonstrate the advantages of professional products, which are a cross-region division of labor economy. More and more new enterprises have constantly been derived from the refinement of cross-region division of labor; the gathering of these forward and backward-connected enterprises and related support structure in the space is conducive to enhancing the regional competitive advantage. Excessive demand generated by "Yiwu Business Circle" and the economy of cross-region division of labor itself, as well as the reduced transaction costs and improved transaction efficiency caused by market size expansion, has greatly promoted the exchange of economic elements between relevant regions. Under the condition that different regions at home and abroad share this large-scale trading platform of Yiwu Small Commodity Market, the regional barriers between the markets and other economic constraints have been weakened or even eliminated continuously. Therefore, there are frequent flows of factors of production (labor, capital, technical knowledge) and the exchange of goods and services between the regions (as shown in Figure 0.3). Under such open conditions, the economic development of the relevant regions is largely influenced by external factors, especially the flow of factors of production, goods, and services between regions. The flow of factors of production will increase the productive capacity of the inflow region, which will pass on the technical knowledge. The strengthening of trade in goods and services between regions can affect economic growth performance in terms of supply and demand. From the aspect of supply, it is beneficial to the deepening of regional division of labor and the effective investment of production factors. From the aspect

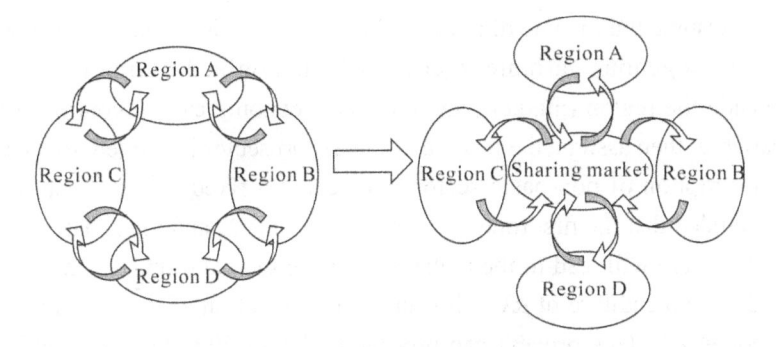

Figure 0.3: Change diagram of traditional regional economy exchanges changing towards sharing market-led regional economy exchanges

of demand, it can expand the output demand. In this process, "Yiwu Business Circle" could expand, radiate, and connect to more domestic and foreign regions.

2.2 Regional economic expansion and "Yiwu Business Circle" expansion

From the regional level, according to the basis of the Masahisa Fujita, Paul R. Krugman, Venables, and the multiplier model, the economic activities in one region can be divided into two categories: one is economic activities that meet the external needs of the region, which is the reason for the existence of the local economy and is called the Export base or Economic base of the region; the other is economic activities that meet the needs of local residents. For a modern highly integrated economy, it is impossible for a region to establish a self-sufficient closed production system, therefore, the purpose of a regional economy is mainly to take advantage of local resources or the occasional formed cycle of accumulation in history so as to offer products or services to large markets outside the region. In this sense, the second type of economic activity is derived or caused by the first type of economic activity, so the second type of economic activity is non-basic for the regional economy.

Assume the income of a regional export sector is X and this income is an exogenous variable, that is, it is determined by the demand outside the region (market), and the local economy cannot control this variable; then assume the income of the export sector is applied to local consumption of non-basic sector products at a fixed rate a. It can be concluded that the first round of export income is X, and after that, local expenditure will lead to the realization of the second round income aX, and the expenditure of aX will lead to the realization of the third round income a^2X. This process can proceed endlessly like this, and can be summed up using a simple equal ratio series to get the income of the region (Y): $Y = \frac{1}{1-a} X$. It shows us that the economic growth of a region depends on the region's external demand (X) for products, as well as the local expenditure (a) after obtaining this part of the income. Of course, this builds on a constant basis of a, and if assuming a is a function of the regional income of the previous period, that is, $at = kY_{t-1}$, and there is a maximum value A, the equilibrium relationship between X and Y can be determined (as shown in Figure 0.4).

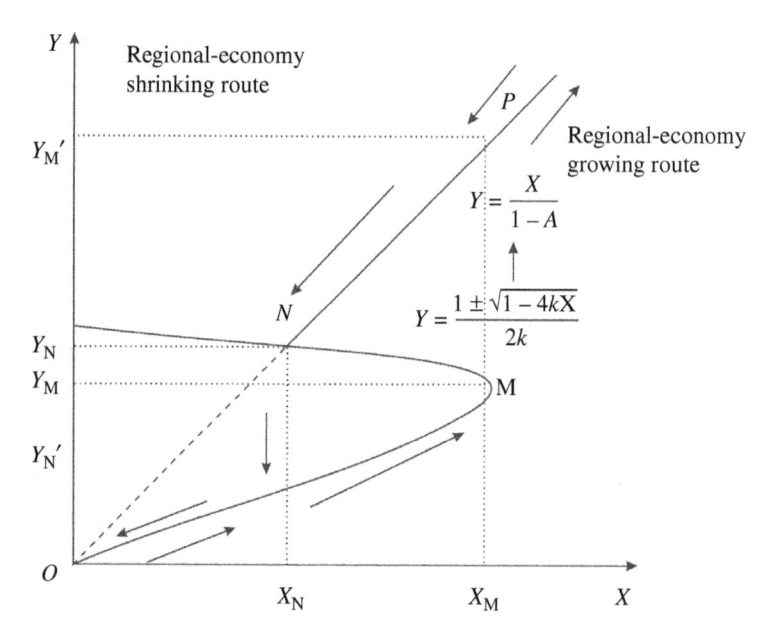

Figure 0.4: **Balance diagram of the regional income and export earnings**

In Figure 0.4, the regional economic growth with the expansion of the export sector is the OM segment of the curve and the NP segment of half line ON. But this raises the questions when the income from the export sector is between X_N and X_M, there are two corresponding regional incomes Y, which are the incomes corresponding to the OM and NP, and which is the real income of the region which is determined by whether the regional economy is in a growing process or a shrinking process. In the process of regional economic growth, when the income of the regional export sector gradually expands from O, the regional income gradually increases along the OM curve; when the regional export sector reaches X_M, the regional economy grows correspondingly to Y_M. At this moment, any small increase of the regional export sector income will bring about a huge regional economic growth; when regional income instantly increases from Y_M to Y_M', the regional economic growth cicada-like change has been completed. Similarly, when the regional economy begins to shrink from the high point, the regional income decreases gradually along the straight line PN as the income of the export sector decreases; and the regional economic growth level declines to Y_N when the regional export sector income decreases to X_N. Similarly, any slight reduction in regional sector income will result in a significant contraction in the regional economy, and regional income will decrease from Y_N to Y_N' at the very moment.

From the above analysis, it can be seen that the growth trajectory of the regional economy is not exactly consistent with its shrinking trajectory. When the regional economic growth reaches point M, the regional economy can burst out, where M is the change point of regional economic growth. When the regional economy shrinks, point N will cause the regional economy to inwardly burst, where point N is the support point of the regional economy shrinking. Therefore, whether the growth of regional economy can exceed the change point is the key to the regional economic growth, which is mainly why reaching the change point can trigger the regional economy to burst out and bring huge regional economic growth; when the regional economic growth exceeds the change point, even if the regional economy is shrinking, as long as the export sector income is between X_N and X_M, the regional economic income is much larger than the export sector with the same income which has not yet been initiated. In this sense, the regional economy is only initiated when the income of the regional export sector exceeds X_M.

It can be seen that it is important for the income of the regional external sector to exceed the change point, and its support to the regional economy is also very obvious. So, how can we make the regional economy reach and cross the point of change? The existence of a large-scale professional market is a good thing. It can increase the reliability of the transaction in three ways to obtain the benefits of a professional economy, for example, first, to increase the number of participants (N) of a regional division of labor collaboration network; second, to reduce the average cost of each transaction at present (q). When the number of participants is large, the average cost (r) of developing business relationships will be reduced. It can be concluded that the function of the reliability of the transaction involves the three abovementioned variables. That is $P = f(N, q, r)$, P and N are positively related, and q and r are negatively related.

If the size[7] of the market is introduced, it is easy to know that the larger the size of the market, the greater the number of traders involved, that is, if S becomes bigger, then N becomes bigger; the larger the market, the smaller the cost to maintain the average cost of existing transactions and the average cost to expand the transactions, that is, if S becomes bigger, q, r become smaller. Thus, it can be concluded that

$$\frac{dN}{dS} > 0,$$

---

[7]The market size here is different from the market size determined by the general market volume, including the information capacity that the market can provide.

$$\frac{dq}{dS} < 0,$$

$$\frac{dr}{dS} < 0.$$

Based on the total differential formula,

$$dP= \frac{\partial P}{\partial N} \, dN+ \frac{\partial P}{q} \, dq+ \frac{\partial P}{\partial r} \, dr.$$

Both sides divided by dS

$$\frac{dP}{dS} = \frac{P}{N} \frac{dN}{dS}+\frac{P}{q} \frac{dq}{dS}+\frac{P}{\partial r} \frac{dr}{dS}.$$

Using the results of the previous analysis, it is easy to conclude that the above formula is bigger than 0, that is, the size of the market is positively related to the reliability of the transaction. You can use Figure 0.5(a) and (b) to represent the relationship between the two: external income of the area X and the reliability of the transaction p are positively related.

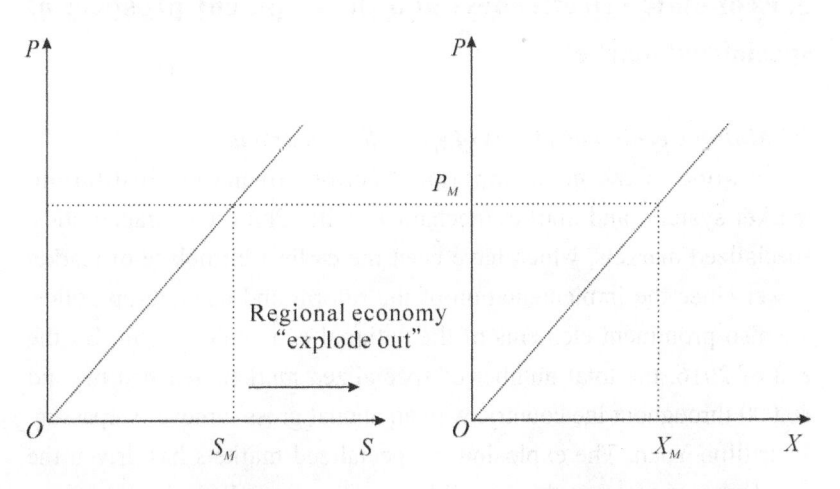

Figure 0.5: (a) Market size and transaction reliability

(b) Export base and transaction reliability

In summary, under the background of the decision-making for the maximization of the interests of the micro-bodies, with expansion of professional market scale, the reliability of the transaction gets higher and higher; as far as the region is concerned, when looking for regional economic growth and trying to cross the point of change, the reliability of the transaction shall exceed P_M in order to make the income from the regional export sector exceed X_M; when the market scale exceeds S_M, the reliability of the transaction will be larger than P_M. As a result, when the professional market scale is over S_M, the regional economy can "explode out" and gradually build a division of labor collaboration network across regions and even across national boundaries. When many regional and economic entities at home and abroad are closely linked with a specialized market, the global division of labor and cooperation network is formed at the core of the professional market. This is the external development mechanism for "Yiwu Business Circle" from the perspective of regional economic expansion.

3. Economic effectiveness and development prospect of specialized markets

3.1 Multiple economic effects of specialized markets

As one of the most important sections of market institution, market system, and market mechanism with Chinese characteristics, specialized markets, which have been the earliest birthplace of market power since the implementation of the reform and opening-up policy, are also prominent elements of the national economic system. By the end of 2016, the total number of specialized markets reached beyond 80,000 throughout the country, with an annual gross turnover surpassing 15 trillion Yuan. The explosion of specialized markets has driven the development of more than 5 million medium, small, and micro-sized enterprises nationwide, which employ over 100 million people. The fact that specialized markets enjoy a long-term existence, development, and prosperity in this country fully suggests that it is an appropriate economic organizational approach that conforms to the development level of productivity within our country ever since its reform and opening-up. Its vitality at least manifests in the following economic effects:

The first one is the combined effect of the deepening of labor division as well as trading efficiency. In terms of enterprises (including medium-sized, small-sized, and micro-sized businesses), due to a small production scale and limited comprehensive strength, building the upstream and downstream integrated production system confronts plenty of difficulties. Commercial entities tend to lack competitive advantages, thus it is an ideal action to implement specialized division of labor and interdisciplinary cooperation. However, the deepening of labor division will also lead to increasing numbers of trades and higher transaction fees. It might even diminish the improvement of production effectiveness brought about by labor division. Such a transaction fee caused by labor division pertains to an internally-generating transaction fee. According to the definition by Yang Xiaokai (1998), internally-generating transaction fees came into being because people contend for the benefits of labor division. Such opportunistic behavior gives rise to inadequate utilization of the benefits or price distortion which falls away from Pareto efficiency in resource allocation. The birth and expansion of specialized markets prompt market capacity to keep growing. Enterprises which used to deal with integrated production realize it is more profitable to enlarge production scale and deepen coordination as well as distribute responsibilities. As a result, they pay more attention to certain links in the production chain. Meanwhile, sections including production & sales, research & development, product design, logistics, and brand operation come to grow apart. In the meantime, specialized markets have a large number of buyers and sellers, which not only adds to the selectivity of transactions but also fully improves the flow of information, thus effectively stifling the opportunistic behavior brought about by information asymmetry. Most administrators of specialized markets play the role of arbitrators

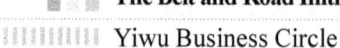
in the third-party regulation structure described by Williamson (1975), providing a guarantee of the implementation of contract fairness and quality supervision for both trading parties, thereby greatly reducing internally-generating transaction fees caused by the lacking information interaction between the two parties. Specialized markets mainly employ a shopkeeper system, in which case sellers virtually offer credit guarantees and property mortgages to buyers in response to their fixed booths. Therefore, in the course of a negotiated transaction, both parties attach importance to the investment of their own credibility as well as the discount of profit expectations in a long-term transaction, which extends cooperation on a long-term basis and cuts down on internally-generating transaction fees. Hence, we can see that specialized markets facilitate the deepening of labor division, reduce transaction fees, and increase trading efficiency simultaneously, which effectively overcomes the contradiction between deeper labor division and increasing transaction fees, manifesting a mixture of combined effect.

The second is the cooperative effect of economies of scale and economies of scope. In terms of medium-sized, small-sized, and micro-sized enterprises, they face a lot of difficulties in achieving economies of scale and economies of scope, not to mention these two types of economic effects tend to contradict each other. In order to achieve economies of scale, business entities have to invest limited resource elements into certain products or some links in the production chain, in which case economies of scope cannot be achieved because it requires the production of multiple products. On condition that enterprises produce multiple products in the hope of achieving economies of scope, their limited resource elements have to be split and utilized separately, in which case economies of scale is hard to form. Specialized markets, on the other hand, provide channels for the two economic effects to coordinate with each other. In a specialized market, professional wholesalers are responsible for communicating supplies and demands. Besides, one wholesaler can provide services for lots of upstream manufacturers as well as downstream purchasing agents. In view of this, numerous enterprises of different sizes, which are all producing the same products, are relatively independent and scattered in space. All enterprises conduct sales by virtue of the same specialized market. As a result, their large scale production and supply capacity surpass independent enterprises and even transnational corporations. Therefore, the external size effect of supply and sales comes into play, with supply and marketing costs being cut and average transaction costs lowered dramatically, finally shaping competitively advantageous wholesale prices.

In the meanwhile, although the products from individual enterprises are relatively homogenized and even focused on certain links of the chain, large quantities of similar products of different specifications produced by similar corporations gather in specialized markets. Buyers can choose freely among relevant lines of products. Thus, seeing all specialized markets as a whole, when the economy of scope surpasses the individual enterprise resource capacity, so to speak, the economic effect of scope cracks the conundrum of enterprises' production scope inefficiency. This shows that, with the help of such an organizational form as a specialized market, enterprises of different scales have achieved the combination of the effect of economies of scale and economies of scope. The abovementioned collaborative economic effects apply not only to manufacturers and wholesalers associated with specialized markets, but also to relevant supporting service enterprises such as storage logistics, financial services, catering & accommodation, recreation & entertainment, intermediary services, and the like. It is because of the large-scale commerce flow, material flow, fund flow, information flow, and everything else brought out by the specialized markets that individual-related supporting enterprises keep expanding their business scales and are able to provide multilevel and diversified services as a whole on the industry level. Moreover, the individual cost of enterprises tends to drop, thereby forming the cooperative effect of economies of scale and economies of scope.

The third is the coexistence of the cluster effect and competition effect. At the beginning of the birth of specialized markets, although it

is only the aggregation of the marketing function, with the scale getting larger and larger, software and hardware optimized and services getting upgraded, and more and more associated economic entities gathering together to provide adequate and systematic services including storage, logistics, catering, accommodation, entertainment, finance, advertisement, consultation, and so forth. Some major specialized markets actively carry out modern financial services represented by supply-chain financing, shop managerial authority mortgage financing, warehouse receipt mortgage financing, RMB cross-border business, etc. Moreover, these markets also provide exhibition services represented by international exhibition & global forum, tourism services such as shopping tours and culture-oriented tours, as well as modern credit solicitation services featuring parallel online-to-offline implementation and diversified integration, etc. Therefore, these major specialized markets gradually become service syntheses conducting various functions including demonstration, negotiation, signing of contracts, payment, logistics, storage, after-sales service, credibility, etc. The aggregation of related economic entities and functions makes it easier for businesses to provide mutual services and support for each other at a lower cost, which improves the competitive edge of upstream and downstream integration, reducing transaction cost, covering searching cost, negotiation cost, contracting cost, enforcement cost, and so forth. In particular, the prestige mechanism caused by spatial adjacency facilitates the conclusion of business and diminishes moral hazards, which is conducive to the establishment of a more steady and permanent cooperation relationship among relevant economic entities. The spatial aggregation of related economic entities also exerts a reinforcement effect on the competitive mechanism. The exchange of extensive and important information as well as other activities including purchases and sales that are carried out between buyers and sellers as well as buyers and sellers due to the aggregation of large numbers of sellers selling the same or similar products, along with numerous buyers in the same specialized market. In the process, the competition among related entities on all levels is inevitable. Particularly the competition among sellers in aspects like prices, qualities, and brands of products is the most intense. It is precisely this intense competition that drives manufacturers to continuously upgrade products and pursue technological innovation, prompting sales entities to constantly raise service standards, thus shaping a competitive mechanism reinforcement effect generated from specialized markets and improving the operational efficiency of the whole supply chain system, ensuring the specialized markets' dominant position in their competition with other circulation channels.

The fourth is the interaction between network effect and conduction effect. The internal economic and social connection within specialized markets form a network structure, namely, a specialized market network. It refers to the aggregation of formal and informal relations established by every subject[8] including business operators, suppliers, purchasers, supporting service institutions, the government, and individuals, which is beneficial to the smooth conduct of market transactions within certain scope of specialized markets in the course of interaction. On the one hand, such a network ties facilitates' resource sharing and complementary advantages, which is conducive to inventing new ideas and new technologies, providing an institutional platform for every subject to get close to an infinitely repeated game. As a result, the behavior of an individual subject cannot escape the constraints of the network developed by themselves in the old days. The network sinks related entities deeply through strategic planning and adjusting

---

[8] The boundary of the professional market network is relatively vague, and it is not limited to the geographical space where the professional market is located. But the main structure of the network is generally located within the space of the location of the professional market. Because all kinds of actors, commodity resources, factors of production in specialized markets flow between different regions. This makes it difficult to ensure that the boundaries of a professional market network coincide with the geographical boundaries of its location.

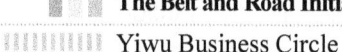
tools, thus conducive to overcoming the opportunistic tendency of concerning subjects. On the other hand, the common culture formed by such network structure is conducive to cultivating mutual trust and cooperation among network numbers, establishing specific circulation channels for knowledge and information exchanges, thus reducing transaction cost. The information passing through specialized markets falls into two such categories, as dominant information and recessive information. Specialized markets pass most information to entities such as manufacturers in the manner of codification. For example, information like the trade leads, price of raw material, or consumer goods can be passed onto corresponding manufacturers through digital methods such as an information index collected by relevant departments. Enterprises can organize and arrange production based on such information. Recessive empirical information mainly disseminates through informal interpersonal communication and contact. For instance, various subjects communicate, haggle, and bargain in the process of transactions in a specialized market, which implicitly passes on information concerning product quality improvement, creative design, functional structure, etc., thus facilitating product innovation and upgrading. Since specialized markets participate in the socioeconomic network constructed by subjects, the cost of such an information transmission effect is relatively low. Its stimulated function towards upstream and downstream innovation further strengthens the network effect of the specialized market, which triggers a more intensive pass-along effect. Therefore, the two of them form then a mechanism for mutual reinforcement.

3.2 The development prospect and orientation of specialized markets

In recent years, domestic and international economic conditions changed dramatically. A new round of global technological revolutions and industrial transformations appear ready to take off, especially in the context of the great development of the Internet marching from a consumer-oriented Internet era to an industry-oriented Internet era step by step. The development of a traditional specialized market faces multiple new challenges such as big data, cloud computing, Internet of Things, 2D barcode technology, and so forth. As a result, marketing has broken time limits substantially. Some manufacturers went over intermediate links including wholesale markets and retailers to confront terminal consumers directly. Therefore, traditional massive wholesale commerce might be influenced tremendously. Against this backdrop, the theory of the demise of specialized markets, which was popular for a while, gave rise to the public attention once again. In the introduction of the Chinese edition of *Yiwu Business Circle*, we raised our doubt about this theory. In the 10 years afterwards, the development of the Yiwu commodities market has proven that we were right about that. Here are some new perspectives on the matter:

We believe the development prospect of specialized markets should be viewed from a dynamic perspective. Knowing from reviewing its development story, the specialized market phenomenon must be seen faithfully as a process which experiences constant change, innovation, transformation, and upgrading. For instance, compared with the first generation of the Yiwu commodity market, the sixth generation of the commodity market, which is also the latest generation, has seen dramatic changes in all aspects from hardware facilities, trading manner to subject levels, commodity composition, management level, and so forth. The market has transformed from a roadside market doing business in the open air to a shopping mall selling competitive products with organic interaction between online sales and offline sales. The original spot trading has been replaced by sales exhibitions and trading orders-based transactions. Cash payment has given way to diversified payment modes including bank transfers, online payment, third-party platform payment, etc. Furthermore, simple commodity trading functions have turned into a compound function covering sales exhibitions, information collection and distribution, price formation, tourism services, product innovation, exchanges of know-how, standard stipulation, regular output, etc. Such tremendous changes would be completely unimaginable at the birth of the Yiwu commodity market.

It is obvious that we must view the future of specialized markets from a dynamic perspective with a developing foresight. We believe that, although the future may bring about a new round of challenges such as the technological revolution, industrial transformation, and business model innovation, as long as specialized markets can fully blend in and adapt to the new trend of economic and social development, go with the new changes in pattern of life and mode of production, and remold its own trading manner, logistics system, information system, and the like by virtue of modern scientific technology, they may enjoy a larger space for development. Besides, a large number of businesses of all sizes scattered at home and abroad still need specialized markets such as sharing platforms to sell goods at lower costs. However, a lot of retailers are having a hard time having a dialogue with manufacturers directly and lack discourse power in merchandise purchases. As a result, they are in need of a specialized market rife with complete competition for commodity purchasing. Thus over an extended period, plenty of new specialized markets will advance with the times in an updated and renewed form in the hope of ushering in a new round of great development and prosperity. Obviously, a multitude of specialized markets will die out sooner or later because of failure or delay in blending in the above-stated development tendency on account of smaller scales, lower subject levels, poor management, and outmoded facilities.

The above-stated differentiated situation has had preliminary manifestation seeing from the practice of the development of specialized markets in China in recent years. A multitude of nationally known large-scale specialized markets represented by China Commodity City in Yiwu are endeavoring to transform from extensive expansion to intensive development by means of innovation function, quality improvement, brand cultivation, internationalization promotion, etc., changing towards modern specialized markets. Other specialized markets are facing plenty of problems such as smaller scale, lower levels, poor overall qualities of operators, worn-out buildings, incomplete ancillary facilities, weak logistic bases in particular, shrinking radiation scope, backward ideas of founders, managers or operators, as well as tenuous brand awareness. It is hard for them to meet up with the demands of adapting to the modern business model, transaction means, and service content innovation. Facing the challenge of the new business model, specialized markets are generally lacking any sense of crisis. Therefore, we believe that in the coming 10 years or so, the development of specialized markets in our country might go over an important shuffle process. Some markets having old trading modes and methods or a slow upgrading process are likely to fade or even perish in the course of market segmentation and integration or get merged and absorbed by other markets, which might lead to a decline in the total number of nationwide specialized markets. On the other hand, the specialized markets which take the initiative to absorb modern technological means, management concepts, and the like to improve their own functions and service levels, are likely to upgrade on many levels including scales, brands, radiation collection capabilities, operation scopes, etc. These kinds of markets expand themselves from regional markets to national markets and even to global markets step by step, changing from merely intermediate links to economic organizations which play unique roles in the overall process of social reproduction.

We believe that the future development direction of specialized markets must comply with the new changes and tendencies of both production and lifestyles. Currently, China has entered the new normal stage of economic development. Its consumption pattern gradually transforms from the stage of mimetic wave-style consumption to the stage where personalized consumption and diversified consumption are leading factors; investment demands change from large-scale intense exploitation and construction to domains involving infrastructure interconnection, new technologies, new products, new types of business, new business models and the like little by little; methods of productive organization change from large-scale batch manufacturing to production featuring miniaturization, intelligence, and professionalization; market competition converts from quantity expansion and price competition to

giving priority to quality, brand, and technology bit by bit. It is clear that the innovative and transformative development of specialized markets, especially the major ones in our country, not only should focus on the advancement of their own hardware and software, but should also adapt to the new business revolution, new tendency, and new changes led by the outburst of modern information technology, coalescing with a series of modern information technology involving Internet, cloud computing, big data, web of things, various business new patterns, and so forth through specialized operation, enterprise operation, standardized management, chain management, etc., achieving revolutionary improvement in aspects like market morphostructure, trading manner, service function, and the like. Specifically speaking, things can be done starting from the following aspects:

The first thing to do is to promote functional innovation by accomplishing the transformation from a commodity transaction medium to a comprehensive service integrator. At present, the function of most specialized markets in China is mainly providing venues for commodity trades represented by commodity display, orders upon negotiation and storage logistics, only part of large leading markets that have multiple functions. The rise and prosperity of the modern service industry brings forward higher requirements for the innovative development and transformative advancement of specialized markets. The trading objects of such markets are no longer limited to commodities, but extended to services. Therefore, the inevitable option for the innovative and transformative advancement of specialized markets is to adapt to the direction of the modern business mode's revolution and innovation, particularly the megatrends of cross-border integration development of various business forms. By means of the innovation model introducing a bunch of other business forms including retail, finance, exhibition, tourism, catering, entertainment, and the like, markets promote service-oriented commodities as well as comprehensive services, forging cross-border integrated service providers, thus enabling specialized markets to not only play the role of value delivery but accomplish the function of discovering, excavating, and creating values. It also requires that traditional market managers must transform towards modern commerce service integrators, focusing on the improvement of modern trading service functions, with capital operation as the connection link, putting forth efforts to build a modernized international trading platform radiating influences across the whole country and even the whole globe via various methods covering online and offline market merging, interconnection between trading and exhibition, financial service innovation, franchise chains, management output, merger & acquisition, etc.

The second is to promote commercial distribution innovation and to accomplish the transformation from an enterprise marketing platform to a brand enterprise exhibition center. At present, the function of most specialized markets in China is to provide a low-cost shared sales platform for medium-sized, small-sized, and micro-sized enterprises including many family workshops, self-employed entrepreneurs, and so on. The buyers are mainly small-scale secondary wholesalers and minor retailers. The commodities circulating on the markets are mostly mid and low-end products. The operators mainly rely on cheap prices and massive wholesale to open up domestic and foreign markets, and as a result, brand construction is comparatively lagging behind. All in all, both trade subjects and trade objects are at a relatively low level, as a result, a series of problems such as virulent price competition, credit sale operating risk, counterfeit and shoddy products, intellectual property infringement, and so forth came into being. For that reason, the top priority is to spare no effort to promote market brand construction. As market operators are generally small-scaled and weak in strength, they may encounter a sea of troubles in taking independent actions in brand-building. Therefore, a lot more attention should go into building and promoting a brand image of the markets, strongly cultivating and introducing brand suppliers, brand purchasers, brand commodities, and the like, guiding specialized markets in a giving way to exhibition centers featuring perfect commodities brimming with brand connotations, and exquisite enterprises step by step along an orderly way.

The third is to boost logistics service innovation and to achieve a smooth transition from a cargo distribution platform to an intelligent logistics & distribution center. By far, most storage & logistics systems of specialized markets in China are comparatively extensive. The fact that some supporting storage & logistics venues are scattered in residential areas has brought out plenty of problems such as potential security issues, traffic congestion, environmental pollution, and so forth. Although a portion of specialized markets have established specific logistics & distribution centers in the course of updating and upgrading, the operating entities of the centers have been shaped from the original joint consignment department for the most part. There are large quantities of centers that are at a small scale with comparatively outdated hardware facilities, business models, management levels, etc., especially less information-based, automatic and intelligent. The completion of business procedures mainly relies on manual work, which has a difficult time adapting to the demands of the rapid development and highly efficient operation of the storage & logistics industry in the context of the great revolution of modern information technology. This problem has increasingly become a considerable letdown for holding back the transformation and upgrading of professional markets. Thus the present situation where the storage & logistics operating entities act on their own free will and compete with each other extensively should be smashed. Besides, a few large professional storage & logistics enterprises ought to be cultivated by integrating resources owned by existing operating entities. Furthermore, the construction of unified intelligent storage & logistics centers should be facilitated, utilizing various modern information technologies and modern storage & logistics know-how including Internet, web of things, cloud computing, etc., in the hope of advancing the construction and development of conventional storage and logistics facilities to accomplish systematization, digitization, interconnection, automation, and intelligence, and coordinating the physical dispersion and information concentration of commodities, finally leading to intelligent high-efficient delivery.

The fourth is to promote the innovation of information flow and to accomplish the transition from information gathering & distribution platforms to big data centers. So far the information service of the majority of specialized markets in our country are mainly focused on the collection and distribution of information revealing supply & demand, prices, industries, policies, etc. A dozen of domestic large leading markets such as Yiwu "China Small Commodity City", Keqiao "China Textile City", Yuyao "China Plastics City", and Linyi Mall have compiled and released marketing information including "the Yiwu China commodity index", "China·Keqiao textile index", "China Yuyao plastic raw material price index", "Linyi mall price index", etc., with domestic and international influence on the rise day by day. These markets have already become prominent channels for their subjects to acquire relevant industry news. However, in general, most specialized markets are unable to or fail to collect, excavate, and use massive transaction data, thus are in no position to provide trading subjects with more accurate and more detailed information services. Therefore, large leading markets should make the most of their own scale advantages and favorable basic conditions to finish the transition from information gathering & distributing platforms to big data centers. Specialized markets intend to provide subjects with more detailed and more accurate information on passenger distribution, supply-demand changes, price fluctuations, storage status, capital flow, cargo transportation, and so forth via cooperating with domestic and international well-known enterprises that enjoy pioneering advantages in the field of development and application of big data such as IBM, Google, Amazon, Baidu, Ali Baba, and so forth, inoculating relevant technologies and resources, carrying out massive collection, storage, counting, excavation, conversion, and utilization on physical markets, warehousing facilities, logistics centers, freight yards, transport vehicles, as well as transaction data on relevant e-commerce platforms.

The fifth is to facilitate the innovation of capital flow and accomplish the transition from capital flow platforms to supply-chain financial hubs. Currently, the financial services provided by most specialized markets in our country are primarily providing necessary support for the fund flow of both contracting parties. A small number of markets attempted to render services involving warehouse receipt collateral and pawns financing of store operation right. The trade parties are primarily engaged in commodity circulation services, generally belonging to asset-light sales agents, minor wholesale dealers, retailers, and the like, lacking related collateral needed in fund-raising. Moreover, in the course of operation, there are low seasons as well as peak seasons, which means every now and again there are demands for short-term capital turnover while the majority of the financial institutions can hardly provide corresponding capital supply services. As a result, the capital supply and demand in the market manifest obvious dislocation, which becomes a great letdown in terms of improving market operational vitality. For that reason, it is advisable to guide, promote, and support the construction of supply-chain finance matching the characteristics of market trading activities. Above all, large leading markets with better development foundations have more reasons to expedite the transition from capital flow platforms to supply-chain financial centers. To be more specific, the advisable practice is to give full play to such advantages of market construction managers as holding a better understanding and an intimate knowledge of business operators, upstream suppliers, and downstream purchasers, especially when it comes to credit evaluation. The idea is to integrate all parties' technical advantages, information preponderance, management advantages, and the like via introducing professional supply-chain financial services, and developing diversified supply-chain financial products specifically targeted based on the characteristics of trading procedures of specialized markets, offering more accurate, more flexible, and more perfect supply-chain financial services, in the endeavor of turning specialized markets into fund pools and industry financial service centers.

III "Yiwu Business Circle" Evolution Trends and Goals

1. "Yiwu Business Circle" core area: World Capital of Small Commodities

1.1 World Capital of Small Commodities' connotation and extension

On December 4, 2015, President Xi Jinping pointed out in the important speech at the closing ceremony of the High Level Dialogue between the Chinese and African Leaders and the Representatives of the Business Community, namely, the Fifth Congress of China African Entrepreneurs that: Yiwu is called the World Capital of Small Commodities. It fully recognizes Yiwu's development achievements and also expresses eagerly expectations of her bright future. For the purpose of Yiwu as the core area of "Yiwu Business Circle", its future evolutionary trend and goal is to be worthy of the name of the World Capital of Small Commodities. The World Capital of Small Commodities means being the core city that takes the lead in the aspects of research and development, design, production, trade, circulation, brand operation, and standard setting and that exerts great influence and re-molding force over the industry chain, supply chain, and value chain of global small commodities. To achieve this goal, the key is to enhance channel superiority, control, and discourse power of Yiwu, to make it occupy dominant positions in core links like small commodities research and development design, brand standard, and sales channels and to improve cross-regional division of labor and cooperation networking based on value association, namely, the ability of "Yiwu Business Circle" to optimize the allocation of resources around the world.

To build the World Capital of Small Commodities, it shall first highlight the features of the "world". As a result, it shall not only fully improve the internationalization level of ideological concepts, policy environment, infrastructure, city functions, talent exchanges, enterprise management, and so on to be connected and integrated into the mainstream of the world economy but also to become a highly open large platform for cross-regional division of labor and cooperation with global shared resource optimization; secondly, it shall highlight the features of "small commodities", the production and trade objects take small commodities, namely, manufactured goods for daily use as the subject and characteristics, focus on small commodities (surely, not limited to small commodities), make high value-added links of small commodities such as research and development, design, brand and standards more exquisite, stronger, better, and larger and achieve seamless connection with small commodities production, circulation bases, and enterprises all around the world; thirdly, it shall highlight the features of "business capital", give full play to channels, business pulse, and network advantages of the Yiwu market connected to the world, construct new systems and new mechanisms that are adaptive to modern trade, form new channels and platforms for organizing import, export and entre-pot trade globally to attract more small commodities production, trading and circulating enterprises to join in the cross-regional division of labor collaboration network of "Yiwu Business Circle". Specifically, to become a real World Capital of Small Commodities, Yiwu needs to construct the following three centers after decades-long efforts:

Firstly, it needs to be the world's leading international commodity trade center. It means to introduce Internet, mobile Internet, Internet of Things, cloud computing, big data, artificial intelligence, 3D printing, smart wear, VR technology, and other recent scientific and technological achievements into the whole process of small commodity trading. It must also construct the world's leading modern display trading system, intelligent warehouse logistics system, integrated big data system, and integrated trade service system to make Yiwu become an International Small Commodity Trade Center, a Circulation Center, an Information Center, and a Price Center with low transaction cost, good credit, which is well-informed, uses new means, and provides good services. First of all, it shall construct the world's leading modern exhibition trading system. Relying on the advantages of the real market and the online market, it shall promote highly-integrated online and offline developments with a focus on linking the entity market facilities into a network through intelligent sensing equipment, conduct networking, intelligentization and digitalization of markets, stores, merchants, and commodities, achieve "network digital trade", develop an intelligent network, intelligent property, intelligent management, intelligent early warning system, and build a "smart business city"; it shall also vigorously promote "Yiwu Shopping" based on the real market to further optimize panoramic shopping mode, such as introducing VR technology to create the market purchasing scenario that simulates the reality, improve merchant purchase and tourist shopping experiences, and provide services like professional market analysis, information translation, trade negotiation, online duty, after-sale tracking, and overseas promotion targeting at the reality of lack of international trade communication and practical operation ability of market operators and small and medium enterprises. Secondly, it shall construct the world's leading intelligent warehouse logistics system,

apply modern information technologies and modern warehouse logistics technologies such as Internet of Things, Internet, and cloud computing to gradually promote systematized, digitized, interconnected, automated, intellectualized transformation, and upgrading of traditional warehouse facilities throughout the city, construct intellectualized public warehouse logistics facilities, combine physical dispersion and informational concentration of commodities, and achieve efficient and intelligent distribution by third party. Thirdly, it shall construct the world's leading integrated big data system. Through cooperation with famous enterprises with leading advantages in development and application of big data at home and abroad, conduct large-scale collection, storage, statistics, mining, and transformation and utilization of transaction data of the entity market, storage facilities, logistics center, freight yard, transportation vehicle, and related e-commerce platforms to form a precise, meticulous, and integrated big data system about passenger flow distribution, supply and demand change, price fluctuation, storage state, capital flow, and freight transport, providing support for decision-making by the related economic subjects, market regulators, party committees, and governments. Lastly, it shall construct the world's leading integrated trade service system, which integrates relevant information about market regulation, customs, inspection and quarantine, foreign exchanges, public security, taxation, judicature, science and technology departments, third party credit evaluation institutions, online trading platforms, financial institutions, and intermediaries. It will create a clear and accurate, traceable, controllable, responsible, online and offline linked, open, shared and integrated trade supervision and service system, promoting trade facilitation and liberalization while improving control and credit-binding forces on the trade risk.

Secondly, Yiwu must construct an internationally famous small commodity research and development design center. That is, to construct the display and exchange platform, property rights trading platform, public service platform for small commodities R&D design through gathering global commodity R&D talents, enterprises, institutions, and conduct upstream and downstream cooperation along the industrial chain through the domestic and foreign first-class R&D capacity for small commodities. On the one hand, based on the existing National Tourism Commodity R&D center, Yiwu Industrial Design Center, Yiwu Korea Design Center, Yiwu Creative Design Center, and Yiwu Creative Park, this transformation will give full play to the guidance of the venture capital of the government, attract and cultivate more small commodities R&D design talent, enterprises, and institutions, encourage and support colleges, universities and enterprises to hold R&D design talent education, training, create a national industrial design public service platform by taking Yiwu Industrial Design Center as the core carrier, further vigorously promote construction and development of the Public Technology Platform, the Small Commodity R&D Center, the Industrial Design Center, the Quality Inspection Center, the Key Laboratory and various public service platforms for the purpose of serving small and medium enterprises, providing research and development services for various economic subjects for the surrounding regions at home and abroad, and developing Yiwu into a source and exporter for small commodities research and development design. On the other hand, it must vigorously support and promote industrial and commercial enterprises, market operators, and so on to adopt many means like business outsourcing, directional entrustment, and transfer of results to conduct cooperation with the research and development design forces of other regions at home and abroad through offline channels and network platforms for the purpose of application instead of ownership; at the same time, it shall consider the reality that high-end R&D design talents are mainly in first-tier cities at home and abroad with good environments for living, work, and startup, and shall vigorously support and promote commercial and industrial enterprises with the strength to set up R&D design centers and purchase R&D design teams so as to achieve optimized allocation of resources globally; it will carry out a global small commodity research and development design competition, set up a "Yiwu Small Commodities Prize", and endeavor to create the small commodities "Red Dot Design

Award" with great international influence; it shall set up a specially small commodities R&D design results trading platform that combines an online and offline presence to attract relevant subjects at home and abroad to conduct transactions. Through the abovementioned efforts, it shall make Yiwu become an applied field and exchange place for foremost small commodities research and development design results. In addition, given the characteristics of small commodities like low unit price, numerous types, fast updating, and easy wear, it needs to focus on links like new materials, technologies, styles, and functions for small commodities R&D design, especially endow products with more fashion elements, cultural elements, and creative elements, make great efforts to develop fashion consumer goods for daily use and cultural and creative industries, integrate the superior humanistic blending between China and foreign countries of Yiwu into product research and development design so as to develop more famous and high quality products that are compatible with traditional Chinese and Western culture, consumption habits, and fashion trends.

Thirdly, it shall be the global leading standard center for small commodities brands. It shall start from different perspectives like product brand, enterprise brand, market brand, industrial brand, and city brand, fully improve the international influence and reputation of the entire brand system of Yiwu, rely on the advantages of the largest global small commodity market and national comprehensive international trade reform pilot, lead the global production and manufacturing of industrial consumer goods, and lead preparation, promotion, and coordination of manufacturing and trade regulatory standards for global industrial consumer goods to make Yiwu the international small commodities brand cluster center, cultivation center, production and trading standard preparation center, and output center. To give play to the advantages of the exhibition and trading platform of the largest global small commodity market and attract more small commodity brand products and enterprises at home and abroad with greater influence, especially more world renowned purchasers and more brand operation headquarters, marketing headquarters, procurement headquarters, and logistics headquarters of large enterprise groups to settle in Yiwu so as to make Yiwu become the brand operation and exhibition center for production and trading enterprises and products for global small commodities. It shall vigorously support and promote brand development of small and medium enterprises and market merchants in Yiwu, cultivate and attract more "small but professional", "small but new", "small but special", and "small but proficient" brand enterprises, wholesalers, and new foreign trade companies or circulation groups with independent brands, overseas marketing channels, and independent research and development innovation abilities. Yiwu must encourage industrial and business enterprises and market merchants to register brands in developed countries and organize production domestically so as to make foreign purchasers and consumers recognize such brands and also give play to production and manufacturing advantages easily. Moreover, it needs to fully improve the market brand, industrial brand, and city brand of Yiwu, because the practice shows that a common market brand is beneficial for promoting joint innovation of technical cooperation and marketing models between market merchants and production enterprises so as to promote constant innovation in technologies through intensified cooperation between the professional market and related industrial clusters, and jointly shape the brand of the professional market through the same kind of enterprises to bring about transformation and upgrading of industrial clusters. Professional market brands will continuously attract productive service industry-like brand marketing and R&D design to enter the market, benefit agglomeration development of medium and high-end service links of related industries so as to form a substitution effect on low-end production, and promote structural optimization, transformation, and upgrading of related industries. As a result, it shall vigorously develop brands of "Yiwu Business Circle", "China Small Commodity City", "Yiwu Small Commodity Market", "Yiwu International Trade City", "Yiwu Small Commodity Index", "Yiwu Trade Fair", and "Made in Yiwu" and enable various economic subjects at home and abroad to conduct

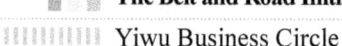

production, trading, circulation, and supporting service activities focused on Yiwu to share the above mentioned brand influence. While promoting construction of a brand system, it also needs to vigorously construct a standard small commodities production and trading system and concentrate efforts on product and market standards. It needs to rely on the foreign trade commodity quality regulation system established with support from the comprehensive reform pilot for the international trade at the national level, further construct and perfect production and trading standard system for small commodities with Yiwu characteristics, and set up a "Yiwu standard" that connects domestic and foreign trade especially when consensus and application are obtained for the product quality standards and trade regulatory standards in the fields of production and processing, online trade, warehousing and logistics, international transportation, and customs inspection for small commodities at home and abroad under market purchase and trade modes. It shall encourage enterprises and industrial associations and so on to establish industrial standards higher than the national standard or export standard and support the transformation of patent technologies with core competitiveness into standardization. It shall set up a QR code quality tracing mechanism for small commodities and develop a quality standard control network that focuses on joint control over links like quality assurance of factory supply source, market operators' certificate inspection, cargo unit inspection, and custom inspection. Through means like output standard, output mode, and output service, as well as intensified cooperation in the aspects of operation, logistics, standards, quality, and the credit system with professional markets and business trading companies of other regions at home and abroad, it shall fully promote the Yiwu market network layout for "China Small Commodities City" and strive to create Tera-scale "Yiwu" market.

1.2 Dynamic mechanism for constructing the World Capital of Small Commodities

Yiwu is a city that bases itself on reform and innovation. To construct a higher level world class "Capital of Small Commodities", the most important mechanism is to gather and rely on various innovation resources and elements at home and abroad and commonly promote overall innovation centered on scientific and technological innovation. In today's world, innovation is increasingly becoming the key to seizing the commanding heights of the international competitiveness of a country, a region, an industry, or an enterprise. President Xi Jinping points out and emphasizes that: "To grasp innovation is to grasp development, and to seek innovation is to seek the future." The fifth plenary session of the 18th CPC Central Committee has proposed the innovation, coordination, green, open, and shared development concept, prioritized innovative development among "five development concepts", and pointed out that innovation is the first driving force to lead the development, and that innovation must be placed at the core position of the overall national development. Yiwu places its hope for building a World Capital of Small Commodities on the basis of integrated development of various modern technological and innovative results, and on the joint promotion of concept innovation, system innovation, management innovation, scientific and technological innovation, industrial innovation, cultural innovation, and social innovation by relevant regions at home and abroad closely related to Yiwu.

To build a World Capital of Small Commodities, Yiwu must rely on the combination of spontaneous endogenous innovation, entrepreneurial activity of the market players, governmental voluntary initiative reform, and innovation measures. Yiwu must also deepen the implementation of an innovation-driven development strategy according to the concept and requirements for innovative development and realize the successful transformation of new and old kinetic energy through accelerating the growth of new kinetic energy with innovation and the improvement of traditional kinetic energy transformation so as to promote innovation in Yiwu's development mode and path, create an innovative city with a strong innovation atmosphere, rich innovative resources, fruitful innovative achievements, developed innovative industries, and powerful innovation strength so as to become a famous "innovative Yiwu". Thus, it shall take improving innovation capability and level as the core, treat the speeding up of economic development mode as the main line, and regard the full promotion of "Yiwu Pilot Project" and other national reform tasks as the key. This will further carry forward the "chicken feather for sugar"[9] business tradition and daring spirit of "the culture of rattle"[10] by taking organic interactions between the new urbanization and the new industrialization as an effective way and taking the construction of innovative talents as the fundamental guarantee. Yiwu will need to vigorously promote new products, technology, design, brands, ideas, and so on brought by public entrepreneurship, rely on technology research and development, creative design, process change, business model innovation; it will also need to comprehensively facilitate market innovation and function upgrading, industrial technology innovation, structural transformation, trade innovation, rule optimization, urban service innovation, and energy level promotion while giving full play to the unique advantages of the gathering of Chinese and foreign

---

[9] In history, Yiwu was densely populated with low per capita cultivated land and poor land. To improve the fertility of the land and increase the output, local farmers made "Maltose" with the sucrose produced by themselves. During slack season, local farmers would shake the rattle and shoulder the cargo load to exchange sugar for chicken feather as the fertilizer to the cultivated land, which is called "chicken feather for sugar". Refer to Lu Lijun, Bai Xiaohu and Wang Zuqiang: *Market Yiwu: From Chicken Feather for Sugar to International Commerce*. Hangzhou: Zhejiang People's Publishing House, 2003, p. 26.

[10] Rattle business culture is the utilitarian philosophy of commercial culture taking the town economy as the carrier and comprehensive reflection of ideas and social customs in the decentralized rural market for business activities, reflecting the hard working spirit of Yiwu people conducting "chicken feather for sugar" by shaking the rattle, tramping over mountains and through ravines and trekking as well as fine quality of being good at discovering, digging, and taking advantage of business opportunities. Refer to Lu Lijun, Bai Xiaohu and Wang Zuqiang: *Market Yiwu: From Chicken Feather for Sugar to International Commerce*. Hangzhou: Zhejiang People's Publishing House, 2003, p. 3.

businessmen and the mutual integration of multinational culture. Finally, there must also be a focus on promoting and facilitating collision and communication between Chinese and foreign multi-culture, thinking, and ideas to provide a source of motivation for innovative activities.

To build a World Capital of Small Commodities, Yiwu must put technological innovation in a more important strategic position, focus on improving Yiwu's technological innovation capability, and give full play to its leading role in the market, industry, trade, urban innovation and development, and urban transformation and development. Thus, it shall speed up construction of major technological innovation platforms, innovation carrier and regional innovation systems, support eligible enterprises and industries to set up industry engineering (technology) centers, R&D centers, and testing centers, support domestic and foreign enterprises, colleges, and universities to construct research and development institutes, key laboratories, and other innovation carriers, and strive to make breakthroughs in key technologies and research and development of generic technologies for major technological innovation projects and production and manufacturing of small commodities. Yiwu will further strengthen the position of the main body of scientific and technological innovation in enterprises, guide high-end innovative talents to enterprises, especially give play to the role of "well-leveraged government investment" fiscal funds and encourage enterprises to be marketed directed with government subsidies and incentives, take application-type technological innovation as a breakthrough, increase technological innovation investment, continuously develop new products, new technologies, and new processes while further making reforms on high benefits, stable guarantee, and a lifetime system of the existing personnel system of the state institutions, set up a sound full-time employment system for civil servants and a special talent system for institutions, promote high-end innovative elements (especially high-level innovative talents) to enterprises, and solve the problems of loose combinations of technologies and economies. Yiwu shall make innovation on talent introduction and the cultivation mechanism to

develop Yiwu into a higher ground for high-level innovative talents, especially attracting and gathering a batch of leading scientific talents, entrepreneurs, high-skill talents, and social management talents, etc., at the forefront of the industry with international vision and capabilities at home and abroad; it shall further promote in-depth and effective implementation of "Yiwu talent" plan, set up a high-level innovative talent service area, provide policy consultation, project declaration, financing introduction, industry–university–research cooperation, industry promotion, and other personalized services, and provide one-stop service for the schooling of children with high-level innovative talents, spouse employment, and talent housing to make these talents "settle, stay and live a better life".

To build a World Capital of Small Commodities, Yiwu must vigorously promote innovative development and transformation of small commodities manufacturing. It shall focus on high and new traditional industries, industrialization of high and new technology, industrial cluster innovation, vigorously promote individualized, quality, and branded development of small commodities manufacturing, and take initiative to explore a high and new international development path. As a result, it shall lay stress on "new, fine and fast", endeavor to make up the shortcome of low added value of products, enhancing the core competitiveness of enterprises and the medium and low-end industry levels. "New" means to focus on new technologies, new format, and new industry, further intensify support and encourage enterprises to introduce advanced production and processing technology, technologies and equipment at home and abroad, set up more provincial or national strategic alliances of industrial technology innovation, facilitate transboundary integration among small commodity markets, small commodities manufacturing, international trade, e-commerce, logistics and express delivery, conventional economic activities, tourist shopping and mobile Internet, big data, cloud computing, Internet of Things, smart wear, and virtual reality technology. "Fine" means to focus on refined, fashionable, and personalized products, vigorously support and encourage tens of thousands of enterprises closely related to the Yiwu market (especially leading enterprises with great comprehensive strength to make the product be the best), design and produce more high value-added products that meet the standard of international safety, environment protection, quality and fashionability, go in-depth to conduct a "famous products in famous shops" project, promote close cooperation between famous brand enterprises and famous retail enterprises at home and abroad to jointly open up the high-end market, and keep up and even lead the consumption trend at home and abroad. "Fast" means to focus on fast manufacturing and fast supply, promote intelligent equipment, automated production, and informationized management of productive enterprises, construct a cooperative supply chain system that integrates upstream and downstream, give the fastest response to the terminal needs so as to adapt to the information age, especially the subversive changes in commercial ecology brought about due to fast e-commerce development, and cultivate and form core competitiveness under a modern business environment. In addition, it shall deepen industry collaboration of other regions related to Yiwu and "Yiwu Business Circle" with a highly open, cooperative, and sharing concept and mechanism, especially for coordinated development between the "Yiwu" market and industry clusters all over the world, explore to set up new cooperative methods, and promote relations between production and marketing to transform from "production, supply and sale" to "sales, production and supply".

2. "Yiwu Business Circle" structure: multi-layer linkage, wide area distribution

2.1 Multi-layer linkage from a regional perspective

At present, although the close correlation between Yiwu and "Yiwu Business Circle" is not subject to absolute influence of factors like geographical location and distances, it mainly depends on value relevance and forming a network like non-circling structure. However, in the forming and development process of "Yiwu Business Circle", the influence of cohesive force and radiant force starts from the surrounding areas to the whole province of Zhejiang, then to the whole country and the world. Even in the new trend of fast-improved current productivity level and production organizing form, distance is still a great factor that affects the transaction costs. Thus, we can make analysis from provincial, national, and global levels. Surely, this analysis order doesn't necessarily mean that the structure of "Yiwu Business Circle" has this layer characteristic, but it is better for us to present to the readers with the correlation between various regions and economic subjects in the business cycle.

Firstly, it is the provincial correlated network. Inside "Yiwu Business Circle", Yiwu keeps closer industry collaboration with many areas in Zhejiang Province. This is because industries and corporate structures in Zhejiang haven't changed the "light, small, and processing" characteristics, especially rural enterprises (including many family workshops and individual craftsmen) that have generally small scales and are unable to set up marketing channels. They have a strong dependence on the low cost and shared sales platform of Yiwu Small Commodity Market and the globally connected business network. Moreover, due to close geographical location, business or non-commercial connections are more frequent. Thus, production and marketing cooperation of both parties can continue for a long time. In the future, given an upgraded business form structure, trade means and service functions of Yiwu Small Commodity Market will have improved quality level, technical content, fashion level, and brand influence of all its traded commodities. It will greatly bring about innovative development, transformation, and upgrading of the relevant industry clusters and SMEs in various areas of Zhejiang closely related to it so as to make Yiwu become the exhibition, marketing center, and brand promotion center for "Made in Zhejiang", which will also provide solid industry support for a new round of great development as well as provide a great leap for Yiwu Small Commodity Market. Surely, due to geographical proximity, with improvement of "Yiwu Business Circle", Yiwu will also conduct more extensive and in-depth cooperation in the aspects of further enhancing resources allocation and regional development integration in various areas of Zhejiang, especially in surrounding areas. Particularly, the planning and construction of Ningbo–Jinhua Railway, Hangzhou–Wenzhou High Speed Rail, Hangzhou–Jinhua–Quzhou Intercity Railway, Jinhua–Yiwu Intercity Bus Rapid Transit System, the construction of Yiwu Railway Integrated Passenger Transport Hub and West Station Freight Hub, the extension of Yiwu Airport and the improvement of the flight area standard, will greatly improve exchanges of personnel, goods, funds, information, etc., between Yiwu, surrounding areas, and other areas in Zhejiang, and speed up construction of the Jinhua–Yiwu metropolitan area and Central Zhejiang city groups taking Jinhua and Yiwu as the core. In this process, Yiwu will develop further in the hinterland.

Secondly, it is a national correlated network. In the process of forming and developing "Yiwu Business Circle", Yiwu and many areas in the country have established close relationships for product sales, logistics distribution, fund settlement, material processing, labor cooperation, government exchanges, and so on, especially many areas that utilize the great influence and reputation of the famous trademark of Yiwu "China Small Commodity City" at home and abroad and create many professional markets named "Yiwu Small Commodity (City)". In the future, with a deepening and expanding "Yiwu Business Circle" and further improvement at the development level, especially with the improvement of the national transportation logistics network, the improvement of the distribution efficiency and reduction in costs, radiation and penetration of Yiwu Small Commodity Market over various regions in the country will be further enhanced so as to promote resources integration and merger and reorganization of a lot of small and medium specialized markets of the same kind throughout the whole country. This will finally form the pattern of Yiwu "China Small Commodity City" and other several large scale professional markets (such as Linyi Mall, Hankou North International Commodity Trading Center, Chengdu International Trade City, Chongqing Chaotianmen

 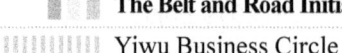
International Trade City) with dominance supplemented through chain operation or flexible cooperation in the professional daily industrial products market. In this process, with Yiwu Small Commodity Market boasting capital, management, talent, and other advantages can take the lead to "go out" through the brand, management, and capital and develop an interregional and cross-industry chain operation. What is more worthy of attention will guide, integrate, and regularize over 200 markets named as "Yiwu Small Commodity (City)" throughout the country based on the first famous trademark for the professional market recognized by the State Administration for Industry and Commerce in November 2014—"Yiwu Small Commodity City"—and construct "Yiwu" market network with closer internal connection. Among connections between Yiwu and various areas in the country, processing with supplied materials is an important means. In the future, with improvement in the development level of "Yiwu Business Circle", there will be a significant change in the way of organization for processing with supplied materials, in the comprehensive quality of the participants, in the grade structure of processing goods, and so on. Especially with active intervention and support of the local governments, the organization level for processing with supplied materials will be greatly improved or transformed from individual free organization to clustered and orderly organization. There will be more skill training, better logistics, distribution, and accommodation of funds and other services, and there will be more sites for processing with supplied materials in Yiwu, which will promote transformation of incoming processing middlemen and practitioners from self-employed individuals to enterprises, and corporate management, which will greatly promote the quality, level, and standards of incoming materials, providing important support for the transformation and upgrading of Yiwu Small Commodity Market.

Thirdly, it is the global correlated network. In the process of outward expansion of "Yiwu Business Circle" and fast development of foreign trade and export, Yiwu has established close exchanges of personnel, trade, culture, science and education, and government affairs with areas from all around the world, especially the countries and regions along the route of the Belt and Road. Generally speaking, focusing on economic and trade relations, many overseas merchants purchase commodities through the platform of Yiwu Small Commodity Market, and many domestic enterprises and operators export commodities through the platform; although the import and entrepot trade in Yiwu has seen rapid development in recent years, more and more overseas commodities enter the domestic market through Yiwu, with the proportion of sales in the market rising year by year while the flow of trade remains an export-oriented pattern. It can be predicted that led by the target of becoming the World Capital of Small Commodities, Yiwu will become an important exhibition and sales platform for worldwide manufacturers of daily industrial products through developing a world-leading modern exhibition and trading system, an intelligent warehousing logistics system, an integrated big data system, an integrated trade management system, etc. in the future. More overseas enterprises will rely on Yiwu to enter the Chinese market or transfer to other countries and regions so as to make commercial intercourse between Yiwu and areas around the globe boast more two-way interactive features. What is worth paying attention to is that the developing of the Belt and Road advocated by China focuses more on a two-way balance of international trade and mutual benefits. As a result, the position of import and entrepot trade will increase day by day, which will be more conducive for Yiwu to give play to the global network of business connection and advantages of a logistics network, and achieve "global purchase and global sale". Benefiting from the promotion of developing the Belt and Road, Yiwu will establish a closer division of labor and cooperation with countries and regions along the route, lay out more commodity exhibition centers, overseas distribution centers, public overseas warehouses, overseas sub-markets, and so on and enhance cooperation in advanced manufacturing fields in developed countries like Germany, the UK, the USA, France, and Italy to jointly set up "International Cooperation Park". The "Park" will rely on the advanced manufacturing processes, equipment, fashion

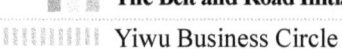

creativity, industrial design, technology research and development, and other advantages of these developed countries to improve the quality and brand of Yiwu; at the same time, through carriers like "Madrid–Yiwu Train", Import Commodity Museum, and Import Commodity Fair, it will provide exhibitions and distribution channels for high quality commodities for the SMEs in these countries and achieve more rapid development for import and entrepot trade of Yiwu.

2.2 Wide area distributed structure from online and offline perspectives

With the rapid development of the Internet and the rise of the digital economy and digital trade, as well as extensive applications of modern new technologies like cloud computing, big data, 3D printing, and smart robotics, it will certainly promote the transformation of standardized and large-scale traditional production to diversified and decentralized production. Distributed self-organizing production of networked and heterogeneous collaboration will gradually replace the traditional large scale centralized mass production. The input structure of the factor will also be changed significantly. Technology-intensive industries have sped up the replacement of traditional labor-intensive industries. Large-scale personalized customization and intelligent manufacturing have become the trend of the development of modern industry. Under this great background, the online and offline markets inside "Yiwu Business Circle" will continuously strengthen mutual promotion and integration of development with further improvement of online market position so as to significantly improve the overall informatization level of the division of labor and cooperation system and speed up the separation of business flow, logistics, capital flow, information flow, and service flow; interactions in various kinds of economic subjects will tend to be invisible and remote, and the transaction process is an increasingly digitized, modularized, and more distributed structure in space.

At present, the domestic and foreign economic subjects forming "Yiwu Business Circle" mostly are SMEs and self-employed households, which will remain the same for a predicted long period. However, the quality and strength of these economic subjects will be gradually improved with expanding of "Yiwu Business Circle". In the process of fusion development and synergistic extension of online and offline markets inside "Yiwu Business Circle", the correlation of offline, online, as well as online and offline cross-regional division of labor cooperation will be closer and more intertwined with each other. For market operators and SMEs with limited scale and strength, there will be many difficulties in conducting online transactions due to restrictions like self-quality, trading habits, and talent resources. Thus, the reasonable choice of fusion development of online and offline markets inside "Yiwu Business Circle" will be constructing a professional middle layer of e-commerce between the market operators and end users and make the Factory to Business to Consumer (F2B2C) mode bigger and greater. The trading objects for upstream F (namely, many operators in the mode of "front shop, back factory" inside Yiwu Small Commodity Market, and small/medium-sized enterprises at home and abroad for agency sales) are mainly purchasers, distributors, retailers, etc., instead of end users. Factories have accumulated rich experience in supply, unitized cargo handling, and business resources all over the world during a long-run process but lack direct sales, after-sales services, and management experience with end users. As a result, it can give full play to the new market based on online and offline fusion as the advantageous exhibition and sales platform for domestic and foreign SMEs, namely, factories, to make great efforts to bring together and cultivate large-scale, professional, and branded Internet merchants and guide and promote domestic and foreign factories and businesses to set up close collaboration. This is to make factories, on the basis of the real market, and business, on the basis of the online market, have complementary advantages and conduct professional division of labor collaboration by focusing on the end user to jointly improve efficiency of commodity production and circulation. In this process, although relevant regions and economic subjects at home and abroad

are hundreds or even thousands of miles apart geographically, they can be more closely related to each other through division of online, offline and integrated labor collaboration by overcoming the space and time limits.

Promoting the important choice of fusion development of the online and offline market inside "Yiwu Business Circle" and expanding to the world also includes combining the way of market purchase and trade achieved by the "Yiwu Pilot Project", cross-cutting e-commerce development, and creating a new mode of purchasing bonded exports in the cross-border e-commerce market. Under the way of market purchase and trade, its transaction characteristics include a low export commodities price, a great variety, faster updating, small single transactions, numerous transaction objects, and frequent transactions, which are very similar to those of cross-border e-commerce. The characteristics of cross-border e-commerce include clear and accurate transaction information, accountable logistics information, and payment information that highly fits the requirements of "the source is traceable, the risk is controllable, and the responsibility can be investigated" for the way of market purchase and trade. Thus, it can create a unique new mode of purchasing bonded exports in the cross-border e-commerce market by closely combining the implementation of the mode of the Yiwu market purchase and trade, development of cross-border e-commerce, and the construction of the bonded logistics center. That is to extend the preferential policies for related and facilitated customs declaration, inspection, exchange settlement, and tax rebate during the process of cross-border e-commerce while utilizing an information platform and tools of cross-border e-commerce to promote business matchmaking and information sharing of the "Internet information platform for market procurement and trade" and "cross-border e-commerce public service platform". At the same time, with the bonded logistics center in the regulatory park, it shall utilize the bonded function to conduct the cross-border e-commerce bonded export business. Export business subjects will declare and deposit the whole or batches of the goods in the bonded logistics center (the eligible subjects can enjoy a tax rebate and the rest are subject to the "no tax and no rebate" policy). When the overseas enterprises and individuals purchase through the e-commerce platform, exports will be inspected and released through relevant regulatory measures in the way of market purchase and trade. The export subjects will regularly incorporate "a list of goods" to be declared to the customs. Surely, it may explore a reverse operation mode and apply the regulatory measures in the way of market purchase and trade into the cross-border e-commerce business.

It can be learned that the target for developing "Yiwu Business Circle" highly fits that of the Belt and Road, which is an open and inclusive, co-built and sharing system. Although Yiwu is the core area for this system, the internal spatial structure and cooperative relationship of "Yiwu Business Circle" are not simply scattered but interconnected like a network. Relevant regions and economic subjects at home and abroad can share the exhibition network, logistics network, capital network, and credit network based on global connection and online and offline fusion at a low cost by accessing the network through one point. It is evident that "Yiwu Business Circle" is very similar to this described network. With the continuous expanding of "Yiwu Business Circle", the internal hierarchy of associations (direct or indirect associated levels of Yiwu Small Commodity Market), associated node (functional trading blocks or units), and associated terminals (various economic subjects) will be increased one by one and the connection strength (similar to bandwidth, including tangible and intangible elements flow) will be larger. In the future, the relevant economic subjects at home and abroad will sell commodities to places all over the world covered by "Yiwu Business Circle" through the local "Yiwu" submarkets, the commodity exhibition center, logistics distribution center, overseas public warehouse, and corresponding e-commerce platforms or purchase commodities from enterprises all around the world. All of this will be integrated into "Yiwu Business Circle" through a cross-regional division of labor cooperation network, namely, providing relevant services like

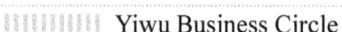

commodity distribution, fund settlement, credit control, and control relying on the international logistics network, capital network, and credit network constructed by "Yiwu Business Circle".

3. "Yiwu Business Circle" evolution goal: value community

3.1 Co-built and shared value ecosystem

The source of human economic activity is to meet the growing demand for material wealth and spiritual wealth which generates creation, distribution, exchanges, consumption, and other processes of value wealth. At the beginning of "Yiwu Business Circle", relevant subjects mainly focused on the value chain of production and supply and marketing (Porter, 1985) for commodities set up by Yiwu Small Commodity Market; later, with extension of the radiation range, the increase of influence and the improvement of channel control of Yiwu Small Commodity Market, it has gradually formed the "value constellation" (Richard Norman and Rafael Ramirez, 1993), where the fixed start of Yiwu Small Commodity Market attracts other members of other galaxies; the rapid development of modern information technology sets up an intangible virtual value chain between many regions and economic subjects inside "Yiwu Business Circle" and has formed a value network with tangible value chains (Slywotzky and Morrison, 1998). This facilitated "Yiwu Business Circle" to march from supply chain and industrial chain collaboration towards value chain synergy and the direction of a value creation system. In the abovementioned process, relevant regions and economic subjects at home and abroad mainly conduct value exchanges, delivery, and creation through commodity trade, industrial cooperation, information interaction, and other methods by taking Yiwu Small Commodity Market as the bond, forming an orderly operating ecological system through interdependence, cooperation, and symbiosis of various components and subjects of "Yiwu Business Circle". In the future, relevant regions and economic subjects inside the business circle will conduct value exchanges, delivery, and creation by further focusing on the demands of end users and even society as a whole. Moreover, with the position of value creation rising, it will form a globally-shared value ecosystem with value creation as an endogenous driving force. This ecological system has at least the following four characteristics:

First, is openness. Being different from a relatively closed global division of labor and cooperation system built at the core of large multinational enterprises (this is generally referred to as "business circle"), "Yiwu Business Circle" is a highly open system and has contained openness, sharing, and non-exclusiveness since the very beginning. The global commodity distribution network, the logistics distribution network, the financing network, the information exchange network, and the credit control network established by it first benefitted the regions and subjects that participated in construction while being open to the other regions and subjects. In the future, it will let more regions and subjects at home and abroad participate in the process of joint value creation. The more the participating regions and subjects, the stronger the abilities for overall value creation. In addition, there will be more value wealth to be shared by various regions and subjects.

Second, is expansibility. It is known from the previous article that the internal elements of "Yiwu Business Circle" are rich and diverse. The correlation between various regions and economic subjects are not only represented in commodity trade relations but also include industrial division of labor cooperation, logistics distribution, financial services, labor cooperation, technology transfer, and government affair exchanges, which makes close ties between Yiwu and other regions of "Yiwu Business Circle" mainly dependent on the value relevance so as to make "Yiwu Business Circle" have infinite expansibility and potential to extend to any country or region in the world. At present, the carriers for value exchanges, delivery, and creation inside "Yiwu Business Circle" are mainly small commodities. In the future, there will be more categories of commodities and services conducting value exchanges, delivery, and creation through this ecological system.

Third, is adaptability. As an ecological value system, "Yiwu Business Circle", in the same way as the ecological system in the natural world, can make continuous self-adjustment and repair according to changes in global economic and social trends in order to adapt to economic ups and downs, separation and integration of politics, and culture changes. Because relevant regions and subjects have adaptability, initiative, and purpose, they may continuously adjust behaviors and rules according to external environment changes so as to "learn", "grow", and "evolve" through constant interaction with the environment. Moreover, this system is extremely stable with a great number of relevant regions, subjects, and abundant cooperation opportunities in various forms. In the future, with more regions and subjects participating, this mutually beneficial and symbiotic value ecosystem will better adapt to the global economic, political, cultural transformation.

Fourth, is synergy. The value ecological system of "Yiwu Business Circle" is set up through synergy and cooperation between various regions and subjects, including the cooperation and mutual benefits between the subject of market transaction and the supporting service subject, the synergistic interaction between the market trading subject, the supporting service subject and market management subject, the government subject, the synergetic symbiosis among the display trading system, the warehousing logistics system, the financial support system, the information interaction system, the industry support system, and the management service system. Synergy and cooperation between them has created an "economic rent", which has enhanced the attraction from other regions and subjects at home and abroad and improved the overall competitiveness of "Yiwu Business Circle". In the future, this synergy will be further enhanced so as to attract more regions and subjects at home and abroad.

3.2 Diversified mode of value creation

As is mentioned above, "Yiwu Business Circle" links together sources for value wealth like land, resources, energy, labor, capital, technology, system, management in global related areas through reorganization and optimal allocation, system innovation, and management innovation to better integrate with elements like resources, energies, labor, and capital to form new supply and create new demands. It could be argued that "Yiwu Business Circle" has enhanced and will further improve the creative ability of value wealth for relevant regions and economic subjects at home and abroad. In the future, "Yiwu Business Circle" will continuously lead and promote collaborative innovation, business model changes, cross-regional element optimization, total factor productivity promotion, etc., through various ways of value creation.

Firstly, it shall improve economic efficiency and reduce cost. With the expansion and promotion of "Yiwu Business Circle", participating economic subjects can conduct commodities circulation and service supply in a broader range, as well as more efficiently, so as to realize value exchanges, delivery, and creation. In the future, with more regions and economic subjects participating, there will be more market opportunities and choices, greater space, and greater range for resource allocation. Given the application of modern scientific and technological achievements and the help of the change in the business model, it will further reduce the economic cost of the entire ecological value system, including the dominant and recessive costs, and especially the cost of friction caused by information asymmetry so as to increase the exchange of value, transfer and create efficiency.

Secondly, it shall improve and create more economic opportunities. Generally speaking, to participate in the global value network, higher economic strength or conditions are usually required. However, "Yiwu Business Circle" has a low entry and exit threshold. This makes many underdeveloped regions without the advantage of

economic development and disadvantaged labor forces participate in the ecological system for global value creation. For example, through processing with supplied materials, the surplus rural labor force (mainly the elderly and women) can participate in this system; some areas lacking industry advantages but with elements like land, resources, and energy or surplus labor can also participate in this value creation system so as to activate the potential of value creation and release social productivity. The significance lies in that it makes many underdeveloped areas and poverty groups have fair opportunities for development. In the future, there will be more and more regions and subjects with economic disadvantages participating in this system, which plays an active role in speeding up development of underdeveloped countries and regions and solving global poverty issues.

Thirdly, it shall greatly improve total factor productivity. With deepening development of value ecosystem established by "Yiwu Business Circle", the total factor productivity taking technological progress, institutional change, organizational innovation, specialization, and collaboration as a power source will be continuously improved. Development modes will be further transformed from extensive growth with high investment in production elements like labor, capital (including plant, machine equipment and inventory), and land (including other natural resources). In particular, institutional innovation and synergy of various regions and subjects inside "Yiwu Business Circle", management innovation and improvement, and business model transformation will not only greatly improve the type, quality, and grade of trading goods but also vigorously improve its brand influence, cultural connotation, and value transmission force; not only will it improve industry chain and supply chain completeness, compatibility, and competitiveness, but it will also improve the integration, control, and synergy of the upstream and downstream value chain; not only will it improve the ability of the overall system to adapt to demand, meet demand, and stimulate demand, but it will also improve the ability to create supply, guide demand, and create demand.

In summary, in the process of repeated game (including face-to-face negotiation, cross-time communication, and informal communication) among relevant economic subjects at home and abroad inside "Yiwu Business Circle", it has gradually set up a new relationship based on value relevance that takes value creation as an endogenous driving force and value identity as a spiritual guarantee. This is quite different from the cold interest relationship between the rational economic men in the hypothesis of classical economics. It is a mutually beneficial symbiotic relationship with warmth, humanity, and trust; at the same time, the governments and departments of relevant regions also actively participate in it and endorse the cooperation for relevant economic subjects inside "Yiwu Business Circle" through communicating and coordinating policies, building a cooperative platform, and providing service support. This relationship will also regularize and punish the behaviors that violate recognized value creation, distribution, and principle of exchanges, which is noticeably different from the relationship between the pure market industry chain and the supply chain dominated by transnational large enterprises. In the future, "Yiwu Business Circle" will not only conduct value in resource allocation, but also set up the universally recognized value resource allocation rules as well as form the rules of the allocation of open and inclusive value resources (the cultural ecology of seeking common ground while reserving differences) so as to break through the constraints of regional borders, ethnic groups, religious culture, and so on. "Yiwu Business Circle" will be sublimated as a cross-value consortium of the cross-regional division of labor cooperation system and become a community of values, making positive contributions to humanity.

Introduction

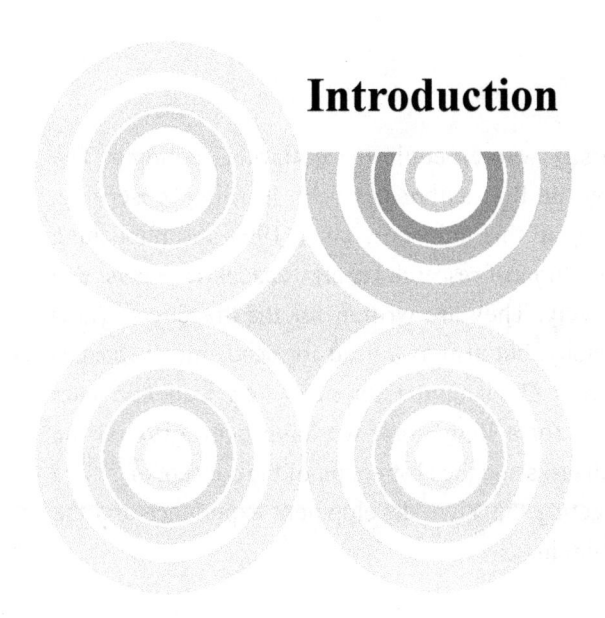

Yiwu is a university where people learn market economy. The academic team led by the first author has been learning, observing, practicing, and thinking in this university since 1993 and publishing our study results in the form of research reports, academic papers, and monographs successively. They are written for the "teachers" (new and old) of this university, but also as a need for academic exchanges between colleagues from Zhejiang and abroad. As an academic team that has studied Yiwu for a long time, we have been granted the corresponding research tasks and the abstraction of the concept of "Yiwu Business Circle", targeting the Yiwu development experience and the issues to be studied there in.

I Formation Background for "Yiwu Business Circle"

Yiwu has a total area of 1,105 square kilometers, over 130 kilometers away from Hangzhou, the provincial capital. It is a county level city belonging to the city of Jinhua.

The small commodity market is the largest characteristic and advantage of Yiwu's economy. The first generation of the small commodity market founded in 1982 only had over 700 booths with only 3.92 million Yuan of annual turnover. Through over 30 years of elaborate cultivation and development, the market system (Yiwu Small Commodity Market for short) has been formed at the core of "China Small Commodity Market City" boasting over 10 professional markets supported by over 30 commodity streets with supporting elements like transportation, property rights, and labor force. At the core and benchmark of Yiwu Small Commodity Market, "Yiwu International Trade City" was awarded the title of the only "quality

and trustworthy market" by the General Administration of Quality Supervision, Inspection, and Quarantine and was the first five-star rated market in Zhejiang. Up to 2016, Yiwu Small Commodity Market had a total area of 5.5 million square meters, boasting 75,000 booths, over 210,000 operating personnel with over 210,000 customer flow volume, and over 1.8 million varieties of commodities for exhibition and sale in the market. Over 65% of proprietors in the market undertake foreign trade business, export over 570,000 standard containers, covering 219 countries and regions all over the world becoming the largest inland customs in the country. The market turnover of "China Small Commodity City" increased from 15.34 billion Yuan in 1998 to 122.6 billion Yuan in 2017. Big dealers, big buyers, and famous brand commodity agents in the market came in a throng, with the proportion of factory direct selling being over 56% and there were over 6,000 well-known general brand agents and general distributors. China Yiwu International Commodities Fair sponsored by the Ministry of Commerce and the People's Government of Zhejiang Province ("Yiwu Trade Fair" for short) has become the third most famous commercial exhibition in China, second to the China Import and Export Fair ("Canton Fair") and the China Trade Fair in terms of influence.

While Yiwu Small Commodity Market continues to prosper, professional markets in some other areas domestically have begun to shrink or even disappear. According to the research results of some scholars of economic history, a lot of industrial wholesale markets that formed at the early stage of industrialization in countries like the UK and the USA mostly disappeared in the middle and late stages of industrialization, which became the realistic basis for the domestic "Demise of Professional Market". However, to view from the over 30 years' development course, Yiwu Small Commodity Market seems to jump out of the historical trap of "extinction". It doesn't have market shrinkage as predicted in the "Demise of Professional Market", but gradually grows into the largest commodity wholesale market in the world with increasingly emerging "Business Circle" characteristics in modern significance due to ever-increasing influence. What makes Yiwu Small Commodity Market jump out of the destiny as predicted in the "Demise of Professional Market" and remain "ever-green" and become the development platform for joint creation, sharing, and prosperity with surrounding areas? In-depth empirical study, to reveal the inner mechanism, point out the future development trend, and propose corresponding countermeasures and suggestions is not only useful for Yiwu Small Commodity Market and the economic and social development of the entire city of Yiwu, but also may serve as reference for sustainable development for other professional markets at home and abroad, which is the background and tenet for us to write *Yiwu Business Circle*.

Market Yiwu focuses on the analysis of the development course of Yiwu Small Commodity Market rated as the "No.1 City in China" from "chicken feather for sugar" to the international trade, revealing the unique path of marketization, industrialization, and urbanization of Yiwu. While this book takes expanding the market order as the main line and illustrates the origin and formation of the small commodity market from the perspective of a professional exchange organization— Yiwu "chicken feather for sugar", local business groups, the innovation behavior of the business group, and the enlightened decision of the local governments; it illustrates the trading efficiency and accumulation effect of the small commodity market from the perspectives of economies of scale, economies of scope, and information economy; it illustrates the optimization and future development direction of the small commodity market from the perspectives of "centralized management over the same category of commodities", the market expansion of combined transport and consignment, and the mode of behavior of Yiwu government; it illustrates the new positioning and "Yiwu Mode" innovation from the perspective of linkage development of the market, industry, and city. In summary, this book primarily focuses on Yiwu Small Commodity Market with perspectives limited to Yiwu itself, which lacks more analysis for division of labor among regions and industries based on

Yiwu Small Commodity Market, and collaboration among various economic subjects. "Yiwu Business Circle", the deepening of research on Yiwu Small Commodity Market and "Yiwu Mode" switches its perspective from analyzing the formation and development of Yiwu Small Commodity Market to the division of labor collaboration with all regions and economic subjects at home and abroad associated with Yiwu Small Commodity Market; broadly, switching the perspective from Yiwu itself to the cross-regional division of labor collaboration network and international exchanges and cooperation at the core of Yiwu is to reveal the process of Yiwu's economy moving from a regional to international stage. In addition, if *Market Yiwu* mainly studies the past and present of Yiwu Small Commodity Market, *Yiwu Business Circle* mainly discusses the future of Yiwu Small Commodity Market and the overall economic and social development of Yiwu. Thus, compared to the deepening and expanding nature of *Market Yiwu*, *Yiwu Business Circle* is far more involved and more difficult than the former. As a result, although we have doubled our efforts to study and write on this subject, there may be a lot of inadequacies in this new book.

II Research Methods and Framework of this Book

1. On the methods of research and discussion

Firstly, this book has mainly learned and applied the method of Marx's *Das Kapital*, namely, the method from concrete to abstract and from abstract to concrete. Other scholars who are involved in writing are also familiar with *Das Kapital*. As a result, the research methods from concrete to abstract and from abstract to concrete have been adopted involuntarily in research and writing. Firstly, starting from the objective economic phenomenon of increasing prosperity of Yiwu Small Commodity Market and promoting the common development of the surrounding areas, we have a more profound perceptual knowledge of producers, distributors, and forwarding agents of Yiwu Small Commodity Market especially in regards to the exchanges and cooperation between Yiwu and other regions through collecting and referring to relevant information and media reports, and combining questionnaires and field visits.

On the basis of full possession of first-hand information, we have proposed the concept of "Yiwu Business Circle" by focusing on the division of labor collaboration network including numerous relevant regions and economic subjects at home and abroad and formed on the basis of Yiwu Small Commodity Market, analyzed the connotation, features, and the formation mechanism for "Yiwu Business Circle" so as to improve the understanding of Yiwu Small Commodity Market and the cross-regional division of labor collaboration network from a sensible to rational stage. Then, based on a large number of field observations, and related reports, data, and cases, we have discussed the formation and development course of "Yiwu Business Circle", especially the status-quo of the cross-regional division of labor collaboration network led by the small commodity market and the behavior characteristics of proprietors, production enterprises, and governments. Moreover, we have revealed the status-quo, promotion measures, and internationalization development influence factors for "Yiwu Business Circle" through analysis of the results of the questionnaire survey. On this basis, we have proposed policy proposals such as achieving development of Yiwu Small Commodity Market towards the high-end level, expanding radiating capability of "Yiwu Business Circle", promoting the transformation of regional economic functions of Yiwu into Central Zhejiang CBD, facilitating international development of "Yiwu Business Circle", and speeding up construction of the innovative international trade city of Yiwu.

Secondly, this book has applied a combination of historical analysis and new economic geography research. It strives to grasp the division of labor collaboration relationship among enterprises, industries, and regions according to the real development course of Yiwu Small Commodity Market. First of all, starting from the four stages of development for Yiwu Small Commodity Market, namely, the initial stage (1978–1987), stable development stage (1988–1991), all-around development stage (1992–2001), and international development stage (2002–till now), we have inquired about "Yiwu Business Circle", which generated and developed in this process, and analyzed its process from the beginning, to the initial formation, and to maturity. At the same time, we have revealed the interactive relationship between the combined transport and consignment market and "Yiwu Business Circle" constantly moving forward from each other. The important role in the formation and development process of "Yiwu Business Circle" was revealed from how the spirit of Yiwu and the commercial culture of Yiwu formed and developed historically. While applying the historical analytical method, we have adopted the research methods of new economic geography and expanded the research perspective of Yiwu Small Commodity Market to the cross-regional division of labor collaboration network formed by focusing on the market, analyzed the network relationship (non-circular relationship) formed by spanning space and geographical order through Yiwu Small Commodity Market by numerous small commodities producers and proprietors at home and abroad, and emphatically revealed the cross-regional division of labor collaboration relationship established between Yiwu and surrounding areas, Yiwu and Central Zhejiang city groups, Yiwu and other domestic regions, and even many overseas areas.

Thirdly, this book has applied the method of combining theoretical research with empirical analysis. First of all, it has expanded the traditional concept of "Business Circle" by relying on relevant theories of political economics, industrial economics, regional economics, new geo economics, etc., and summarized the connotation of "Yiwu Business Circle". Then, it has deeply analyzed the economic rationality of the cross-regional division of labor collaboration network at the core of Yiwu Small Commodity Market from the theoretical perspectives of division of labor and specialization, effect of economies of scale, and effect of market cluster; it gives a theoretical explanation of rationality for "Yiwu Business Circle" on the basis of research on reducing transaction costs in small commodity markets, the effect of increasing returns to scale, promoting professional division of labor, inducing industrial agglomeration and promoting regional cooperation, and so on. While conducting theoretical research, this book has also adopted an empirical analysis method. The academic team for this book has also paid close attention to relevant reports of TV stations, radio, newspapers, networks, and other media and obtained numerous cases in addition to going deep into Yiwu for a long time, observing directly, participating in, and experiencing the formation and development of "Yiwu Business Circle" so as to provide the support of empirical materials for analyzing the formation process, the development status quo, and future trend of "Yiwu Business Circle". At the same time, authors have also designed questionnaires for the small commodity market proprietors and producers, conducted data analysis on 6,363 copies of valid questionnaires, and came to a conclusion of the status quo of "Yiwu Business Circle", key measures for improving "Yiwu Business Circle", and influencing factors for the international expansion of "Yiwu Business Circle". Many cases are referred in the discussion of the promising and innovative international trade city. It has revealed the important role of the promising initiatives of the government, the self-dependent innovation of the small commodities proprietors and producers, and the construction of "Yiwu Business Circle".

2. Framework of this book

In addition to the Introduction to 2019 Edition and the Introduction, this book also includes five chapters and one conclusion.

Chapter One is the connotation and features of "Yiwu Business Circle". This chapter firstly introduces and analyzes the traditional concept of "business circle", expands on the traditional concept of "business circle", and defines the connotation of "Yiwu Business Circle" through a comparative analysis of "Yiwu Business Circle" and the traditional "business district"; then, regarding the main components of "Yiwu Business Circle", it conducts an analysis on the aspect of the market system at its core, the fundamental supporting industries, a group of businessmen who play a key role, a secure logistics network, etc.; finally, it reveals four main features of "Yiwu Business Circle", namely, the objects of transaction being mainly small commodities, the linkage development of business, trade, and industry, the international expansion of the division of labor collaboration network, and the network's non-circle structure.

Chapter Two covers the division of labor collaboration network of "Yiwu Business Circle". This chapter proposes the content of developing an interregional division of labor collaboration, inter-provincial division of labor collaboration, and international division of labor collaboration at the core of Yiwu Small Commodity Market inclusive in "Yiwu Business Circle" as a cross-regional division of labor collaboration network from the core of "Yiwu Business Circle"; Chapter Two also analyzes the rationality of the division of labor collaboration network by applying the economic theory of economies of scale, economies of scope, transaction cost, industrial cluster, etc.; finally, it discusses the great significance of the expansion of "Yiwu Business Circle" for bringing about construction of Central Zhejiang city groups, promoting regional coordination of urban and rural areas in the whole province, promoting coordinated development of China's Eastern–Central–Western Regions, and conducting international exchanges and cooperation.

Chapter Three is the path and mechanism for the formation of "Yiwu Business Circle". This chapter firstly discusses the process of the beginning, to the initial formation, and to maturity undergone by "Yiwu Business Circle" accompanying the development of Yiwu Small Commodity Market, and analyzes the core and dynamic action played by Yiwu Small Commodity Market; then, it studies the path of the regional expansion of "Yiwu Business Circle", highlights the support of Yiwu combined transport and consignment market for "Yiwu Business Circle" and great leading role of Yiwu business culture for the development of "Yiwu Business Circle"; finally, it illustrates the formation mechanism for "Yiwu Business Circle" from economies of scale, economies of scope, and large-scale markets due to commercial population clustering, market driving specialized division of labor, division of

labor further inducing industrial agglomeration, and a market network promoting cross-regional division of labor collaboration, etc.

Chapter Four covers the development trend and strategy for "Yiwu Business Circle". This chapter firstly proposes the idea of improving the radiating ability of "Yiwu Business Circle" from promoting Yiwu Small Commodity Market to becoming the price formation center, information release center, and logistics center; then, based on the inner trend of function transformation and promotion of Yiwu Small Commodity Market and "Yiwu Business Circle", it illustrates the connotation, conditions, and architecture of building Yiwu into Central Zhejiang CBD; at last, it analyzes the internationalization of "Yiwu Business Circle" and the city positioning of Yiwu's international business and trade city.

Chapter Five covers the construction of "Yiwu Business Circle" and innovative international business and trade city. This chapter firstly discusses the decisive significance of three independent innovative modes, namely, original innovation, integrated innovation, and re-innovation after introduction, digestion, and absorption; then, it analyzes the connotation, features of the innovative international business and trade city, and the significance of its construction over expansion of "Yiwu Business Circle" and the realistic foundation for Yiwu to construct an innovative international business and trade city; at last, it proposes the countermeasures for constructing the innovative international business and trade city from ramming up the foundation of innovation and creating an environment for innovation, cultivating innovative enterprises to expand the innovation industry, and gathering innovative talents to stimulate innovation power.

The conclusion expands on "Yiwu Business Circle" and the "Yiwu Development Experience". In our opinion, expanding "Yiwu Business Circle" is indispensable from the "Yiwu Development Experience", which has been evaluated and analyzed in this context. Firstly, by combining the practical experience of the academic team in participating in the market construction and economic development personally over the past 10 years, it has analyzed the mode of thinking, the key to the formation, the organizer, and highlight of the practice for the "Yiwu Development Experience". Secondly, it proposes the countermeasures and suggestions for expanding "Yiwu Business Circle" and innovating on "Yiwu Development Experience" from the perspectives of the development model, independent innovation, market drive, talent market, and harmonious society.

The preliminary research results of this book were used as research reports and submitted to the leaders of the Provincial Party Committee and Government in the form of the Committee Member's Proposals by the Advisory Committee on Economic Construction of Zhejiang People's Government. They then received the attention and approval of Xi Jinping, the then Secretary of the Provincial Party Committee. For the first draft of the book, Xi Jinping directed the office of the Provincial Committee to organize the research group to summarize "Yiwu Development Experience". The first author and his collaborator professor Wang Zuqiang were invited to participate in this work. The research group summarizes the development experience into six points, where "Flourish Business and Build City, Connecting Trade with Industry, Radiation Effects, and International Development" are placed in a very prominent position. We also take initiative to connect further researches on "Yiwu Business Circle" by summarizing "Yiwu Development Experience".

Ⅲ Main Innovation Points of this Book

1. Propose the concept of "Yiwu Business Circle" for the first time

"Yiwu Business Circle" illustrated in this book is fundamentally different from the "business circle" in retailing and means that all economic subjects and regions are closely related to Yiwu Small Commodity Market or enterprises, including forward product sales area, backward industrial support area, and the resulting cross-regional division of labor collaboration networks. Formation and development of "Yiwu Business Circle" has inseparable relations with Yiwu Small Commodity Market, which to a great extent depends on the functioning and upgrading of business form. It is because of the cost advantages of Yiwu Small Commodity Market brought about by economies of scale, economies of scope, and division of labor based on specialization that the development of division of labor based on specialization and collaboration has been encouraged, and the birth of the cross-regional division of labor collaboration network at the core of the market—"Yiwu Business Circle" has been promoted; with the development and perfection of the market function and the upgrading of market form and structure, division of labor based on specialization and industrial clusters promoting each other results in the continuous evolution and development of "Yiwu Business Circle". As a result, common characteristics of economic subjects and regions that can be included in the scope of "Yiwu Business Circle" are as follows: they might rely on the platform of Yiwu Small Commodity Market to sell their own products to all parts of the country and bring about development of industries with local advantages or purchase small commodities from all around the country or abroad, conduct processing with supplied materials, carry out labor service export, undertake industry transfer, attract investment and promote business, seek inter-regional cooperation, and expand to the overseas market through Yiwu Small Commodity Market. Yiwu Small Commodity Market plays a critical role in this process and constructs a huge division of labor collaboration network that connects numerous economic subjects and relevant regions like producers, traders, and forwarding agents at home and abroad—"Yiwu Business Circle".

2. Illustrate basic characteristics of "Yiwu Business Circle"

These basic characteristics are as follows: (1) The object of transaction in "Yiwu Business Circle" is mainly small commodity. The small commodity market is the source for its birth and "Yiwu Business Circle" always focuses on the production and sales of small commodities, achieving linkage development of the business, trade, and manufacturing industries. Although some market proprietors began to turn to the production and sale of other products after completing primitive accumulation of capital, so far, inside "Yiwu Business Circle", small commodities are still the most competitive and representative products for production or sales. (2) Linkage development of business, trade, and industry. "Yiwu Business Circle" takes Yiwu Small

Commodity Market as its core, brings about industry development through the market, and the market is supported by the industry. This "trade and industry linkage" development mode not only exists in Yiwu but is also reflected in the division of labor collaboration relationship between Yiwu and surrounding counties, cities, and other regions. On the one hand, this is related to government policy choices and promotion. On the other hand, it is the demand and embodiment of the market economy law of capital operation. (3) "Yiwu Business Circle" presents the trend from the market and the region to their international development. It is difficult to distinguish the initial "Yiwu Business Circle" and Yiwu Small Commodity Market strictly in the form and scope. As the function of the small commodity market is increasingly perfect, and is functioning with gradually enhanced radiation capacity, it promotes "Yiwu Business Circle" to expand from the surrounding areas to the other regions; after the internationalization level of small commodity market is improved, the scope covered by "Yiwu Business Circle" shows obvious cross-regional, international characteristics. (4) A network with a non-circle structure. The traditional "business circle" is usually divided by the distance to a shopping mall and the geographic location of a supermarket, showing an apparent circle structure. However, due to the richer components of "Yiwu Business Circle", its internal form of economic linkage is more diverse. It not only has linkage in commodity trade but also has industry division of labor, collaboration, logistics, finance, and other supporting services, which make the tightness of its internal connections depend not mainly on geographic location, distance, and other factors, and show an irregular network structure.

3. Propose to construct Central Zhejiang CBD

The functional transformation and promotion of Yiwu Small Commodity Market will make Yiwu march toward the goal of a Central and Western Zhejiang Central Business District (Central Zhejiang CBD for short). In this book, we expand the concept of a traditional "business circle" from the urban level to regional level. The Central Zhejiang CBD as we said also has the functions of the CBD in traditional theories such as business activities, financial services, information consultation, and economic radiation; from the perspective of the construction process and the formation mechanism, there are also similarities between them. However, the concept of Central Zhejiang CBD is distinctly different from the small urban regional attributes of the traditional business center. It has necessarily expanded the geographic scope of the CBD, namely, the traditional business center concept which focuses on the concentration, communication, and combination of traffic, logistics, capital flow, and information flow in a particular region of the city. The Central Zhejiang CBD highlights intersection and integration of manpower, commodity, capital, information flow, and so on in the economic regions included in and affected by "Yiwu Business Circle". As a result, we understand the connotation of Central Zhejiang CBD as: the business intensive area that serves the entire Central Zhejiang city groups as well as Central and Western Zhejiang construction and development by taking Yiwu's main urban area as the main area, market guidance and government support as the main drive, a modern service and headquarters economy with business office, science and technology innovation, finance, insurance, convention, trade, modern logistics, and legal consultation as main formats, and information processing of Yiwu Small Commodity Market as the main content. We believe that we should grasp the development trend of the regionalization and internationalization of the service scope of the business center instead of simply restricting the business center mechanically to a particular geographic area of a large city. Surely, development of the business center itself requires a certain degree of concentration because an overly dispersed region will inevitably lead to a reduction in business efficiency. Thus, combined with the existing conditions of commercial facility construction and the business center related index in Yiwu City, through carrying on the strong points and counteracting the weaknesses, mutual exchanges and sincere cooperation between cities, counties, and districts of the Central and Western Zhejiang as well as of the Central Zhejiang, especially through unremitting efforts of Yiwu, it is absolutely possible to develop Yiwu's main urban area of approximately 100 square kilometers into a Central Zhejiang CBD.

It is especially exciting that the goal of constructing a "Central Zhejiang city group" has attracted more and more attention from the cadres and masses of the entire Central and Western Zhejiang areas, who have gradually formed a consensus and put the same ideas into practice. To form Central Zhejiang and give full play to the important task of promoting the development of the whole central and western regions of Zhejiang, the key lies in that all cities, counties, and regions shall develop regional characteristic industries to achieve complementary advantages and form the strong resultant force of Central Zhejiang city groups. To this end, Jinhua Municipal Committee and Government have proposed the general idea and "gathering of (Jinhua–Yiwu) main axis" is one of the keys to it. We believe that this is an important decision that gives full play to the advantages of politics, location, talent, resources, etc. of Jinhua, and the business and trade advantages of Yiwu to be combined and promoted. It is the only road for expanding "Yiwu Business Circle", deepening "Yiwu Development Experience", and constructing the "Central Zhejiang city groups". In a sense, it can be said the date of gathering of "main axis" is the rising tide of creating the "Central Zhejiang city groups".

4. Propose to construct an innovative international business trade city

Highlight the role of Yiwu Small Commodity Market over formation, development, future expansion, and improvement of "Yiwu Business Circle" by combining the reality of Yiwu's developed trade industry and highlighted internationalized features with the requirements of changing the way of growth, innovative development mode, and building an international trade city, and propose the idea of building an innovative international trade city. Independent innovation has decisive significance over the construction of "Yiwu Business Circle". The formation and development process of Yiwu Small Commodity Market and "Yiwu Business Circle" is full of innovation, which is the result of a series of independent innovation activities. It is because the masses, enterprises and governments dare to break through the bondage of old stereotypes and make innovations. A series of independent innovation activities such as "chicken feather for sugar", street market, "Four Permits", "Flourish Business and Build County (City)", quota tax, centralized management over the same category of commodities, government regulation separated from management, "Promoting Industry by Commerce", "Connecting Trade with Industry", and building an international business and trade city have been initiated. In particular, the original small commodity market and proposal of "Four Permits" policies, "Flourish Business and Build County (City)" strategy, and the strategic goal of an international business and trade city have laid the core and foundation for "Yiwu Business Circle"; the integrated innovation strategies of "Promoting Industry by Commerce" and "Connecting Trade with Industry" bring about integration of industry with market, support market with industry, integrate advantages and functions of the market and industry for mutual complementarity and mutual prosperity, promoting division of labor collaboration based on specialization in enterprises, industries, and regions, and facilitating the formation and development of Yiwu Small Commodity Market and "Yiwu Business Circle". In addition, many SMEs in Yiwu make reinnovation based on introduction, digestion, and absorption so as to make Yiwu be able to gradually replace Guangzhou, Shenzhen and become the center for circulation, exhibition, information, and manufacturing of domestic small commodities, make Yiwu Small Commodity Market improve the ability to gather resources at home and abroad ever-increasingly, have a batch of technology-based SMEs get rid of the conditions of simple imitation and OEM, gradually develop independent brands and technologies, and promote "Yiwu Business Circle" to expand towards internationalization. As a result, vigorously developing independent innovation and constructing an innovative city are the fundamental ways to achieve the goal of an international trading city.

IV Significance of Research on "Yiwu Business Circle"

The research conclusion of "Yiwu Business Circle" in this book raises a question on the "Demise of Professional Market" widely popular at home and abroad and at least provides a counterexample for research. Those supporting the "Demise of Professional Market" believe that the development of a professional market exists when the enterprise scale is too small, unable to have their own sales channels but have to reduce the unit product sales cost through the public platform of the professional market; with competition bringing the survival of the fittest and with the strength of the surviving producers on the market increasing, they will gradually get rid of the trading place of professional markets, "nibble" at the original professional market through constantly expanding and consolidating their own sales network, which results in the final demise of such professional markets. The following phenomena in the modern history of developed countries such as the UK and the USA provide the basis for the "Demise of Professional Market": in many industries, some big enterprises have set up their own logistics and distribution departments and exit from the original traditional professional markets; the emergence of modern logistics enterprises has replaced the original commodity and means of production and undertakes the main function of product circulation. Some famous professional markets in history (such as Manchester textile market) indeed have been long gone. Analysis and research of this book reveals that Yiwu Small Commodity Market will not only die out, but shows a growing trend of vigorous development and reveals the objective reality and internal mechanism for evolution of "Yiwu Business Circle". It can be concluded from this, on the one hand, that Yiwu Small Commodity Market has crossed the "three trading" stages and developed to the purchase order trading stage (it is estimated that at present, trading order in Yiwu Small Commodity Market accounts for 70%, wholesaler trade for 20% and spot trading 10%). This new development trend has broken through the historical trap described in the "Demise of Professional Market". On the other hand, China's industrialization and urbanization levels are still far from those of the European and American countries. Large and scattered small and medium-sized enterprises need to make use of the professional market to sell products on the platform of quasi-public products, however, it is difficult for a large number of small and medium-sized retailers to talk directly with the production enterprises, and they lack the right to speak in the purchase of goods and need to purchase goods through a fully competitive professional market. As a result, in a very long period of time, the mode of "small enterprises + small dealers + large markets" also has strong practicality in China. The economic development stage determines the inherent demand for the public trading platform such as the professional wholesale market, which is an important reason for the continuous flourishing of Yiwu Small Commodity Market. Moreover, the formation and development process of Yiwu Small Commodity Market and "Yiwu Business Circle" are full of independent innovation, especially regarding the original innovation and integrated innovation activities. This series of innovations help

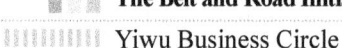

Yiwu Small Commodity Market and "Yiwu Business Circle" constantly obtain new development impetus and radiate new vitality so as to break through the fate of "Demise of Professional Market".

Yiwu Small Commodity Market and "Yiwu Business Circle" are important components in the embodiment of the "Yiwu Development Experience" and are the models for professional market integration, transformation, and promotion[1] in Zhejiang. Exploration and discussion about "Yiwu Business Circle" in this book not only reflects the "Yiwu Development Experience" takes "adhere to flourish business and build cities, promote industry linkage, focus on urban–rural integration, facilitate harmonious development, enrich profound culture, strive for a promising party and government" as its main content, but also expands and deepens the "Yiwu Development Experience" from the perspective of cross-regional division of labor collaboration, includes exchanges and cooperation between Yiwu, surrounding counties and cities, Central Zhejiang city groups, other provincial regions and other regions at home and abroad into the vision of the "Yiwu Development Experience". It not only provides countermeasures and suggestions for the future development of Yiwu Small Commodity Market and economic society by revealing the inner mechanism and law for the formation of "Yiwu Business Circle", but also provides experience for reference to the professional wholesale market of other regions at home and abroad in terms of cross-regional division of labor collaboration and development; especially, it has certain reference significance for constructing the Central Zhejiang city groups, promoting coordinated development of urban and rural areas in Zhejiang Province, and the coordinated development of China's Eastern and Western Regions. For the purpose of Zhejiang, with a lot of professional markets, it is very important to avoid the historical destiny of "Demise of Professional Market" in the future. The experience of constructing a cross-regional division of labor

---

[1]Refer to Lu Lijun: On the Strong Province of Modern Commerce and Trade in Zhejiang. *Business Economies and Management*, 2005 (8).

collaboration network and promoting the small commodity market's development and improvement, and the interlinked and mutually-supporting structures of enterprise clusters, industrial clusters, and market groups within serve as certain reference significance for keeping market prosperity through continuous innovation activities, benefiting from the division of labor based on specialization through enhancing cross-regional division of labor collaboration relationship in order to optimize allocation of regional resource elements, and breaking the bottleneck in development.

The analysis and research of "Yiwu Business Circle" in this book reveals the future development trend of Yiwu Small Commodity Market and the "Yiwu Mode", which has important reference value for large business and trade logistics enterprises such as Commodities City Group, Hopeful Group, International Logistics Center, as well as small commodities proprietors, small commodities producers, and other market subjects and governments for reasonable strategic choice, adopting corresponding measures according to the law of objective development, and effectively coping with difficulties in development. For example, the discussion on key measures for improving "Yiwu Business Circle" makes the government and many proprietors and enterprises become aware of the importance of improving the internationalization level, optimizing the economic development environment, and enhancing operating capabilities to obtain corresponding countermeasures and suggestions; analysis about the influencing factors of internationalization expansion will help Yiwu cope with the challenge of internationalization better and speed up the pace of integration with the international community; discussion about the high-end development of the small commodity market and expansion of radiation ability of "Yiwu Business Circle" provides a way of thinking for the future development and upgrading of Yiwu Small Commodity Market and further play and promotion of popularity of the radiation capability of "Yiwu Business Circle"; discussion on Central Zhejiang CBD provides a new way of thinking for the construction of Central Zhejiang city groups

and socio-economic development of Central and Western Zhejiang; discussion about independent innovation and the innovative international business and trade city illustrates the future development trend of Yiwu, which helps the government and many small commodity producers and dealers fully understand the nature and significance of independent innovation, continue to adhere to the overall development strategy of "Flourish Business and Build City", and form the new way of thinking for achieving its goal of creating the international business and trade city through promoting the upgrading of the small commodity market, enhancing the radiation capability of "Yiwu Business Circle" and achieving social sustainable development of Yiwu's economy with independent innovation.

Chapter **1**

Connotations and Features of "Yiwu Business Circle"

A precise understanding about the connotations and features of "Yiwu Business Circle" is the foundation of its related studies. Many people may be apt to interpret the meaning of "business circle" according to its literal meaning. However, "Yiwu Business Circle" itself is a new concept, different from a "business circle" in the traditional sense. In view of its unique components, the understanding about "Yiwu Business Circle" should not be confined to the business field. Moreover, it is also inadvisable to simply take it as a regular "circle" structure. As a consequence, this chapter firstly defines the connotations of "Yiwu Business Circle" through the analysis on the difference between "Yiwu Business Circle" and the traditional "business circle", subsequently introduces several basic elements of "Yiwu Business Circle", and ultimately expounds the features of "Yiwu Business Circle".

I

Connotations of "Yiwu Business Circle"

1. Traditional concept of "business circle"

Business circle, also known as the "commercial space" or "company operation circle", refers to the scope from which commercial companies could attract consumers. On the part of companies, business circle means the space of business activity where they could provide commodities and services to consumers; on the part of consumers, a business circle is a space which creates convenience for their purchase behaviors. The "business circle" concept in a traditional sense could be divided into a narrow one and a broad one. A business circle in its narrow sense usually refers to the geographic scope in which certain large-scale retail stores or supermarkets attract their consumers to go shopping in. For instance, if residents living within a five-mile distance to a certain hypermarket are accustomed to buying commodities there, then the business circle scope of that hypermarket is five miles. A business circle in its broad sense refers to

a certain economic area which has developed business industry with great consumption potential attracting a substantial number of consumers. In general cases, such type of economic area is in the prosperous district of a metropolitan. Centering around a local shopping mall or business district, an economic area could form and radiate its business emissive power in all directions.

According to the status of the economic area, the "business circle" in a broad sense could be divided into the primary business circle, the secondary business circle, and the peripheral business circle. A primary business circle generally indicates such an economic area which has a group of important large-scale shopping centers, shopping malls, supermarkets, department stores as well as surrounding small-scale shopping malls, supermarkets, or grocery stores. A secondary business circle usually means the business district is composed of peripheral shopping centers, shopping malls, supermarkets, and department stores outside of the primary business circle. Besides the inferior appeal to consumers, it also has relatively dispersive consumer sources. A peripheral business circle is the business district composed of shopping centers, shopping malls, supermarkets, department stores, convenience stores, and specialty stores outside of the secondary business circle. Compared with the secondary business circle, it has fewer consumers and more dispersive consumer sources. The business circle is not in a rounded shape, but in an oval or multilateral round shape instead.

According to traditional theory, there is a limit to the development of a business circle. Whenever a certain business circle reaches the saturated state, competition within the circle turns extraordinarily ferocious and even perfervid. At such a moment, the deterioration of the business operation environment will lead to the mass exodus of consumers, which later directly results in the decline of business revenues per unit. In these conditions, it is imperative to control the construction of business facilities within the business circle. In order to judge whether the business circle has reached the saturated state, the saturation index could be used for measurement according to the following formula.

$$S = \frac{C \times E}{F},$$

where S is the saturation index, C is the total number of consumers, E is the average purchase amount of every single consumer, and F is the business operation area of shopping centers, shopping malls, supermarkets, and department stores within the business circle.

Supposing the normal business volume of shopping centers, shopping malls, supermarkets, and department stores within a certain business circle in a certain year is 20,000 Yuan per square meter, the number of target consumers is 2 million, per capita purchase is 6,000 Yuan, and the existing business operation area is 1 million square meters, then the saturation index of this business circle calculated in accordance with the abovementioned saturation index measurement formula is

$$(6000 \times 200) \div 100 = 12000 \text{ Yuan/square meter.}$$

The volume per square meter in the business circle reduces 8,000 Yuan. This means that the business circle has reached the saturated state and it is inappropriate to introduce new business facilities.

In view of the research targets, the scope covered by a traditional business circle is principally the scope for business companies to attract consumers and the rational arrangement of the business industry for passenger flow, excluding any consideration about economic relation in backward and forward linkages. The research problem studied in this book is a regional economic problem. Although the concept of "Yiwu Business Circle" concerned here has a connection with the traditional business circle, the following analyses will indicate its unique connotations.

2. Expansion of the concept of "business circle"

Pursuant to the above analysis, the traditional concept of "business circle" mainly means the circle is constituted by business behaviors, or is the geographical area where consumers of a certain company that provides specific commodities or services are living in. In addition to the hierarchy, the business circle also possesses superposition, irregularity, and dynamics features. In history, the size of a business circle is often decided by consumers' purchase behaviors and shops' operation ability. In modern times, besides the disparity in region, operation scale, operation species, operation business state, and urban transportation vehicles among business network points, scope, form, consumer distribution intensity, and demand features also vary from one another among these business circles. Therefore, subject to the influences from all sorts of factors, a certain business circle possibly is of large or small size and has diversified forms of expression during different operation periods.

This book refers to the word "business circle" in traditional theory and expands it to the new concept of "Yiwu Business Circle" to study the regional and industrial economy's development in Yiwu. According to this book, due to the similarity between Yiwu's radiation functions for surrounding regions via the development of business industry and large-scale business center's "business gravitational field" in the traditional business circle, the research decides to refer to the concept of "business circle" and expands from city layout and business industry layer to area layer. This research defines the cross-area labor division collaborative network formed centering around Yiwu Small Commodity Market as "Yiwu Business Circle" out of the considerations in the following few aspects:

Firstly, the people of Yiwu used to follow the tradition of "chicken feathers for sugar" in history. After reform and opening-up, the rise of Yiwu's economy started with individual business. From the first small commodity street vendors to the current international business city, successive Yiwu Municipal Committees and Governments always regarded the small commodity market as the leading momentum of Yiwu's socio-economic development in both the strategic selection and policy orientation such as "Flourish Business and Build City", "Promoting Industry by Commerce" or "Connecting Trade with Industry". It shows that the business industry always seizes the dominant status and plays the role as the foremost driving force in socio-economic development across the city.

Secondly, the large-scale development of modern industry in Yiwu started in the mid-1990s. The reason is that the beginning of industry is inseparable from the primitive accumulation of capital, while the primitive accumulation of industrial capital of Yiwu is inseparable from the development of the small commodity market. At present, nearly all private entrepreneurs aged above 50 are individual vendors or operators in the small commodity market. In a manner of speaking, the industrial capital accumulation process in Yiwu is actually the development process of the small commodity market. Some major operators have accumulated capital, consumer groups, marketing networks, and market operation experiences by going through arduous hardships in market operation over the years. They manifest their sensitive smell, flexible brain, rich capital, professional technology, and advantages in other aspects.

Thirdly, the leading role of the tertiary industry in Yiwu's economy far exceeds its proportion in GDP. The industrial economy of Yiwu is dominated by the light industrial commodity. The formation of advantageous industries in accessory, clothing, sock, blanket, textile, zipper, tape, artware, and printing has an intimacy with the development of the small commodity market. It is definitely not a simple industrial transfer and agglomeration process for Yiwu to transfer from the previous "buying and selling of China-made commodity" to subsequent "buying and selling of global commodity" and shape its own industrial support. This includes the inherent tendency of technical progress

and industrial promotion. While to a large extent, it is the outcome of market competition. Exactly due to the driving functions of the small commodity market, there springs up a group of outstanding performers in the same industry at home and abroad from local Yiwu companies, such as major corporate groups represented by Mona, Lanswe, Neoglory, and True Love. These companies mostly benefit from the platform and window role of Yiwu Small Commodity Market in the initial stage and conduct business trading with traveling merchants from different places at a rather low cost. They only establish their own marketing network when the companies develop to a certain scale. However, these companies still maintain the close contact with the small commodity market just as before. As a result, a fundamental conclusion could be drawn that the external function of the market as a public trading platform is the critical condition of the growth of many industries and companies of Yiwu.

Fourthly, Yiwu is now trying to develop into an international business city. This city positioning fully indicates the significant status of the business industry in Yiwu's socio-economic development. Therefore, the study on Yiwu's economy should start with its market and business industry. Along with the deepening of exchanges and cooperation between Yiwu and other regions at home and abroad, the market-based cooperative relation turns more intimate and flow of capital, talents, and technology turns more frequently. Consequently, examining the cross-area economic interaction and mutual development history between Yiwu and other businesses and the formation of correlated backward and forward industrial links could reveal the mechanism and secret of Yiwu's economic take-off and make rational predictions on its future development tendency. More importantly, it has significant theoretical and realistic means to accelerate Yiwu's development, propel the construction of the city agglomeration in Central Zhejiang, and facilitate provincial and even nationwide urban–rural harmonious development.

To sum up, due to the great differences from a traditional business circle, the concept of "Yiwu Business Circle" should be redefined. By proposing the concept of "Yiwu Business Circle" and endowing it with new connotations different from the traditional "business circle", the research on the one hand fully considers the unique economic development history of Yiwu driven by the business industry, and on the other hand expects to innovate research perspectives and methods based on existing research results and offer more references to urban–rural harmonious development theory and practices throughout the study on "Yiwu Model".

3. Definition of "Yiwu Business Circle"

In view of the growing intimacy and deepening labor division collaboration relation between Yiwu and surrounding regions, other related areas, and economic entities at home and abroad, the research considers that Yiwu has formed a small commodity market-centered cross-area labor division collaboration network distinct from a traditional business circle—namely the so-called "Yiwu Business Circle" mentioned in the book. To be precise, "Yiwu Business Circle" refers to all economic entities and areas in close economic ties with Yiwu Small Commodity Market or companies at home and abroad, including both forward product marketing areas, backward industrial support areas, as well as the resulting cross-area labor division collaboration network. Next, common features shared among these economic entities and areas subject to the scope of "Yiwu Business Circle" will be set forth. Based on the platform of Yiwu Small Commodity Market, they either sell their commodities to all places or purchase small commodities from other places at home and abroad to directly and indirectly serve for the two abovementioned main subjects. Apart from trade contacts, more and more exchanges and cooperation in the field of production, finance, and information have been progressively realized via the platform functions of Yiwu Small Commodity Market. The small commodity market exerts a critical and pivotal role during this circulation process. In other words, numerous domestic and overseas traders and producers connect with one another through various ties and form the giant cross-area labor division collaboration network centering around the city's small commodity market, namely the concerned "Yiwu Business Circle" in this book.

While implementing the overall development strategy of "Flourish Business and Build City", Yiwu city realizes the rapid development of its local industrial economy and especially its small commodity market, and finally gives rise to the primary layer of "Yiwu Business Circle" with more extensive radiation scope via "Lead Business to Industry" "Promoting Industry by Commerce" and "Connecting Trade with Industry". Driven by the enormous market power, Yiwu's surrounding areas, Yangtze River Delta, Northeast China, Southwest China, Central China, and other areas in China have been increasingly making more close economic contacts with Yiwu, and in the meantime, relevant logistics, information flow, and capital flow keep being expanded. On the whole, the growth and development process of light industry in many areas have countless ties with Yiwu Small Commodity Market. On the one hand, because commodities sold in the small commodity market come from all provinces, cities, autonomous regions in China, and even foreign countries, it builds up the marketing platform for multitudinous domestic and overseas companies to expand their market space and pushes forward the development of featured advantageous industries in surrounding and other areas of China. In this sense, Yiwu Small Commodity Market is actually an important window by which Chinese companies can integrate with the international society and pioneer the international market. On the other hand, Yiwu Small Commodity Market has become a famous small commodity purchasing center at home and abroad. Nearly thousands of well-known shopping malls and circulation companies in China directly procure commodities every year, and more than 10,000 foreign merchants from over 100 countries and areas across the globe dwell in Yiwu permanently to engage in the small commodity procurement business. It is clear that the development of Yiwu Small Commodity Market has produced tremendous economic rise in numerous related areas at home and abroad. In turn, other areas also support the fast advancement of the small commodity market and overall economic society of Yiwu by virtue of economic exchanges and cooperation in diverse means.

As mentioned above, either in connotations or in spatial scope, "Yiwu Business Circle" has fundamental disparity different from the "business circle" referenced by the business retailing industry. It is more like a "big business circle" concept. As a market-centered cross-area labor division collaboration network, its formation and development has close intimacy with Yiwu Small Commodity Market. The unique functions exclusive of the small commodity market hasten the emergence of "Yiwu Business Circle", while it continually takes shape and consolidates along with the improvement and exertion of Yiwu Small Commodity Market functions and the promotion of business operation and structure. As a consequence, the formation and development of "Yiwu Business Circle" relies on the function exertion and business operation upgrade of Yiwu Small Commodity Market to a large extent. On the part of production companies, out of consideration for cost factors, it is a necessary tendency to choose a workplace close to the market. When a large-scale trading market gathers a substantial amount of population, capital, technology, and resources, the inherent return-seeking driving force of production factors makes single market trading functions hardly satisfy the requirements of an overall labor division collaboration network anymore. Under such circumstances, improvement, promotion, and expansion constitute new development momentums in the next round of developments of market size, business operation, and functions. During the market-industry interaction and promotion process, "Yiwu Business Circle" surpasses the scope of traditional market trading functions and simultaneously forms a cross-area labor division collaboration network via the improvement of informatization and networks. Within this network, the small commodity market acts as the core and numerous local and surrounding industrial clusters offer it support. The two form mighty outward emissive power in mutual development. The structure of "Yiwu Business Circle" could be inferred from Figure 1.1.

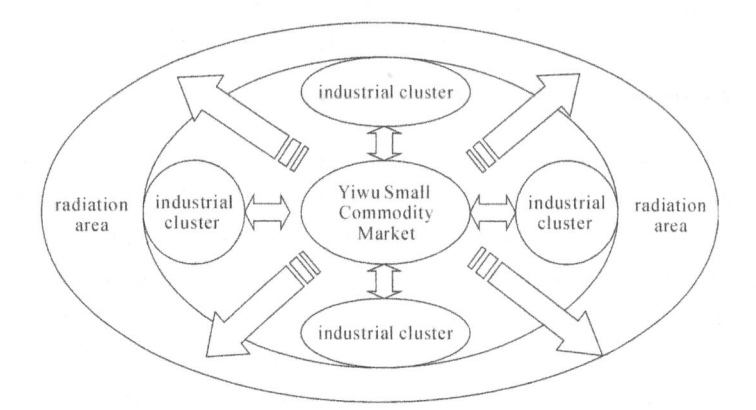

Figure 1.1:   "Yiwu Business Circle" structure chart

As shown in Figure 1.1, Yiwu Small Commodity Market plays the core role. It is also the source and momentum of "Yiwu Business Circle". The primary influence of "Yiwu Business Circle" is mainly confined to the internal small commodity market, namely the innermost small circle. Later on, together with the continuous expansion of market size, the returns to scale effects turn prominent and corresponding trading expenditures have been greatly lowered so that substantial industrial clusters gather in relatively large scope in the surrounding area. At the same time, with support from these industries, market radiation ability is further enhanced. A much wider labor division collaboration network, namely "Yiwu Business Circle", hereby takes shape when the market radiates market, industrial, and other related areas through product and information output. During the formation process of "Yiwu Business Circle", forms of contact among all economic entities become more and more diverse. In the initial exchange field, there gradually appears a more complicated and superior form via the simple commodity procurement and supply relation in the Yiwu market, such as labor division cooperation relation in the production field, exchanges and communication among governments, and all-round economic relations in the finance and information fields. The layer structure exhibited in Figure 1.1 is the abstract expression for a business circle core and non-core. In reality, the real geographical state of "Yiwu Business Circle" is not in such a regular layered distribution structure, but an interlaced network structure instead. Please refer to the description about "network-shaped non-layer structure" features in Section III (p. 151) for more details about the specific business circle area's distribution state.

II   Components of "Yiwu Business Circle"

1. Market system of "Yiwu Business Circle"

"Yiwu Business Circle" symbolizes the expansion of market order essentially. By virtue of the function of market mechanism, factors within the "business circle" such as market subjects, commodity, capital, talents, and information could rationally be allocated and flow. "Yiwu Business Circle" is constituted by lots of factors which have various statuses and functions in the business circle. Among which a sound market system is the radical premise for the market mechanism to play a role. Different categories of markets mutually connect with, rely on and restrict one another to form the organic synthesized market system. The formation of the market system is in need of certain conditions.[1]

---

[1]See Lu Lijun, Bai Xiaohu, Wang Zuqiang: *Market Yiwu: From Chicken Feather for Sugar to International Commerce*. Hangzhou: Zhejiang People's Publishing House, 2003, p. 112.

The first condition is the rich category of relevant commodity species, the second condition is huge quantity and scale, and the last condition is the intrinsic connection among all parts in the system. Apparently, the active force which drives the formation and development of "Yiwu Business Circle" comes from Yiwu Small Commodity Market. Consequently, within "Yiwu Business Circle", the market system exists in the central place (namely, Yiwu Small Commodity Market as shown in Figure 1.1).

The significant meaning of "Yiwu Business Circle" to regional economic development should be attributed to its full exertion of the market mechanism which enables rational and effective economic operation. While a sound market system is exactly the foundation for this mechanism to exert such functions, the market system does not take shape in one day since it also follows a progressive process. During the development process of Yiwu Small Commodity Market, when trading scale greatly expands and professional entities differentiate from the common breeding matrix, the uniform market system made up by plenty of relatively independent professional markets would come into existence.[2] The initial market system is principally made up by each professional small commodity market and supporting transportation and property rights market. Accompanied by the growing expansion of small commodity trading scale, a stable commodity source becomes the root of development in Yiwu Small Commodity Market. In such cases, localized production becomes a necessary requirement. Because production companies agglomerate to form the industrial cluster, numerous factors which provide supporting services for the market such as the labor market, technical market, information market, and transportation market also spring up one by one. Correspondingly, the market system in "Yiwu Business Circle" simultaneously undergoes a

---

[2]See Lu Lijun, Bai Xiaohu, Wang Zuqiang: *Market Yiwu: From Chicken Feather for Sugar to International Commerce*. Hangzhou: Zhejiang People's Publishing House, 2003, p. 114.

development process from the individual to the whole, from simplicity to diversity and from primary level to advanced level. These markets which offer supporting services to the small commodity market have a significant role in the exertion of the business circle's functions. Due to this, the market system in "Yiwu Business Circle" not only contains all sorts of small commodity markets, but also includes transportation, intellectual property, and factor markets.

The agglomeration phenomenon of similar professional markets in this space is called a "market cluster".[3] In this sense, it can also be said that the "market system" mentioned in this chapter is also shown in the form of "market agglomeration". However, besides all sorts of professional small commodity markets, the market system also includes professional streets, factor markets, and other related contents. Either as the supplement or as the support of professional markets, the market system possesses more economic integrality. At present, "Yiwu Business Circle" has formed a relatively sound market system which takes International Trade City (Futian Market) as the center, over 10 professional markets and 30 professional streets as the support, as well as the transportation market, intellectual property right market, labor force market, technology market, and information market as the support. The organic connection among these factors could be revealed from Figure 1.2. The figure shows that supporting markets including the factor market, property right market, logistics, and transportation market mainly serve for the small commodity market. Thus, the formation of the overall market system originates from the expansion of the small commodity market, and other markets develop by providing services for it. The two markets altogether make up the market system in a primary–secondary and successive relation.

---

[3] See Bai Xiaohu: Economies of scope and economies of scale of Yiwu specialized market cluster, *Finance and Trade Economy*, 2004, (2).

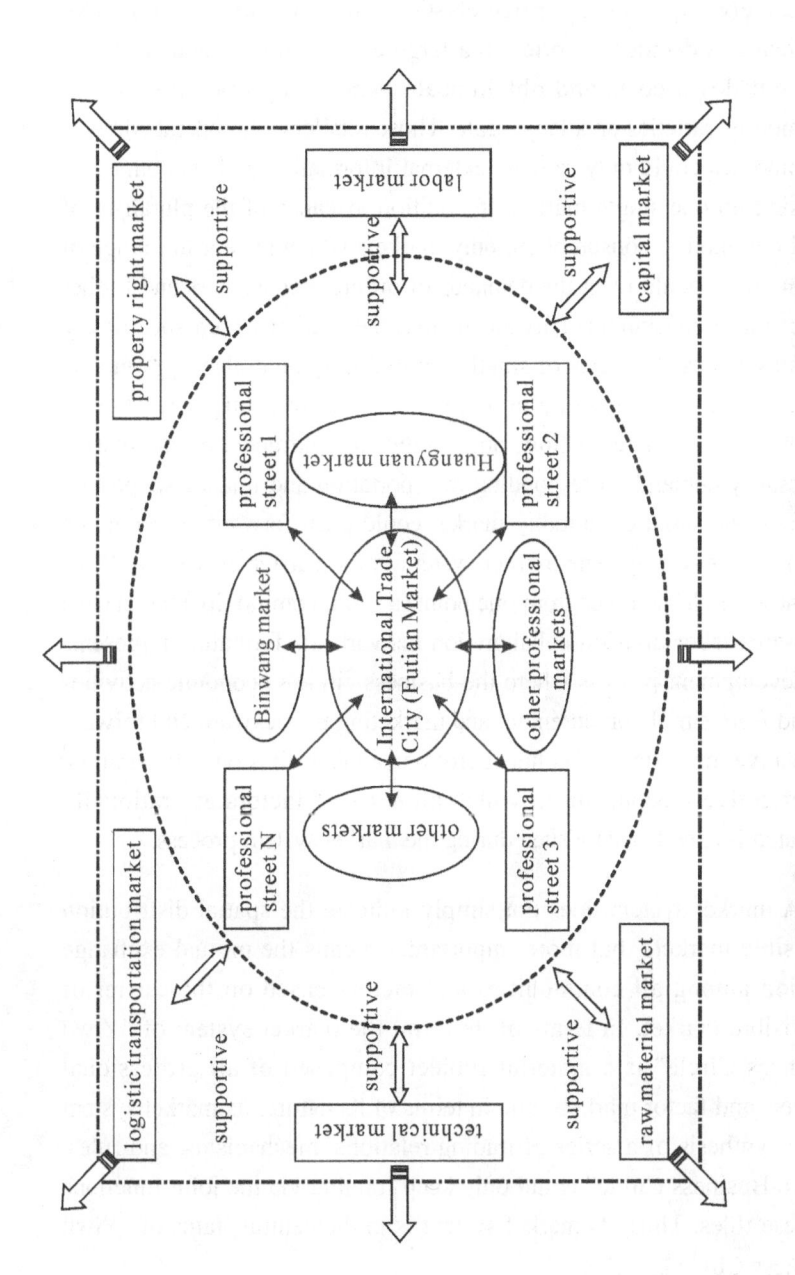

Figure 1.2: Core of "Yiwu Business Circle"—Yiwu Small Commodity Market system chart

Since small commodities are labor-intensive products that have a relatively large demand price elasticity, their market's competitive advantage is decided by price to a large extent. Single retailers could only cut down costs and obtain scale benefits by operating single commodity varieties on a large scale. Those retailers who operate diverse commodities could only retrieve external information and economies by focusing on one single market. In addition, because of the pluralism of small commodity consumption, only markets which have a full range of commodities could meet the demands of different consumers and further attract more consumers. This means that the market which specifically operates different species of small commodities could also agglomerate and acquire certain scope economies. Because a large number of passenger flow, material flow, and capital flow attracted by the market necessarily demand corresponding transportation and finance supporting services, the small commodity market could push forward an economic boom across society. The market system is the carrier by which "Yiwu Business Circle" evolves from one point (a small commodity market) to a cross-area labor division collaboration network. Its formation represents the development process where the business circle's economic activities extend from simple procurement and marketing to backward and forward correlative industries and conduct cross-area labor division collaboration. An effective mechanism in which all sorts of factors are rationally allocated is exactly established during the market system process.

A market system does not simply indicate the spatial distribution of visible markets, but more importantly means the mutual exchange relation among all commodities and factors based on the carrier of the visible market. In terms of its form, the market system of "Yiwu Business Circle" is a material subject composed of all professional markets and factor markets; and in terms of its nature, its market system is the synthesis of a series of trading relations, mechanisms, and rules. "Yiwu Business Circle" could only keep running via the joint functions of these rules. Thus, its market system is in the central status of "Yiwu Business Circle".

2. Support industry of "Yiwu Business Circle"

The factor of support industry has a fundamental status in "Yiwu Business Circle". Without the support industry, pure large-scale market cluster would never constitute as "Yiwu Business Circle". As an economic system driven by business industry, a stable commodity source is the basic component which could ensure sustained development. As a consequence, the traditional support industry of "Yiwu Business Circle" is a backward small commodity manufacturing industry in the business field. This is also the intrinsic reason why Yiwu's economy steps onto the road of "Connecting Trade with Industry" after its start in the small commodity market. During the formation process of "Yiwu Business Circle", Yiwu primarily gathers lots of industrial clusters in local and surrounding areas via the appeal to small commodity products and its provision of cheap and stable commodity sources guarantees the sustained development of the market. In this way, "Yiwu Business Circle" gradually takes shape and rapidly develops. However, when production and marketing reach a certain scale and level, pure manufacturing support fails to satisfy industry promotion and reformation requirements, and some newly emerging supporting service industries gradually develop to new support industries.

Throughout the historical development process, the traditional support industry in "Yiwu Business Circle" has been a small commodity manufacturing industry which directly provides commodity sources for small commodity trading, among which clothing, textile, accessory, toy, hardware, printing, and wool spinning are representative advantageous industries. Accompanied by the upgrade of market form and industry, all sorts of market-oriented industries continue to develop and expand. For instance, exhibition, logistics, and distribution gradually turn to be new market-oriented industries following the business industry and small commodity manufacturing industry. The common feature of these industries is that they generate from the direct service for the

small commodity market. While gradually turning mature on account of the development into a small commodity market, these industries in turn offer potent support to its further promotion and development. In the time of fast expansion in the business industry, small commodity manufacturing industry, and market-oriented industry, considerable horizontal support industries such as financial insurance, transportation, tourism catering, and information service also grow quickly and provide forceful guarantees for connecting the entire "Yiwu Business Circle" commodity manufacturing and the marketing system.

Among traditional support industries in "Yiwu Business Circle", the most fundamental industries are all sorts of local, surrounding, and nonlocal industrial clusters and companies which offer commodity sources to Yiwu Small Commodity Market. Because its intrinsic features determine fewer limitations from natural resources, the business industry has greater mobility. It is not reliable for an economic system to simply build connection through commodity procurement and marketing relations, for the reason that any possible rise of business costs or instability of commodity sources would easily lead to market depression in the economic system. However, since the manufacturing industry has higher requirements on resources, technology, talents, capital, and other factors and possesses relative stability, the influences of a single factor such as business costs rise on the whole economic system will be weakened and the stability of the business industry-centered economic system will be largely improved once backward industrial distribution establishes a favorable interaction relation with the surrounding market.

The industry support of "Yiwu Business Circle" not only comes from small commodity manufacturing industry clusters in the city and local area, but also from other areas which provide professional processing services for Yiwu companies. As a general rule, these areas have rather low economic development levels and industrial levels. The main source of revenues for local residents is agricultural production. Actually, local residents could earn higher revenues than from agricultural production and accumulate industrial personnel resources and capital by engaging in processing services for the Yiwu markets and companies. With cheap labor prices, these areas find an effective means to cut down on manufacturing costs for the central "Yiwu Business Circle" on the condition of growing prominent factor restrictions. Also, they become the orientation of industrial transfer for internal advanced areas within "Yiwu Business Circle". Therefore, the support industry has significant influence on the rational flow and allocation of production factors and the harmonious development of the regional economy. By the increasing degree of internationalization in Yiwu Small Commodity Market, spatial distance no longer has more difficulty in hindering the rise of logistics efficiency. Many overseas companies are now becoming the industrial support for "Yiwu Business Circle" and in the meanwhile, considerable overseas commodities circulate in Yiwu Small Commodity Market via this channel. Based on more diversified commodity varieties, these overseas companies seek more direct economic benefits through incorporating into the labor division collaboration system within "Yiwu Business Circle".

Accompanied by the growing increase of small commodity manufacturing and the degree of trade internationalization, and the convergence of great quantity of personnel, material flow, capital flow, and information flow, many service industries such as exhibition, finance and insurance, tourism catering, transportation, and information service seek promising development opportunities. The rise of these industries should be, on the one hand, ascribed to the demands for small commodity manufacturing and trading, and on the other hand ascribed to their identity as newly emerging industries and new economic growth points. In this sense, these support industries will produce vital support functions in future development of "Yiwu Business Circle". In the meantime, by means of the general application of information technology, traditional support industries in "Yiwu Business Circle"

manifest increasingly benign growth momentum and provide new-round momentum for the further expansion of the overall business circle after transformation and upgradation.

Because the market system-centered "Yiwu Business Circle" has sought forceful industrial support, the overall economic system is set up on a solid operating foundation and accordingly seeks fast and stable development in combination with the full exertion of market vitality.

3. Merchant groups of "Yiwu Business Circle"

The third important component of "Yiwu Business Circle" is the merchant group, namely its key personnel factor. During the full formation and development process of "Yiwu Business Circle", it is the most proactive pusher and foremost beneficiary. Accordingly, to learn about the development process of the merchant group is to learn about the development process of "Yiwu Business Circle" in some sense.

By reference to existing research findings concerning "Yiwu Model", while exploring the reasons for the development of Yiwu Small Commodity Market, many scholars hold the opinion that local residents' business customs and regional merchant groups[4] in Yiwu make up an important research topic. The term "merchant groups" in the book do not simply denote "Yiwu merchants".[5] As for the historical course, "merchant groups" correlated with "Yiwu Business Circle" not only

---

[4] See Wang Zuqiang: The expansion of market order and the growth of specialized trading organizations: A case study of "Market Yiwu". *Journal of Zhejiang Shuren University*, 2004, No. 2.

[5] See Lu Lijun, Bai Xiaohu, Wang Zuqiang: *Market Yiwu: From Chicken Feather for Sugar to International Commerce*. Hangzhou: Zhejiang People's Publishing House, 2003, p. 74. In the book's discussion of regional merchant groups, Yiwu merchants are mainly divided by geographical features; and the merchant groups mentioned in this book are measured by the degree of economic connection, which is beyond the concept of geography.

include merchants from surrounding areas in Yiwu (such as Dongyang, Yongkang, Pujiang, and Zhuji) who play a vital role in the small commodity market development process, but also include merchants who come from all places to do business in Yiwu when it becomes the largest small commodity market in China, and merchants who come from overseas countries to build up close business connections with Yiwu Small Commodity Market and industries when it becomes an international business city.

With regard to the regional features of merchant groups, those Yiwu farmers who used to shake the drum-shaped rattle and carry the sugar on shoulders with a pole could be taken as the predecessors of merchant groups. The most prominent feature of these farmers engaged in "chicken feather for sugar" should be their sense of organization, which ultimately leads to the appearance of the professional trading organization of "sugar-knocking group". After the reform and opening-up, local merchants in Yiwu changed from itinerant traders to shopkeepers and gradually established the small commodity market. A number of businessmen from local areas and even farther areas joined in this group to mutually promote the prosperity in the small commodity market.

During this historical period, although there also sprang up small commodity markets similar to Yiwu's in surrounding areas with identical or better geographical position and basic conditions, the city still retains nearby merchants and attracts a group of merchants from farther areas to join in this group due to its ideal business environment, hospitable and plain folk customs, quick returns and small margins profit-making mode, and non-repulsion of nonlocal merchants. This point could also be used to explain the reason why other counties and cities similar or superior to Yiwu could not rapidly form a small commodity market like Yiwu.

Nowadays, following the continuous expansion of foreign trade business, Yiwu has gradually become an international business city

and one of the areas which have the highest export-oriented degree in Zhejiang's economy. This tendency inevitably forces the merchant groups in support of "Yiwu Business Circle" development to increasingly present internationalization features and obviously surpasses the contents covered by the concept of "Yiwu merchants". Accordingly, the geographical features of "Yiwu Business Circle" merchant groups are not limited to Yiwu. It includes merchants from other areas of China and overseas, Yiwu merchants in nonlocal areas and overseas, as well as nonlocal merchants who keep close business contacts with Yiwu.

In accordance with the industrial features of merchant groups, the merchant groups in "Yiwu Business Circle" started with the business industry. After developing to a certain stage, some of them turned to open up stores and some brand companies, and further, did not rely on the previous small commodity market. Because of the prosperous development of service industries represented by the transportation industry, real estate industry, and catering industry activated by market development, practitioners in these industries also became organic components of "Yiwu merchants". In brief, as decisive personnel factors in "Yiwu Business Circle", "merchant groups" act as the source of vigor in the formation and development of "Yiwu merchants".

4. Logistic network of "Yiwu Business Circle"

The logistics network in "Yiwu Business Circle" experiences a revolutionary process from inferior layer to superior layer. In the very beginning, an important advantageous factor beneficial to the rise of the small commodity market was Yiwu Railway Station. Owing to the stronger transportation ability and relatively convenient transportation conditions, Yiwu Railway Station greatly lowered the transportation costs for small commodities. At the same time, earlier market distribution apparently presented the geographical features close to Yiwu Railway Station. Moreover, since Yiwu Railway Station has high working efficiency, low charges, good reputation, and is hospitable to nonlocal merchants, it becomes an important unloading terminal for the nonlocal commodity in Central Zhejiang and brings about huge personnel and material flow. While activating the fast prosperity of the small commodity market, it pushes forward the advancement of relevant support service industries and further generates enormous propelling functions on the development of Yiwu's society and economy.

Under the background of the further expansion of the small commodity market scale, the professional consign market[6] rises in response to proper times and occasions. Consign business is the byproduct of the small commodity market. As a result of inconvenient commodity transportation in the initial market development stage, few rickshaw pullers established a professional consign department to transport small commodities and operate a united translation of railways and highways in 1985. From then on, the consign industry realizes orderly development subject to government regulations. The highly efficient operation of Yiwu's small commodity logistics system ensures the fast development of the market.

From the perspective of time, before the formation of "Yiwu Business Circle", supportive logistic systems in the small commodity market still belong to traditional logistics. Its prime function is transportation and storage. However, together with the reformation and upgrade of market and industry, simple transportation and storage functions could not meet the demands of market development, while the popularity of modern logistics creates the possibility for further development of the market in general and the fading of the "professional market" that once took place in western developed countries.

Up to now, "Yiwu Business Circle" has developed to be a well-operated and high-efficiency logistic network and acquired scale

---

[6]See Lu Lijun, Bai Xiaohu: The expansion of the cooperative group—a case study of the changes in the system of Yiwu united consignment market, *Economic Research*, 2000, No. 8.

benefits similar to market agglomeration. Just like the small commodity market network, Yiwu's logistic network reduces the cost via scale development and furthermore encourages the fast development of its small commodity market by attracting logistic businesses from surrounding areas to centralize in Yiwu. Under the mutually reliant enhancement mechanism between a small commodity market and logistic network, the logistic network already becomes an integral organic component of "Yiwu Business Circle".

Based on the giant logistic network and business in Yiwu, although it is simply a county-level city, it obtained the approval to establish the customs office which provides a full set of port services such as customs clearance, thus greatly facilitating the development of the foreign trade business and creating huge convenience for the expansion of "Yiwu Business Circle" radiation scope and improvement of corresponding radiation power. Nowadays, Yiwu has become the largest logistic center in the Central and Western Zhejiang area and its logistics industry has become another backbone industry that includes the business and manufacturing industries. The logistic network of "Yiwu Business Circle" spreads over the whole country and many places in the world. The realization of storage, processing, information, testing, and logistic distribution functions has crucial meanings to the normal operation and further promotion of "Yiwu Business Circle".

To sum up, among all factors which make up "Yiwu Business Circle", if it were regarded as a human body, then its market system would be the heart and blood vessels, the industry support, the skeleton, the merchant group, the brain, and the logistic network, the muscles and nerves. It is exactly these prime tissues that constitute a full and vigorous "Yiwu Business Circle".

III Features of "Yiwu Business Circle"

Being such a highly energetic economic system, "Yiwu Business Circle" necessarily has its own distinctive features, which could be proven by the small commodity-dominated trading objects, connection between business and industry, internationalization of a labor division collaboration network, and the non-layer structure of a network shape. Next, the following description will start with the analysis on the first feature.

1. Small commodity-dominated trading objects

Small commodity primarily refers to daily consumer goods most prominently characterized by their feature of "smallness". As for commodity form, this feature is displayed by small volume, small area, and lightweight. As for production, this feature is displayed by small capital scale,

small scale of production, and small product output.[7] A small commodity has a wide range of other features including low unit price, great variety, frequent use, fast upgrade, and difficulty in standardization. Before the development of economies reached a certain height, consumers usually took price factors into account when buying small commodities, but brand appeal was less attractive. Some people attribute it to the low industrial level of a small commodity. Because of its simple production processes, low requirements in invested capital scale, and high substitutability between capital factors and labor factors,[8] small commodities are suitable for Yiwu's weak initial industrial base but rich labor resources. This is also the basic evidence for Yiwu's economy to start with small commodity trading and follow the development path to become a global small commodity distribution center supported by small commodity production. From small commodity trading to small commodity production, all industrial selections in "Yiwu Business Circle" are decided by objective factors. The formation of "Yiwu Business Circle", which originates from a small commodity market and surrounds small commodity production and sales, signalizes a major progress in the business and production industry. Although "Yiwu Business Circle" has the full capacity to produce other products together with the completion of capital accumulation in some major markets, the most competitive and representative trading objects remain small commodities either in production or sales now.

At present, although many entrepreneurs in Yiwu have accumulated adequate capital to develop other industries, large-scale heavy chemical industry and other industries in surrounding areas do not have any

---

[7]See Lu Lijun, Bai Xiaohu, Wang Zuqiang: *Market Yiwu: From Chicken Feather for Sugar to International Commerce*. Hangzhou: Zhejiang People's Publishing House, 2003, p. 113.

[8]See Lu Lijun, Bai Xiaohu, Wang Zuqiang: *Market Yiwu: From Chicken Feather for Sugar to International Commerce*. Hangzhou: Zhejiang People's Publishing House, 2003, p. 98.

significant advantages in both natural resources, technical and human capital due to the limitations caused by objective conditions. Even some areas included in "Yiwu Business Circle" within geographical range or with economic ties might have the proper conditions to develop into a heavy chemical industry or other industries (such as Ningbo), or a small commodity production and trading industry which supports the formation and development of "Yiwu Business Circle" on the whole will remain in the mainstream status for a rather long term. To be sure, in spite of the dominance of small commodity trading objects within "Yiwu Business Circle", it does not exclude the possibility for each area to develop other industries. Clearly, with growing influences of "Yiwu Business Circle", plenty of companies at home and abroad rely on Yiwu Small Commodity Market to expand its trading channel. Among commodity varieties circulating in the small commodity market now, artware, household appliances, and textile have far exceeded the primitive scope of "small commodity". Therefore, a small commodity mentioned here is not the "small commodity" in a strict sense. On the contrary, a commodity within "Yiwu Business Circle" still primarily presents the feature of smallness, but does not rule out the possibility of any drastic changes in commodity shape in the future.

Along with the transformation and improvement of market and industry, high-tech and branding of small commodity is the necessary tendency for future industries in Yiwu and surrounding areas. "Yiwu Business Circle" has sufficient historical experience, information, technology, institution, and mechanism advantages in small commodity production and sales. Small commodities would still have a large market as long as it makes technical transformations, propels industrial upgrades, and improves industrial layers.

2. Connections between business and industry

Driven by business industry, Yiwu Small Commodity Market and economy in the core of "Yiwu Business Circle" activates industry with the market and supports the market with industry. It gradually takes shape and develops by means of the joint advancement of both business and industry. According to the law of market development, an inevitable requirement of capital is to convert from the business field to the industry field. In particular, after the early and mid-1990s, considerable business capital in Yiwu started to convert to a small commodity production industry. A large group of private entrepreneurs and merchants took advantage of the available information and sales network to expand to industry and accordingly triggered over 20 distinctive small commodity production industries represented by the socks, accessories, and zipper industries. Throughout the boom of these industries, Yiwu ushered in a bilateral interaction, interdependence, and mutual prosperity situation where the market activated industry, and industry supported the market. The development of industry manifests the growth of total industrial output value, while the development of business industry reflects the growth of annual business volume in "China Small Commodity City". Please refer to Table 1.1 for more detailed data.[9]

Table 1.1: Statistical table of annual total industrial output value in Yiwu City and annual business volume in "China Small Commodity City"

Year	Total industrial output value in Yiwu city (10,000 Yuan)	Annual business volume in "China Small Commodity City"(10,000 Yuan)
1982	13,908	392
1983	19,798	1,444
1984	30,754	2,321

---

[9]Data source: Refer to Yiwu Statistical Yearbook (1999–2005) for gross industrial output value; See Lu Lijun, Bai Xiaohu, Wang Zuqiang: *Market Yiwu: From Chicken Feather for Sugar to International Commerce*. Hangzhou: Zhejiang People's Publishing House, 2003, p. 44, Table 1.1 for annual turnover of "China Commodity City".

Continued

Year	Total industrial output value in Yiwu city (10,000 Yuan)	Annual business volume in "China Small Commodity City"(10,000 Yuan)
1985	40,793	6,190
1986	49,367	10,029
1987	70,882	15,380
1988	96,127	26,500
1989	110,695	39,000
1990	152,936	60,600
1991	199,101	102,500
1992	306,090	205,400
1993	610,001	451,500
1994	1,199,551	1,021,200
1995	1,374,685	1,520,000
1996	1,582,263	1,846,800
1997	1,737,250	1,451,100
1998	1,968,389	1,534,000
1999	2,214,438	1,753,000
2000	2,558,488	1,928,900
2001	2,853,356	2,119,700
2002	3,313,241	2,299,800
2003	4,026,154	2,483,200
2004	4,925,000	2,668,700
2005	5,930,000	2,884,800

After drawing two statistical broken lines for the total industrial output value of Yiwu city and annual business volume in "China Small Commodity City",[10] it is apparent that around 1995, the proportion between business and industrial output value had evident transformation (Figure 1.3). This proves that during the joint development process of the two parties, the development of business industry precedes that of industry and lays the foundation for the development of industry. However, the development of industry is the necessary condition to push forward the development of business industry. In business–industry joint development, industry depends on and provides services for business industry. Exactly under the lead of business industry, industrial output values rapidly increase. During this process, proper government policy guidance is established on the objective law of economic growth.

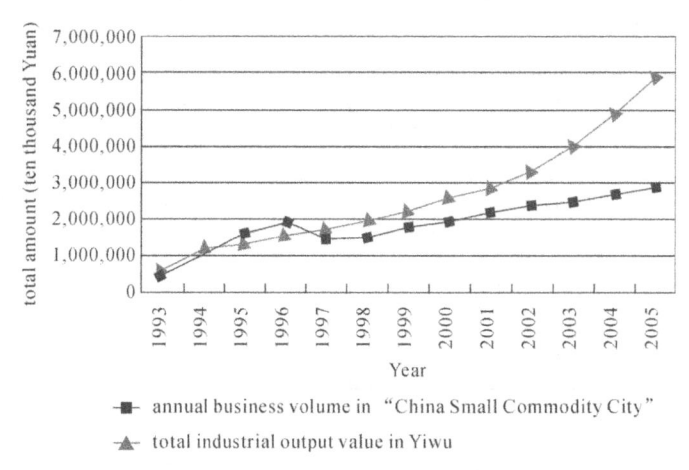

Figure 1.3:   Business and industry joint development chart in Yiwu City

---

[10]The total volume of commerce and trade in Yiwu is obviously larger than that in "China Small Commodity City". The annual turnover of "China Small Commodity City" is used to compare with the total industrial output value of Yiwu City. On the one hand, this is because the development of "China Small Commodity City" is an epitome of the development of the trade industry in Yiwu. On the other hand, it can also explain the status of Yiwu Small Commodity Market in the whole Yiwu business district.

In recent years, along with the continuous upgrade of Yiwu Small Commodity Market and the appearance of some new type of business modes, higher requirements have been proposed on the technical contents in small commodities. This further encourages the primitive small commodity production industry to improve the quality of small commodities via technical transformation. Additionally, the reliance on land, water, electricity, natural resources, and other factors severely restricts further development of a traditional production industry. It is also essential to introduce high-tech products and push forward technical innovation to initiate a low-consumption, non-pollution, and new high-tech production industry. The upgrade of the production industry in turn enhances the global competitiveness of Yiwu Small Commodity Market, thereby continuously extending the international influences and radiation scope of "Yiwu Business Circle".

3. Internalization of labor division collaboration network

The formation and development of "Yiwu Business Circle" is inseparable from the small commodity market. Starting with the small commodity market, "Yiwu Business Circle" develops into to a cross-area labor division collaboration network and now moves forward in the direction of internationalization. As a consequence, this feature could be used to describe the development tendency of the whole "Yiwu Business Circle".

Throughout the development history, Yiwu did not have close ties with external areas and the scope of the market activities was still limited within Yiwu. This means that the small commodity market of "Yiwu Business Circle" initially remained in the nurturing stage. Exactly due to the expansion of small commodity market's radiation scope, Yiwu continues to enhance the connection with the outside world and progressively forms "Yiwu Business Circle". However, accompanied by the rise of substantial industrial clusters supported by the small commodity market industry, the scope of "Yiwu Business

Circle" expands from the circulation domain to the production domain. At this time, "Yiwu Business Circle" actually turns from one point (small commodity market) to multiple points (market + industrial cluster). Economic vigor in this area is given full play, owing to the interaction between business and industry, and in the meantime, the peripheral and external radiation of commodity-based industrial competitiveness further gives rise to the progress of industrialization, deepens cross-area labor division, and finally forms the cross-area labor division collaboration network. Nowadays, with unceasing promotion of the degree of internationalization, the coverage scope of the business circle's labor division collaboration network presents cross-area and internationalization features in the territory and diverts from a business and light production industry to a modern service industry.

Four factors which make up "Yiwu Business Circle" also embody internationalization features.

(1) In terms of market system, what exists originally is a single small commodity market. After relocation, reformation, and upgradation, many other markets are derived with varying scales when the single market continues to expand. Among others, factors, logistics, and property rights markets are indispensable parts during the formation and development process of "Yiwu Business Circle". Unceasing growth of the quantity of all sorts of markets and expansion of distribution scope towards local or surrounding areas in Yiwu facilitate the internationalization tendency.

(2) In terms of support industry, even if the source of small commodity comes from all areas of China in the preliminary entrepreneurship stage, real industry support for "Yiwu Business Circle" could only take shape when industrial clusters gather in local and surrounding areas of Yiwu. A simplistic procurement relation is invalid in the industrial chain formed by the production of small commodities in Yiwu, for the reason that in case of any possible rise of business costs,

production companies will always hold the impetus to seek a new sales channel. Industry could only be called support as long as production has specific purposes (namely, for whom to produce). Out of the existence of the giant platform of "Yiwu Business Circle", more and more companies actively seek the connection with Yiwu Small Commodity Market, and accordingly fabricate the industry support for "Yiwu Business Circle" in an objective manner. By far, this mechanism has expanded nationwide and worldwide from the local and surrounding areas of Yiwu. Only industry-supported internationalization could authentically incarnate the internationalization tendency of "Yiwu Business Circle".

(3) In terms of merchant groups, it is clearly important to notice business merchants' geographical features and the internationalization tendency of merchants in local and surrounding areas pursuant to the description of their geographical features in the above analysis on components.

(4) In terms of logistic networks, logistics and business flow should be unified as a whole in accordance with the generality of market trading activities. Though they might go through different paths via the completion of new functions such as information technology application and logistic distribution, it comes down to maintaining the consistency between logistics and business flow in the end. When trading subjects (merchant groups) become increasingly internationalized, the internationalization of a logistics network naturally happens without extra efforts.

4. Non-layer structure in network shape

On the basis of the intimacy of economic ties, a traditional business circle could be divided into a core business circle, a secondary business circle, and a peripheral business circle. The layer-structure in a traditional business circle is mainly divided according to the distance of geographical positions. Because the strength of economic ties is inversely proportional to the distance of geographical position, or in

other words, much closer distance leads to a more intimate relation, the traditional business circle usually demonstrates an overt layer structure. However, with the improvement of transportation facilities and the application of information technology, influences of distance factors on economic ties weaken day by day and intangible information flow is nearly free from the restriction of distance. Thus, "Yiwu Business Circle" does not have a layer structure which is formed in line with the distance from geographical positions to a central business circle.

"Yiwu Business Circle" has more abundant components than traditional business circles, therefore, economic ties among subjects have more affluent expression forms through the forward and backward extensions in the industry chain and the mutual development across areas and industries. In addition to business trading contacts, there also exist many other ways of developing contacts including industrial labor division, collaboration, logistics, finance, and other support services. The diversity of internal economic contact forms within "Yiwu Business Circle" leads to the fact that the intimacy of economic ties is not simply or mainly decided by geographical status or distance, and corresponding economic ties present an irregular network-like structure. For instance, in comparison with other places in China, some overseas markets, sellers, or producers usually have more intimate connections with Yiwu. Though they are in a relatively remote position far from "Yiwu Business Circle", they are in the central status in the economic relation network. Now that some areas far from Yiwu (such as Quzhou, Lishui, as well as Shangrao in Jiangxi Province) have realized the propelling functions of the Yiwu market for its local economy, they already came up with development thinking modes such as "connecting with Yiwu" at an early time and possibly have higher intimacy with Yiwu's market than those cities and counties closer to Yiwu. Consequently, though "Yiwu Business Circle" centers around Yiwu and gathers a batch of layered industrial clusters and professional markets, it is not in a layered structure like the traditional business circle but is actually in a network-shaped structure established via economic ties.

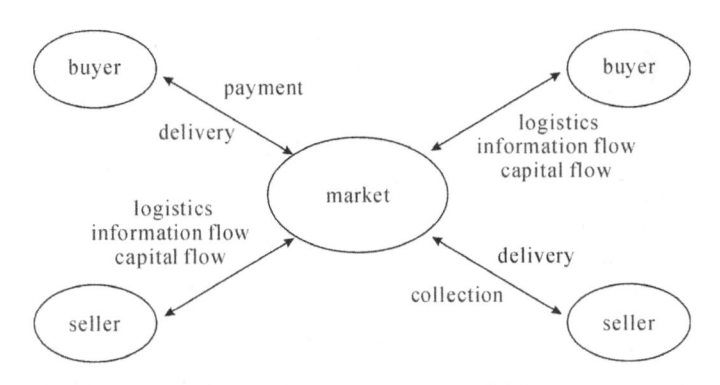

Figure 1.4:   Traditional trading relation chart

The network-shaped structure of "Yiwu Business Circle" could also be understood from the perspective of a logistics network. Traditional commodity trading will accomplish success after realizing the convection between logistics and capital flow through market negotiation and contract signing between sellers and buyers, wherein the former takes charge of delivery and the latter takes charge of payment. During this process, a general commodity is usually brought by sellers in the market and taken away by buyers after acceptance inspection. The consistency between logistics and business flow can be seen in Figure 1.4.

Nevertheless, due to the emergence of modern logistics, particularly third-party logistics, commodities could be directly transported from the place of production to the place of sale. By acquiring commodity information in the market, sellers and buyers could conclude agreements across remote distances, and commodities could be directly transported to the third place from the place of production. After the formation of "Yiwu Business Circle", some subjects establish firm cooperative relations via long-term business contacts so that the information is transmitted between sellers and buyers explicitly. As the common platform is integrated in the whole system, the foremost function of market is to work as an information distribution and exhibition center

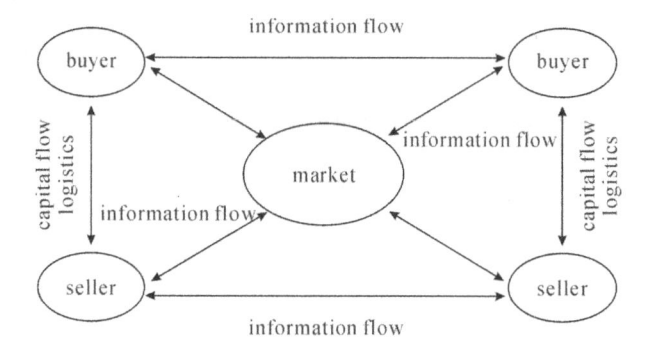

Figure 1.5: **"Yiwu Business Circle" network-shaped trading relation chart**

which separates logistics and information flow. Please refer to Figure 1.5 for more details.

The above four features of "Yiwu Business Circle" are distinct from traditional business circles and general industrial clusters. Based on the definition for the "Yiwu Business Circle" concept in this book, "Yiwu Business Circle" has much wider components and involved fields than traditional business circles and general industrial clusters. It more eminently highlights the communication and cooperation functions among different subjects inside "Yiwu Business Circle" as a whole. At the same time, as a certain abstract economic system based on regional economic development in Yiwu, "Yiwu Business Circle" comes from the small commodity market and benefits from the local government. It could be said to be a superior form.

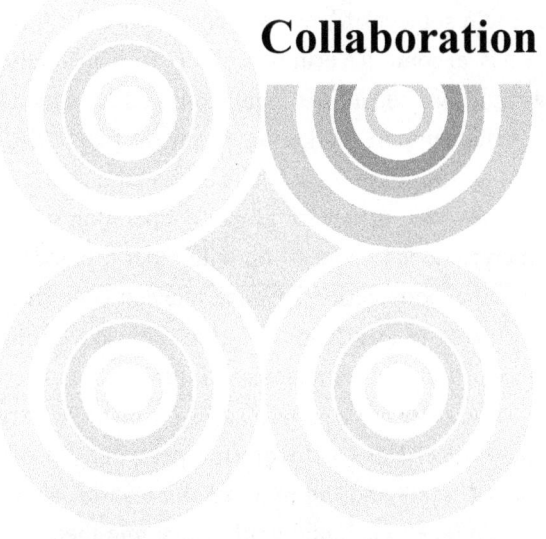

Chapter 2

"Yiwu Business Circle" Division of Labor Collaboration Network

Yiwu Small Commodity Market is the core of "Yiwu Business Circle", the main manifestation and support carrier of which are physical markets like International Trade City, Huangyuan Market, and Binwang Market. Since Yiwu Small Commodity Market was named as "International Small Commodity City" by State Administration for Industry and Commerce in 1992, the economic activities around the market have become the main subject of Yiwu's economic life. To this day, the whole of Yiwu has become a veritable "International Small Commodity City". As a result, we regard the small commodity market and the leading industries that support market development like trade, convention and exhibition, and logistics as a whole and as the core of "Yiwu Business Circle". This core, the interregional cooperation with other provincial cities, interprovincial cooperation with other provinces in the country, and international cooperation between relevant countries and regions have constituted the Division of Labor Collaboration Network for "Yiwu Business Circle". This chapter will further illustrate the rich connotation of "Yiwu Business Circle" as a Cross-regional Division of Labor Collaboration Network from the perspectives of the core of "Yiwu Business Circle" and the regional division of labor collaboration of "Yiwu Business Circle", and apply economic theories such as economies of scale, transaction costs, and industrial clusters to analyze the rationality of this division of labor network.

Core of "Yiwu Business Circle": Yiwu Market and Yiwu Industry

I

1. New features and new functions of "Yiwu Business Circle"

The common features of economic subjects, industries, and regions that can be included in the scope of "Yiwu Business Circle" are as follows: they may rely on the platform of Yiwu Small Commodity Market to sell products to all parts of the country or purchase small commodities from all over the country and even from abroad. In this circulation process, Yiwu Small Commodity Market plays a pivotal role. Through over 30 years' development, qualitative changes have taken place in the small commodity market as the core of "Yiwu Business Circle" in continuous innovation, and some new features and functions have been created:

Firstly, the regional influence of the market develops internationally. Yiwu Small Commodity Market has an obvious tendency to internationalize the circulation of goods with the number of existing export countries and regions reaching 219, basically covering every corner of the world. Through connecting similar markets in Cologne of Panama, Dubai of the United Arab Emirates, Brazil, Chile, and other places, it has enhanced the position of Yiwu Small Commodity Market as one of the international commodity distribution centers. Diversification of the main subject of export and the diversification of export commodities make extroversion of the market reach over 60%. More importantly, the center of gravity of exports has gradually shifted from third-world countries to developed countries. According to the statistics of customs trade volume in 2005, the USA has become the largest exporter of Yiwu Small Commodity Market, followed by the United Arab Emirates, Russia, Ukraine, R. O. Korea, Japan, and so on.

Secondly, the market format is advanced and modernized. By promoting the development of market gradient, a multi-level pattern of co-existence and co-prosperity has been formed; it has adopted measures like withdrawing booth and changing the store to transform the market hardware facilities, expand the unit operating area, and improve the operating environment so as to promote rapid development of a new batch of emerging industries; the common development of the public stalls, boutiques, specialized areas, and the collection of exhibition and service in one of the foreign trade offices has changed the traditional model of the store and promoted the innovation of the business; International Trade City is equipped with high-tech management hardware, central air conditioning, electronic monitoring, and an automatic fire alarm system, etc., and the trading environment has been greatly improved. With the continuous improvement of the hardware facilities in the physical market, Yiwu has successfully opened up an invisible market on the Internet using modern information technology. With establishment of the Internet Network Information Company for the International Small Commodity City, "www.sunbu. com", and B2B e-commerce service fulfillment, it has formed various service functions like trading platforms, search engines, payment intermediaries, distribution centers, and supporting services, providing more convenient business services for the market subjects.

Thirdly, the service function of the market is branded and individualized. At present, Yiwu Small Commodity Market has been transformed from the traditional sales of the product to the sales force. It gathers a lot of consumer information and transmits them to different manufacturers. In addition, manufacturers can promote their own products and brands through the market. The market transmits product information such as variety, specification, quality, and price to the consumers, and then feeds back the consumer's demand information to the manufacturers. The manufacturer organizes the production according to the orders of the merchants, and pays the advertising fee to the merchants according to the orders, while the merchant does not charge any additional cost to the consumers besides the commodity price. This face-to-face, centralized way of publicity is more interactive than the way large media ads are used to create corporate brands; compared with the establishment of its own marketing system and franchised store, the professional market has nearly unlimited consumer groups; its low cost makes it similar to "free lunch", which is more attractive to small and medium enterprises that can't afford to pay a huge amount of advertising. As the scope of the "business circle" of the market is expanding gradually, more and more manufacturers both at home and abroad strive to use the influence of the market to propagate themselves. With the development of the market function transformed from the traditional trading of large and homogeneous products to the branding, the individualized function of the market is becoming more and more prominent.

2. Industry development supporting the core of "Yiwu Business Circle"

Looking at the development process of the small commodity market, business and trade are the foundation of Yiwu's economy, which has promoted the development of industrial and regional cooperation, and in turn promoted the prosperity of the market, thus forming "Yiwu Business

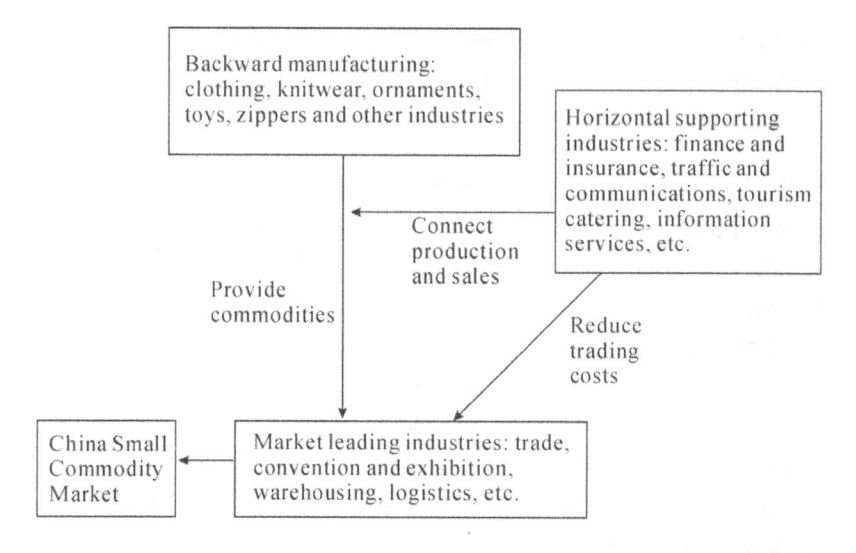

Figure 2.1: Core industry support structure map for Yiwu Small Commodity Market

Circle" with the linkage effect. This phenomenon can be figuratively compared to "nuclear fission": The market is a huge reactor and it has triggered a continuous fission of the factors of production, such as capital, manpower, and information. Thus, it has become a modern industrial structure leading to the third industry, as well as the modern small commodity manufacturing industry, which leads the consumption trend at home and abroad. While the trade, exhibition, logistics, warehousing, and so on are the leading industries in the market, which embody the main functions of the market, the small commodity manufacturing industry is the backward industry of the market that provides products for the market. Finance, communication, information, etc. are horizontal industries, providing services for market trading and the connection between sales and production (refer to Figure 2.1).

2.1 Market leading industry

The direct reason why Yiwu Small Commodity Market can become the largest in the world is the rapid development of commerce and trade, which is the root of the increasing prosperity of the market.

Business is inherently impulsive in flow and opening, inevitably to seek a breakthrough. With the expansion of scale and influence, some periods may even grow exponentially so that business and trade not only support the development of "Yiwu Business Circle" core, but also become the key to expanding the "Yiwu Business Circle".

The convention and exhibition industry is the concentrated expression of the influence of the market. Since the "Canton Fair" and East China Fair are the embodiment of the Pearl River Delta and Yangtze River Delta market influence, and because the two are in an important position in China, they in a sense also reflect the whole Chinese Market. However, as a county city, if Yiwu intends to hold a convention and exhibition, and if it is not supported by broad market potential, then it is at very high risk and unlikely to succeed. At present, more than 80 exhibitions are held every year in Yiwu, and the "Yiwu Fair" has become the third largest commercial convention and exhibition in the country. In general, exhibitions are often held out of the needs of local government and market players to expand their influence and promote local products. The more and more flourishing of the "Yiwu Fair" is not only required to satisfy the needs of the Yiwu government and Yiwu merchants themselves, but they are also the common demands of many small commodity buyers and producers at home and abroad. They need such a platform to show their products and information, and to find the products and information they need. The exhibition economy is the extension of the development of "Yiwu Business Circle" in nature and adds a finishing touch of power to the development of the small commodity market as the core of "Yiwu Business Circle" in the interaction. Its centralized display function and the daily transaction function of the small commodity market are combined to push "Yiwu Business Circle" to a higher level.

Logistics warehousing is essentially a supporting service industry for the development of business and trade, but "Yiwu Business Circle" has the characteristics of a large quantity and wide range

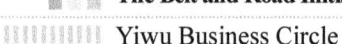
in the production and sale of small commodities. Thus, logistics warehousing has formed an organic whole with business and trade on the first day of the formation of Yiwu Small Commodity Market and "Yiwu Business Circle", and becomes one of the leading industries supporting the core of "Yiwu Business Circle". At present, in China, the logistics warehousing of the small commodity market has the largest business volume inland of China in addition to the international freight forwarders of famous ports like in Shanghai, Ningbo, Qingdao, and Dalian. From the point of combined transport and consignment to the international logistics center, we can see the shadow of expansion of logistics warehousing and institutional innovation in Yiwu with each expansion of the small commodity market and "Yiwu Business Circle".

2.2 Backward manufacturing industry

To view from the perspective of Yiwu Small Commodity Market, the manufacturing industry is the backward industry of the market. Therefore, many professional markets in China usually follow the road of "a manufacturing to professional market". Most of them support the development of the market by developing strong commodity production; Yiwu, on the other hand, went out of the way of "professional market to manufacturing", that is, "Promoting Industry by Commerce". There is no good or bad difference between the two roads, but their economic conditions, regional culture, and characteristics of the times determine the different development paths. "Lead Business to Industry", "Promoting Industry by Commerce", and "Connecting Trade with Industry" are great features of Yiwu Small Commodity Market. In line with the development of the market, the development of Yiwu's industry has gone through the transformation process from single to multiple, from low level to high level, and gradually formed the industrial development pattern of "Small Commodities, Big Industries, Small Businesses, and Large Clusters".

In the early 1980s, Yiwu Small Commodity Market was emerging and there was no support from the local industry. After years of capital accumulation, some merchants began to set up family workshops and small businesses. The large-scale development of modern industry in Yiwu started in the middle of the 1990s. Many high grade, famous enterprises have also come to the fore since then. Relying on the government's guidance and the role of market platform, Yiwu has formed the pattern where the market drives industry and industry supports the market, two-way interaction and co-existence, and prosperity. At present, the city has more than 20 distinctive small commodity manufacturing industries with great innovative capabilities, leading the trend at home and abroad with world market influence, forming ornament, clothing, knitting, hosiery, zippers, handicrafts, toys, cosmetics, cultural products, and other dominant industries, where the production and sales of industries like hosiery, knitted underwear, toys, cosmetics, and handicrafts account for over 30% of national production and sales, zippers account for over 50%, while ornaments account for over 70%.

2.3 Supporting service industry

In addition to the manufacturing industry being directly driven by the market, modern services such as finance, insurance, logistics, warehousing, leasing, information, and accounting are also increasingly developed. In recent years, large shopping malls, office buildings, high-end hotels, banks, and other facilities are increasing. Eight of the 20 largest shipping groups in the world have set up branches or offices in Yiwu, far away from the ocean. The development of the above supporting services industry, in turn, has made the small commodity market and the manufacturing industry supporting the market's prosperity. In the future, with the further development and upgrading of Yiwu's business and trade, the expansion of the scope of "Yiwu Business Circle" and the extension of the industrial chain will bring huge demands to the financial insurance and information service industry both in scale and depth; therefore, financial insurance and information services will play an increasingly important role in the transformation and upgrading of the production and trading function

of Yiwu Small Commodity Market, and become one of the leading industries in the core of "Yiwu Business Circle". In addition, other production and life supporting services, such as tourism and catering, will also play a more and more important role in the economic life of "Yiwu Business Circle".

The driving of the market to the industry is not only shown in quantity but more importantly is shown through the fierce market competition, the broad market platform, and the keen information feedback mechanism. It will promote the quality of industry to be improved faster, "forcing" enterprises to quickly find the direction of the adjustment of the product and the industrial structure, and strive to break through the limit of the quantitative growth. This is mainly reflected in the transformation of the industry, promotion of technology, expansion of the scale of the enterprise, continuous emergence of well-known enterprises, and the increasing improvement in the quality of the operators. For example, after the overproduction of the middle- and low-grade wool, shirts, and other products in the textile industry, some wool spinning enterprises will produce special flame retardant wool, and a batch of shirt factories will produce more seamless underwear with a higher added value; when straw industry exports suffer more and more international trade barriers, they will improve the level of technology, set up factories according to the international pharmaceutical companies' GMP standard, and organize production so as to make the products reach the Carrefour, Wal-mart, Metro, etc., almost all the famous international supermarket chains.

"Yiwu Business Circle" Division of Labor Collaboration Network Form

1. "Yiwu Business Circle" interregional division of labor collaboration form

When the radiation of Yiwu Small Commodity Market to the related industries has been implemented into the region, the specific geographical form of "Yiwu Business Circle" will be formed. To adapt to the development of market and industry, the development process of the expansion of "Yiwu Business Circle" follows a regional radiation from the near to the distant. When implementing the overall development strategy of "Flourish Business and Build City", it has formed the core layer of "Yiwu Business Circle" through "Promoting Industry by Commerce" and "Connecting Trade with Industry" based on the development of local business, trade, and manufacturing and relied on the division of labor collaboration within the surrounding counties and cities and

in Zhejiang. The radiation range of Yiwu Small Commodity Market is getting wider and wider.

Block economy, professional market, and private enterprises are the three characteristics of Zhejiang's economy. Due to the increasingly fierce competition in the market, some regional industrial base commodities have flowed more to Yiwu Small Commodity Market. It is one of the concrete manifestations of the economic transformation and promotion of Zhejiang's economic transition from a regional blocky economy to a regional division of labor collaboration. Through in-depth investigation, it is found that one of the main sources of commodities in the small commodity market is the surrounding counties and urban areas (refer to Table 2.1). This is an important feature of "Yiwu Business Circle", and it is also a rational choice made by Yiwu and the surrounding counties. This is due to the fact that Zhejiang is a large province of light industry in the country, and in the production of small commodities, Zhejiang has a certain advantage compared with other provinces. The regional division of labor and cooperation between the surrounding areas of Yiwu and Yiwu itself is mainly based on Yiwu Small Commodity Market to conduct the processing or selling of local products. Through various forms of communication and cooperation, the surrounding counties have developed their own industries using Yiwu Small Commodity Market as a shared trading platform. At the same time, they support the development of the market with their own regional characteristic industries. This is the important condition and foundation for the formation and development of "Yiwu Business Circle".

Among provincial interregional cooperation, Hangzhou and Ningbo, with their unique advantages of air and sea transportation, have become an important channel for the export of Yiwu's small commodities, which forms the logistics cooperation network among Hangzhou, Ningbo, and Yiwu. The core of the "iron triangle" has greatly enriched the three-dimensional level of logistics in "Yiwu

Business Circle", and has provided a solid material basis for the establishment of "Yiwu Business Circle" in the international market by Yiwu Small Commodity Market. In terms of industry support, Jinhua–Quzhou–Lishui Industrial Belt and Wenzhou–Taizhou Industrial Belt are most closely in time with the market. The two major industrial belts, especially the manufacturing enterprises of Wenzhou–Taizhou Industrial Belt, have traditional advantages in the production and processing of small commodities, and have certain influence both at home and even internationally, where Yiwu Small Commodity Market has formed this disperse influence into a joint force. In the small commodity market, the influence of brand expansion does not come at the price of Wenzhou, Taizhou, Yongkang, Dongyang, and other regional brands. Local products in the market form a mutual promotion between the two brands, to enhance a win–win situation with their unique characteristics while continuously enhancing the quality of their own regional brands. It should be said that the division of labor between Yiwu and some neighboring counties is not innate, such as Wenzhou clothing, Taizhou plastic hardware, Yongkang hardware, and Shaoxing cloth. At the very beginning, the local professional market and Yiwu Small Commodity Market had more competition than cooperation with each other; they would inevitably snatch the source of goods and some even became irreconcilably opposed and stuck in a zero sum game. However, when the decline of the Wenzhou button market became apparent, many traditional professional markets in Zhejiang appeared to slow down or even decline to varying degrees in the development of the market, Yiwu Small Commodity Market has taken a new role in the market, and has completed a role in the replacement of the local professional market. Like the current home appliance industry, when home appliance marketers such as Gome and Suning Appliance expanded, they inevitably formed a kind of interdependence and mutual promotion alliance with household appliance manufacturing enterprises.

Table 2.1:   Exchanges and cooperation between Yiwu and other cities, counties and districts in Zhejiang Province

Major cooperative areas			Related industry	Regional division of labor collaboration
Jinhua City	Jinhua city level	Main urban area (including development zone)	At present, it has formed a cluster of knitting, ornaments, leather goods, clothing, electric tools, and other industries. It is becoming an influential manufacturing base in Zhejiang Province; every step of the economic development zone is closely related to the Yiwu market. A large number of enterprises in the region are engaged in small commodity processing. Their products go all the way to the world through the Yiwu market.	Sell local products through the Yiwu market platform, while selling obtain information from the Yiwu market and master market demand.
		Wucheng District	Bedding, shoes and hats, handicraft fans, papermaking, color printing, and packaging, flowers and plants, beads, headgear, Chinese knots, dried flowers, greeting cards, toys, braids, wigs, belts, woolen fabrics, candle cores, etc., where Chinese knots and wigs have accounted for 2/3 of the market in Yiwu; the processing area has covered the whole area and has processed more than 30 kinds of products. At present, there are 351 economic men; the monthly number of persons involved in processing is close to 30,000; the total processing fee for processing with supplied materials was 114 million Yuan in 2003, ranking the first place in Jinhua.	Yiwu enterprises set up bases in Wucheng; set up "window" in Yiwu, publicize Wucheng enterprises, products, actively guide enterprises to create their own brands.
		Jindong District	Among more than 2,300 enterprises in the region, 1/3 rely on the Yiwu market, 1/11 annual sales of the Yiwu market come from the products of Jindong District; of the 149 enterprises signed in the Jinsanjiao (Golden Triangle) Economic Development Zone, more than 100 are from Yiwu; there are 325 of 510 administrative villages in the whole region with more than 9,800 households and 18,000 people engaged in processing supplied materials. The annual processing fee is 65 million Yuan.	Take orders and process with supplied materials.
	Yongkang		Yongkang hardware takes the Yiwu market as an important window of its own, accepting its rich information and using its marketing channels. In the first hardware and electrical trade fair in Yiwu, more than 170 hardware enterprises from Yongkang attended.	Through the Yiwu market platform, complement each other's advantages and sell local products.

Continued

Major cooperative areas		Related industry	Regional division of labor collaboration
	Dongyang	There are tens of thousands of people in the Yiwu market for business from Dongyang, and hundreds of companies have set up windows in the market, involving thousands of products. Nan Ma straw mats, Qian Xiang leather bags, Huashui "Chinese knot", bedding, clothing, and other industries all rely on the Yiwu Market; 60 of 74 administrative villages with 63% peasant households are engaged in producing Chinese knots; foreign businessmen directly place orders to Qian Xiang leather goods in Yiwu, while purchasing raw materials like zippers and leather materials for the leather goods and bags from Yiwu; Yiwu almost monopolized middle and low-end suit market.	Sell local advantage products through the Yiwu market platform.
	Lanxi	At present, main products are daily chemicals, towel textiles, and 50% of the 600 million towels produced by 600 towel manufacturers are sold through the Yiwu market. At present, there are 20 towel enterprises with booths in Yiwu Binwang Market; bicycle accessories, new printing and packaging products, rubber and plastic, highly processed products, new field fine chemical products, and other industries are also actively moving towards the domestic and foreign markets through the Yiwu market; 25 towns (sub-districts) with more than 40,000 people are engaged in Yiwu's processing with the supplied materials industry, and the annual processing fee is close to 100 million Yuan.	Connect the Yiwu market through the linkage with the Yiwu market, and the processing of incoming materials and so on, obtain information from the Yiwu market, grasp the market demand and become an important production and processing base for Yiwu small commodities.
	Pujiang County	Of the 30,000 people in the county who are doing business outside the country, there are more than 4,000 in Yiwu; crystal, padlock, quilt, and other industries have special stalls in the Yiwu market; 10% of the crystal products are sold directly from Yiwu to home and abroad. The sales volume of foreign trade in Yiwu has reached more than 200 million Yuan. More enterprises have signed orders in Yiwu, and the products are shipped directly in Pujiang. Of the more than 30 quilt shops in the Yiwu market, 20 are operated by Pujiang people.	Sell local advantage products through the Yiwu market platform.

Continued

Major cooperative areas		Related industry	Regional division of labor collaboration
	Wuyi County	Hardware and electrical appliances, cultural and educational supplies, sunny umbrellas, sports goods, leisure tourism craft gifts, edible fungi, and other high quality agricultural products from other industries are sold to the whole world through Yiwu; more than 4,000 people in the county are engaged in the processing of incoming materials, mainly ornaments, craft gifts, and clothing; hot spring ecotourism.	Sell local advantage products through the Yiwu market platform.
	Pan'an County	1/3 of the workforce, namely 30,000 people, are engaged in the processing industry for the Yiwu market, processing products like bags, headdresses, beads, hook bags, crafts, holiday lights, wooden crafts, knitting crafts, cushion, toys, packaging; the products of local resources for processing are wallpapers, wood beads, bamboo, and wood products; and the products of local enterprises' diffusion processing are mainly Christmas gifts, clothing, and so on. The headdress flowers and ribbons accounted for 80% and 75% of the Yiwu market and beads accounted for 50%; it introduced investment funds of 100 million Yuan from Yiwu in 2004; the No.1 Central Zhejiang Tea Market was invested by Yiwu businessmen.	Vigorously develop the raw material processing business, sell the local advantage products through the Yiwu market platform, and some brokers have been on the way of production, supply and marketing through the processing with supplied materials.
Other counties and cities in Zhejiang	Hangzhou	As of April 22, 2006, Hangzhou Customs "Yiwu–Hangzhou–Beijing" two transit export channels have been running for 4 months with accumulative 62 dispatches of "Yiwu–Hangzhou" truck, airline, shipping, customs export goods cargo up to 11,150 pieces, weighing more than 262 tons; the Chun'an County Bureau of Science and Technology set up the liaison office in Yiwu, and Jiande county held the "Yiwu–Jiande Incoming Processing Business Matchmaking Meeting".	Yiwu has exported commodities through the Hangzhou Airport, and some counties and cities undertake the processing of Yiwu materials.

Continued

Major cooperative areas		Related industry	Regional division of labor collaboration
	Ningbo	Sinotrans Ningbo Int'l Container Transportation Co., Ltd. set up an office in Yiwu to carry out the transportation business for Yiwu goods; Ningbo Port Bureau, and Yiwu Shipping Development Corporation set up Kai Yuan International Logistics Co., Ltd. jointly and introduced port advantages into Yiwu; the standard container export of Beilun port accounts for more than 1/10th of the total import and export; Yiwu Commodity Direct Selling Center in Chenghuangmiao Shopping Square is the "window" of Yiwu in Ningbo; most products of famous clothing companies like Ningbo YOUNGOR, Shanshan, and Chairman are sold at home and abroad through Yiwu; over half of Cixi home appliances are sold to Europe, America, and Middle East. Yiwu is one of their largest domestic sales markets. At the same time, the products are sold to the domestic and foreign markets on the platform of "Yiwu Fair" and the small commodity market.	Yiwu export goods through Ningbo port and logistics advantage, and advantage goods are sold at home and abroad through the Yiwu market.
	Wenzhou	The main related industries are pen making, toys, luggage, lighters, leather shoes, zippers, etc.; Yongjia Qiaoxia toys go to the world through Yiwu; the Yiwu market is the most important sales channel for Wenzhou lighters and razors and the sales of shaver in Yiwu accounted for about 40–50% of the total sales volume; Yiwu, Chengdu, Wuhan, Shandong, and other places have become the main distribution centers of Wenzhou pen products, especially Yiwu has become a place of strategic importance. 30 scale enterprises, including the four major "Chinese pen making kings", have set up sales windows in Yiwu; Wenzhou shoes are never without the development of the Yiwu market, the two created the great scenes of the footwear industry; 50% of Pingyang Zhenglou gift industry is radiated to the domestic and foreign markets through Yiwu, Zhenglou Gift City, known as "Small Yiwu", learned from the experience of Yiwu; the plastic accessories at the Yongjia Qiaotou support the Yiwu ornament industry, and the Qiaotou ornaments are also sold through Yiwu market. The Yiwu market makes the Qiaotou button and zipper industry undergo redevelopment; Wenzhou glasses industry turned to high-grade, gradually quietly withdrawing from the Yiwu market.	With the help of the Yiwu market platform, the dominant industries accumulate the original capital and promote the replacement of the products at home and abroad, provide raw materials and semi-finished products for related industries in Yiwu, promoting the subsequent rise of button and other industries, but there is also the condition that the eyewear industry fades out of the Yiwu market.

Continued

Major cooperative areas	Related industry	Regional division of labor collaboration
Shaoxing	Through Yiwu, textile fabrics are sold to Dongyang, Yongkang, Yiwu, far away to Russia, the Middle East, and so on; in Yiwu knitting market, Zhuji socks, shirts, and trousers occupy the market with great shares, and half of the stalls are run by Zhuji people. Zhuji pearl enterprises are in the implementation of brand development, in addition to Hong Kong as its bridgehead, Yiwu has also become a platform for business owners. The Yiwu market achieved the initial Shengzhou tie industry, and as the industry matured, Shengzhou China Tie City replaced leading position of Yiwu tie market; the combined transport and consignment market of Keqiao China Textile City is only the second domestic consignment market after Yiwu, and it can be said to be established by the Yiwu people. 85% were Yiwu people before 2000, and now 53% of the people are also from Yiwu.	Advantage industry relies on the Yiwu platform to go to domestic and foreign markets, driving the development of the local professional market.
Taizhou	The main related industries are handicraft gifts, pumps, toys, hats, etc.; the handicraft industry and the market in Xianju are well developed, but the annual promotion costs are too high, and the Yiwu market is becoming a new platform. There are 400 pump enterprises in Wenling Daxi that have distributors in Yiwu and participate in "Yiwu Fair" to promote products through sales window in Yiwu; 50% of Wenling hats are sold in the Yiwu market; eyeglasses occupy 95% of the Yiwu eyeglass market, and 37% of the domestic market; Taizhou plastic products occupy half of the Yiwu market, and more and more businesses land in the Yiwu market. Others sell online through related small commodity networks.	Advantage industry relies on the Yiwu platform to go to domestic and foreign markets and also improves the level of local industries.
Jiaxing	The main related industries include electronic toys, plastic utensils, clothing, wool textiles, and furniture. Jiaxing's major markets also dispatch designated personnel to visit and learn about Yiwu's experience in marketing and management.	Sell goods through the Yiwu market; attract investment from Yiwu merchants; learn from each other's experience in the market.

Continued

Major cooperative areas		Related industry	Regional division of labor collaboration
	Huzhou	The main related industries are handicrafts, bamboo chopsticks, textile fabrics, and logistics. In Zhili of Huzhou, Zhili Shopping Mall, Zhili Children's Clothing Mall, Zhili Cotton Cloth City, Zhili Children's Clothing Accessories Market, Zhili Building Materials Wholesale Market, and other markets, traveling merchants and abundant commodities have formed the huge logistic system which leads to the whole country. The giant Zhili logistic network is in the market network weaved by Yiwu merchants.	The local dominant industries interact with the Yiwu market, and the Yiwu merchants invest in the local industry.
	Quzhou	Daily necessities, arts and crafts, cosmetics, knitwear, hardware tools, electronic appliances, bags, office stationery vigorously develop the processing industry; the annual processing business has reached 400–500 million Yuan through the Yiwu market; the Quzhou auction industry entered the Yiwu market for improvement; approximately 200 plus Quzhou nannies work in Yiwu; Longyou bow knot, birdcage, cool mat, bamboo handicraft, printing oil, red ink paste, seal, inkpad, etc., mostly enter the international market through Yiwu; Changshan Huyou go out of the mountains through the Yiwu market; Jiangshan high-grade cement, Kaihua plastic also rely on the Yiwu market to develop vigorously; at present, Kaihua has more than 20,000 employees working or doing business in Yiwu, accounting for about a quarter of the total number of migrant workers in the county.	Vigorously develop the processing business, sell local advantage products, and export labor services through the Yiwu market platform.
	Lishui	The main related industries are pens, bamboo chopsticks, wooden toys, swords, celadon, black pottery, etc.; the pen industry with an annual sales revenue of 610 million Yuan leaps into the top three in the domestic industry, and half of them are sold through Yiwu; Qingyuan bamboo chopsticks are sold to all parts of the country and even around the world using chopsticks through Yiwu, "Suncha" in Yiwu has set about building a first-class logistics center for greater development; for purpose of complementary advantages, it creates a "shopping tour" together with Yiwu; Yunhe wooden toys and Suichang black potteries have bases for production in Lishui and take orders in and sell products through Yiwu; Longquan sword sold through the Yiwu market accounted for 1/3 of Longquan's output.	With the help of the Yiwu market platform, the dominant industries are moving towards home and abroad, complementing advantages and developing shopping tourism.

Continued

Major cooperative areas		Related industry	Regional division of labor collaboration
	Zhoushan	The main related industries are small plastic, screws, textile, clothing, shoe making, pen making, etc. Most enterprises are more or less related to the Yiwu market, and the products are sold to all parts of the country through Yiwu.	Sell products by mainly relying on the Yiwu Market.

2. "Yiwu Business Circle" interprovincial division of labor collaboration form

Since the reform and opening-up, the great achievements of Zhejiang's economic development have attracted the attention of the people at home and abroad. The media mentions "Yiwu market" the second most, just behind "Wenzhou businessmen". Among many other areas in the country, some introduce Yiwu small commodities, some refer to the Yiwu experience in the development of the establishment of the market, some attract the Yiwu people to make direct investments in the establishment of the market, some sell local commodities through the small commodity market, while others use local location advantages to set up the Yiwu sub-markets. More border and port cities act as the "terminals" of the small commodity market for commodity export (refer to Table 2.2).

The commodities in the market come from almost all provinces, municipalities, and autonomous regions in China, and almost all provinces and cities in China become the outlet of Yiwu's small commodities. Through various forms of regional division of labor and cooperation, Yiwu Small Commodity Market has a wider range of radiation. Under the great leading role of the market, development of light industry enterprises and the growth process of the Yangtze River Delta and Northwestern, Northeastern, Southwestern, Central, Southern China, and many other areas have been linked with the small commodity market, which in turn are supported by other areas and the rapid development of the economy and society of the whole city takes place with economic exchanges and cooperation in all forms. Such huge volumes of commodity trading make the output form of commodities in the market change gradually. Its product display and information exchange functions weaken the market and even the local commodity transaction function, and the quotation, order, customs declaration, and so on are becoming the main trading behaviors of Yiwu Small Commodity Market.

Table 2.2: Exchanges and cooperation between Yiwu and some provinces and cities in China

Major cooperative areas	Related industry	Regional division of labor collaboration
Beijing	Beijing Yiwu Commodity Wholesale Market only had around 550 business booths around 2000, but the daily passenger flow was up to 7,000 or 8,000 people at a time, with more on weekends; Tianyi Market is a leader in the wholesale market of small commodities in Beijing. Yiwu stocks have more than 70% market share in Beijing Tianyi Market.	Mainly introduce small commodities from the Yiwu market and Yiwu people to set up market locally.
Shanghai	Shanghai Chenghuangge Small Commodity Market takes Yiwu as the main source of goods; small commodities from the Yiwu market make up 50% of the market for the Fuyoumen Small Commodity Market (Fuyoumen Building); Shanghai and Yiwu's advantages are complementary to expanding the tourism market, and the Yiwu Railway Station will have on average 1,000 guests from Shanghai every day.	Mainly introduce small commodities from the Yiwu market and Yiwu people to set up market locally.
Chongqing	80% of socks in Chongqing are from "Yiwu Manufacturing". Yiwu socks are all over the markets, supermarkets, and large and medium-sized wholesale markets in Chongqing. Yiwu shirt accounts for 70–80% of the sales of shirts sold in Chongqing Chaotianmen Wholesale market; Chongqing Yiwu Xinghe Ornaments Market is the largest ornament market in the southwest.	Mainly introduce small commodities from the Yiwu market, and Yiwu people to set up market locally and learn about Yiwu business management and operation mode.

Continued

Major cooperative areas	Related industry	Regional division of labor collaboration
Hong Kong, Macao, and Taiwan	Yiwu ornament not only has advantages in design, quality, and price, but also has led the international trend in style. It is very popular in Hong Kong; for the development of Yiwu's convention and exhibition industry, large conventions and exhibitions can be held in Hong Kong and international brands can be created by relying on the Hong Kong information channel. Hong Kong has perfect convention and exhibition facilities, advanced management concepts, and high-quality exhibition talents; with the further implementation of CEPA, Hong Kong and Yiwu exhibition industry cooperation is facing great opportunities hitherto unknown. On August 4, 2004, the government of Yiwu held the "Promotion Meeting of China Yiwu International Small Commodities Fair" in Macau and achieved complete success. Now, the small commodities in Yiwu have come into the daily life of the people in Taiwan and enjoy a high reputation there. From the "Ten Yuan Shops" to "Hundred Yuan Shops" in Taiwan to small vendors everywhere, Yiwu small commodities are everywhere. In the aspects of decoration, daily necessities, and wedding supplies, Yiwu's small commodities have a high share in Taiwan. The Taiwan Businessmen Association of Yiwu has more than 200 members. It has a special Taiwan Pavilion in the International Trade City. There are more than 80 booths, and more than 60 Taiwanese businessmen in business. There are more than 600 Taiwanese businessmen buying goods here every day.	Mainly introduce small commodities from the Yiwu market, refer to the Yiwu experience, and conduct cooperation with Yiwu regarding conventions and exhibitions, or make direct investment in Yiwu for integrated industry and trade development.

Continued

Major cooperative areas	Related industry	Regional division of labor collaboration
Jiangsu	Xuzhou Xuanwu Market promoted a series of market culture construction through learning Yiwu and won the titles of Jiangsu Model Market, Fair and Just Market, and so on; it rose to sixth in the national top 100 markets, with Yiwu hosiery accounting for 90% of its sales.	Mainly introduce small commodities from the Yiwu market and refer to the Yiwu experience for setting up a market.
Guangdong	Over 50% of Christmas gifts in Yide Road Boutique Street are from Yiwu; there are 21 combined transport and consignment lines between Yiwu and Guangzhou, and the goods shipped from the Yiwu market to Guangzhou every day are very huge in volume; many toys in Guangdong are sold through the Yiwu market. In the Yiwu International Trade City, high and medium grade plastic toys, electric toys, and jigsaw puzzles are basically Guangdong goods, with an annual turnover of 3 billion Yuan, accounting for 20% of Guangdong's total sales; more and more enterprises in Guangdong are beginning to open overseas markets with the aid of the Yiwu market; in recent years, some factories in Guangdong have taken more and more orders from the Middle East, Africa, Eastern Europe, and other places, many of them take such orders through the Yiwu market; from Yiwu to Shenzhen, there are goods of 10 wagons per day, totaling about 100 to 130 tons; from Shenzhen to Yiwu, there are goods of 15 wagons per day, totaling about 200 tons.	Guangdong has a huge industrial base, Yiwu has a huge commercial market, and there are obvious complementary advantages; mainly export commodities through the Yiwu market platform, expand the market, and exchange information; learn from Yiwu's experience of establishing the market, and introduce the capital export of Yiwu merchants and the business circulation industry.

Continued

Major cooperative areas	Related industry	Regional division of labor collaboration
Shandong	About 80% of the commodities in Qingdao Jimo Small Commodity City are from Yiwu; Weifang Yiwu Hezhong Website has become an important online trading platform between Weifang and Yiwu; Weihai International Trade City–Shandong Wendeng Small Commodity Wholesale Market takes Yiwu as an example and intends to build a northern "Yiwu"; Qingdao's plush toys, knitted underwear, copper crafts, sea crafts, and other products have shown great vitality through the Yiwu market; 80% of the commodities in Heze Huadu Market are from Yiwu, with 40 tons of goods purchased from Yiwu Small Commodity Market every day, radiating eight districts and counties in terms of wholesale.	Mainly introduce small commodities from the Yiwu market and Yiwu people set up market locally.
Fujian	Yiwu small commodities such as head flowers, ornaments, shirts, socks, and ballpoint pens have become popular in Changtai County Small Commodity Market and Commercial Center. The knives, zippers, tableware, and sporting goods produced in Changtai County continue to be shipped to the Yiwu market for sale. In the Changtai Small Commodity Market with more than 300 stalls, nearly 1/4th of the stalls have Yiwu small commodities, and more than 10 stores of over 100 stores in Changtai Commercial Center operate Yiwu products.	Mainly introduce small commodities from the Yiwu market.

Continued

Major cooperative areas	Related industry	Regional division of labor collaboration
Heilongjiang, Jilin, and Liaoning	Most of the small commodities in markets and supermarkets in Dalian come from Yiwu. Yiwu small commodities have become the main commodities in Dalian Department Stores, and the consignments from Yiwu to Dalian have become the green passage for the transport of goods between the two places; on average, 5 carts of 150 tons of Yiwu commodities are transported to Shenyang daily. Most of the commodities purchased from Yiwu in the Northeast are transported to Shenyang by special cars; more than 70% of the socks in Shenyang Wuai market, one of the top 10 wholesale markets in the country, are from Yiwu.	Mainly introduce small commodities from the Yiwu market, learn from Yiwu experience in setting up market, and accept capital output from Yiwu.
Sichuan	In Chengdu Lotus Pond Market, there are many Yiwu people starting business here, and many well-known brand products in Yiwu are very popular in the market of Lotus Pond; more than 2,800 people in Yiwu are doing business in the Lotus Pond Market. Products of many well-known brands have been sold here, and the general agent and the general agency have been established here; in the shirt city of the market, Yiwu brand shirts occupy half of the market share and nearly 60% of the stores are operated by Yiwu people; Yiwu's consignment industry runs through the arteries between the Yiwu market and the Lotus Pond Market in Chengdu, with four lines and four sites.	Mainly introduce small commodities from the Yiwu market, refer to the Yiwu experience in setting up a market, and have a lot of Yiwu merchants settle in local markets.

Continued

Major cooperative areas	Related industry	Regional division of labor collaboration
Hubei	Over 90% of goods in Changjiang Market are directly from the Yiwu market; Yiwu shirts, dresses, picture frames, crystals, imitation plants, furniture furnishing articles, socks, arts and crafts, clocks, and watches occupy a big market share of the Yichang region through Changjiang Market and are also doing well in Sichuan, Chongqing and other provinces and cities.	Introduce small commodities from the Yiwu market; introduce Yiwu merchants; refer to Yiwu's successful experience, and be in line with Yiwu market.
Hunan	Fashion tourist commodities, stylistic toys, craft ornaments, knives, flower ornaments, headscarves, wood carvings, and so on in the Old Street of Fenghuang, Xiangxi Autonomous Prefecture, are almost entirely from Yiwu; in Changsha Gaoqiao Market, Yiwu commodities can be seen everywhere. Market statistics show that in the current Gaoqiao market, 60% of the commodities of small department stores come from the Yiwu market, where knitted products account for 70%, while the stylistic toys products reach 80%; clothing, department stores, shirts, underwear, and other small commodities in Zhuzhou Market mainly come from Yiwu and occupy the leading position in the market, and many market operators are Yiwu people.	Introduce small commodities from the Yiwu market, introduce Yiwu merchants; utilize Yiwu brands and the commodity effect; refer to Yiwu's successful experience, and actively be in line with the Yiwu market.

Continued

Major cooperative areas	Related industry	Regional division of labor collaboration
Inner Mongolia	Nearly half of the more than 200 commodities operating in the largest wholesale market in Inner Mongolia come from Yiwu, especially those with large sales such as swords; some market investors raise funds and draw on the experience of Yiwu to establish the market; most of its operators in Yiwu Small Commodity Wholesale Market, Xianghe Market, Hengchang Market, Rongxing Market, etc., in Hohehot Municipality take the promotion and sale of "Yiwu small commodities" as the selling point; the dairy industry enterprises in Yili, Mengniu grow stronger through the Yiwu market; the sales network set up by Yiwu businessmen in Inner Mongolia promotes local development of small commodities traders and makes them rich, bringing about profound changes to their concept.	Mainly introduce small commodities from the Yiwu market and refer to Yiwu's experience in setting up markets.
Henan	In Henan Province, 50% of daily consumer goods in the largest integrated commodity wholesale trade center are from Yiwu; in Henan, the wholesale markets of Yiwu small commodities are mostly in Zhengzhou. According to incomplete statistics, in Yiwu, on average, there are seven customers in each booth operating in Zhengzhou.	Mainly introduce small commodities from the Yiwu market and refer to Yiwu's experience in setting up markets.

Continued

Major cooperative areas	Related industry	Regional division of labor collaboration
Xinjiang	Xinjiang's grape and other melon fruits enter into the majority of China's ordinary families through the Yiwu market; Xinjiang Trade City, the first sub-market of Yiwu "International Small Commodity City", introduces Yiwu commodities to the north and south of Tianshan and 90% commodities of the market are from Yiwu. Socks and shirts are all from Yiwu; Yiwu small commodities are sold to Russia, Pakistan, the United Arab Emirates, and other countries through the Changzheng Wholesale Market.	Mainly introduce small commodities from the Yiwu market, set up markets, output advantage products like melon and fruit; utilize northwest border to sell Yiwu commodities to the surrounding western and Western Asia countries.
Qinghai	The Xining Yiwu Trade City established by Yiwu people is known as "Yiwu". It has become the synonym for the Yiwu brand. 70% of nearly 10,000 commodities come from Yiwu, and there are 40,000–50,000 passenger flows per day.	Mainly introduce small commodities from the Yiwu market; make direct investment in setting up markets, and help merchants with financial difficulties by offering small-sum guaranteed loans.
Tibet	Tromsikhang Market in Lhasa, Tibet, is the largest wholesale market in Tibet with more than 2,000 stalls and tens of thousands of goods. More than 90% of the thousands of goods sold on the second floor of the market are from Yiwu Small Commodity Market. Merchants continue to send Yiwu commodities to Lhasa to enrich the Tibetan market.	Mainly introduce small commodities from the Yiwu market and output local products through the Yiwu market.

Continued

Major cooperative areas	Related industry	Regional division of labor collaboration
Gansu	In 1994, Yiwu merchants set up Lanzhou Yiwu Trade City in Lanzhou. At present, there are 3,000 stalls with an area of 60,000 square meters and tens of thousands of product varieties, and the market is quite prosperous.	Mainly introduce small commodities from the Yiwu market and make direct investment in setting up markets.
Shaanxi	One third of the 3,000 stalls in Xi' an Kangfu Road Market, known as the "No.1 Market of Northwest China", are operated by Yiwu people; the Yiwu brand is famous here with products entering in all supermarkets; the distribution network of Yiwu socks covers the whole northwest.	Mainly introduce small commodities from the Yiwu market; Yiwu merchants settle in local markets. A lot of northwest general agents for Yiwu commodities distribute products to the surrounding areas.

3. "Yiwu Business Circle" international division of labor collaboration form

The Division of Labor Collaboration Network of "Yiwu Business Circle" well-reflects the non-circle structure of the business circle. The USA is the world's biggest consumer market of most commodities and makes no exception of the Yiwu Small Commodity Market. It has become the largest exporter of goods for the small commodity market and Europe has become its largest export market. For countries with great demand for commodities, such as the United Arab Emirates and Russia, Yiwu has become the main division of labor collaborator that remedies their insufficient domestic production, which makes these countries become one of the main export areas of Yiwu small commodities. From the current situation, Yiwu increases its export to some areas with great demand for small commodities and a favorable domestic trade environment has rapidly formed on a large scale. For Africa, South America, and other countries, the market potential has not been fully tapped. In recent years, Yiwu's exports to developed countries are often plagued by trade barriers, some of which are due to low science and technology content and failing to comply with local import standards; some are discriminatory barriers set up by the local government in the interest of protecting domestic industries and employment. Thus, to further expand the Division of Labor Collaboration Network of "Yiwu Business Circle", the city needs to start from improving the quality and technology of our own small commodities and give play to business ability of Yiwu businessmen to expand the international market continuously.

To be a real International Division of Labor Collaboration Network for "Yiwu Business Circle" and achieve the target of "purchase and sell goods globally" through the Yiwu market, we shall "go out" while paying attention to "introduce in". There are three aspects involved. The first is the introduction of merchants. Yiwu must become a commodity city that gathers global businessmen. Only in this way can we gather global commodity information. The second is the introduction of technology, including product standards and patterns. This is an important way for Yiwu products to transform from international popularization to national individualization in the global trade. Only in this way can we produce more products that are suitable for every country's culture and consumer preferences. The third is the introduction of the source of goods. To become a global small commodity sales center, it is necessary to gather global small commodity production information and small commodity patterns. The introduction of goods is mainly based on the introduction of commodity information, that is, to provide a space for commodity display to overseas goods through samples and other forms. Table 2.3 shows the output of Yiwu small commodities to the whole world.

Table 2.3: The output of Yiwu Small Commodities to the whole world

Main sales areas	Related industry	Regional division of labor collaboration
The USA and other areas of North America	In 2005, the USA became the largest exporter of small commodities in Yiwu. The main products were socks, handicrafts, and ornaments. In 2005, European and US merchandise exports accounted for 35% of the city's total exports and developed economies such as Europe and America have become the main export markets of Yiwu small commodities.	Output commodities; Mengna and other major enterprises are registered enterprises and set up offices in the USA, expanded the US market, and established strong trade relations with large transnational supermarkets such as Walmart; small- and medium-sized commodities can enter the US market, even the entire North American market, through the McCullen Free Trade Zone.
Western Europe	In 2005, Europe has become the largest market for the export of Yiwu commodities. Through attending the famous European conventions and exhibitions such as 2006 Frankfurt, gifts, office supplies, and beauty salon development (intention turnover fetched nearly 30 million USD) and Offenbach Asian Living (nearly 20 million USD), Yiwu companies latest and best products were exhibited, improving the visibility and reputation of the market, which is increasingly attractive to the European Union and other developed regions.	Export commodities; hold exhibitions, attend European exhibitions, collect extremely rich foreign trade information, and sign foreign trade contracts; understand the development trends of related industries and look for international gaps.
Russia, Ukraine, and Eastern Europe	In 2005, Russia was the top three Yiwu commodity exporters for 3 years in a row, accounting for 1/10th of the total export of Yiwu. Main products are clothing, textiles, followed by cosmetics, hardware, Christmas supplies, plastic products, etc. At present, more than 80 production and circulation enterprises in Yiwu do business with Russian businessmen year in year out, and Yiwu has one of the world's five sub-markets in Ukraine.	The Yiwu market has strong complementarity with Russia and Eastern Europe. It has developed from the former border trade to the direct purchase, the foreign trade order, the factory direct sale, and so on.

Continued

Main sales areas	Related industry	Regional division of labor collaboration
Arab countries such as the United Arab Emirates	In 2005, 4,555 Arabs chose to live in Yiwu; in 2005, 30,000–40,000 Arabs came to Yiwu for procurement; in 2005, the Arabs spent 116 million USD on the export of Yiwu small commodities to the Middle East, and more than 400,000 varieties of small commodities in Yiwu became their targets. Like foreign Chinatowns, Arab Street is also formed because of the large number of Arabs who live in Yiwu.	Arab traders buy commodities in large quantities in Yiwu; Yiwu sells goods directly through famous exhibitions in Arab regions such as Dubai.
East Asian countries such as Japan and R. O. Korea	During the World Cup, Yiwu became a land of "treasure hunt" for Japan and R. O. Korea businessmen; Yiwu commodities including hats, telescopes, picture frames, handicrafts, key chains, and trumpets were hunted by foreign businessmen, forming a stable trade relation. At present, there are more than 8,000 foreign businessmen in Yiwu, among which there are over a thousand of Korean merchants and about 400 Japanese merchants in Yiwu to purchase commodities from Yiwu Small Commodity Market. Japan and R. O. Korea are the two countries with the largest number of shopping tourists in Yiwu's market. Each year, about 10,000 R. O. Korean tourists and 8,000 Japanese tourists come to Yiwu for shopping tourism.	Mainly R. O. Korean and Japanese businessmen directly purchase in Yiwu; the government teams went to Seoul, Kagoshima, Osaka, and Tokyo for shopping tourism promotion activities.

Continued

Main sales areas	Related industry	Regional division of labor collaboration
Pakistan and other South and Southeast Asian countries	In 2005, more than 1,200 Pakistani businessmen were in Yiwu, and registered over 200 enterprises. Yiwu's Christmas products are exported to more than 160 countries in the world, but more than 80% went to India, Pakistan, and the Middle East.	South Asian merchants purchase goods in the Yiwu market; Yiwu people set up sub-markets in Pakistan, directly selling the commodities of Yiwu.
South Africa and other African countries	Through trade middlemen, small commodities such as toothbrushes, knitted goods, toys, Christmas gifts, cultural and educational products, and hardware tools are exported. In 1998, "South Africa China Small Commodity Wholesale Center" was completed, but due to public order and other reasons, there has been no great development.	Mainly indirect trade; the function of Yiwu's sub-market is not fully reflected.

Economic Rationality of "Yiwu Business Circle" Division of Labor Collaboration Network

III

1. Division of labor and transaction cost savings

As a cross-regional division of labor collaboration network, the competitiveness of "Yiwu Business Circle" lies in the effectiveness of the allocation of resources. Through the division of labor and specialization, the transaction cost and information cost are saved, and economies of scale are obtained, so that the resources can quickly and effectively flow and configure within "Yiwu Business Circle", the radiation capacity of the commercial circle is continuously enhanced through the globalization of trade, and the radiation range is continuously expanded. Yang Xiaokai, a famous Chinese economist, holds that the scope of market is the result of the division of labor and specialization, which determines not only demand but also supply. Therefore, the division of labor must be used to further expand the market. The scope and depth of the market is the fundamental property of modern economic development, and the transaction cost is the by-product through coordinated division of labor in the market itself, the resource allocation, and the continuous evolution of the associated organism. So long as it is a market economy under the condition of division of labor, there will be transaction costs.

1.1 "Yiwu Business Circle" market transaction fee

Transaction costs can be divided into two categories according to the causes: exogenous transaction costs and endogenous transaction costs.

Exogenous transaction costs refer to those expenses that occur directly or indirectly during the transaction process, which are generally tangible and have nothing to do with the economic distortion caused by the conflict of interests between the decision-makers. Inside "Yiwu Business Circle", because there is a large, efficient market, the exogenous transaction cost for searching for product information, price information, and for trade negotiations is low through the market, so there is not much room for the cost of exogenous transactions.

Endogenous transaction costs mainly refer to the transaction costs caused by moral hazard, adverse selection, and other opportunistic behaviors, which are related to people's decision-making.

The influence of endogenous transaction cost over equilibrium division of labor network size and the economic development is more significant than that of exogenous transaction cost. This is because the endogenous transaction cost is the decision by the individual, their choice of system, and their contractual arrangements. No matter "Yiwu Small Commodity Market" or "Yiwu Business Circle", in their early stages of development, trade means and tools were not the most advanced at the time, and relatively exogenous for a county-level city of Yiwu. The technical conditions of trade were also basically restricted by the technology level of development of society as a whole. So, in the face of external transaction cost, the trading subjects of "Yiwu Business Circle" could only follow the footsteps of the times, their self

initiative is quite limited, and there is still a big gap compared to some developed areas. Because the transaction costs for the cross-regional division of labor collaboration network of "Yiwu Business Circle" are mainly endogenous transaction costs, it is of great significance for "Yiwu Business Circle" to reduce the endogenous transaction costs. The transaction system based on the social capital such as Yiwu's own commercial culture plays a key role in reducing transaction costs. In the development course of Yiwu Small Commodity Market and "Yiwu Business Circle", there has been a phenomenon of market disorder and businessmen cheating customers. There are two ways to solve this problem: market information release and long-term mechanism establishment. The specific measures taken by the small commodity market are as follows: in order to make consumers compare the quality and price of products easily, and to avoid fraud, the same kind of goods are displayed in a centralized way through centralized management over the same category of commodities; by means of credit commitment and assessment and a scoring system, the influence of a business fraud is prolonged, thus offsetting the incentive for merchants to make profits through short-term behavior.

1.2 Coordination mechanism between internal division of labor and transaction costs inside "Yiwu Business Circle"

Under a certain division of labor structure, the relationship between endogenous transaction cost and exogenous transaction cost is reciprocal. For example, if the terms of a contract are complete, it can effectively reduce the endogenous transaction cost, but the contract will require a higher cost, that is to say, increase the exogenous transaction cost; if the clauses are not complete, it can reduce the exogenous transaction costs, but will lead to the increase of endogenous transaction costs such as opportunism. In a credit market, due to rare opportunistic behavior, the endogenous transaction costs are kept low, and the transaction costs are mainly determined by exogenous transaction costs.

There is a conflict between division of labor based on specialization and transaction cost: although the division of labor based on specialization can reduce the production cost, due to the increase in the number of transactions, the transaction costs (specifically the exogenous transaction cost) rise. Therefore, coordinating the relationship between the two is very important for the effective function of "Yiwu Business Circle". From the previous analysis, we can see that there is a critical point between division of labor based on specialization and transaction costs. Before the critical point is reached, marginal transaction costs are low enough, and division of labor based on specialization can make the integrated effect of both of them positive; after the critical point, division of labor based on specialization can increase production cost instead. "Yiwu Business Circle" has been in a state of preceding the critical point for a long time. In the process of division of labor and specialization, transaction costs increased slowly and gained the advantage of specialization, which is one of the internal reasons for the flourishing of the small commodity market in the past 30 years.

1.3 Influence of market network over transaction costs inside "Yiwu Business Circle"

The role of market network in improving economic efficiency, reducing costs, particularly in terms of transaction costs, is almost unquestionable, even revolutionary.

Market networks can greatly reduce transaction costs, and more accurately, market networks can greatly improve transaction efficiency, which is mainly reflected in the average value of all transactions in the entire market network; as a whole, the transaction costs are not necessarily reduced. Due to the topological nature of the market network, a small increase in the number of trading corners may lead to the increase in the number and frequency of transactions by geometric multiples, and the overall transaction costs may also rise. Figure 2.2 shows how trilateral transactions increased to quadrilateral transactions:

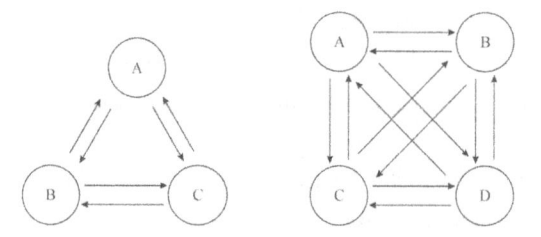

Figure 2.2: How trilateral transactions increased to quadrilateral transactions

In the trilateral transaction, the tradable time is 6, and in the quadrilateral transaction, the tradable time is 12; after the network expansion, the kinds of tradable products increase and the exogenous transaction costs increase significantly; as the complexity of the transaction increases, the amount of information that needs to be obtained also increases, and the overall risk of the transaction may increase too, so the capacity and transaction costs of the entire market may rise. However, due to the increase in the number of transactions, the transaction efficiency may be improved as long as the cost of the average single transaction is reduced.

1.4 Model of transaction cost reduction for Yiwu Small Commodity Market[1]

Lower transaction costs mean higher transaction efficiency. In a market network, the efficiency of the transaction (P) is proportional to the number of participants (N) in the market network, and to the probability of each participant obtaining the transaction (r) in the market network; but it is inversely proportional to the cost rate per transaction (q) of the average labor cost of developing a business relationship (c), which can be expressed as the following quantitative model:

---

[1] This model simplifies Yang Xiaokai's professional division of labor on specialization model, omits the derivation process, and gives the conclusion directly.

$$P = F(1/q, 1/c, N, r)$$

At the same time, through the derivation, we can get the following three conclusions: (1) when N is a large number, the reliability of division of labor can be improved by reducing the average cost rate of developing a business relationship; (2) by increasing the number of participants in the network, the network generates an investment synergy effect, thereby improving the reliability of the transaction after division of labor; (3) at present, the maintenance cost rate of each transaction is reduced, which can improve the reliability of division of labor.

After the first few years of development, Yiwu Small Commodity Market quickly formed a certain scale. Then, through repeated relocation, renovation, and expansion, it has maintained a rapid growth rate and ranked first for 10 consecutive years in domestic market transactions. In such a context, the commercial population in the small commodity market is gathering in large numbers, with continuous increases in the number of transactions and frequency. c and q in the corresponding model decrease sharply, while N and r increase greatly. Under the combined action of the above factors, the transaction cost of the market is greatly reduced. Most of the small commodity producers choose the market transaction as the main way of product circulation rather than relying on the self-built marketing network. The result of this market-oriented choice is also an important manifestation of the function of "Yiwu Business Circle".

2. Effect of economies of scale

At the beginning of Yiwu Small Commodity Market, its function depended mainly on the large scale of the commodity quantity, so that the price of unit commodity was greatly reduced, so as to attract merchants from all over to purchase in Yiwu. As the small commodity circulation system in the country was not smooth at all then, the commodities in the small commodity market were simple and the

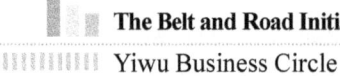
quality was not high. However, the products were popular among rural consumers, which caused the market to grow and develop gradually, bringing about rapid economic growth to entire Yiwu. Since then, with increasing types of commodities and the declining cost of collecting information for the procurement of the small commodity market, one of the main reasons why many customers love the market is that they can buy almost all commodities here for a decent price without rushing about, which leads to great saving on the cost of procurement.

In the framework of monopolistic competition, using the Dixit–Stiglitz model (DS model) of the production function, one can explain the above phenomenon. In this model, there are three departments, namely, final products, intermediate products, and research and development. The production function of the final product is $Y=(H_Y, L, x) = H_Y^\alpha L^\beta \sum_{i=1}^{\infty} x_i^{1-\alpha-\beta}$, where H_Y, L, and x_i are human capital (used for the final product sector), simple labor, and intermediate inputs; the intermediate goods sector would use some resources (such as capital) and the new design, and production of intermediate goods as the final product. It is assumed that every unit of intermediate product needs capital of units, because the production of intermediate products is symmetrical with the production function of the final products, so the output of each intermediate product should be the same under equilibrium conditions, which is recorded as $\bar{x}$. If the intermediate varieties decided by the Research and Development Department is A, then, $\sum_{i=1}^{A} \eta \bar{x} = K$, namely, $\bar{x} = K/N\eta$. $Y = H_Y^\alpha L^\beta K^{1-\alpha-\beta} \eta^{-(1-\alpha-\beta)} N^{\alpha+\beta}$ can be obtained by substituting $\bar{x}$ in the production function of the final products department.

The above production function shows that even if three inputs, namely, human capital, H_Y, labor, L, and capital, K, remain the same (like new classical assumptions, these inputs are homogeneous in output), increasing varieties of intermediate products, N, can also lead to a sustained growth of output and social welfare improvement. It can be stated that, even if Yiwu Small Commodity Market is a high degree export-oriented economy, its endogenous growth factor is still very important. From the initial period of "chicken feather for sugar" to street vendors wandering about the streets selling needles, plastic toys, lighters, and so on, and then to operating small commodity ventures in booths, the spontaneous formation of the small commodity market has occurred in Yiwu, finally forming the International Trade City today after over 30 years of development. Because the raw materials and processes for producing small commodities are very similar, some different kinds of intermediate products of the final products are even the same. Therefore, the production of different small commodities to one place can achieve economies of scale. With the increase of the commodity category in Yiwu Small Commodity Market, the quantity of intermediate products in the process of manufacturing small commodities increase and the endogenous growth factor of "Yiwu Business Circle" also plays a role at the same time.

In addition to the large-scale product category and quantity, Yiwu Small Commodity Market can also obtain economies of scale in the collection and processing of information; the more complete commodity category also makes the market and the surrounding industrial clusters obtain economies of scope. Because of such economies of scale and scope, the national or global cross-regional division of labor collaboration network at the core of the Yiwu Small Commodity Market, namely, "Yiwu Business Circle", exists.

3. Market cluster effect

Industrial cluster is the product of division of labor based on specialization. It is a form of industrial layout chosen to reduce the transaction cost caused by specialization and to obtain the increasing returns generated by division of labor. The development of industrial clusters is a gradual accumulation and self-enhancement of the system evolution process; its dynamic mechanism of self-enhancement comes from the division of labor based on specialization generated by increasing returns. When the degree of specialization (time shared

for the production of a product by the producer) is high enough, a high level of division of labor between the producers of products of different manufacturers, agencies, and other companies appears. If all transactions in the same place are more efficient than those scattered in multiple locations, there exists an industrial cluster. On the one hand, the marginal cost of production decreases with the deepening of division of labor (the number of transactions increases), which is also the greatest benefit of specialization; but on the other hand, due to the transaction cost being increased as the division of labor deepens, the efficiency of the division of labor depends on the marginal production cost and marginal cost curve intersection (i.e., the above critical point). If the division of labor efficiency declines with the deepened level of labor division, the division of labor is not enough to offset the benefits of the increased marginal transaction cost, at this point, then the vertical integration of the internal division of labor between enterprises is the best choice. Conversely, if the division of labor efficiency is improved and the advantage of division of labor is greater than the increased marginal transaction cost, the cost of collaboration between the enterprises is lower than that of vertical integration within the enterprise, which is the inner motive power of industry cluster formation. The production enterprises within the scope of "Yiwu Business Circle" have spontaneously formed the industrial cluster around the market due to guidance of Yiwu Small Commodity Market, making it an inevitable requirement to raise the level of specialization, reduce production cost, and improve the industry's competition ability. This is because "Yiwu Business Circle" provides a highly efficient trading network inside the business circle, so that the enterprise keeps a lower transaction cost while the division of labor based on specialization is deepened, so that the benefits of the division of labor based on specialization are obtained, and the production cost is reduced.

There is an interactive relationship between division of labor based on specialization and industrial clusters. The development of division of labor leads to the expansion of the division of labor network and trade networks. If the division of labor-related transactions are concentrated in one region, the positive network effect of division of labor will become greater, thus improving transaction efficiency. Transaction efficiency is helpful to solve the conflict of the division of economic and trading costs due to space expansion, promote the evolution of division of labor, bring about greater positive network effects, increase aggregate income due to division of labor, and attract more and more enterprises to gather in the region, leading to the formation and expansion of the cluster. In other words, the geographic concentration of the transaction is required by the division of labor, and the size of the division of labor depends on the efficiency of the transaction, and the efficiency of the transaction depends on the geographic distribution of the industry. Therefore, the transaction efficiency, the degree of transaction concentration, and the level of division of labor interact with each other and are determined in the market competition. The interaction between them, the positive feedback mechanism for the positive network effect of the division of labor, and the improved efficiency of centralized trading promote clustering and the deepening of division of labor, achieving the desired division of labor and regional distribution equilibrium eventually under resource constraints. In "Yiwu Business Circle", there is another form of interaction—market cluster and specialized exchanges. The above two pairs of interactions involve the production and exchanges, and thus have a strong similarity. Within the scope of "Yiwu Business Circle", through the interaction between the small commodity market cluster and the specialized exchange, economies of scale and specialized economy of exchange are obtained; therefore, the interaction between the surrounding industrial cluster and the specialized division of labor is driven, and economies of scale and specialized economy of production are obtained. It is the combination of these two interactions that make "Yiwu Business Circle" complement them in production and exchanges and become the driving force of "Yiwu Business Circle" function.

In theory, in order to solve the conflict of specialized economy and transaction costs due to space expansion, promote the evolution

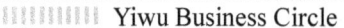

of division of labor, bring about greater specialized positive network effect, and increase the aggregate benefit, it is required to find a kind of organization form, which cannot only reduce the transaction cost, but also avoid the organization cost of the transaction. This kind of organization form is the market division of labor network. "Yiwu Business Circle", the cross-regional division of labor collaboration network, in solving the division of labor and transaction costs, is also fully indicative of the future development trend of the economy of Yiwu Small Commodity Market and the entirety of Yiwu. With the acceleration of internationalization and informationization, the radiation and scope of the tangible market, to a certain extent, can't continue to expand due to the limitation of space, nature, and other objective conditions, so the tangible market leans more and more toward the intangible market transition. In the future, the market's radial force and competitiveness, which is unlikely to rely mainly on further expansion of hardware conditions to seek improvement, must rely more on internationalization, informationization, and environment, and other soft factors for support. "Yiwu Business Circle" itself is a cross-regional division of labor collaboration network established by relying on the original tangible market. It also has the advantage of being similar to the invisible market, and can be expanded indefinitely; at the same time, it has a strong internal organization, and can find a good binding point between reducing the transaction costs and deepening the division of labor, so as to inject new vitality into the future development of "Yiwu Business Circle".

Basic Function of "Yiwu Business Circle" Division of Labor Collaboration Network

1. Bring about construction of Central Zhejiang Megalopolis

"Central Zhejiang Megalopolis", taking Jinhua urban district as the core, is formed of four cities, namely, Yiwu, Yongkang, Dongyang, Lanxi Cities, and Pujiang, Wuyi, Pan'an Counties, and a number of central towns. At present, it has formed a regional urban economic circle with respective characteristics, advantages, and greater integrity. Urban agglomerations are culturally linked, complementary, and dynamic.

From the perspective of the international development experience and trend, the megalopolis is the main driving force to promote the economic development of a country or region. The megalopolis can form huge effects of industrial agglomeration and effects of economies of scale, and its rise

significantly drives the economic development of a country or region. The construction of the Central Zhejiang Megalopolis is an inevitable requirement for further promoting of the development of the central and western regions of Zhejiang by leaps and bounds, speeding up the integration of urban and rural areas, and making it a new growth point of Zhejiang's economy. At present, the traditional economic growth mode in the central and western regions of Zhejiang, the limited resource elements, and the environmental carrying capacity are difficult to adapt to the trend. The demand of economic development and construction of the Central Zhejiang Megalopolis will promote the central and western regions of Zhejiang to form the industrial structure of division of labor collaboration, orderly competition, dislocation development, and enhance the comprehensive competitiveness of industries and regions. It will also promote the mutual protection of the ecological environment, environmental pollution control, promote the coordination of population, resources, and environment, and realize the comprehensive and coordinated sustainable development of the economic society.

To achieve the role of bringing about leapfrog economic development of the central and western regions of Zhejiang, the Central Zhejiang Megalopolis needs to first enhance its economic development strength and cultivate an economic development pole with a strong agglomeration and radiation function; Yiwu's international market advantage and prosperous trade, industry, and modern service industry make it possible for it to become one of the main economic development poles of the Central Zhejiang Megalopolis. In particular, increasing development of "Yiwu Business Circle", the cross-region division of labor collaboration network at the core of Yiwu Small Commodity Market, will further enhance the agglomeration and radiation effect, attract more domestic and foreign advantages and high-end resource elements, and enhance the ability of technology innovation, knowledge innovation, system innovation, and so on of the Central Zhejiang Megalopolis, promote the transformation of economic structure adjustment and growth mode, and facilitate the adjustment, upgrading, and optimization of industrial structure.

"Yiwu Business Circle" links all counties and cities of Central Zhejiang Megalopolis more closely through Yiwu Small Commodity Market to make various regional subjects of the Megalopolis conduct division of labor collaboration by focusing on the market. The Megalopolis integrates the overall resources through modes like free flow of all kinds of elements, industrial gradient transfer, and the construction of a processing base so as to fully utilize resources of regions with less developed economies. This includes land, water, electricity, and labor forces, making up for the resources and ecological environment disadvantages of the developed regions; at the same time, by utilizing the economic advantages of the developed regions, it will promote accelerated development of the less developed regions, finally achieving the goal of enhancing the overall sustainable development ability of the Central Zhejiang Megalopolis.

Construction and development of "Yiwu Business Circle" will continuously solidify the division of labor collaboration relationship among cities, counties, and districts of Central Zhejiang Megalopolis, and enhance their exchanges and cooperation to gradually form the industrial division of labor collaboration network with dislocation development, complementary function, and advantage sharing. This will avoid vicious competition within the megalopolis, achieving the target of harmonious coexistence, mutual promotion, and common prosperity. With the radiation of "Yiwu Business Circle", the expansion and agglomeration of the driving range and the enhancement of the diffusion function, it is possible to promote the establishment of regional brands in the Central Zhejiang Megalopolis. Through the enhancement of the overall strength, the position in the regional development strategy and spatial layout of the province is strengthened, and the regional economic group which can keep up the pace with the three metropolitan groups of Hangzhou, Ningbo, and Wenzhou is formed.

2. Promote regional coordination of urban and rural areas in the whole province

2.1 It is beneficial to speed up the economic and social development of Central and Western Zhejiang and promote the less developed areas to get rid of poverty and increase wealth

The construction and development of "Yiwu Business Circle" enhances the overall economic strength of the cross-regional division of labor collaboration network at the core of Yiwu Small Commodity Market while expanding the radiation effect on the surrounding area day by day, and strengthening the driving effect continuously; in particular, Central and Western Zhejiang, due to their geographical location, will first receive this radiation and driving effect. The construction and development of "Yiwu Business Circle" at the core of Yiwu Small Commodity Market will attract domestic and foreign high-end talents, technology, and other elements of resources involving the role of market agglomeration and guidance, and will make up for the lack of high-end factor resources in the region through the radiation effect; the development will give timely feedback regarding the information of market supply and demand, guide the adjustment of enterprises in Central and Western Zhejiang, optimize the product mix, and produce more famous, special, superior, and new products that meet the needs of the market. With continuous progress in the construction of "Yiwu Business Circle", its industrial structure will be adjusted and upgraded gradually, it will promote industrial gradient transfer to the surrounding less developed areas so as to undertake industrial transfer for the less developed counties and towns in Central and Western Zhejiang, conduct the business of processing with supplied materials, and create good conditions for processing bases and export source bases. Accompanied by the popularity, business, and capitals brought by the further expansion of "Yiwu Business Circle", it will attract more domestic and foreign capital to pay attention to Central and Western Zhejiang, which are rich in resources, boast vast geographical areas, and promote the joint development of new types of scenic tourism, ecological agriculture, and leisure industries, making the resource advantage of Central and Western Zhejiang into an industry advantage; while strengthening its economic strength, it will broaden the fields of mountain and sea cooperation and create the necessary economic base conditions for joint technical breakthrough, transformation of scientific and technological achievements, labor cooperation, and talent development. The continuous enhancement of radiation and driving effect of "Yiwu Business Circle" will also put forward higher requirements for the quality of talented personnel, thus urging Central and Western Zhejiang to further strengthen the training of talents and introduce them to provide the necessary manpower and intellectual resource support for economic and social development. It can be seen that the construction and development of "Yiwu Business Circle" will greatly promote the full play of the ecology, land, labor, and other resource elements in the region and turn it into a realistic economic growth and competitive advantage, as well as form a new bright spot for economic growth so as to narrow the gap between the above-mentioned regions and the coastal areas of Northeast China, achieving the goal of coordinated regional development of the whole province as soon as possible.

2.2 Through typical demonstration, the coordinated development of the urban and rural areas of the province will be promoted, and the integration process between the urban and rural areas will be accelerated

The construction and development of "Yiwu Business Circle" will prompt the cadres of some other areas to understand the essence of the development experience of "nursing the agriculture by industry, enhancing the agriculture with business, urban areas helping rural areas, and urban and rural mutual promotion" in Yiwu City. That is to promote the coordinated development of urban and rural areas by first achieving breakthroughs in the development concept and transforming the supporting strategy of "blood transfusion" into "hematopoietic", and enhancing the initiative of farmers, agriculture, and rural areas to change their development status. To enhance agricultural self-development capacity, improve the efficiency of agricultural production objectives, through the city, the nurturing role of industry, and the service role of the third industry, it shall adjust and optimize the agricultural product and industrial structure, promote the agricultural technological progress and upgrading of equipment, and expand sales channels of agricultural products, so as to achieve the goal of agricultural production efficiency. It is necessary to perfect the investment mechanism of rural infrastructure construction, broaden investment channels, encourage industrial and commercial capital to invest in rural infrastructure construction and develop efficient ecological agriculture, and perfect the corresponding investment return mechanism. The construction and development shall promote the establishment of villagers' self-government system, financial system, and supervision system, and optimize the soft environment of economic and social development; it shall try to broaden the channels of increasing farmers' income, absorb a large sum of rural surplus labor force through the development of rural industry and trade services, cultivate a large number of private entrepreneurs through the development of the market, breaking all kinds of barriers between urban and rural areas, so that farmers and citizens can share the fruits of economic and social development. In particular, with the development of "Yiwu Business Circle", it will first promote the pace of rural development in the surrounding counties of Yiwu, so that the core area of the business circle, Yiwu City, and rural areas will achieve coordinated development and urban–rural integration, which will be gradually expanded to the urban and rural coordinated development and integration of the Central Zhejiang Megalopolis and the entire Central and Western Zhejiang. This will provide a greater experience for reference and play a greater role in the demonstration for promoting urban and rural coordinated development of Zhejiang Province and other areas throughout the country.

3. Promoting the coordinated development of the eastern, central, and western regions of the country

3.1 Drive the construction and development of the commodity markets in the central and western regions

The formation and development of "Yiwu Business Circle" makes its radiation and driving effect diffuse gradually, exerting a direct driving effect over the economic and social development of Central and Western China. The commercial capital accumulated in the development of Yiwu Small Commodity Market, the core of "Yiwu Business Circle", actively seeks investment in Central and Western China and sets up industrial and commercial enterprises and small commodity markets; especially in the national implementation of the "Western Development" and "Rise of Central China" strategies, a large number of Yiwu businessmen set up dozens of sub-markets in Central and Western China like Shanxi, Shaanxi, Hubei, Hunan, Chongqing, Sichuan, Ningxia, Gansu, Qinghai, Xinjiang, and other provinces, municipalities, autonomous regions; these markets take the "parent market" of Yiwu Small Commodity Market as the base and build a commodity distribution and information transmission system between the two places, linking the function of "Yiwu Business Circle" and the development of the local economy together. The central and western regions provide important carriers for "Yiwu Business Circle" to expand market space there and extend the division of labor collaboration network while activating the local market potential, providing a better platform for sales of local products, promoting the local employment, growth of private entrepreneurs, enhancing public awareness of the market, and playing a great guiding and driving role over the development of local agricultural production, finance, transportation, information, consulting, catering services, and so on.

3.2 It provides an important platform and carrier for the development of old industrial bases in the central and western regions and Northeast China

With the construction and development of "Yiwu Business Circle", its radiation effect will be expanded continuously and the cross-regional division of labor collaboration network will be gradually extended to relevant cities and counties of Anhui, Jiangxi, Fujian, and even Shanghai, Jiangsu, Guangdong Provinces. It has become a more powerful and influential cross-province economic community, thus creating closer division of labor collaboration with other parts of the country. With the expansion of radiation scope and ability of "Yiwu Business Circle", its ability to gather a domestic and foreign business atmosphere, popularity, and capital will be further enhanced to provide better product sales, information exchange platforms, and international channels for the rest of the country. In particular, the western region, which is rich in natural resources and energy, and the central and northeast regions where heavy industry is more developed, can better rely on the function of Yiwu Small Commodity Market, the core of "Yiwu Business Circle" to convert its own resources and energy advantages into industrial and competitive advantages. This area can expand the domestic and international market space for local characteristic products through this sales platform, raise the visibility of local products and industries, and establish and publicize products or regional brands. Through timely feedback of market demand information to guide industrial and agricultural production, adjust and optimize the industrial and product structure, and produce products that are truly marketable, the efficiency of industrial and agricultural production will be improved. Through labor export, it will transfer a large number of surplus labor force, broaden the distribution channel of workers, and raise the income level of farmers. The development of "Yiwu Business Circle" will create more favorable conditions for the old industrial base in Central, Western and Northeast China, especially the countryside to undertake the industry transfer of eastern coastal areas, processing with supplied materials, development of natural resources, to carry out investment promotion, and capital introduction.

3.3 Inject the driving force for the economic and social development of the central and western regions

At present, the core areas of "Yiwu Business Circle", namely, Yiwu and the surrounding areas, see ever-increasing commercial density, increasingly fierce market competition, together with the rising cost factor and the restriction of industrial development space. Thus, the marginal income of capital has begun to decline, and some of the business capital accumulated in the market development is seeking new investment routes and space. Because of the low investment density, low market competition pressure, cheap factor resource price, huge potential consumption demand, wide reserve development space, and preferential macro policy in Central and Western China, they have become the preferred targets for industrial and commercial capital investment in the eastern coastal developed areas. These capital output and subsequently industrial gradient transfers bring advanced technology, equipment, and management experience to Central and Western China, while greatly promoting the change of concept of the regions regarding development, which is of great significance over the innovative development mode and training of thought for the regions. Due to the construction and development of "Yiwu Business Circle", there are included a series of innovation activities, such as private capital accumulation in the development of the small commodity market that are transformed from business to industry, linking industry and business, strengthening agriculture with business, and investment in urban infrastructure construction so as to bring about rural industrialization, agricultural modernization, and urban–rural integration. Many cities in Central and Western China have weak financial and material resources, and private economic development is not comparable to that of the East. Thus, to accelerate the urbanization process and narrow the gap with the East, we need to learn from the innovation concept and practical experience in the development of "Yiwu Business Circle" in order to strengthen the market mechanism based on the role of institutional innovation, with an open attitude to attract a wide range of overseas capital to participate in the construction of the region. In the radiating and driving play of "Yiwu Business Circle", and under the impetus of the local reform and opening-up policy, it will promote development and utilization of resource, energy, and the cultivation of an advantageous and characteristic industry in Central and Western China; it will establish the resource and energy bases, speeding up the development of ecological agriculture, profitable agriculture, ecological tourism, red tourism, etc.; it will broaden sources of financing for local industrial development and infrastructure development, and improve the production and living conditions of the masses; it will promote effective realization of the development and function of talent resources and improve the overall quality of the labor force; it will vigorously promote the adjustment, optimization, and upgrading of local industrial structure, change the way of economic growth, strengthen the comprehensive strength of local economic and social development, and gradually narrow the gap with the developed regions, so as to promote the realization of the strategic objectives such as "Western Development", "Rise of Central China", and "Revitalization of Northeast China".

4. Expand international exchanges and cooperation

Since China's reform and opening-up to the outside world, Guangdong has become one of the most active provinces for international exchanges and cooperation. After the 1990s, with the development and construction of Pudong New Area, Shanghai has become one of the core cities of our country's foreign exchanges and cooperation, and its international status is rising rapidly and it gradually has become the trend of Asia and the international economic center. Policy support is the important reason why the exchanges and cooperation between the two regions are very active, and from the present development situation, foreign trade in the two regions has been shown to be mainly characterized by the introduction from the developed countries, and the key factor to support its external exchanges and cooperation is the huge domestic market behind it. Yiwu's foreign exchanges and cooperation show different features. From the beginning, Yiwu had no policy support from the central government, and was solely driven by the interests of enterprises and businessmen. This has led to the stronger independence of Yiwu's businesses and businessmen in the complex international market. Because of its flexibility and mobility in the international market, it is more extensive in the area of exchange and cooperation. From the development process, Yiwu used the huge domestic market to establish its own development basis and strengthen itself. Yiwu's international exchanges and cooperation development process are processes of expanding the international market continuously. One of the most important reasons for Yiwu to attract foreign merchants is not a large domestic market, but their foreign markets, because they can find commodities and information needed by their markets in Yiwu. As a result, from the perspective of regions, various nodes in the international division of labor network of "Yiwu Business Circle" refer to the subjects of equality in the market. Whether it is the USA, Europe, the Middle East, or Africa, in the eyes of Yiwu, those with larger markets are the key cooperation areas. However, Yiwu itself stands at the high end of sales and production, which makes the international division of labor collaboration network of "Yiwu Business Circle" have some functions which are not obvious in other parts of our country.

The international division of labor collaboration network of "Yiwu Business Circle" is developed by relying on the small commodities. Superficially, the production and processing technology of small commodities is not high, which is strong in substitution, and is at a disadvantage and bottom position in international division of labor collaboration. This is also an important reason why foreign trade in many other areas has been facing technical and tariff barriers in recent years. With the establishment of Yiwu Small Commodity Market as the international center, there is already a very close connection between the components inside "Yiwu Business Circle". It can be said that the rise in the price of Yiwu's small commodities will directly lead to the increase in cost of living in many areas such as Europe, the USA, and the Middle East. Moreover, due to the extensive market region of "Yiwu Business Circle", the influence of the developed countries on the setting up of various barriers will be offset by the increasing expansion and development of China's market. Surely, this is not to say that Yiwu's commodity production doesn't need technological innovation or product and industry upgrading. The rise of the Yiwu commodity market to information, standards, and other high-end fields makes it more prominent in the international commodity market. The advantages of Yiwu Small Commodity Market cannot be replaced by other regions in short periods and it is this irreplaceability that many of the world's large-scale commodity purchasers and procurement agencies focus on in the market for commodities, and from the present situation, such a strong position is still further strengthened.

The flow of "Yiwu Business Circle" is not only goods, information, and technology, but also cultural exchanges and collisions. This is reflected in local Yiwu where the streets are lined with the Korean, Indian, Arabian, Italian, American, etc. style restaurants, and foreign merchants in different clothing and colors, which is a manifestation of Chinese and foreign cultural exchanges. The government of Yiwu has offered to make foreign investors "become" internal businessmen, which is not only to provide foreign investors with a good shopping and entrepreneurial environment, but also to make foreign investors develop a sense of cultural identity. This kind of cultural identity is not the indoctrination of oriental culture, nor the occupation of other culture. It is a culture of inclusion and diversity based on our own characteristics. Similarly, Yiwu people all around the world not only promote the hard working, thrifty oriental culture and the unique business culture of Yiwu, they also bring the international advanced cultures and advanced business ideas back to Yiwu, which has promoted the cultural exchanges among different regions in "Yiwu Business Circle". This cultural exchange is successful in the light of the good situation of attracting foreign merchants and the exchange of foreign businessmen with Yiwu.

Formation Path and Mechanism of "Yiwu Business Circle"

The development of Yiwu Small Commodity Market can be divided into four stages, beginning with the early 1980s: the embryonic start-up stage (1978–1987), the steady development stage (1988–1991), the comprehensive expansion stage (1992–2001), and the internationalization stage (2002–now). In each of the above stages, the market's characteristics, functions, subjects, radiation radius, etc., all tend to develop toward higher levels and wider areas. With the continuous growth of the small commodity market, "Yiwu Business Circle" has also gradually gone through a process from incubation to the initial formation, and then to the maturation. This indicates that the development and upgrading of "Yiwu Small Commodity Market" and "Yiwu Business Circle" are mutually influential and interdependent. Thus, to reveal the formation path and mechanism of "Yiwu Business Circle", we must grasp two clues: the first is the formation and development of the small commodity market, and the second is the relevant factors that play an important role in the formation and expansion of "Yiwu Business Circle".

I — Formation of "Yiwu Business Circle"

1. Several stages of "Yiwu Business Circle" formation

1.1 Sprouting of Yiwu Small Commodity Market and the incubation of "Yiwu Business Circle"

In the embryonic start-up stage (1978–1987), Yiwu Small Commodity Market generally experienced a transition of three generations of commodity markets[1]: The first-generation

---

[1] See Lu Lijun, Bai Xiaohu, Wang Zuqiang: *Market Yiwu: From Chicken Feather for Sugar to International Commerce*. Hangzhou: Zhejiang People's Publishing House, 2003. The book divides Yiwu Small Commodity Market into five generations, namely the first generation: Huqingmen Market, Niansanli Small Commodity Market; the second generation: Xinmalu Small Commodity Market; the third generation: Chengzhonglu Market; the fourth generation: HuangYuan Market Phase I; and the fifth generation: Huangyuan Market Phase II, Binwang Market, International Trade Mall.

small commodity markets include the Huqingmen and Niansanli markets that were opened in 1982. They are, strictly speaking, merely the prototypes of small commodity markets with very simple stalls and very few trade varieties. Due to the scarcity of merchants at that time, the formation of the agglomeration effect was impossible, and the Niansanli small commodity market was eventually incorporated into Yiwu Small Commodity Market that was located in Choucheng. The second-generation small commodity market, which was established in 1984, realized the transformation from "street market" or "straw hat market" to "field market", with more than 2,740 kinds of commodities. The circulation sphere gradually spread out across the country and surrounding counties and cities and radiated to other provinces and cities. By 1985, the number of stalls increased to 2,874, and the turnover was 61.9 million Yuan. The third-generation small commodity market, established in 1986, featured ample business space and ever-complete commodity categories. A three-dimensional management service system was initially formed with 4,096 fixed stalls and 1,387 temporary stalls, which recorded a market turnover of 153.8 million Yuan by 1987.

In the early days of the reform and opening-up, the "fast ice" of a planned economy was broken first in the field of industrial daily necessities because the civilians needed a convenient and cheap way of purchasing products in the context of a "shortage economy". Due to the long-term policy of "emphasizing production over circulation" under the planned economy, the "waiting for customers" mode of operation adopted by the state-owned collective commercial and trade enterprises was hard to change in a short period of time, which lead to the disjunction between production and sales, especially the huge gap between supply and demand in daily necessities. It was precisely this "gap" which made the pedlars in Yiwu see a business opportunity. Besides, it also prompted the formation of a "street market" for the distribution and dispatch of goods. On the one hand, the then state-owned enterprises did not produce products oriented toward market, but adopted a unified purchase, marketing, and phasing-out by the state, thereby resulting in a large backlog of commodities. On the other hand, there was no channel for the majority of consumers to get in touch with the enterprises. Having sole reliance on state-owned stores and supply & marketing cooperatives obviously makes it difficult to meet the tremendous demand brought by the implementation of agricultural household contract responsibility system, which offered Yiwu's traditional pedlars an unprecedented space for development. Their development became an inevitable result of the combination of the "chicken feather for sugar" tradition with the characteristics of the times in Yiwu. However, the transportation and communication conditions were seriously backward at that time. In addition, the majority of commodities sold were daily necessities such as toothpastes, towels and shoes, and the main mode of sales was retail. Therefore, the pedlars' procurement and sales activities were centered primarily around Yiwu, which tended to expand towards the surrounding counties and cities, the entire Zhejiang Province, as well as the neighboring provinces. During this period, although simple commodity exchanges and circulation between Yiwu and neighboring provinces and cities took place through pedlars' village-going and household-visiting business practices, they only played a role in circulating products and regulating supplies due to the limited content and scale of exchange. Yiwu Small Commodity Market had little impact on the economic development of surrounding counties and cities. However, it is undeniable that this phase is of great significance to the formation of "Yiwu Business Circle". Because it is precisely such a bold attempt to break through the shackles of a planned economic system for a developing commodity economy that has contributed directly to the sprouting of the small commodity market, which subsequently became the core of "Yiwu Business Circle".

With the further betterment of the national economy and the implementation of the textile & light industry priority policy by the state, the civilians' basic consumption demands for daily necessities have turned to the primary consumer goods such as garments, headdresses, bedding, and knitwear. Their demands for commodity types increased, and they also began to impose certain requirements on quality. Especially in 1982, Yiwu County Party Committee and

Government opened the first generation of the small commodity markets, and the pedlars and distribution stalls started to develop rapidly, thereby getting rid of the original and almost primal way of purchase and sales. The purchase and sales volumes also increased rapidly. The purchase suppliers and the sales demanders began to stabilize and expand gradually. Under the influence of consanguinity, affinity, and geographical relationship, the number of people engaged in the production and sales of small commodities soared, thereby forming the corresponding industries. At that point, Yiwu's transportation and communication conditions were somewhat improved, and the sales territory also expanded to the surrounding counties and cities. In terms of sales mode, both retail and wholesale could be found. In particular, the establishment of a third-generation small commodity market has strengthened the economic ties between Yiwu and its surrounding counties and cities to a greater extent. Such an economic connection was no longer reflected merely in the level of commodity exchanges, but also in more contents such as the production, division of labor, cooperation, and flow of human resources. The strengthening and deepening of the ties have provided the basic economic foundation and environment for the incubation of "Yiwu Business Circle".

In this stage, the civil-induced institutional change is the main drive for the development of Yiwu Small Commodity Market. Despite the continuously expanding market scale, its status as the national small commodity circulation center has not yet been established, and the "Yiwu Commercial Circle" was also in its initial incubation period. A fundamental basis for this judgment is that through the joint efforts of "shopkeepers" and "pedlars", the trade volume of small commodities had been quite huge at that time, and the sales territory had also been rather vast, in which the small commodity market was at the core. In the same period, the private specialized markets in Wenzhou and other regions also boomed. The specialized markets in various regions had their respective specialties, which played certain pivotal roles in different fields. In this stage, the influential sphere of Yiwu Small Commodity Market had already spread to the surrounding counties, cities, and even further beyond. The market was the most prominent one among numerous private specialized markets in Zhejiang Province, while "Yiwu Business Circle" centering on it was yet to be formed literally.

1.2 Development of the small commodity market and formation of "Yiwu Business Circle"

After the concerted efforts of the private sector and the government, Yiwu Small Commodity Market gradually formed to a certain scale and began to enter a stage of steady development (1988–1991). During this period, the size of the venue, the total number of stalls, the types of commodities, the annual turnover, etc., continued to grow steadily. By 1991, the annual turnover of the market already rose to 1.025 billion Yuan, ranking first in the country in terms of similar markets and becoming the nation's largest small commodity market. The radiation scope of "Yiwu Business Circle" was not limited to the neighboring provinces, which also had a huge impact on the "Three Northern Markets" in the northeast, northwest and north of China.

During the comprehensive expansion stage (1992–2001), the phase I project of the fourth-generation small commodity market was completed in 1992, with more than 7,100 new stalls, which truly realized the transformation from "field market" to "indoor market". In the fourth-generation phase II market built in 1993, a total of 7,000 new stalls were set up. In 1995, the Binwang Market, which was generally the same level as the Jiyuan Road fourth-generation small commodity market, was established. The business area of Yiwu Small Commodity Market soared from 13,600 square meters in 1985 to 460,000 square meters, and the market turnover surged from 61.90 million Yuan to 15.2 billion Yuan. During this period, the overall market function was gradually improved, and the market participants were increasingly diversified, forming a grand pattern of "buying and selling throughout the country". In the mid-to-late

1990s, China's economy as a whole contracted. In addition, impacted by the Asian financial crisis in 1997, the small commodity market was undergoing adjustment and consolidation. There was no significant increase in the premises or scale of market, and the total annual sales even declined. This was also a manifestation of structural contradictions caused by rapid development. Afterwards, with the deepening and expansion of industrial restructuring, Yiwu Small Commodity Market once again developed with strong momentum, showing its core position in similar markets, with the market size and radiation capability both far beyond other specialized markets. By 2001, there were eight markets with a turnover of over 1 billion Yuan in Wenzhou, exhibiting an annual total turnover of 18.359 billion Yuan. The Daily Commodity Mall in Luqiao, Taizhou, had a turnover of 11.621 billion Yuan, while Yiwu Small Commodity Market had a turnover up to 21.19 billion Yuan. At that time, similar markets in Wenzhou, Taizhou, and other regions were not only considerably weaker in scale than Yiwu Small Commodity Market, but their product transaction prices and goods sources also began to be affected by Yiwu heavily.

During this period, two major market conglomerates were formed in Yiwu Small Commodity Market: Huangyuan and Binwang. The market scale further expanded, commodity categories increased, and the three-dimensional management service system was already formed. Meanwhile, the reformations in market management, business operation, marketing methods, and other aspects were in steady progress, which greatly improved the level of market. Yiwu Small Commodity Market has risen to fame since then, not only were the related industries in surrounding counties and cities developing increasingly around it, but the commodities from other parts of Zhejiang Province and coastal provinces were also introduced one after another. Furthermore, based on this, a number of distinctive industrial clusters were fostered, which indirectly promoted the development of markets and industries in peripheral regions. On provincewide and nationwide scales, a cross-regional division of labor and collaboration network centering around the small commodity market, i.e., "Yiwu Business Circle", had basically taken shape, which had a close economic relation with the market and its firms (including both forward product sales and backward industrial support).

1.3 Internationalization and maturation "Yiwu Business Circle"

After 2002, Yiwu City set an overall goal of building an international business city, which began to establish an iconic "International Trade Mall" market, thereby further upgrading the market's hardware and software environment, so that the small commodity market could step into a new stage of internationalization (2002–now). At present, the outward degree of Yiwu Small Commodity Market has reached over 60%, thus initially forming a new international business pattern of "buying and selling global commodities". The core position of the market in the national small commodity production and circulation has been firmly established.

As the fifth generation of Yiwu Small Commodity Market, the International Trade Mall has greatly improved the market operation environment and opened up a vast space for the further development of the market. The medium to high-end commodities from all over the country have been exported continuously nationwide and even around the world via the window of Yiwu Small Commodity Market. In addition, foreign goods that account for about 5% of the total turnover have been imported. At present, the development of Yiwu Small Commodity Market has been quite mature, which is gradually transitioning to a new phase in which the commodity market and the information market are valued equally. In particular, the International Trade Mall no longer takes spot trading as the sole or main function, whose product display, information exchanges, and other functions become the fundamental reason for the continued prosperity and development of the market. The main market activities have shifted from the retail and wholesale of products to information processing

and business offices. The modern service industries such as finance, insurance, real estate, and advertising have enjoyed rapid development, and a significant number of large domestic and foreign companies have set up their offices here for handling business information, thus transforming Yiwu from a trade center located in Central Zhejiang to a business center. When examining the world's six major metropolitan areas with a concept of "circle", we can find that for economic or urban circles like New York, Paris, and Tokyo, their interior cores such as business center all assume the functions of information centralization and release. Therefore, in this stage, with the increasingly prominent information release and business functions of Yiwu in the production and circulation of small commodities, "Yiwu Business Circle" has begun to enter a mature phase. Certainly, the real maturation of "Yiwu Business Circle" requires further continued improvement and perfection in these two aspects in the future.

2. Pivotal driving function of the small commodity market in "Yiwu Business Circle"

From the late 1980s to the early 1990s, various kinds of specialized markets were flourishing everywhere in Zhejiang Province. These specialized markets took different development paths. For example, the former famous Wenzhou Yongjia Qiaotou Button Market and the Yueqing Liushi Low-voltage Appliance Market in Zhejiang were over the hill, while the Yiwu "China Small Commodity Store", the Haining China Leather Mall, etc., became large-scale specialized wholesale markets with powerful radiation, great influence, and strong competitiveness. Compared to many other specialized markets in the province, Yiwu Small Commodity Market basically has no special advantages in terms of external conditions. Nonetheless, it is precisely in Yiwu, which has neither geographical advantages nor industrial competitive edges, that you will find the small commodity market with strongest radiation, highest turnover, and most diverse trade categories fostered in the country (see Figure 3.1).

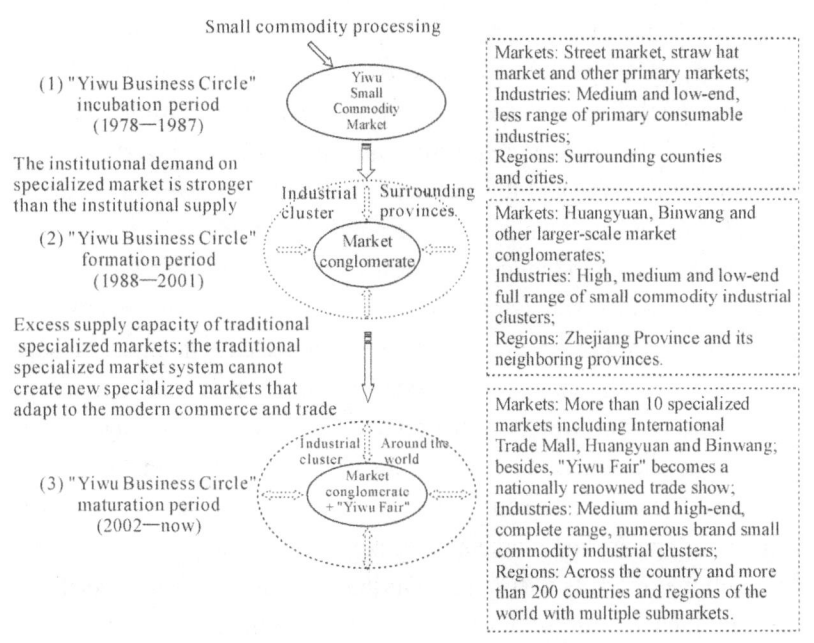

Figure 3.1: Driving role of Yiwu Small Commodity Market in the development of "Yiwu Business Circle"

There are also quite a number of other related domestic works. For example, Zheng Yongjun[2] believed that from the perspective of institutional supply and demand, the development of specialized markets will go through the following four stages. In the first stage, the society's institutional demand for specialized markets is significantly stronger than the institutional supply, and the main bottleneck restricting the development of specialized markets is the institutional supply shortage. In the second stage, the specialized markets' institutional supply capacity is in line with the degree of society's demand for specialized markets. In the third stage, the institutional demand of specialized markets is weakened, while the supply capacity of traditional specialized markets is in surplus. However, due to the lack of functional innovation in

---

[2] See Zheng Yongjun: Prospects and countermeasures for specialized market development in Zhejiang. *Marketing Herald*, 1999, No. 4.

specialized markets, the traditional specialized market system cannot create any new specialized markets—the institutional supply of a modern specialized market that adapts to modern commerce and trade. In the fourth stage, with the adjustment of specialized markets' institutional demand and the restructuring and functional innovation of specialized markets themselves, the number of traditional specialized markets is reduced to the level compatible with the traditional economic sector, whereas the supply capacity of modern specialized markets will also be compatible with the modern economic sector. It should be said that at present, the majority of specialized markets in Zhejiang are in the process of transition from the second stage to the third stage, i.e., a period from the opinion that "institutional supply capacity of specialized markets adapts to the demand capacity" to the opinion that "institutional demand of specialized markets is weakened, while the supply capacity of traditional markets is surplus". During this period, many specialized markets lack functional innovation, and are unable to create a new specialized market system that meets the development requirements of the modern commerce industry. As a result, they have somewhat declined or even closed down. Yiwu Small Commodity Market, in contrast, has made a breakthrough in this regard, not only becoming the world's largest small commodity market, but also forming "Yiwu Business Circle" centering on it, which involves the production and circulation of almost all daily necessities industries and products, covering the whole country and stretching across the world.

The first author of this book believes that[3] a large number of distinctive, dynamic, and supported specialized wholesale markets in Zhejiang, represented by Yiwu Small Commodity Market, will never decline due to the modernization of commerce and business practices, techniques, and tools. On the contrary, it is bound to be naturally merged into the torrent of modern commercial circulation

---

[3]See Lu Lijun: Upgrading of "great province of market" to a "strong province of modern commerce circulation". *Journal of Business Economics*, 2005, No. 8.

after integration, transformation, and upgradation. However, we should also realize that there are at most only three or four markets with similar scales, forms, and increasingly modernized functions as Yiwu Small Commodity Market throughout Zhejiang Province, while most other specialized markets remain in a state where the Yiwu market had been from the 1980s to the early 1990s. Therefore, the integration, transformation, and upgrading of the existing specialized markets are an inherent requirement of Zhejiang Province for building a "strong province of modern commerce and trade". According to Wang Zuqiang,[4] the driver of regional economic development in Yiwu is marketization rather than industrialization. Owing to the businessmen's collective action and the government's enlightened decision-making, Yiwu has become the largest circulation center for small commodities in China. The advantage of the "Yiwu Mode" lies in the specialization of transaction modes. The specialized transaction of small commodity markets has formed the information economy of scale, external economies of scale, and the economy of scope, thereby establishing a low-cost advantage of Yiwu's small commodities. Later, the sound interaction between market order expansion, growth of specialized exchange organizations, and industrial agglomeration enables Yiwu to have its unique industrialization and urbanization path. Taking Yiwu Small Commodity Market as a typical case, Bai Xiaohu[5] studied its mechanism for dynamically coordinating economies of scale and of scope by regarding specialized markets as a "conglomerate", in order to explain the overall development of a specialized market conglomerate. Furthermore, he empirically studied the evolution of specialized market conglomerates in three stages: market origination, stall wholesale, and

---

[4] See Wang Zuqiang: The expansion of market order and the growth of specialized trading organizations: a case study of "Market Yiwu". *Journal of Zhejiang Shuren University*, 2004, No. 2.

[5] See Bai Xiaohu: Economies of scale and economies of scope of specialized market conglomerate in Yiwu. *Finance & Trade Economics*, 2004, No. 2.

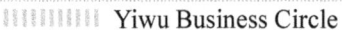
market planning. Bao Weimin and Wang Yisheng[6] argued that since the Song Dynasty, a pattern of town economy has formed in some parts of China. Yiwu Small Commodity Market boomed, driven by the specialization that resulted from social division of labor. The market, in turn, promoted the economic growth and prompted the transformation of a town economy to a market economy, during which the change of traffic conditions has played a key role in the development of Yiwu's commodity economy. Therefore, the formation of the "Yiwu Mode" is also the result of regional historical development. According to Sun Jie, Gu Kejian and Xu Tao,[7] the competitive advantage of market models in developed areas represented by Yiwu Small Commodity Market is, from a static perspective, reflected primarily in the low-cost advantage based on a certain degree of differentiation. From a dynamic perspective, the market models in developed areas will still have strong dynamic competitiveness in a certain period of time in the future due to economies of scale and external economy. However, they are also facing serious challenges because of the presence of a non-efficient equilibrium state caused by prior entry and path dependency, as well as other supportive subsidy policies that local governments may take. Markets in developed areas should not pay too much attention to low-cost competition, whose way out lies in rethinking the strategic positioning of markets. They should break through low costs to create significant differentiation advantages by upgrading and improving market models so that they are hardly imitable for emerging markets and thus maintain higher levels of profitability in the future competition.

In our opinion, there are two major reasons for the serious lack of functional innovation in the specialized markets. The first reason is

---

[6] See Bao Weimin, Wang Yisheng: Yiwu mode: a historical study from the town economy to the market economy. *Zhejiang Social Sciences*, 2002, No. 5.
[7] See Sun Jie, Gu Kejian, Xu Tao: Competitive advantage, external economies and sustainable development of markets in developed areas in China: a case study on Yiwu Small Commodity Wholesale Market. *China Soft Science*, 2004, No. 10.

lagging theoretical research. Most scholars in the theoretical circle have realized that the function and position of traditional specialized markets will tend to be weakened in the economic system. However, in-depth theoretical research on the future development direction and operation mode of specialized markets is lacking, especially regarding the evolutionary regularities of specialized markets themselves. Some of the existing works tend to focus simply on the evolution of specialized markets, while relating it less to the research of enterprises, industries, and the regional economy, thus resulting in a serious insufficiency of theoretical knowledge about institutional innovation in specialized markets. The second reason is the lack of modern operating and managerial personnel in many specialized markets, which leads to a serious scarcity of innovation subjects for a specialized market system. It is precisely in the above two aspects that Yiwu merchants walk at the forefront of China with their own pragmatic attitude, although from today's point of view, the development and promotion of Yiwu Small Commodity Market still needs further theoretical innovation and support from a large number of modern management personnel. It must be pointed out that the essence of the small commodity market development experience lies in the private sector instead of papers and writings. We can never underestimate the spontaneous private innovation behavior and the market grasping ability of Yiwu merchants who are rich in entrepreneurship. Innovation is the fundamental driving force behind the emergence and development of Yiwu Small Commodity Market and "Yiwu Business Circle", which includes the innovation of management tools and the innovation of the government management mechanism. Porter's diamond model holds that there are four key factors that determine the competitiveness of a country or a cluster: factor conditions, related supporting industries, corporate strategies, and structure and rivalry. In addition, opportunities and the government also play respective roles on the four key factors in their

own way, thereby affecting competitiveness.[8] The primary difference between Porter's theory and the traditional theory of comparative advantage is that it believes that a region's initial resource endowment does not necessarily bring competitive advantages, while innovation is the major factor contributing to the formation of a cluster's competitive advantage. From the perspective of the formation of Yiwu Small Commodity Market and "Yiwu Business Circle", it is the innovation that made Yiwu take the lead in establishing a small commodity market by adapting to the requirements of economic and social development as early as the days of the debate on having a planned or market economy in China. Meanwhile, the important carrier for establishment and development of a market economy system is the market—mainly the commodity market.

Yiwu merchants have played a key role during the development of Yiwu Small Commodity Market and "Yiwu Business Circle". In the late 1970s and early 1980s, the relative backwardness of Zhejiang's daily necessities production forced the market operators to step throughout the province and even the whole country to practice trade activities without any concerns for hardships. The long-term "chicken feather for sugar" trade has endowed Yiwu merchants with hard-working, shrewd, bold, and courageous traits. Yiwu merchants actually gathered the popular daily necessities from all over the country to Yiwu by carrying them on shoulders with a pole, then sold them to the country and even the world via Yiwu Small Commodity Market. Although all this seems very incredible today, the successful practice of the market has demonstrated that behind Yiwu merchants' hard work, a deeper level of advantage is their ability to grasp the market allocation of resources. This ability, when developed to a higher level, will be the entrepreneurial spirit.

---

[8]See Michael Porter: *Competitive Advantage of Nations*. Beijing: Huaxia Publishing House, 2002.

Expansion of "Yiwu Business Circle"—Yiwu Logistics Market

II

1. Emergence and development of logistics market

Many scholars consider that the logistics market in Yiwu is a relatively independent market parallel with Yiwu Small Commodity Market. It should be noted that such an understanding is not accurate enough. Chapter 2 already mentions that the logistics and warehousing industry, as the leading industry in the small commodity market, is an important part of the core of "Yiwu Business Circle". In this chapter, we point out more clearly that the logistics market is the natural extension of the small commodity market's development, which emerges, grows, and eventually becomes an integral part of it. The logistics market has evolved from the original freight service or freight market. Since the emergence of cross-regional transactions in the small commodity market, transport has become an inseparable part of small commodity trade. When the freight market is very

small, people naturally regard it as a part of the commodity market; and when it begins to develop rapidly and forms its own scale, people are increasingly aware of its own business development law. In addition to the uniqueness of Yiwu's freight market development, the Yiwu logistics market began to appear as an independent form. However, it is precisely the uniqueness of Yiwu's logistics market that determines its important position as a part of Yiwu Small Commodity Market. In Yiwu, where the geographical location is not very advantageous and the volume of commodity transport is very huge, both the emergence and development of a logistics market are closely dependent on the small commodity market. From the first day of its inception, its management subjects and objects are intertwined with the transaction subjects and objects of the small commodity market. Meanwhile, the superficial independence is an impression left on people due to its unique intermodal mode and huge transport scale. Concerning the development and internal mechanism of Yiwu's logistics market, the companion book *Market Yiwu: From Chicken Feather for Sugar to International Commerce* has made detailed research.

In this new book, the reason why we should separate the logistics market from Yiwu Small Commodity Market for analysis is that the development of the logistics industry is an important driving factor during the regional expansion of "Yiwu Business Circle", in which the logistics market plays a pivotal role. The emergence and development of the logistics market satisfy the realistic needs for the constant expansion of "Yiwu Business Circle". With the development of the small commodity market and the expansion of "Yiwu Business Circle" to broader areas, the original way of shouldering goods or via car and train adopted by traveling merchants can no longer meet the needs of market development. In May 1985, a villager from Sanlitang Village, Choucheng township of Yiwu, took the lead in setting up a cargo transport agency from Yiwu to Nanjing Pukou Highway, which became the first logistics point of automobile cargo transportation in Yiwu. On October 27 of the same year, the storage and distribution station of Yiwu opened passenger and freight transportation services from Yiwu to Shanghai and Changshu, respectively. The opening of these three lines marks the birth of Yiwu's logistics industry, which has also accelerated the nationwide expansion pace of "Yiwu Business Circle". By the end of 2005, Yiwu had 398 logistics agencies, more than 130 railway lines for freight traffic, and 235 unloading terminals for foreign goods. Meanwhile, five railway lines for baggage and parcel were opened successively targeting Northeast, Northwest, Southwest China, and Guangzhou, Beijing. Railway stations in Shanghai, Hangzhou, Jinhua, Pujiang, and Yingtan all had transfer stations in Yiwu, with a daily freight volume of over 8,000 tons. In terms of air and waterway transportation, there are currently over 1,000 standard containers shipped from Yiwu to the Middle East, Africa, Europe, and other parts of the world via the ports, inland ports, and airports of Shanghai, Ningbo, and Shenzhen nearly every day.

2. Management mode of logistics market

Since its formation, the logistics market has gone through three rounds of rectification, in 1990–1991, 1994–1995, and 1998–2000, respectively. It implemented the ceiling and floor prices for each logistics line and point; it also practiced the risk contract responsibility system for each line and point according to the principle of "Approved Base, Fixed Ratio Growth, Excess Retention, and Shortage Self-Compensation" and standardized the operation of logistics lines and points through annual assessment.

Supply management. The Provisions on the Management of Goods Supply in Yiwu implemented by Yiwu Municipal Government clearly states that any logistics goods supply occurring within the territory of Yiwu is all included in the scope of uniform standardized management except for the self-produced, self-marketed, and directly-shipped products from the factories, mining companies, and institutions. The Provisions also stipulate that the unlicensed transport of merchandise within the Yiwu territory to the adjacent areas in pieces is prohibited. Where a person or an event in violation of the freight management

provisions is found, the logistics agency has the right to report it to the transportation management office, which is then handled by the inspectors dispatched by the office. The logistics agency should not canvass the cargoes, not deal with the violators in private, so as to avoid triggering conflicts and causing confusion in the industry.

Freight rate. Initially, the ceiling price was approved uniformly by the price control department. After the third rectification, a single-line and multi-point threshold opening were once adopted, and after the occurrence of vicious competition, the department approved the floor price. The transportation management implements stringent supervision and heavy penalties generally in accordance with the freight rate provisions. The overcharged lines and points will be punished with a warning and fine of 5,000 Yuan for an overcharge of over 5 Yuan upon the first verification, and will be deprived of business qualification upon the second verification. Those that overcharge over 100 Yuan will be immediately deprived of business qualification.

Line & point management. The logistics agencies are subject to assessment by the transportation management office according to the term of operation provided in the contract agreement and the letter of responsibility. Those who pass the assessment and have paid the taxes and market development & construction service charges approved by the government are allowed to continue the contracted operation, while the disqualified lines and points are reopened to public bidding.

Insurance claims system. Since 1995, the transportation management office has guided the insurance undertakers to join hands with the logistics agencies to strengthen insurance claims settlements over the traveling merchants' cargoes, which has also introduced the relevant claims settlement system. The loss of fully insured goods will be compensated at 100% by the insurance company, while the loss of uninsured goods will be compensated at 10 Yuan/kg to the travelling merchants by the logistics agency. A pattern of settling claims is gradually formed, in which the logistics agencies purchase insurance at the claims division of the insurance company on a full truck load or monthly basis after collecting premiums from the travelling merchants. The insurance company's claims division may also dispatch stationed personnel at the logistics agencies for direct acceptance of insurance on a voluntary basis from the travelling merchants. If a logistics agency does not purchase insurance from the insurance company, it should make a public commitment to the management department and travelling merchants that it is responsible for full compensation upon the notice of loss. The cargo insurance claims system adopting the above three modes of operation greatly reduces the economic loss of logistics agencies and travelling merchants during the cargo transportation process and improves the safety of cargo transportation.

Strict rectification for ensuring market security. In 1998, Yiwu Municipal Party Committee and Government revoked the security division of the transport management office and established the Municipal Public Security Bureau Police Station for Public Transportation, in order to safeguard the social order of the logistics industry. The public transportation police station practices the policy of "comprehensively tackling problems at both roots and symptoms, combining punishment with prevention" over the logistics industry, and has signed the social order responsibility agreement with various logistics agencies, thereby effectively safeguarding the normal operation of the logistics market.

3. Role of logistics market in the regional expansion of "Yiwu Business Circle"

As the government took control over the entry of Yiwu's logistics market initially, the local supply once continued to outflow. However, after the third rectification, the government liberalized the logistics market, not only completely changing the previous outflow of supplies, but also attracting the supply of goods from other regions. This has greatly strengthened Yiwu's position as a regional logistics hub and enhanced its radiation capability, thereby expanding the area of "Yiwu

Business Circle". Local business operators and some companies in neighboring counties and cities even ship the full carloads to Yiwu, which are then transported to various regions. Compared to other regions, the freight market in Yiwu has obvious competitive advantages in the following three aspects. The first is the diversified service content, which includes all kinds of services such as domestic, international, highway, railway, air, waterway, fast, regular, and express transportations. The second is the superior transportation network of the freight market, which covers large and medium-sized cities and regions all over the country. The third is the relatively low freight rates and the satisfactory information and insurance services. The freight radiation chart, which consists of more than 130 radiation lines centering Yiwu's local logistics market, vividly outlines the regional network of "Yiwu Business Circle".

The shrewd logistics operators of Yiwu have not only made the local logistics industry flourish, but also developed logistics lines along the wholesale markets across the country since the early 1990s to create the nation's largest cargo transportation network. The logistics agencies in Zhejiang's Tongxiang, Luqiao, and Jiangsu's Changshu are mainly run by Yiwu natives; the logistics agencies at the Shaoxing China Textile Mall are almost monopolized by Yiwu natives; and nearly 50% of 500 logistics agencies in Guangzhou are run by Yiwu natives. According to preliminary statistics, currently there are 93 logistics companies established by Yiwu natives in the province outside the city, employing more than 1,200 people. There are 386 logistics companies established in various cities outside the province, which employ more than 4,200 people, and at present, there are also a large number of operators who are engaged in international logistics. So in a manner of speaking, where there is a market, there are Yiwu natives engaged in logistics services. Some of the consignors or logistics providers from Yiwu are consolidating step by step on the world map, having set up distribution centers (transfer stations) in major cities such as Guangzhou, Harbin, Urumqi, UAE's Dubai, Brazil's Rio de Janeiro, and Russia's Nakhodka. After the goods arrive at these places, the merchants distribute them to the neighboring countries or regions via the local land, sea, and air channels.

As Yiwu Small Commodity Market began to step towards internationalization, Yiwu, as the world circulation center for small commodities, has led the rise and development of the international freight industry. The development of the industry, in turn, has further promoted the internationalization of Yiwu Small Commodity Market, thereby enabling the regional distribution of "Yiwu Business Circle" around the world. In December 2005, Air China Cargo and Yiwu International Logistics Center jointly launched the trucking service from Yiwu to Hangzhou to realize the ground extension of exporting international flights. Meanwhile, Yiwu Customs Office and International Logistics Center also opened a two-way rail–sea intermodal transportation route to Ningbo Port, so that the cargoes from Yiwu can directly depart without the approval of Ningbo Customs. This eliminates the intermediate link between the port and the inland customhouse, thereby saving the shipping time and shipping costs considerably for companies. The rapidly developing international freight industry and the fast, convenient international freight routes have become the solid backing for Yiwu Small Commodity Market to radiate all over the world, thus creating the most direct path for the expansion of "Yiwu Business Circle" in the world.

Ⅲ Leading Role of "Yiwu Business Circle"—Yiwu Business Culture

1. Connotations and essence of Yiwu business culture: Yiwu people and Yiwu spirit

The origin of Yiwu's business culture can be traced back to the grand background of the great significance of Eastern Zhejiang Practical School's utilitarian philosophy, which is constituted by the three schools Yongkang, Jinhua, and Yongjia and has profound influence in Zhejiang on the formation of Zhejiang business culture. However, under the same business cultural origin, why has Yiwu's business culture been able to create unique business prosperity? Clearly, Yiwu's business culture has its distinct qualities, which have played an important role in the formation and development of "Yiwu Business Circle".

1.1 Yiwu native's unique characters

Located in Central Zhejiang, Yiwu lacks location advantages. The land is mostly mountains and hills, without many plains, so its natural resource endowments are poor. As early as the Qing Dynasty Qianlong years, Yiwu natives had begun to do a "chicken feather for sugar" small business. The long distance, heavy load, high risk, and low profits of the "chicken feather for sugar" business have developed the "diligence, studiousness, uprightness, and courageousness" spirit unique to Yiwu people. After the reform and opening-up, it was exactly those "disciplinants" who had traded "chicken feather for sugar" first spawned the idea of doing small commodity business and opening a small commodity market.

In terms of cultural tradition, Yiwu is influenced deeply by the Eastern Zhejiang Practical School represented by Lü Zuqian, Ye Shi, etc. This is manifested mainly as the unique characters of Yiwu people. The first is the fighting spirit daring to travel from place to place; the second is the adherence to righteousness, to regard impartiality and profit as equally important, to value business ethics, to keep integrity, and to avoid fraud; the third is the business philosophy of "earning ten percent when others earn ninety percent", and making money on the premise that others are profiting. If "Yiwu Army" is the historical origin of Yiwu businessmen's uprightness and braveness, then "Qiaotang Sect" is the school training Yiwu natives on the business tradition.[9] Thus, "Yiwu Army" and "Qiaotang Sect" became Yiwu's two most typical group representatives. It is precisely by the unremitting endeavor of "pioneering" private entrepreneurs and individual business owners that Yiwu has become a very competitive commercial city, which has fostered the world's

---

[9] See Lu Lijun, Bai Xiaohu, Wang Zuqiang: *Market Yiwu: From Chicken Feather for Sugar to International Commerce*. Hangzhou: Zhejiang People's Publishing House, 2003, p. 57, 70.

largest small commodity wholesale market and became a city with harmonious urban and rural development.

1.2 Essence of Yiwu business culture

Yiwu merchants' profound business tradition has set the rough outline and direction for the present economic development mode of Yiwu. Yiwu natives have an innate business awareness, which is inseparable from their traditions. Undoubtedly, Yiwu's traditional business culture has played an important role in the development of the small commodity market. Yiwu's business culture shares many similarities with the basic requirements of a modern market economy, which is reflected mainly in the following aspects:

1.2.1 Unique economic values

In the early stage of reform and opening-up, China's traditional social values began to get hit by the new era. The values centered on traditional ethics and morality, which have been passed down for thousands of years, were facing revolutionary changes. Inspired by the Communist Party of China's policy of reform and opening-up, the revolution of Yiwu people's values took place in advance. The values were centered on economic values first boarded in the historical stage of Yiwu Small Commodity Market. Yiwu people's unique economic values are especially manifested clearly in two periods. During the period of market establishment, they skillfully used "time difference", "space difference", and "information difference" to achieve the goal of "faster, newer, and cheaper products than rivals". After the rise of the market, they also gained the "technological gap" and "management gap" through study to achieve the goal of "more superior, expensive, and special products than rivals".

1.2.2 Universal adventurous spirit and strong social mobility

Entrepreneurship requires risk taking. No risk, no profit; and high risk, high returns. Compared to other regions, Yiwu businessmen grow up travelling with their parents, who develop an adventurous spirit and are able to adapt to unfamiliar surroundings quickly. They are highly capable of bearing uncertainties in the future and dare to take risks for legitimate business interests. More importantly, Yiwu's social environment allows and tolerates failure, where the losers who strive for success are admired. They admire the unsuccessful people who dare to fight hard. Many people are not afraid of failure. Even if they have failed with heavy debts, they try to "make a comeback" and often achieve their goals.

The rise of Yiwu Small Commodity Market and industrial cluster is very closely related to the high social mobility of the local people. In the early days of the reform and opening-up, Yiwu people, with their superior horizons and key information, already started to create small businesses all over the country. They accumulated capital while collecting various forms of information. Once the time was right, they brought the information they heard and saw, together with the know-how, funding, experience, and projects accumulated during business practices to their hometown to run individual businesses. After the stalls and businesses were thriving and the capital was abundant, many proprietors took business trips abroad to seek business opportunities in the international market. They even set up markets, stores, and companies abroad, in sharp contrast to people from many other places who were merely accustomed to farming in their hometowns. Since China has been in the traditional agricultural society for a long period of time, people are generally "attached to their native lands" and are reluctant to leave their primary relationships to migrate to other places. Yiwu people, on the other hand, are at the national forefront in terms of "going global".

1.2.3 Business tradition combining competition with integrity and inclusiveness

Yiwu businessmen are not only good at competition and dare to confront it, but they can also value integrity, tolerate competitors, and are used to fair competition among peers, which is the key for numerous companies and individual operators engaged in the

manufacture of the same products to compete, cooperate, and coexist in the same markets or regions. For example, the sock industrial cluster in Yiwu can gather several of the world's largest sock groups, which are closely linked to the cultural tradition of combining competition with integrity and inclusiveness. There are as many as 8,000 foreigners who have been doing long-term business in Yiwu. They can take root in Yiwu under the impact and blending of various cultures, which are inextricably linked to the local business tradition of combining competition with integrity and inclusiveness.

1.2.4 Valuable learning spirit

After some Yiwu people bring back the information from outside to run their own businesses or projects, others learn and follow their examples upon seeing broad market prospects and possible profits, thereby resulting in industrial clusters formed by many manufacturers of the same products or commercial clusters running similar products. Currently, with the growing internationalization of markets, many Yiwu natives have been studying computer science and foreign languages one after another. Such a common practice has endowed Yiwu with a learning society trait represented by "learning by doing".

1.3 Yiwu spirit of advancing with the times

"Diligence, studiousness, uprightness, and courageousness" are part of the "Yiwu Spirit" outlined by the municipal party committee in 1989 through soliciting opinions from all levels of the masses in the city. In practice, the municipal party committee and the municipal government, along with the citizens of the city, continue to give new meanings to the "Yiwu Spirit". In 1992, the "Market Spirit" of "industriousness, integrity, persistence, and pioneering" was refined. It is precisely such a powerful personality that has cast the brilliant achievements of today's Yiwu. The times are advancing, and the people's ideologies are changing, so the humanistic spirit must also keep pace with the times. At present, the following four changes are particularly noteworthy in the actual context that helps the Yiwu Spirit keep pace with the times. The first is that Yiwu has initially become an international commerce and trade city featuring small commodity circulation, display, information, and manufacturing. The second is that Yiwu has become an immigrant city in the real sense. The third is that Yiwu residents' income level and quality of life have been greatly improved, at least for those who have stepped into the well-to-do level early. The fourth is that Yiwu is in the golden period of development, a period of economic transition and frequent contradictions, which leads to an ever-growing economy, social conflicts, and new problems, as well as the fierce collision of various ideas and concepts. Such an obvious change has taken place in these times. This requires a new spirit of the times that can lead people's minds, which gives rise to a grand discussion on the expression of "Yiwu Spirit" in the new era.

According to the expressions collected so far, "integrity", "inclusiveness", and "boldness" are the core words, and we think this is in line with reality. Yiwu's privately-run businesses are the economic pillar of the city. Entrepreneurs' understanding and views on the Yiwu spirit may be more strongly representative. Some entrepreneurs believe that the "New Yiwu Spirit" should be described as "dare to create the best in the world". From the "chicken feather for sugar" economy to opening the "street market", then to building the world's No. 1 small commodity market now, Yiwu people are not afraid of enduring hardships and getting tired, they dare to contend with the risk, thus creating an extraordinarily new spirit of Yiwu people. Some entrepreneurs also believe that the new "Yiwu Spirit" should be described as "thrifty, sincere, open, and daring" because for the development of Yiwu, thriftiness is the basis, sincerity is the norm, opening-up is the belief, and daring is the motivation. Some foreign businessmen think that the "Yiwu Spirit" is reflected more in diligence and integrity; while others consider that "harmony" is the foundation for everything in Yiwu. Due to the extensive participation

of society, the significance of the new "Yiwu Spirit" is not merely the solicitation of several expressions. More importantly, it strengthens the common belief of all new and old Yiwu residents through such a discussion and gathers more force to create new glory. In August 2006, the CPC Yiwu Municipal Party Committee released the document ([2006] No. 10), calling for further cultivation and promotion of the new-era "Yiwu Spirit" of "diligence, studiousness, uprightness, courageousness, integrity, and inclusiveness" throughout the city.

Yiwu has a saying: "Guests are the bringers of prosperity", which is a true reflection of Yiwu people's "integrity, inclusiveness, courageousness, and common prosperity" mentality under the influence of modern business culture.

2. Leading role of Yiwu business culture in expansion of "Yiwu Business Circle"

Although Yiwu people are no longer the only behavioral group for business activities in "Yiwu Business Circle", we can see that Yiwu's business culture is embodied everywhere in these activities. It is the internal gene embedded in business activities that leads the expansion of "Yiwu Business Circle". Next, we will make further analysis from the aspects of Yiwu business culture's spiritual, ethical, and marketing cultures.

First of all, from the perspective of Yiwu's business ethics culture, Yiwu people inherit the Chinese nation's fine tradition of respecting loyalty, filial piety, chastity, and righteousness while accepting the philosophical thinking of utilitarianism, thus forming spiritual traits of overlooking power, valuing righteousness, persevering, and stressing commitment. Meanwhile, such a simple, straightforward, righteous, and decent humanistic spirit accumulates to form a unique folk custom in Yiwu. Yiwu people generally have the sense of humility and mutual benefit in their daily life. These business customs, as well as the spiritual qualities within them have created Yiwu people's business ethics culture of valuing both morality and profits, observing business ethics, staying honest and trustworthy, and achieving mutual benefits. It is precisely because of the influence of such a business ethics culture that Yiwu Small Commodity Market has set up its own gold signboard of integrity and inclusiveness, thereby avoiding the path of decline or even collapse walked by some small commodity markets in other regions due to the proliferation of inferior products and frequent credit crises. Meanwhile, owing to such a modest, win–win cooperation spirit of Yiwu merchants, they have joined hands with a growing number of partners, and "Yiwu Business Circle" has also been expanding gradually in this regard.

Secondly, from the perspective of Yiwu's commercial spiritual culture, the Yiwu people, who are deeply influenced by the traditional philosophy of utilitarianism, bravely carried the goods on their shoulders with a pole to travel extensively under the pressure of real life. This seemingly primitive and simple early commercial activity cultivated the Yiwu people's unique fighting spirit of daring to take risks and seeking their fortune. It is precisely under the influence of such a daring commercial spirit that the businessmen of Yiwu walk out of Yiwu to other places in China and the world. Yiwu's small commodities have also been flown to almost every corner of the world. From this point of view, Yiwu Small Commodity Market, as the core of "Yiwu Business Circle", has connections with other regions within the circle that is not merely a cohesive model of "strengthening attraction internally and actively approaching externally". Yiwu businessmen themselves expand outward and radiate actively, which is an important factor in the formation of "Yiwu Business Circle".

Finally, from the perspective of Yiwu's marketing culture, the "Qiaotang Sect", which was born along with the early barter form of "chicken feather for sugar", is responsible for the organization and coordination of small commodity sales. We can say that the

organizational division of labor, marketing skills, and marketing ideas of "Qiaotang Sect" have been initially equipped with some of the basic elements and functions of modern business marketing. Characterized by low price, wide variety, huge quantity, and intense competition, most manufactures and sellers of small commodities have to take a "small profits but quick turnover" strategy. To achieve quick turnover, a basic way is to expand the volume of trade and improve the market share through business cooperation with dealers in other regions. In the meantime, there is also the need to exercise some control over the quality of such quantitative expansion by emphasizing the closeness and efficiency of cooperation. It is precisely under such a pressure of "profitability only by selling more" that Yiwu businessmen have gradually spread the influence of Yiwu's economy to many parts of the country and the world through extensive, effective cooperation and pursuance of market expansion. In other words, the actual conditions and needs of small commodity sales in Yiwu have contributed to the formation of Yiwu's marketing culture with an extreme connotation of expansiveness and cooperation. Under the guidance of such a marketing culture, the influence of Yiwu merchants, Yiwu small commodities, and the Yiwu economy have spread outward step by step.

If the traditional Chinese business culture is "virtue-based" and the western business culture is "finance-based", then Yiwu's business culture is a good combination of the two. Equal emphasis on righteousness and profit is the foundation for the existence of Yiwu Small Commodity Market. Struggle and expansion are the basic forms for the development and growth of the market, which are also the necessary ways of forming "Yiwu Business Circle". Cooperation, inclusiveness, and efficient, harmonious organization, on the other hand, ensure the tightness of "Yiwu Business Circle" network, making it more realistic. Today, this unique business culture of Yiwu has spread rapidly throughout the country, radiating the business culture further. The expansion of Yiwu business culture is reflected mainly in Yiwu merchants' establishment of Yiwu trade markets throughout the country, as well as the country's learning of Yiwu's development experience. Yiwu businessmen have set up trade markets in places like Beijing, Shanghai, Chongqing, Xinjiang, Gansu, and Shandong. Meanwhile, provinces like Sichuan, Hubei, and Hunan learned from Yiwu's experience to set up local markets by attracting Yiwu merchants and importing Yiwu small commodities.

It should be pointed out that although Yiwu has created its own "business prosperity", it has not actually formed its own "business civilization" up to now. In particular, it still has a long way to go in terms of improving the quality of market players and building a business civilization. Yiwu's business culture is the essence of its further development. We believe that through inheritance, promotion, and innovation, Yiwu merchants will surely build a business civilization that is in line with the requirements of the new era, thereby setting an example for the commercial development of the entire country and even the world.

Formation Mechanism of "Yiwu Business Circle"

IV

1. Formation of large-scale market by commercial population gathering

The formation of "Yiwu Business Circle" is a process of continuous evolution and development with Yiwu Small Commodity Market as the source and impetus in which the cost advantages are brought about by market economies of scale and economies of scope, and specialized division of labor is gained while reducing transaction costs and a cross-regional division of labor cooperation network is formed through the mutual promotion between specialized division of labor and industrial clusters.

The development of commerce and trade must be premised on the gathering of popularity, while Yiwu's commerce and trade-based development model is closely related to the dense population-location condition and the business tradition of Yiwu people. After understanding the national supply and demand information of commodities, the "chicken feather for sugar" and "carrying pole" pedlars, who once travelled extensively, changed their "traveling" business mode into a "settled" business mode, thereby forming the initial commercial population of "Yiwu Business Circle"—Yiwu merchants. Afterwards, with the formation and development of the small commodity market, the local commercial population of Yiwu increased rapidly through the demonstration effect of relatives and friends. Meanwhile, many wholesalers and retailers in the surrounding areas and all over the country have also gradually taken Yiwu Small Commodity Market as a purchasing base, thus leading to the gathering of a substantial commercial population in Yiwu.

With its high proportion of commercial population, Yiwu Small Commodity Market has become a subregion with a strong ability to attract commercial populations in the region. It has gathered a large commercial population, which provides the subjective condition for its development into a national circulation center for small commodities. The rapid concentration of traders is a great driving factor for the vigorous development of the small commodity market. Meanwhile, the enormous attraction produced by the market's development has also led a large commercial population in and around the province to gather in Yiwu, thereby promoting the formation and development of the entire "Yiwu Business Circle".

Owing to the development of Yiwu Small Commodity Market, a lot of transaction costs have been saved for the operators of stalls (companies) within it and the domestic and foreign merchants. Under the premise of traditional neoclassical economics that the price is the only dimension of product identification, the market competition is strengthened since numerous operators of the same types of products are concentrated in the same area, thereby forming lower market prices. This enables the purchasers to find the satisfied "low price" more quickly, thus shortening the price search time, accelerating the market transaction

speed, reducing the market transaction cost, and expanding the market transaction volume. The enlargement of market transaction scale in turn further attracts the entry of more operators into the trading space, thus making the competition more competitive, accelerating the transaction speed, while the transaction costs continue to decline, and the efficiency of market transactions is further enhanced, so that the profit-making space of all parties have been constantly expanding. Meanwhile, as the centralized transaction can greatly reduce the transportation cost and improve the efficiency of information transmission in the market, it can also greatly reduce the exogenous transaction costs resulting from the conflicts of interest among non-policymakers that are incurred directly or indirectly during the transaction process. Since it is easier to perfect the market trading system and management rules in a relatively concentrated geographic area, strengthening the management and regulation of Yiwu Small Commodity Market can greatly lower the moral risk of all parties involved in the transaction and reduce the adverse selection of violating the market trading rules and other opportunistic behaviors. Thus, the endogenous transaction costs resulting from the conflict of self-serving decision-making by all parties in the transaction are also significantly reduced.

2. Market-led specialized division of labor

Although the regional economy is a smaller system compared to the national economy, the presence of the market and the evolution of labor division are, similarly, indispensable conditions for economic growth. In fact, the existence and expansion of Yiwu Small Commodity Market are the necessary conditions for the cross-regional division of labor and cooperation among the central and western parts of Zhejiang Province, the entire province, and some other parts of the country to promote the formation of "Yiwu Business Circle".

It is precisely the highly efficient Yiwu Small Commodity Market which keeps the transaction costs low after detailed division of labor, so that the specialized production of enterprises becomes profitable.

As the market size continues to expand, its industry-driving role further enhances, and the production scale of specialized labor division enterprises reaches the critical point of economies of scale accordingly, thereby not only further reducing the cost of production, but also letting Yiwu Small Commodity Market stand out from similar markets. Due to the effect of increasing returns to scale, the flourishing market has promoted the development of a cross-regional division of labor network, i.e., "Yiwu Business Circle". As Yiwu Small Commodity Market continues to expand in size by combining regional resources, the effect of scale has led to an enhanced transaction efficiency. As the effect of increasing returns to scale expands, the interregional division of labor and coordination of production become a more favorable economic activity, which drives various economic entities and regions associated with the market to further carry out specialized division of labor and collaboration around the market. This allows "Yiwu Business Circle" to grow steadily and expand continuously.

3. Division of labor-induced industrial agglomeration

Under constant relative productivity, relative preference, and relative population size between regions, the improvement of market transaction efficiency is bound to prompt the transition of a self-sufficient mode of production to a localized division of labor, which would then evolve into a complete division of labor. Therefore, when the surrounding regions of Yiwu make the labor division decisions around its small commodity market, the determinants for the degree of labor division are not only associated with the factor endowments in respective regions, but also to a large extent, closely related to the transaction efficiency of the small commodity market. Since the market is orderly and well developed, with prominent transaction efficiency, the division of labor between Yiwu and the surrounding areas has become a rational choice for entrepreneurs.

After Yiwu Small Commodity Market becomes the main channel for sales of products for many enterprises, manufacturers also prefer

to relocate their production departments as close to the market as possible in consideration of a series of "cost factors" such as reducing transportation costs, in order to obtain a price advantage in the competition. During the gathering of large numbers of manufacturers around the market, similar manufacturers can concentrate on one place to benefit from the specialized division of labor, thereby further widening the competition gap between firms within and outside the clusters. This attracts the firms outside the clusters to migrate close to and even integrate into the clusters because the industrial layout around the market shows a distinct massive economic feature. Clearly, the formation of industrial clusters is also the result of a rational choice by firms in the market. After the formation of industrial clusters around Yiwu Small Commodity Market, the industrial foundation of "Yiwu Business Circle", a cross-regional division of labor and cooperation network, has also formed.

4. Market network promotes regional cooperation

Due to the existence of a large-scale market, i.e., the small commodity market in Yiwu, the economy of the city and surrounding regions exhibits a significant outward trend. Correspondingly, the proportion of the region's exports in the entire economy is also larger than other regions, and the forward and backward linkages between the region's industrial clusters and the market are closer as well. Concerning the form of linkages, some underdeveloped areas provide a cheap labor force for Yiwu firms through the processing of materials supplied from Yiwu Small Commodity Market without actual labor export. Some areas with their own developing industrial clusters, on the other hand, offer an abundant supply of goods by selling products directly via Yiwu Small Commodity Market. Although there is no superior government that plans the cooperative relations between Yiwu and surrounding areas in terms of an administrative division, under the function of market mechanisms, these regions have spontaneously established a mutually beneficial win–win mechanism based on the division of labor and cooperation.

On the contrary, due to the "lock-in effect"[10] in Yiwu Small Commodity Market, the original market has been strengthened and consolidated. The "lock-in effect" means that the possibility of other regions developing new markets at cheaper costs is "locked" because the initial transaction costs are higher than the average transaction costs of Yiwu Small Commodity Market. The development of new markets in the surrounding areas not only cannot lower the transaction costs of local enterprises, but also is likely to bring shrinkage due to the "polarization effect"[11] of Yiwu's market (in fact, some similar markets near Yiwu are shrinking or have already shrunk). This also further encourages the surrounding areas to choose to become integrated with Yiwu Small Commodity Market to pursue division of labor and cooperation with Yiwu rather than striving to establish a new market network. During the formation and development of "Yiwu Business Circle", the rapid growth of regional economy was merely an external manifestation of the function of the labor division and cooperation mechanism. Its root lies in that the business opportunities brought by Yiwu Small Commodity Market lead the city and its surrounding areas to rapidly form a cross-regional labor division and cooperation network centering around Yiwu's market, i.e., "Yiwu Business Circle", through specialized division of labor and industrial restructuring. This promotes the rapid growth of foreign trade in the region.

From a practical point of view, the development of Yiwu Small Commodity Market has promoted the formation of a cross-regional network of labor division and cooperation, i.e., "Yiwu Business Circle",

---

[10]See Sun Jie, Gu Kejian, Xu Tao: Competitive advantage, external economies and sustainable development of the markets in developed areas in China. *China Soft Science*, 2004, No. 10.

[11] A pair of concepts put forward by Hirschman of the USA: "Trickle down effect" and "polarization effect". Specifically, the positive impact of regional growth pole on the economically backward peripheral areas is called the trickle down effect, while its negative impact is called the polarization effect.

mainly from the following three aspects, which has also facilitated its functions. Firstly, the development of the small commodity market has greatly increased the number of participants in the labor division and cooperation network in the region. This is because the low-cost, "share-based" trading platform it provides has attracted large numbers of domestic and foreign operators to gather, thus prompting the manufacturers, wholesalers, and other business entities to actively establish close contacts with the market, and prompting the input of substantial commercial capital into the market transactions. With the expansion of transaction scale, the effect of increasing returns to scale becomes more pronounced, thereby attracting more operators to join the network, further refining the division of labor and deepening the cooperation. Secondly, the development of Yiwu Small Commodity Market has reduced the cost-per-transaction rate for all parties involved in the division of labor and cooperation across the regions. This enables them to trade by gathering within a particular area and using certain logistics distribution centers to match the communication network, thereby greatly lowering transportation costs. Because commodity price information is concentrated in Yiwu Small Commodity Market, both buyers and sellers can find transaction partners in a relatively short period of time, which reduces the transaction costs. The increase in the number of both trading parties offers a wider space for the choice of transaction partners. After several games, the acts that violate the market rules will be abandoned, thereby reducing the additional transaction costs caused by moral factors. Thirdly, the development of Yiwu Small Commodity Market has helped reduce the average cost for maintaining business relations among firms. This is because with the expansion of market size, the market-centered division of labor and cooperation continue to deepen, various economic entities' level of specialized production and sales increase, their mutual dependence enhances, and their cooperation intention becomes more apparent. With the increase in the number of transactions by all parties involved in the cross-regional division of labor and cooperation, the mutual understanding and trust between them are enhanced. Additionally, after multiple repeated games, the large-scale markets' potential binding power on the aforementioned parties to observe the market rules continue to strengthen, and the market trading environment is optimized, thereby significantly reducing the parties' risk protection expenditure originally spent for maintaining inter-firm business relations. In short, through the above three paths, Yiwu Small Commodity Market has increased the number of participants in the cross-regional labor division and cooperation network, cut the transaction costs after the division of labor, and improved the efficiency of labor division and coordination, so that the increase in overall benefits brought by cross-regional labor division and cooperation exceeds the rise of costs, thus promoting its formation and development.

To sum up, it is precisely the incomparable advantages of Yiwu Small Commodity Market in both scale and efficiency to other regions that have resulted in the formation of a cross-regional labor division and cooperation network centered around it—"Yiwu Business Circle".

Chapter **4**

"Yiwu Business Circle" Development Trend and Strategies

Yiwu Small Commodity Market's functions are a core and a hub for the growing "Yiwu Business Circle". Thus, for research on the development strategy of "Yiwu Business Circle", we must take the market as the starting point, the improvement of the market function as the main line, and the expansion of the market space and function extension as the direction. As the function and spatial scope of the small commodity market expand outward from inward, the development trend of "Yiwu Business Circle" includes three levels: firstly, it is the Yiwu market itself, namely the small commodity market and relevant industries, that continuously move to the high-end level; secondly, it is the regional level, namely where Yiwu shall strive to build itself into a business district in the central and western regions of Zhejiang, which is not only the result of regional economic division of labor, but also further enhances the need of a regional economic division of labor; thirdly, it is the international level, which is the inexorable trend for further development of the trading platform and stable trading relation of Yiwu Small Commodity Market all over the world. This chapter aims to explore the development strategy of "Yiwu Business Circle" around the above development trend.

High-end Market and "Yiwu Business Circle" Radiation Capability Extension

I

1. Price formation center

If Yiwu Small Commodity Market is compared to an enterprise, then the Yiwu market has basically realized the goal of being bigger and stronger by relying on the domestic market and has been expanding to the international market on the basis of the domestic market. Thus, it has established its status as one of the international small commodity trading centers. Therefore, unlike many enterprises that rely on the domestic market to attract foreign investment, the Yiwu market has been rising to the high end of the international market; price changes can directly or indirectly affect the prices of small commodities around the world. At present, although Yiwu Small Commodity Market still faces problems like similar product design and low quality, however, if there will be a batch of famous enterprises like Neoglory, Mengna, Lanswe, and NDL, they will influence through Yiwu Small

Commodity Market and may to some extent become a price maker. At that time, the small commodity market is not only a "Price Summary Center", but also will become the "Price Formation Center", so as to attract more famous enterprises to settle in and form a virtuous circle.

If the core competitiveness of first-class enterprises is the standard, then the first-class market must have the ability to set prices; only in this way, Yiwu Small Commodity Market can become the leader in similar domestic and foreign markets, and play a "barometer" role to the fluctuation of commodity prices in the whole country and even the world.

At the end of April 2006, the Ministry of Commerce began to issue and broadcast the "China Business Weather Forecast", the wholesale price index of consumer goods for daily use in Yiwu (referred to as the "Yiwu Index"). It was the only consumer goods wholesale index promoted in the "Yiwu Fair" in 2006. The "Yiwu Index" will regularly issue the "price index", "prosperity index", and other market real-time characteristics and trends of Yiwu Small Commodity Market at home and abroad. It can be predicted that it will be a China index that will affect worldwide small commodity wholesale, inventory, logistics, popularity, and especially the formation mechanism of the market price. Then, through the commodity price formation and guide mechanism of the "Yiwu Index", a sign of disturbance of Yiwu Small Commodity Market can affect the general merchandise price across the ocean just like a butterfly can flutter its wings over a flower in China and cause a hurricane in the Caribbean. It is expected that the establishment of the "Yiwu Index" will surely promote Yiwu Small Commodity Market to march toward the goal of the global small commodity price formation center.

2. Information release center

Since the late 1980s, the "scale + low price" advantage of Yiwu Small Commodity Market has attracted merchants from all over the country, and further promoted the super-conventional development of

Yiwu Small Commodity Market. In the 1990s, due to the further scale expansion of the market and the rise of personalized demand, a large explosion occurred regarding the amount of market supply and demand information, putting forward the serious challenge to the traditional transaction mode of cash, spot commodities, and scene. Thus, some experts believed that Yiwu's previous "cellular mode"—the market concentrated trade economy with more than 50,000 peddlers each year flying across the country like bees collecting market information (gather honey), and then "buying national goods and selling national goods", was already in deadly danger.[1] In the traditional marketing mode, each purchaser and supplier faced many customers and even customer bases, and when the number of buyers and suppliers exceeded a certain limit, the exchanges of information became chaotic. All over the country, all kinds of specialized markets spread, which not only divided up the market share, but also intended to replace Yiwu Small Commodity Market as the national small commodity distribution center. In such a situation, Yiwu Small Commodity Market has entered a relative adjustment period (1996–2000), there has been no significant increase in the market's business field, and the annual sales volume has even declined. The root cause lies in that the traditional market information interaction mode has failed to meet the market demand.

At the end of the last century and at the beginning of this century, the "digitization strategy" of Yiwu Small Commodity Market greatly expanded and promoted the function of market integration of production factors, and formed a modern market information interaction mode; the market has finally gotten rid of the predicament and stepped into the stage of internationalization (since 2002) and gradually formed the trade pattern of "buy global goods and sell global goods".

---

[1] See Wang Rulin: "Four major difficulties in Yiwu informatization" completely mistook the prescription for the wrong medicine, *Zhejiang Online News Network*, March 29, 2005.

Yiwu Small Commodity Market has gathered a large amount of consumption information, which is the main basis for manufacturers to decide what to produce and how much they produce, so as to drive manufacturers to continuously segment the market and improve products and industrial structure. In addition, manufacturers can promote their products and brands through the market so as to realize the interaction between consumers and producers throughout the market. The market will feed back product information, such as varieties, specifications, quality and price of products to the customers, then feed back the demand information of consumers to the manufacturers. Then, manufacturers will organize the production according to the merchants' orders, and pay merchants an "advertising fee" depending on such orders while merchants will charge consumers no more in addition to commodity prices. Compared with the way of promoting the enterprise brand by using large media advertising, this kind of face-to-face and centralized publicity is more interactive in the small commodity market. Compared with enterprises establishing their own marketing system and specialty stores, specialized markets have an almost unlimited number of consumers, and its low cost makes it almost a "free lunch", and is certainly more attractive to small and medium-sized businesses that can't afford to pay large advertising fees. Due to the growing "business circle" at the core of the market, more and more domestic and foreign manufacturers strive to use the influence of the market to promote themselves, consumers are willing to accept in a large market all kinds of different manufacturers' product information, thus forming a constantly expanding product information transmission channel.

In the future, with the construction and development of "Yiwu Business Circle", the move from "selling commodities" to "selling information" will become a major transformation and promotion of the function of Yiwu Small Commodity Market. The market has applied information technology to various areas of market circulation, becoming a "digital market"; more and more production operators will become practitioners for informatization, continuously mining the hidden wealth. In 2005, the city was carrying on broadband network transformation construction in stages to each transaction block of the small commodity market; the "China Commercial Port Network" has become the network exhibition center for more than 3,000 SEMs, integrating 19 categories of information resources of 150,000 varieties of Yiwu commodities, and established three versions, namely Chinese, English and Korean. It has fulfilled the service of being a "China Small Commodity Digital City", and built the online virtual market interactive with the real market, so as to let market operators have both a physical booth and online intangible market stalls at the same time, promoting the popularization and application of electronic commerce.

In the process of construction of "Yiwu Business Circle", based on the strong market information demand of upstream small and medium-sized production enterprises, the function of Yiwu Small Commodity Market has been expanded, transforming from the original function of "selling commodities" to both "selling information" and "selling commodities". This kind of transformation is the result of the overall market effect and is not artificially imposed. While maintaining vigorous commodity trading, the market will change from merely acting as an intermediary of commodity circulation to giving more play to the intermediary function of information flow and transmitting the manufacturer's product information to relevant enterprises and consumers through intermediary activities such as display. Because of the function of electronic ordering and information network system, the market plays an intermediary function through information transmission, and transmits the information of many consumers to the producers after collection and analysis. Manufacturers produce orders according to consumer demand information, and commodities can be transmitted to consumers through a more convenient path. In this process, many small and medium-sized enterprises which have

no ability to establish their own global marketing system have found an effective way to feed back and collect information with the help of the internationalization of information exchanges in Yiwu Small Commodity Market in order to achieve the goal of landing all over the country and even the world. The higher the quantity of information in the small commodity market, the stronger the function of this path; the stronger the function is, the more the information exchanges of both supply and demand sides are, with the two reinforcing each other, thus forming a virtuous circle. For example, in the toy trading area of Yiwu International Trade City, merchants and vendors signed a supply and sales order. A few minutes later, the millions of dollars' worth of wooden toy production order "flies" through the network to a toy factory in Yunhe Wooden Toy Industrial Zone and production is immediately organized, which was difficult to imagine in the past. More manufacturers have completed commodity trading in a short period of time through virtual market platforms such as "China Commercial Port Network" and "China Small Commodity Digital City". The improvement of efficiency due to informatization brings benefits to every link of the transaction. In fact, not only are small and medium-sized enterprises using the function of the market, but many large enterprises will also benefit from the information function of Yiwu Small Commodity Market.

Accelerating informatization is a strategic choice to improve market adaptability and international competitiveness of enterprises, and it is a powerful driving force to lead and transform traditional enterprises to achieve leapfrog development, and is also an important measure to enhance the core competitiveness of enterprises. Similarly, informatization of Yiwu Small Commodity Market mainly turns a modern market network into a new business format through large-scale application of network technology, and makes the function of the market experience revolutionary changes through enhancing information display and communication. This results in decreasing information costs, and realizing the high speed transmission and full sharing of information, for buyers and sellers to clinch a deal in the shortest path connection, and at the fastest speed. In a homogenous competitive market environment, the only way to stay ahead is to keep opponents from catching up. For Yiwu Small Commodity Market, the goal is to expand the margin of tangible market as far as possible, keep the advantage of low cost to the "freezing point" that peers can't bear; at the same time, the influence of "Yiwu Business Circle" is extended to the whole world by using the cross-regional division of labor collaboration network to construct the intangible market.

3. Logistics center

With the increasing improvement of transportation infrastructure, Yiwu has established export express passages to Shanghai Port and Ningbo Port by road, railway, air and sea, gradually making itself the transport hub of Central Zhejiang. The logistics infrastructure tends to be perfect, forming the Jiangdong freight market, Xuefeng road freight market, and Yiwu International Logistics Center.

However, to view from the requirements for construction and development of "Yiwu Business Circle", the development of Yiwu's logistics industry still has a large gap. Firstly, the informatization level is not high, the scale of enterprises is generally small, the technical equipment and management tools are relatively backward, the service network and information system is not yet sound, and there is a lack of a public platform with logistics resources. Secondly, the industry organization is not standardized, the number of transportation lines is large but the network is slow without sufficient communication between each other, reducing transportation efficiency. Thirdly, the service function is not sound, limited basically to transportation, warehousing, and distribution, and has not been expanded to early logistics planning. Fourthly, there is a lack of freight yard and the layout is unreasonable. Lastly, there is a professional personnel

shortage, a lack of a good training system, and the introduction of talent is difficult.

When the network information transaction in the market replaces or partially replaces the original spot transaction, and the direct communication between the merchant and the producer is realized, it will be very difficult for only one manufacturer to face tens of thousands of customers at home and abroad for the realization of commodity trade. Therefore, the innovation of market nature is needed through the construction of the logistics distribution center. The logistics distribution center has an effective distribution service radius, and beyond availability, other regional logistics centers or enterprises' network resources can be used. Similarly, local network resources can be used by other regional logistics centers and logistics enterprises to share resources. Yiwu has the world's largest wholesale market for small commodities, and is located in the connection part between the eastern and central regions of Zhejiang Province with transportation becoming more and more convenient. Establishing a distribution center by relying on the small commodity market is beneficial not only to the development of the small commodity market itself, but also to the development of the economy in the central and western regions of Zhejiang and even the whole Zhejiang Province. In this regard, the development of Yiwu's logistics industry is a natural extension of the product market in the distribution field and is matched with the small commodity market, which is a huge and competitive economic system. Intermingled with the development of the logistics industry and the market in Yiwu, the experience accumulated in marketing management, with a large number of management personnel providing rich management resources for construction of the logistics center, and constantly promoting informatization construction in recent years has provided a basic information platform as well (see Figure 4.1). For Yiwu, the comparative advantage of the integrated transaction management cost savings has become a reason to build a logistics center.

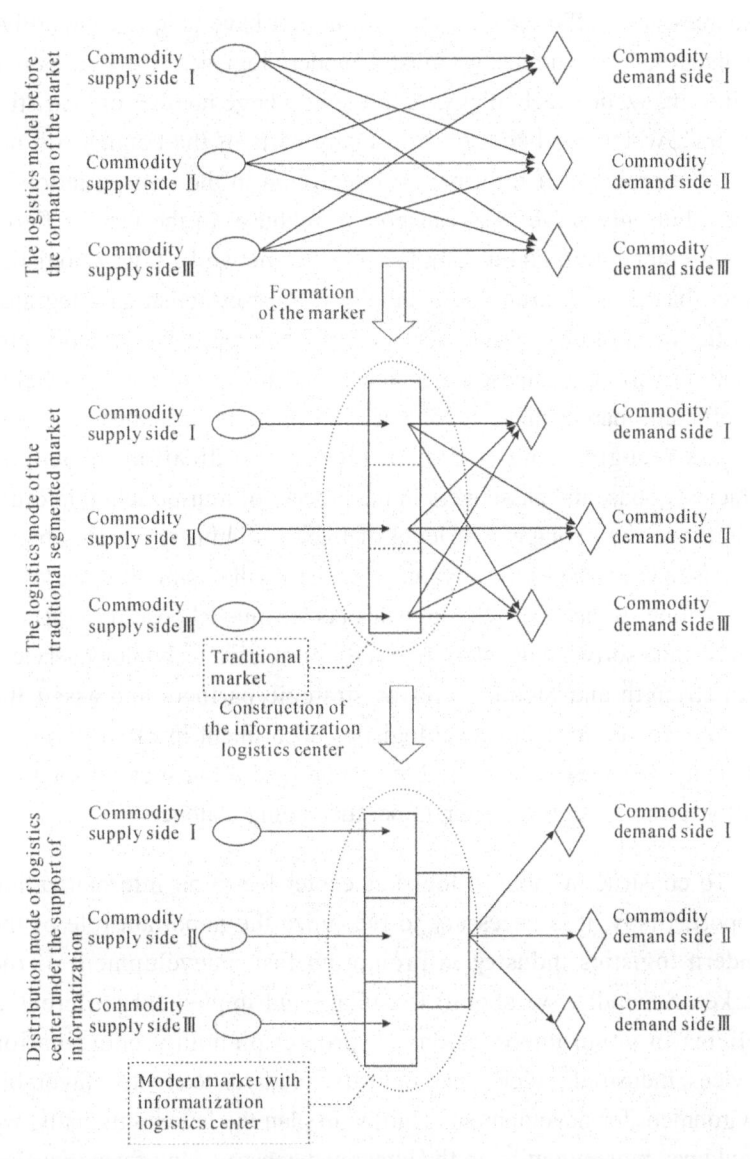

Figure 4.1: The change and comparison of logistics mode

As a transportation and storage distribution center, the land resources and traffic location of Yiwu do not have unique competitive advantages, so Yiwu must establish a modern logistics center supported by informatization technology. At present, a large number of "logistics centers", which are being built in many parts of the country, do not solve the problem of information integration in the transportation of goods, but only serve as a transport warehouse. In the face of fierce market competition and a complex logistics network, Yiwu's logistics center, based on information technology, must establish an integrated logistics management system that supports comprehensive development, adapts to various business types and operation modes while realizing the efficient management of logistics information, introduces business process reengineering and the effective coordination of people, vehicles, goods, and passengers in the process of transportation in order to improve the management level of logistics industry, creates better benefits, and enhances the advantage of the small commodity market in competition. In addition, the logistics center must choose providers of professional software development and information technology services with strength and technologies as strategic partners and assist the logistics center and enterprise logistics department in establishing an efficient warehouse, a distribution system, and a logistics information platform through collaboration rather than going it alone.

To construct a modern logistics center based on informatization support, firstly, it is necessary to recognize the important role of the modern logistics industry in promoting faster development of the market. Secondly, we should formulate and implement preferential policies in government guidance, project planning, coordination services, industrial policies, and industry standards to create a favorable environment for development. Thirdly, to plan the layout rationally, we should pay more attention to the integrated construction of warehousing facilities and transportation yard. Fourthly, efforts should be made to introduce leading enterprises in the logistics industry and build a logistics industry system combining large and small and medium enterprises (SMEs) to meet the logistics needs of various aspects and levels. Fifthly, it is required to speed up the informatization construction and utilize modern information technology, endeavor to build a regional and industry logistics public information platform, support enterprises to introduce talents, and improve its own ability by applying advanced technology and concept transformation. At present, we should pay more attention to the cultivation of third-party logistics enterprises, so as to change the mode of logistics operation mainly based on individual business households, and strive to realize the transformation of the consigned market to the modern logistics center.

II Transformation and Promotion of Regional Functions—Central Zhejiang Central Business District (CBD)

1. Construction of Central Zhejiang Central Business District (CBD) and "Central Zhejiang Megalopolis"

Yiwu Small Commodity Market is the core and hub of "Yiwu Business Circle", which requires Yiwu to undertake the important task of constructing the Business District for Central and Western Zhejiang, namely Central Zhejiang Central Business District (CBD) for short. The regional functions in Central Zhejiang Megalopolis are complementary to each other and subject to division of labor and the industries have their own characteristics and advantages, especially Yiwu, which has the world's largest small commodity market. The induced polarization effect of Yiwu Small Commodity Market makes the resources of Central Zhejiang Megalopolis and Central and Western Zhejiang and other relevant regions continuously flow into this region, promoting the prosperity of the small commodity market.

The prosperity of the market produces a radiation effect to output the raw material processing business and cultivate men of business and local start-up enterprises to drive the economic development of the surrounding counties, so as to make the counties and cities in Central Zhejiang, whether Yongkang or Dongyang with a developed economy or Wuyi or Pan'an with a less developed economy, establish a close economic connection with Yiwu, gradually constructing a regional division cooperation network with Yiwu Small Commodity Market as the core.

Superficially, Central Zhejiang Megalopolis is a collection of four large cities, namely urban Jinhua, Yiwu, Dongyang, Yongkang, and Lanxi, and small cities such as Pujiang, Wuyi, and Pan'an, but from the perspective of the essence and connotation of it, as a new urban form, Central Zhejiang Megalopolis is not natural state distribution of urban geography, but a new form of productivity layout taking industry as the tie. It is an organic whole based on an industry collaboration network and a specific distribution form of all kinds of resources in the region, with new features and functions different from the simple sum of cities. Its internal organic connection is one of the basic features of Central Zhejiang Megalopolis. Therefore, the overall function of Central Zhejiang Megalopolis has far exceeded the function of Jinhua, Yiwu, and other individual cities. At present, any city of Central Zhejiang Megalopolis is not fully functional as the core city. It can only form an independent urban system that can be kept abreast of it in the competition of Hangzhou Bay Cluster and Coastal Urban Agglomeration of Wenzhou as a functional unit. In Central Zhejiang Megalopolis, Jinhua City hosts the region's political, economic, cultural, science, and education centers and is the second major information center of Zhejiang. Yiwu, Yongkang, and Dongyang have become the important economic growth poles in the region, relying on the small commodity market, hardware market, and construction industry. Lanxi is the old industry base and main energy supply city for Central Zhejiang and small cities such as Pujiang, Wuyi, and Pan'an which have great potential in the development of special agriculture and leisure tourism. At the same time, it is not only necessary to set up an industry system of organic connection within Central Zhejiang Megalopolis, but also to protect the natural environment and establish the ecological compensation mechanism according to the natural, economic, and social foundation of this region so as to realize the matching and balance of a regional ecological and economic system. Therefore, in the construction and development process of Central Zhejiang Megalopolis, it is necessary to take the total amount and utilization of natural resources, population growth, and the structure and characteristics of labor resources into account in the broader context so that it is possible to grasp the law of socio-economic development in the region from the macro perspective, system, and vision while making Central Zhejiang Megalopolis have a relatively stable self-regulation ability. Natural stability is a good barrier to external disturbance, and has a good recovery ability after its own coordinated development has been broken. Facing the change of objective factors, it has the advantages of adapting to its own development trend and making active and effective reaction, thus providing a powerful guarantee for the sustainable development of Central Zhejiang Megalopolis and the whole area.

In recent years, inside Central Zhejiang Megalopolis, a development trend of strategic cooperation, resource sharing, and industrial interaction among different cities has shown good momentum and produced great economic and social benefits. The whole megalopolis' infrastructure continues to improve, and the "Half Hour Economic Circle" of cities, counties, and districts of Central Zhejiang Megalopolis has initially taken shape with the basic realization of rapid development of external traffic, convenient regional traffic, and urban and rural traffic connections. Economic complementation and mutual promotion among cities, counties, and districts inside Central Zhejiang Megalopolis are becoming more and more obvious. For example, the purified Shafan water in Wucheng District of Jinhua flows into Jindong District Golden Triangle Development Zone, which has been troubled by water for years; 50 million cubic meters of Dongyang Hengjin reservoir water per year injects "happy water" for Yiwu; Yiwu people have sent a large batch of foreign merchants to Yongkang Hardware Expo and Yongkang provides skilled workers for Yiwu which is suffering from "Technical Worker Shortage"; Pujiang County has moved "Crystal Festival" to Yiwu; Wuyi and Pan'an have obtained a batch of orders from adjacent cities and counties like Yiwu and Yongkang; Jinhua has built the Jinpan Development Zone on the outskirts of the city to become a window open to the outside world and a new economic growth point; Jinhua has accelerated the expansion of the city and solved the problem of unemployment for thousands of residents.[2] In short, due to the rapid rise of Central Zhejiang Megalopolis and the cooperation, sharing and interaction between the regions, it has given full play to the overall advantages of Central Zhejiang Megalopolis, and promoted the overall prosperity of the megalopolis and the cross-leap development in Central and Western Zhejiang.

The construction and development of Central Zhejiang Megalopolis provides a new idea for the development of Yiwu Small Commodity Market and "Yiwu Business Circle". From the point of view of the regional division of labor collaboration, Yiwu, with its realistic advantage in business and commerce, has the ability to integrate the business activities of Central Zhejiang. The gathering of such business activities deepens the division of labor collaboration between Yiwu and other counties and cities of Central Zhejiang, forming a fixed layer at the core of Yiwu in Central Zhejiang. Such a fixed layer shares the partial function of Yiwu, strengthens and improves the agglomeration and radiation function of "Yiwu Business Circle" to the whole area, which is conducive for "Yiwu Business Circle" to achieve a higher level of development. Thus, the construction of Central Zhejiang Central Business District in Yiwu not only strengthens its own commercial function but is also an effective development path for promoting regional industrial transformation and

---

[2] See Xu Xiaoen: Resources sharing in depth, the win–win mechanism of Central Zhejiang Megalopolis develop towards maturity. *Zhejiang Daily*, 2006-01-06.

improvement of the central and western regions of Zhejiang by relying on the fixed layer of "Yiwu Business Circle".

2. Connotations of Central Zhejiang CBD

2.1 Concepts and expansion of CBD

We will take the function elements of "Central Business District" as the core connotation in this chapter and extend the area as a form of representation so as to promote the concept of CBD from the urban level to the regional level. Central Zhejiang CBD, as we referred to it, also has the functions of business activities, financial services, information consulting, economic radiation, and other functions of the central business district in traditional theory. From the point of view of the building process and formation mechanism, the two are similar, which can be discussed as the same thing. The existing theory can be used to explain the emergence and development of Central Zhejiang CBD to a certain extent. However, it is different from the relatively narrow urban area attribute of the traditional business center. The concept of Central Zhejiang CBD proposed by us makes necessary expansion of the composition of CBD in the regional space according to the cross-regional division of labor collaboration network of "Yiwu Business Circle". The traditional concept of the central business district emphasizes the concentration, communication, and combination of people, logistics, capital flow, and information flow in a particular area of the city, while Central Zhejiang CBD emphasizes the convergence and integration of manpower, logistics, capital flow, and information flow in the urban area of Yiwu, which is the core economy in the economic regions included in and affected by "Yiwu Business Circle". Our expansion of the CBD concept is based on the following considerations: (1) The appearance of a central business district is due to the development of a city or regional economy, which needs a relatively concentrated core area to condense the economic energy and reduce the commercial cost. In the central and western regions of Zhejiang, given the ever-larger and more complex exchanges of goods, resources, and information resulting from the construction of Central Zhejiang Megalopolis and development of modern economy, certain requirements for construction of a CBD have been proposed. In particular, Yiwu's urban area, as a core area of "Yiwu Business Circle", undertakes the function of integrating the business information of the whole business circle, and the development of "Yiwu Business Circle" needs a relatively concentrated area to deal with business information. In Central and Western Zhejiang, a metropolis like Hangzhou, Ningbo, or Wenzhou has yet to be formed. Therefore, the existing model of establishing a CBD within metropolitan areas in the world is obviously not suitable for Central and Western Zhejiang. It is necessary to break through the definition and mode of the traditional central business district and expand the definition of central business district on the basis of the actual demand brought by the development of the regional economy. (2) In Central Zhejiang, the trend of taking "Jinhua–Yiwu" as the main axis of development is increasingly obvious. The two most important cities fully play their respective advantages, carry on the strong points, counteract the weaknesses, and support each other to make the Yiwu Business District of Central Zhejiang become possible. (3) Looking at the existing central business districts in the world, the most important content in a CBD is economic control, and Yiwu is the first choice to build Central Zhejiang CBD because of its economic control and ability to influence. (4) From the current situation in Central Zhejiang, Jinhua, considering its position as the center of politics, culture, science, and education, has the following tasks: firstly, it shall continue to strengthen the position and function of the abovementioned "four centers" and make the inner core of Central Zhejiang Megalopolis become stronger; secondly, it shall enhance division of labor collaboration and industry linkage with surrounding developed cities and help surrounding less developed counties and cities establish their own development strategies and leading industries to build "Greater Jinhua" together. Yiwu, as a county city under the jurisdiction of Jinhua City, has the most abundant commercial resources,

and has formed its own unique development path and advantages. If it can be built into a Central Zhejiang CBD, it will greatly enhance the influence of "Greater Jinhua". (5) From the perspective of the international experience, many metropolises in the world have the trend of making the CBD geographically deviated from the centers of politics, culture, etc., and instead formed multi-center and networked modes. For example, in Paris, with the construction of La Défense, the city's central business district has actually become independent from the old urban area and Shanghai's business district is a combination of the traditional business district in Puxi and the e-commerce center in Lujiazui, Pudong (E-CBD), which complement each other and are both indispensable. As a result, taking into consideration the future trend of the megalopolis' construction, we will not restrict or exclude any possibilities regarding the direction of the diverse network development of a regional expansion of the CBD.

2.2 Formation mechanism of Central Zhejiang CBD

The CBD follows certain rules in the evolution of function and space. From the perspective of formation dynamics for the CBD, it may experience three kinds of evolution mechanisms in the process of construction and development: the spontaneous growth mechanism, the mandatory transformation mechanism, and the adaptive intervention mechanism.

2.2.1 Spontaneous growth mechanism

Most CBDs follow the law of market economy in the embryonic stage of growth in order to develop spontaneously and orderly, and have their inner and potential elasticity. Urban traffic, location, religion, and politics are the intrinsic motivations of this spontaneous growth. Under the premise of social and economic stability, the CBD based on this mechanism has strong stability, its space develops in the extended plane form, and the relationship with the whole city is natural and harmonious. Under the action of this mechanism, the development of CBD is slow and continuous.

2.2.2 Mandatory transformation mechanism

Under the circumstances of drastic changes in society (such as major decision-making changes, wars, major disasters, etc.), a CBD will develop under a mechanism dominated by mandatory transformation. A CBD may be forced to move regionally or make an internal structural adjustment under the pressure of some strong external force. For example, after our country made the important decision to develop the Pudong New Area, the financial and trade center of Shanghai was built in the Lujiazui area, opposite to the Bund of Shanghai, which made the CBD of Shanghai jump in space. Under the mandatory transformation mechanism, the development of the center of an urban business district appears as a passive mutation status.

2.2.3 Adaptive intervention mechanism

This is the CBD development mechanism between spontaneous growth mechanism and mandatory transformation mechanism. This kind of mechanism means that due to the influence of all kinds of development powers, the development of the city has exceeded a certain limit, but the spontaneous growth mechanism does not easily realize the corresponding transformation of the CBD at this time. Therefore, we must adjust the construction of the CBD through scientific intervention measures to meet the requirements of urban development. The main difference between the adaptive mechanism and the mandatory transformation mechanism lies in the degree of intervention. In general, the implementation of this mechanism is based on the existing urban business agglomeration of government departments, and actively cooperating with relevant policies to facilitate the formation of business district in the short term. The adaptive intervention mechanism makes the CBD not only inherit the history of the city style and context, but also makes improvements and innovations in the space forms, functions, contents, etc., according to the development momentum of the urban economy. At present, the development mechanism is commonly used in the construction of the CBD in major cities of each country over the world.

From the perspective of international experience, a simple mandatory or spontaneous mode does not exist. This is because although the business and administrative offices can be separated, modern business, particularly business centers involved in international business for most of the major initiatives, are difficult to complete and be independent from the government; at the same time, the construction of the business center must be influenced by the urban planning, the tax policy, and so on. Jinhua City Government and Yiwu City Government have played a crucial role in the cultivation and construction of Yiwu Small Commodity Market. In the current scenario and for the future of Central Zhejiang CBD, it must also conduct active and effective adaptive intervention so as to accelerate the process of constructing Central Zhejiang CBD, to strengthen its agglomeration and radiation function. Due to the original development lag, the urban infrastructure of Yiwu is in a large-scale construction period. Without proper government intervention, the disorder of urban construction is highly likely to exist. Therefore, whether from the view of the international experience or the actual situation, the most likely ideal way for Yiwu to build Central Zhejiang CBD is to adopt the adaptive intervention mechanism. Yiwu is not likely to be supported by state level policy like Shanghai Pudong to mandatorily build a flat land into a CBD within a short period of time, and its own financial capacity is insufficient to support the huge amount of money needed for the construction of the CBD infrastructure; the period of spontaneous formation of the CBD is too long and today, regional competition is very fierce. Once the opportunity is missed, it will have a negative impact on the economic and social development of all the Central Zhejiang regions and even lead to the gradual decline of "Yiwu Business Circle", which is moving towards maturity. Therefore, on the basis of Yiwu Small Commodity Market with the International Trade City as the core, supplemented by policy support after about 10 years' efforts, it's absolutely necessary and possible to build Yiwu's main urban area initially into the Central Business District of Central Zhejiang.

2.3 Connotations of Central Zhejiang CBD

The proposal of the concept of the "Central Zhejiang CBD" better reveals the close relationship between co-existence and complementarity among cities, counties, and districts of Central and Western Zhejiang: Yiwu Small Commodity Market as the core to the surrounding areas provides huge business support. Other surrounding areas, relying on the market, develop manufacturing or other special advantage industries based on division of labor so as to form the cross-regional collaboration network at the core of Yiwu Small Commodity Market in Central and Western Zhejiang. Accordingly, the Central Business District of Central Zhejiang can be understood as this: the concentrated business district that serves the entire Central Zhejiang Megalopolis and Central and Western Zhejiang, taking Yiwu's main urban area as the main area, market leadership and government support as the main power, business office, science and technology innovation, finance, insurance, exhibitions, trade, modern logistics, law consulting, and other modern service industries and the headquarters economy as the main formats, and information processing of Yiwu Small Commodity Market as the main content. We promote the concept of Central Zhejiang CBD to the regional level because at present the central and western regions of Zhejiang lack a metropolis and the economic structure and special status of Yiwu's main urban area make it possible to give play to the main functions of a CBD. Our philosophy is to grasp the regional and international development trend of the business district service scope, and determine the location and regional scope of the business district with the practical function rather than simply and mechanically limiting the business district to a geographical area of a large city. Of course, the excessively dispersed CBD area will inevitably lead to the decrease of business efficiency, and the development of the business district itself requires a certain degree of concentration. Therefore, taking the International Trade City as the core, about 100 square kilometers of Yiwu's urban area will be the main area of Central Zhejiang CBD, which is not only beneficial to give full play to its unique popularity,

business, and capital advantage, but also can be well combined with the existing Yiwu business facilities, which can basically meet the relevant business district index required.[3] We will explain the relevant statements above with further connotations as follows:

"Taking the business office, technological innovation, finance, insurance, exhibitions, business trade, modern logistics, legal consulting, other modern services, and headquarters economy as the main formats": the business district is the product of the modern economy. It is a centralized place of company headquarters or regional headquarters, as well as banks, insurance companies, R&D centers, accounting firms, intermediary organizations, and so on. Most of these institutions are engaged in the modern service industry, especially producer services. In addition to serving the local people's life, they mainly provide production services for mutual coordination and communication for fields like research, development, production, and sales after elaborating the division of labor under the modern production conditions. Enterprises that specifically produce material products will move from the business district to the periphery, thus realizing the agglomeration of the modern service industry in the core area; the traditional tertiary industries will remain partially in the core region, but they are not the subject of the business district, and part of the traditional tertiary industries will be required to be upgraded or eliminated due to failing to adapt to the requirement of modern economic development.

"Taking information processing of Yiwu Small Commodity Market as the main content": in Yiwu, it is necessary to firmly establish the core position of the small commodity market, which is the biggest advantage for Yiwu to stand out in Zhejiang, even the whole country, and is the

---

[3]Mainly Murphy's index, including: Central Business Height Index, CBHI for short, which means total central business district building area/total building base area; Central Business Intensity Index, CBII for short, which means total area of construction area of the central business area/total building area.

foundation for constructing Central Zhejiang CBD. Moreover, almost all business activities in Yiwu are centered on the small commodity market, compared with the business districts in other big cities. At this level, Yiwu Small Commodity Market is also the supporter and carrier of Central Zhejiang CBD. The traditional specialized market mainly deals with the sale of goods. In the process of face-to-face traditional trading, there is not much room for business activities. Compared with the limited number of goods, the amount of information is almost unlimited. Therefore, once the function of the small commodity market is changed from simple commodity trading to commodity trading and information exchanges, the explosion of information will provide huge space for the increase of business activities, so as to provide substantive contents for the construction of a business district. In today's small commodity market, commodity trading is only one of the many economic activities that take place in search of commodity information, negotiation of trade, logistics distribution, financial insurance, legal advice, and so on. Thus, the construction of Central Zhejiang CBD must seize the core of information processing in the small commodity market. At this point, the future development direction of Yiwu's main city is not only Central Zhejiang CBD, but also the business district of the whole "Yiwu Business Circle", and its function will be radiated to the whole country and even the whole world.

"Taking market leadership and government support as the main power": business activities are first and foremost market behaviors. Therefore, the construction of Central Zhejiang CBD must be dominated by the market and give full play to the role of enterprises, especially large and medium-sized private enterprises, encourage them to change the mode of production for specialized division of labor, to separate the design, research and development, and sales from the specific production links in the region. It must encourage them to set up headquarters or an office within the business district to continuously extend the value chain through the supporting services in the business district. The construction of the business district cannot be separated from the construction of office buildings, network facilities, water, and electricity infrastructure, etc. Without scientific planning, it is difficult to imagine. Therefore, the government must strengthen guidance, actively participate, and conduct scientific planning in the process of building a business district. And given the growing regional influence and international influence of Yiwu Small Commodity Market, business dependence on government affairs will be further enhanced, so the government support to the construction and development of the business district plays a vital role. "Market leadership and government support" is not only the compliance of economic law, but also the natural selection of the adaptive intervention mechanism.

"Serving the entire Central Zhejiang Megalopolis and Central and Western Zhejiang": a business district must have certain regional influence, even international influence. Given its important status in Central Zhejiang Megalopolis and "Yiwu Business Circle", Yiwu is duty-bound to take on the task of serving the construction and development of Central Zhejiang Megalopolis and Central and Western Zhejiang with its special business district function. Without such positioning, it is bound to limit its development scale and development direction, and it is really difficult to build Central Zhejiang CBD. Therefore, Yiwu must seize the industry chain, taking the market as the core, expand the industrial links, improve the level of industry, constantly output its influence to Central and Western Zhejiang and other cities in "Yiwu Business Circle", and expand their information, business consulting, and other functions. This play of the functions must be based on modern communication technology, greatly improve the efficiency of the business offices' affairs and their decisions to attract more corporate headquarters and other agencies to settle in, and continuously enhance the capacity and its sphere of influence.

3. Conditions for Yiwu to build Central Zhejiang CBD

Because of long-term development and government's active guidance, Yiwu has created relatively significant advantages in the economy, society, location, transportation, policies, and so on compared to other cities of Central Zhejiang Megalopolis regarding construction of Central Zhejiang CBD.

3.1 Overall economic advantages

Based on the analysis of the driving effect of the core cities in Zhejiang Province on the three economic zones, it can be seen that the core positions of the core cities in Northern Zhejiang, Eastern Zhejiang, and Southern Zhejiang are similar to those of Hangzhou, Ningbo, and Wenzhou. Yiwu has become the most economically intensive and most popular city in the central and western regions of Zhejiang in terms of most business activities.

3.1.1 Comparison of three economic zones

At present, the Hangzhou Bay Economic Zone is the region with the strongest development foundation and the highest degree of economic integration in Zhejiang province, which determines that it will bear the brunt of the challenge in the transformation of the economic growth mode.

The Wenzhou–Taizhou Coastal Economic Zone has experienced the track of economic growth decline. An extensive endogenous economic growth mode and "intergenerational lock" in the industrial structure adjustment once became the restraining factor for the sustainable economic growth of the Wenzhou–Taizhou Coastal Economic Zone. It is dominated by a labor-intensive processing industry with a great economic endogenous nature, but the core competitiveness based on the independent innovation ability and its own brand is weak. The economy declined at a time when the country strictly controlled the macro policy influence of land use, tightening credit and competition at home and abroad. This means that the Wenzhou–Taizhou Coastal Economic Zone is at the critical moment for the transformation of economic growth as the Hangzhou

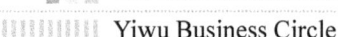

Bay Economic Zone and needs to attract a large number of advanced technologies, management, ideas, and capitals of developed countries and promote the comparative advantages that rely on low cost into the competitive advantages that rely on knowledge as soon as possible through being able to "attract foreign capital through private enterprises and combine private enterprises and foreign capitals".

The Central and Western Zhejiang, comprising by Jinhua, Quzhou, and Lishui, is the Inland Economic Zone, which started the process of economic integration late and is one of the loosest economic links in the three economic circles. In contrast to the other two economic zones, most of the county and urban areas of the Inland Economic Zone need to address the pending core issue for regional economic development: how to establish and implement the local practical development strategy of Yiwu and avoid the detours passed by other areas? In face of the increasingly competitive situation of the regional economy, municipalities, counties, districts, and the relevant aspects of the Inland Economic Zone have increasingly understood the great significance of promoting resource integration in the Inland Economic Zone and taken action actively. For example, discussions on theories of coordinated development of the Inland Economic Zone are increasingly rich and transport integration in the Inland Economic Zone has begun to be implemented. Especially, guided by the major decisions made by the Provincial Committee of the CPC and the Provincial Government such as construction of Central Zhejiang Megalopolis and taking the new road of urbanization, discussion on the economic and social development strategy of the Inland Economic Zone is being vigorously developed, and it presents the momentum of the two-way positive interaction between practice exploration and theoretical research.

3.1.2 Core city comparison

Hangzhou is the core city of the Hangzhou Bay Economic Zone and is Zhejiang Province's political, economic, and cultural center. Its GDP, added value of the second industry and tertiary industry, total social fixed assets investment, total retail sales of social consumer goods, total value of import and export, and the actual use of foreign capital are in first place among the cities of the three categories of economic zones in Zhejiang, showing strong economic strength and driving force for the economic zone. Ningbo, as another core city of Hangzhou Bay Economic Zone, promoted by the development strategy of "Flourish City with Port" and "Five Linkage", has achieved great progress in port development, the rise of harbor industry, and elaborated international trading platform and played a leading role in opening to the outside world and economic development in Zhejiang.[4]

Wenzhou is the core city of the Wenzhou–Taizhou Coastal Economic Zone and its economy is in a steady and rapid development period with a prominent leading position in the industrial economy. The per capita GDP is the highest among the cities in the region. Regional GDP, exports, and other indicators are not inferior to Hangzhou–Ningbo; although the city's foreign trade exports are affected by international trade friction and export product structure fluctuations, as a whole they have maintained a relatively rapid growth momentum. It is the fastest-growing part of the three major needs. At present, the focus of Wenzhou's economy has been transformed from "the expansion of quantity" to "industry promotion" and investment. In general, it shows strong competitiveness.

In Central and Western Zhejiang, the development trend prospect for the two adjacent cities Jinhua and Yiwu is promising. In terms of industry, Jinhua's industrial economy is growing faster, while Yiwu's trade and service industries are more developed. But from the perspectives of

---

[4]See Lu Lijun, Yang Haijun: *Study on the Construction of Ocean Ningbo—A Powerful City of Marine Economy*. Beijing: China Economic Press, 2005, pp. 222–226.

main economic indicators like GDP, per capita GDP, total investment in fixed assets, the total retail sales of social consumer goods, total imports and exports, and the actual use of foreign capital, Jinhua and Yiwu are not as good as Hangzhou and Ningbo, and are also slightly weaker than Wenzhou.

Although the development of the Inland Economic Zone started relatively late, it is possible to make a stronger late-mover advantage if we can make more reasonable strategic choices from now on. The material basis of this late-mover advantage is firstly, the further development of Yiwu Small Commodity Market; secondly, it is the development of manufacturing along Jinhua, Quzhou, and Lishui highways and Zhejiang–Jiangxi railway. Generally speaking, manufacturing is the main driving force for economic development. Compared with the two large coastal economic zones, the Inland Economic Zone is at a disadvantage in the development of advanced manufacturing, but its development of manufacturing is promoted thanks to the driving effect of Yiwu Small Commodity Market, taking a different path from the traditional development mode. In this sense, Yiwu Small Commodity Market is the biggest advantage of the Inland Economic Zone. If Yiwu achieves the goal of becoming the Central Zhejiang CBD, it means that the economic development in the central and western regions of Zhejiang has taken a new step, which has become a new growth point in Zhejiang's economy, making significant changes to the contrast between the Inland Economic Zone and other economic zones. Therefore, relying on the market to promote the business and trade service industry, and then drive the development of the manufacturing industry, is the breakthrough point and key point for obtaining the late-mover advantages by the Inland Economic Zone.

3.2 Industry support advantages

In the construction theory of a business district, the urban location theory of "central ground" believes that the city and the surrounding area are a cooperative symbiotic system, which is the true portrayal of the cooperative relationship between Yiwu and other counties and cities in Central and Western Zhejiang: Yiwu provides huge business support to the surrounding areas at the core of the small commodity market and other surrounding areas rely on market division to develop the manufacturing industry and promote development of Yiwu Small Commodity Market so as to form the cross-regional division of labor collaboration network at the core of the market. At present, when the commercial and trade circulation industry that plays a leading role continues to develop in Yiwu, modern service industries like finance, exhibition, insurance, tourism, culture, information, and real estate are increasingly developed, Yiwu has became the third largest logistics center in Zhejiang Province after Ningbo and Hangzhou; in turn, the development of the supporting service industry has led to a more prosperous manufacturing industry and a manufacturing industry that supports the development of the market so as to spontaneously form the supporting modern service industry chain that matches the consulting service industry, taking the domestic and foreign large companies or agents as the core and being guaranteed by the financial insurance enterprises. All of these provide strong support for the construction of Central Zhejiang CBD in Yiwu. Based on the location advantage and the characteristics of the industry layout, according to the principle of "high starting point, high standard, high speed, high benefit", Yiwu has planned two industrial belts, namely Northeast Yiwu and Southwest Yiwu, covering an area of over 200 square kilometers. The northeast industrial belt focuses on developing high-tech and competitive industries such as export products processing, clothing, knitting, and printing; the southwest industrial belt will build a modern and international manufacturing base with international competitiveness that takes small commodity manufacturing as the core and matches service industries like logistics distribution and technology research and development.

3.3 Hardware facility advantages

Firstly, it is transportation. Yiwu City, guided by the construction of big traffic and promoting the great development, has made remarkable achievements in improving transportation infrastructure and developing the transportation market, and is becoming one of the traffic hubs in Central Zhejiang. The highways radiate in all directions and Yiwu has formed a "ten minute traffic circle" at the city level. Zhejiang–Jiangxi Railway Multi-track passes 42 kilometers through Yiwu and is the national railway artery. At the same time, Yiwu Railway Station has been newly upgraded to the first-grade station, and its size and facilities are top-class in the county (city). There are three departure trains and over 110 trains passing by and stopping at the station. 4C Class Civil Aviation Yiwu Airport is the second county (city)-level medium-sized airport in the nation and more than 10 air routes to Guangzhou, Beijing, Shenzhen, Shantou, Fuzhou, Xiamen, Nanjing, Zhengzhou, and other cities have been in service. At present, the city has formed a far-radiating, long-range, efficient, and convenient three-dimensional transportation network which is basically consistent with the allocation of productive forces and the source density of passenger traffic, providing favorable conditions for the construction of Central Zhejiang CBD.

Secondly, it is post and telecommunications. Yiwu's post and telecommunications industry has made "super-conventional and leap-type" development. 24 postal establishments and more than 60 integrated postal service kiosks have been set up to build a convenient postal service network. In particular, brilliant achievements have been made in the construction of "digital Yiwu". The country's first county-level Internet node, the first broadband education network in the country, the clearest "China Commercial Port Network" e-commerce platform in domestic business model, the first rural optical fiber access network in the province, the first township-level TV conference call network in the province, and the second "telephone city" in the province have been built.

Thirdly, it is commercial facility. The newly built International Trade City will have broadband access. A large number of hotels, business office buildings, modern residential areas, and lots of places of communication are also distributed in this region and surrounding areas, forming a good business environment. Yindu Hotel is the first four-star city business hotel in Central Zhejiang, located in the bustling business district, and sets up a new model of luxury hotel with its rich, elegant, and complete hardware facilities, perfect services, and high standard management. Kaixin Grand Hotel is a standard four-star international business hotel located in the 21st century business district, with convenient transportation, and all guest rooms are equipped with computers and access to the Internet through optical fiber to provide a convenient business service space. Business districts, shopping centers, and multi-functional conference rooms are also available and fully functional. The four-star Ocean hotel located near the International Trade City, and the four-star Jindu Hotel and Shandu Business Hotel near the municipal government and Xiuhu Square provide very convenient conditions for the reception of domestic and foreign merchants.

Fourthly, it is other facilities in the city. Yiwu will construct a batch of city landmarks such as the Central Business District, Xiuhu Square, and Meihu Convention and Exhibition Sports Center at the core of the International Trade City through key engineering projects, forming unique urban individuality of the commercial city. To speed up construction of the urban traffic network, it has completed the five vertical and five horizontal urban main roads and express routes from the central urban area to several central towns. In order to strengthen the construction of urban greening and beautification, and starting from the old city reconstruction, namely the construction of Xiuhu Square, a 13-kilometer-long riverside corridor has been developed. The lighting project of "one corridor, three roads, and six bridges" has been carried out to improve the city image. In succession, the second water plant and water diversion project of Badu Reservoir were completed, and 200 million Yuan was paid for the purchase of nearly 50 million tons of water rights per year from Dongyang Hengfan Reservoir. At present, the city's daily water supply capacity is up to 150,000 tons, ensuring the production of water to the city, and electricity supply is increasing by more than 27% annually, which basically meets the needs of social and economic development. Through "three wastes" discharge control, the urban household garbage disposal rate and smoke control area coverage both reached 100%, with the air quality of urban residential area up to the secondary standard. With the processing capacity of 70,000 tons of sewage treatment works, it undertakes treatment of urban industrial and domestic sewage, and plays a positive role in the improvement of urban environment quality and the promotion of the sustainable development of Yiwu. In September 2006, it has passed the inspection and acceptance check for the national environmental protection model city and received praise from the relevant national departments.

3.4 Soft environment advantages

Compared with hardware, the soft environment is untouchable, but ubiquitous. Thus, it plays a greater positive role in the construction and development of Central Zhejiang CBD.

3.4.1 A business culture that combines tradition with modernity

The motivational force of the regional economy is a regional culture that has formed the unique business culture based on the combination of traditional business and modern trade, which is the intrinsic motivation for Yiwu to become the world-famous small commodity city. Traditional commercial culture, combined with modern business senses and concepts, makes Yiwu Small Commodity Market and its merchants go out of the country and to the world. The tolerance of the people of Yiwu is evident from the policies and attitude towards outsiders. Taking "Neoglory" (Holding) Group as an example, its 5,300 employees come from 23 provinces and cities, 14 ethnic groups, and less than 1% are real Yiwu people. Even if the people in Zhejiang are counted, "locals" still account for less than 10%. The integrity of Yiwu people is more manifested in cooperation and benign competition between businessmen. They believe in win–win situations and avoid price wars. It is not hard to imagine that for small commodities with such low technology content and high labor intensity, if there is price war from the start, it is impossible to become bigger and stronger.

3.4.2 Strong support from the superior leadership and the surrounding counties and cities

The relevant departments of the Central Government, as well as the Zhejiang Provincial Party Committee and Government, the Jinhua Municipal Party Committee, and the successive leaders of the Municipal Government, have paid great attention to the construction of Yiwu Small Commodity Market and the economic and social development of the city, which is the most important support conditions for constructing Central Zhejiang CBD. Under the loving care and guidance of superior leadership, in recent years, Yiwu city leaders pay more attention to reducing business costs, optimizing the economic environment, and strengthening regional cooperation to make Yiwu Small Commodity Market better serve the economic development of the surrounding counties. The surrounding area has been increasing the recognition of the small commodity market, and many cities, counties, and districts have adopted "keep in line with Yiwu" and "integrate into Yiwu" as an important development strategy.

3.4.3 A loose policy environment

In recent years, many specialized markets that flourished for a while have declined and even disappeared, but Yiwu Small Commodity Market has kept its lasting advantages. One decisive reason is the open and loose policy environment provided by the Yiwu Party Committee and the Government, and one of the most distinct symbols was the overall development strategy of "Four Permits" and "Flourish Business and Build County" proposed in 1982 and 1984, respectively. More importantly, in the following successive party committee, government leaders have kept along the path of "Flourish

Business and Build County (City)" for more than 30 years, and can put forward and implement the focus of the overall development strategy and target according to the actual situation of different periods. In 2002, the CPC Municipal Committee and Municipal Government leaders put forward the direction of the market internationalization. After several years of efforts, the latest "version" of Yiwu Small Commodity Market, namely the "International Trade City" with modern equipment and new transaction mode sprang up, marking the transition from a traditional specialized market to a modern wholesale and trade market. Yiwu government organizations at all levels regularly solicit opinions and suggestions from foreign merchants to improve examination and approval efficiency, improve service level, and enhance the investment environment so as to become the first choice for investment in Central and Western Zhejiang for well-known enterprises at home and abroad, which have accelerated the internationalization of the economy and laid a good foundation for the early stage development and later development of the central business district.

4. Framework of "Central Zhejiang CBD"

The characteristics of the business district are contained in a variety of contents and forms, and there are historical, traditional, ethnic, local, new, and modern characteristics. For Central Zhejiang CBD, it shall not only fully consider the city's own characteristics but also pay more attention to the division of labor collaboration with surrounding areas so as to give play to its radiating and driving effect in the economic development of Central and Western Zhejiang. For constructing Central Zhejiang CBD, Yiwu must be closely tied to the International Trade City, and other small commodity markets. This is because the current business activities of Yiwu are mainly transactions of small commodities. It can be predicted that the development of business activities such as finance, insurance, information, and consulting is also on the premise of the constant upgrading of small commodity trade.

Central Zhejiang CBD to be constructed in Yiwu shall form and give play to four major business functions guided by the small commodity market, namely, an international convention and exhibition center, regional economic headquarters, a regional financial center, and a knowledge information center.

4.1 "Yiwu Fair" and international convention and exhibition center

Along with the accelerating internationalization of Yiwu Small Commodity Market, Yiwu's convention and exhibition industry has witnessed a rapid rise and has become an important growth point in the city's economic development. The convention and exhibition industry has not only promoted the economic development of Yiwu and the construction of the city, but also improved the carrying capacity of Yiwu to the internationalization of the regional economy, and become an important symbol of the formation of "Yiwu Business Circle". In fact, the convention and exhibition economy has become an inevitable choice for the construction of Central Zhejiang CBD and International Trade City.

As a regionally central city, there are certain difficulties in developing the convention and exhibition industry with international standards in Yiwu. Surely, the level of the international convention and exhibition is determined not only by the urban size. For a city with a certain economic strength, as long as it has an international advantage in one aspect, it is possible to run an international convention and exhibition. Compared with other cities at home and abroad, Yiwu is rich in resources and developed in business, trade, and circulation. It is the world's largest commodity market place, and it can be said that it is an exceptional condition for her to develop the convention and exhibition industry. Taking Yiwu as a strong support, the convention and exhibition industry has started from scratch, from small to large, experiencing rapid development since the middle of the 1990s. Furthermore, under the guidance of government policy, Yiwu's convention and exhibition industry has established the goal of internationalization, specialization, and diversification in the early stage of development.

In 2005, the "Yiwu Fair" with "small commodity and new life" as the theme, attracted 1,700 companies from more than 20 countries and 25 domestic provinces, municipalities, autonomous regions, which set up 3,000 booths in 10 large exhibition areas. The exhibition of commodities was dominated by small commodities with distinctive features and was favored by buyers; the exhibitors were mainly manufacturing enterprises, which were attractive to buyers. The standards and levels of exhibitors have been significantly improved, including 270 overseas enterprises, 53 famous enterprises above the provincial level, 18 countries with well-known trademarks, and more than 30% of well-known enterprises. The number of buyers increased greatly, the purpose of the exhibition was diversified, focusing more on collecting market information, and the domestic and foreign repurchasing rate was more than 70%. The exhibition layout level and service capacity of the exhibition were faster, and 70% of merchants expressed extraordinary satisfaction or satisfaction. Buyers and sellers gained a lot of business opportunities, with a turnover of 8.098 billion Yuan. Through various exhibitions, conferences and activities, it has propagandized the new Yiwu, promoted the business, trade, and circulation industry, promoted the opening to the outside world, and has realized the comprehensive development of the economy and trade, science and technology, culture, and tourism. Among them, the "Shanhai Collaboration Exhibition Area" was designed to connect economically developed areas with less developed areas and open up channels for the purposes of common prosperity with 217 participating enterprises from Jinhua, Quzhou, Lishui, Zhoushan, and other places with 261 booths and 34 collaboration projects successfully worth a total amount of 340 million Yuan, involving multiple fields like industry, business, trade, tourism, material processing, and labor cooperation. It can be said that the annual "Yiwu Fair" as a brand of Yiwu played a great role in strengthening cooperation and exchanges with cities, counties, and districts in the central and western regions of Zhejiang, promoting the construction of Central Zhejiang CBD and the formation and development of "Yiwu Business Circle".

At the same time, the interaction between the exhibition and the fair was realized. It has hosted more than 50 international and national conferences, such as the annual meeting of the Chinese mayor and the wealth forum. It has improved the level of professionalism in the exhibition and enhanced the content and effect of the exhibition, leaving the two to complement each other. Now, driven by the "Yiwu Fair", a batch of professional exhibitions for hardware, toys, ornaments, and stationeries rises successively, which has formed the pattern of the interactive brand exhibition and small and medium-sized exhibitions,[5] reaching a considerable scale with good economic and social benefits. Among them, the Toy Fair, Hardware Fair, Ornament Fair, Stationery Fair, Handicraft Fair, and other fixed batch of fairs have gradually become the support projects of Yiwu's exhibition industry. Its unique market exhibition advantages also attract the attention of professional exhibition companies in Shanghai, Hangzhou, Suzhou, Shenzhen, Nanjing, and so on. They occupied Yiwu's market one after another.

In the future, the development of Yiwu's exhibition industry still insists on the direction of internationalization, specialization, diversification, and regularization. "Yiwu Fair" has been one of the three largest commercial brand exhibitions in the country and rated

---

[5] Main exhibitions include China Yiwu International Small Commodities Fair (hereinafter referred to as "Yiwu Fair"), Yiwu Hosiery Underwear Clothing Industrial Equipment Exhibition (hereinafter referred to as "Hosiery Machine Exhibition"), China Yiwu (International) Hardware Appliances Fair (hereinafter referred to as "Hardware Fair"), China (Yiwu) Toys and Children's Products Fair (hereinafter referred to as "Toy Fair"), Yiwu Housing Industry (hereinafter referred to as "Housing Fair") and China Yiwu (International) Ornament Fair (hereinafter referred to as "Ornament Fair").

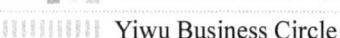

as the largest, the most influential, and the most productive small commodity trade exhibition, but its scale, grade, and international level are not yet the same as the "Canton Fair". Among them, the average foreign trade opportunities per booth (the number of visitors divided by the number of booths) is 7.2 for "Canton Fair" and only 5.8 for "Yiwu Fair", the difference of which is significant. Another advantage of the "Canton Fair" is that it has a large number of brand pavilions, which is another weakness of the "Yiwu Fair". However, "Yiwu Fair" also has its advantages. First, it has the strong industrial support of Zhejiang's light manufacturing enterprises. For the enterprises participating in "Yiwu Fair", 99% of them are manufacturers, which achieve source purchases with low cost. Second, the exhibition period of "Yiwu Fair" is in the renewal period of the autumn "Canton Fair", which formed the staggered development. "See samples at the fair and place orders in Yiwu" is the first choice for many foreign merchants. Third, participating in "Yiwu Fair" must give full play to their own advantages while learning from the advanced experience of domestic and foreign well-known exhibitions. In particular, it is required to seize the focus of internationalization and attract more well-known domestic and foreign brands and products. Meanwhile, it is necessary to make full use of the resource conditions, such as venue and popularity, to set up new professional exhibitions in due course, and to attract more large-scale domestic and foreign exhibitions to settle in Yiwu relying on the brand advantages of the "Yiwu Fair".

4.2 Regional economic headquarters

In the short and medium term, Yiwu is not as an attractive option as Shanghai, Hangzhou, or Ningbo to introduce a large batch of high-level headquarters, so we should focus on the headquarters of private enterprises both inside and outside the province, especially within Central and Western Zhejiang. It is expected that, with the further advancement of economic system reform, private enterprises will usher in a new round of good opportunities for development. Those providing a better platform for the development of private enterprises in the future and even in the whole country will occupy the heights of economic and industrial development. To view from the actual situation of Central and Western Zhejiang, on the one hand, many private enterprises have now entered the second stage of startup after years of development. Improving the level of industry and the management level is imminent. Such improvement is inseparable from the external information and support of human resources, and Yiwu can just provide such a platform. On the other hand, to view from the industrial level, at present, the capital scale or production scale of private enterprises in Central and Western Zhejiang are relatively small, and most of them have not been able to enter CBDs of Shanghai, Hangzhou, Ningbo, and other metropoleis. Yiwu can meet the real needs of private enterprises in Central and Western Zhejiang due to its relatively low business costs in information, finance, talent, logistics, technology, and other aspects. Yiwu is growing constantly and these enterprises will be further developed through the platform of Yiwu, which is an interactive win–win situation. In fact, through 40 years of reform and opening-up, Yiwu has shown the trend of establishing regional headquarters of domestic and foreign enterprises. Inside Yiwu Small Commodity Market, big dealers, big purchasers, and famous brand products come in a throng with the direct selling proportion of manufacturers up to 56% and the number of general agents and dealers of well-known brands reaching more than 6,000. Therefore, in long and medium terms, Yiwu can completely attract well-known national enterprises and even global multinational company headquarters to settle in with their market advantages and complement advantages of Shanghai, Hangzhou, Ningbo, and other cities, together forming the national and international CBD networks.

4.3 Regional financial center

Generally speaking, there are three basic conditions for the formation of regional financial centers: one is the gathering place of the economy, the second is the gathering place of financial institutions and financial talents, and the third is the gathering place of information. Yiwu now has strong regional financial competitiveness, a large capital supply and demand capacity, as well as a relatively perfect financial organization system. In comparison with other cities in Central and Western Zhejiang, Yiwu has obvious advantages in building a regional financial center.

In line with the region's financial needs, Yiwu aims to build a comprehensive, regional and financial center that is multi-level and symbiotic with the construction of a financing center, a small and medium-sized enterprise financing center, an agricultural development financing center, an investment and financing center, and a refinancing center as the main subjects. It will integrate the financial industrial center, financial market center, and financial supervision center, taking the city and surrounding counties as the core and radiating Central and Western Zhejiang. The formation of the regional financial center of Yiwu not only takes time, but also needs the support of economic and trade development. Therefore, we must proceed from the following three aspects: (1) Further improve the economic strength of Yiwu and the radiation ability to the surrounding areas. The establishment and development of the financial center cannot be separated from the highly developed industrial structure with a strong external economic effect. To become a regional financial center, Yiwu must rely on the small commodity market, optimize the industrial structure, improve economic operation quality, and enhance the comprehensive economic strength of the city. (2) Establish a perfect social credit system based on the government's integrity and efficiency. The market economy is a credit economy and economic efficiency, good social credit, and high efficiency are guarantees for establishing a normative market economy order, and are also the essential conditions for constructing a regional financial center. From the perspective of credit and efficiency structure, the government's credit and efficiency are keys. Without good government credit and efficiency, it is impossible to establish a good social credit and efficiency system. Therefore, to establish a regional financial center, it is necessary to establish a sound social credit system, and the first step is to build a more honest and more efficient government.

(3) Strengthen financial infrastructure and personnel development. Building a regional financial center and strengthening the construction of financial infrastructure is the premise, and the establishment of a system is the guarantee. Only with a complete financial infrastructure, a sound financial system, and a good social and financial order, can it actively resolve and reduce financial risks, improve the standardization level of financial industry management, and ensure a healthy financial center. According to the current development situation of Yiwu's industrial economy and financial markets, it must speed up the development of the currency market, taking commercial banks as the main subjects, actively attract joint-stock banks, foreign banks, and financial institutions to set up branches in Yiwu, gradually forming a banking system led by state-owned commercial banks, taking joint-stock commercial banks as the main subjects complemented by small and medium-sized private banks. It must also gradually establish and improve the insurance market and the modern financial service center taking other non-bank financial institutions as services and intermediaries. It will train and introduce a number of high-level financial professionals to provide financial human capital with core significance for the construction of the financial center. At present, an important gap between Central and Western Zhejiang and the developed eastern coastal areas is that the financial system is not perfect enough. Yiwu should attract various financial institutions at home and abroad based on relatively developed regional finance and become a dense financial area with sound institutions and a strong radiation force. In turn, it shall strengthen the capacity of capital absorption, improve the efficiency of allocation, and finally build Yiwu into a financial center of Central Zhejiang.

4.4 Regional information center

The research and development ability of science and technology has been a weak link in most enterprises in Yiwu. On the one hand, because the dominant industry of Yiwu is dominated by the traditional industry, many enterprises start from family-based workshops without giving much attention to technological accumulation and

technological learning, or without being willing to undertake great risks of technological research and development. On the other hand, the city has not yet established a sound scientific and technological innovation environment, or a fair and equitable commercial credit environment. Enterprises rely on technology for a long time with woefully inadequate independent innovation abilities including original innovation, integrated innovation, introduction, digestion, absorption, and re-innovation. Therefore, many industries present the situation of "low, small, and scattered", which can only be in the middle and low ends of the international industrial chain. Today, Yiwu is moving towards becoming the International Trade City. To build Central Zhejiang CBD, it is necessary to resolve the problem of technical research and development, otherwise the whole Yiwu economy will be like "the giant without muscles", that is big and strong but unable to bear the task of leading regional economic development. Therefore, the future focus of Yiwu in terms of independent innovation consists of the following. Firstly, we will vigorously implement the talent strategy, encouraging all kinds of innovation. Secondly, we will focus on the common technologies and key links of certain industries and carry out joint efforts to tackle key problems. Thirdly, we will accelerate in creating a fair and just environment to encourage creation, building a better image and attracting more domestic and foreign enterprises to invest and start a business in Yiwu.

Among the factors contributing to the unprecedented prosperity of the modern metropolis' CBD at home and abroad, talent is a decisive factor. Yiwu's economic development has gone through a stage of primitive accumulation of capital, but more importantly, the technology and talent shortage is still severe. First of all, it is necessary to improve the quality of the entrepreneurs and the market operators. In particular, scientists, financial experts, senior management personnel, engineers, and technology researchers are in severe shortage. To address this, enterprises must "go out and bring in" and not just sit and wait for foreign merchants to purchase, but take the initiative to face the international market, bringing the talents and advanced management concepts in all aspects. Secondly, it is required to implement the strategy of "New Yiwu people", to gather and retain talents. There are only just more than 600,000 local people in Yiwu, even though they all engage in business, the number is no more than 600,000. Therefore, Yiwu should be open-minded and sincerely treat every person who starts a business and works in Yiwu so as to make them accept the culture of Yiwu, accepting them as the "New Yiwu people", not just as outsiders doing business or working in Yiwu.

In general, CBDs are integration points of all international and domestic economies, thus boasting an enormous amount of information, with all kinds of information bases, databases, and information networks that are connected, converged, gathered, and accumulated here, which continuously consolidates and strengthens the information function of CBD. Informationization injects new vitality into Yiwu Small Commodity Market and makes it once again enter a period of steady development. With the improvement of regional integration and the international level, a strong market agglomeration function and an extensive range of radiation make the scale of business activities of Yiwu expand constantly, and the amount of information rise rapidly. This puts forward higher requirements for the function of information service in the market, especially more professional technicians, market information personnel, and related technologies. At present, in Yiwu, network companies with computer network technology as the selling point come into being at the right moment and provide relevant network technology and consulting services. However, it is difficult to sufficiently grasp the present situation of the enterprise by only studying the existing network companies and one cannot truly exclude the difficulty and anxiety in realizing informationization in enterprises. The future of informationization will focus on the integration of relevant information resources and improve the ability of enterprises to use information. Also, it will continue to give play to the inherent advantages of the control and release of information of the world's largest small commodity market, further expand the scope and field of regional services, and constantly cultivate and strengthen the function of the information center of Central Zhejiang CBD.

Internationalization of "Yiwu Business Circle" and Positioning and Development of Yiwu City

III

1. Internationalization trend of "Yiwu Business Circle"

The existing research results show that when the elements' (especially the labor and land) advantages are gradually weakened, it is the basic trend of the future evolution for "Yiwu Business Circle" to approach internationalization through the establishment of cross-regional division of labor collaboration at the core of the market. As a trading center, Yiwu cannot be satisfied with being in the leading position in the domestic small commodity wholesale market. It must also take the first-class design of products and services, the first-class brand, and the first-class quality to enter the international market. At the same time, we should note that there are still many shortcomings in industrial development, technological innovation, and urban management in the market upgradation and scale expansion.

Therefore, we must learn from the advanced experience of developed countries in the market economy.

Yiwu, located in the Inland Economic Zone of Central and Western Zhejiang, gives full play to the small commodity market advantage, expands the development space, and takes a different path of internationalization. The conditions for the formation of "Yiwu Business Circle" are as follows: firstly, that it shall increase the number of market participants; secondly, it shall expand the market trading variety and scale; thirdly, it shall shorten the search time of commodities. After 40 years of development after the reform and opening-up, Yiwu Small Commodity Market has basically established its domestic and foreign trading platform and stable trade relations; the number of market participants and trading products and size have increased greatly. Along with the advancement of the development of traffic communication and informationization, it has broken the limit in space and time and made the average transaction cost of the multinational cooperation cheaper, paving the way for global cooperation, which is the inner impetus for the internationalization trend of "Yiwu Business Circle".

To view from the city as a whole, the urbanization process of Yiwu City and the development of Yiwu Small Commodity Market are synchronous. After five generations of the small commodity market, the accumulation of various elements of the "flat effect" has been initially formed with regional capital, information, technology, and labor force being further concentrated in Yiwu. Yiwu has the largest specialized market cluster of small commodities in the country, competes with all kinds of categories, and has formed a large and well-informed network of small commodity circulation through "centralized management over the same category of commodities". Under the support of the small commodity market, the position and role of Yiwu in regional economic development will be further consolidated and improved, making it a regional center of commodity circulation, the window of international trade, a specialized production area, a capital settlement center, and an investment and financing center. Especially considering the circulation of small commodities, Yiwu Small Commodity Market is not only the domestic small commodity circulation center but its influence is also expanding to the overseas markets. When the whole country spared no effort to expand its international market and China's manufacturing industry swept across the world, Yiwu Small Commodity Market attracted a large number of international customers using low prices, a new style, fast updates, and good quality so as to occupy a place in the global industrial division of labor. From the perspective of private economic development, Yiwu has become one of the most developed cities (counties) in Zhejiang Province, and is going through the whole country to go into the world.

Internationalization is an important means for "Yiwu Business Circle" to continuously expand its scope and improve its level. Internationalization brings more producers and consumers to Yiwu Small Commodity Market so as to reorganize the industrial division of labor and sales system for original domestic small commodity production. In the era of the changing consumption concept and constant product innovation and economic globalization, Yiwu must make industries and the market develop further towards internationalization, grasp the pulse and trend of industry development in order to keep itself at the forefront of industrial innovation, and become Central Zhejiang CBD so as to affect other domestic regions of the country. Also, internationalization gives Yiwu the opportunity to convey its own consumption idea and development concept to the world, to expand the scope of "Yiwu Business Circle", and to mine the depth of "Yiwu Business Circle", making it become one of the world's small commodity design, development, and sales centers. No matter it's information output or input, internationalization can further strengthen the core status of Yiwu and strengthen the control and influence of "Yiwu Business Circle".

2. Internationalization of "Yiwu Business Circle" and development of Yiwu City

At present, "Yiwu Business Circle" has basically formed, gradually developed, and gone deeper towards internationalization. In this new situation, how will Yiwu continue to lead the development trend of the small commodity market and go ahead in the country? We believe that in the future, Yiwu Small Commodity Market will transform its basic functions into product display—negotiation—take orders—arrange production nationwide—export so as to become a real international market. At that time, in a certain sense, domestic small and medium-sized enterprises will enter the international market without having to establish their own sales system abroad by only entering Yiwu Small Commodity Market. To this end, Yiwu needs to re-examine the development direction of the small commodity market and the functional orientation of the city from the international perspective of "Yiwu Business Circle". Yiwu leaders at all levels, all types of industrial and commercial enterprises, general merchants, and all cadres and masses must be awake to realize that through the construction and development of "Yiwu Business Circle", Yiwu is forming an open economy that can "arrange raw materials and sales in markets abroad and vigorously develop processing industries for export". However, it also needs to have the international markets and a highly open city to really integrate into the world industrial chain. Thus, the construction of the "International Trade City" should and must be the development direction of Yiwu. In October 2002, the newly built Futian Market was officially named "Yiwu International Trade City" by Yiwu Municipal Party Committee and Government, which has shown the ambition of Yiwu people to build an international trade city.

Yiwu establishes the strategic goal of "International Trade City". It shows that with the formation and development of "Yiwu Business Circle", the urbanization and modernization of Yiwu has entered a new era. The establishment of the goal of "International Trade City" is beneficial to the distribution and processing of small commodities from all over the world, and to the promotion of the organizational form of the small commodity market, thus further promoting the internationalization of "Yiwu Business Circle". Generally speaking, the international trade city refers to a city with obvious radiation, influence, and control in the trade industry in the world's division of labor system. The international trade city should have the following basic characteristics: firstly, the business sector must have great influence in the world, which is the core feature of an international trade city; secondly, it needs to have modern urban infrastructure, which is the foundation of the international trade city; thirdly, is the internationalization of the urban function, which is the inherent requirement of the international trade city. On this basis, Yiwu must rely on the further development and improvement of the commodity market to attain great achievements in the following aspects: firstly, it is to form comprehensive economic strengths and strong international competitiveness by becoming an international small commodity distribution center, an exhibition center, an information center, a manufacturing center, and a research and development center; secondly, it is to form Central Zhejiang CBD with a large scale and strong service capacity; thirdly, it is to form a highly developed cultural cause and frequent international exchanges.

3. Basic framework of Yiwu International Trade City

Construction of the international trade city is a full range and high quality urban development process, not just the expansion of urban area and increase of urban resident population. More importantly, it can advance further expansion of "Yiwu Business Circle".

3.1 The core and symbol of the international trade city: international small commodity circulation center and international trade city

3.1.1 International small commodity circulation center

The small commodity market is the lifeblood of Yiwu's economy and the construction of the international trade city is the key to expand Yiwu's international market share of small commodities and build Yiwu

into an international small commodity distribution center. Therefore, it is necessary to further improve the market system. Firstly, it shall actively expand the international market, continue to implement the diversification strategy, strengthen the promotion of related industries and business entities, especially the introduction of international brands. It shall do a good job in the relocation of the non-staple food market, reconstruct the Bingwang Market and Huangyuan Market, and accelerate the expansion and relocation of the capital goods market. According to the principle of staggered development, classified clustering, support and complementarity, and centralized management over the same category of commodities, it shall conduct scientific layout, overall planning, and reconstruction of a specialized street. Secondly, it shall accelerate the construction of "digital market" and build an international sales network. Thirdly, it will vigorously develop the exhibition economy, continue to raise public awareness and level of "Yiwu Fair", and make breakthroughs in the organization, participation member's level, the quality of visitors, and goods, forming relatively stable business groups, and cultivating a batch of strategic and management personnel with high professional and technical levels. Fourthly, it shall actively develop the exclusive distribution, general agent, chain distribution, e-commerce, and other modern trade and distribution methods, vigorously promote the diversification, intensification, and modernization of market management means and ways of trade. It shall actively open up the relevant professional transaction area and small commodity raw material market, transform the existing market booths, implement the booth expansion into shop, vigorously develop the street market, and promote the combination of the street market and the market. Fifthly, it shall vigorously promote the diversification of foreign trade operators, ways of trade, export commodities and export markets, speed up the construction of supporting facilities, management organization, and service organization, further improve the service system of foreign trade, try all means to expand commodity exports, and expand the international market in full range. Sixthly, it shall integrate the existing logistics resources and plan and construct a modern logistics park with

complete functions, integrating business flow, logistics, information flow, and capital flow with a high starting point and high standards and form a joint-stock logistics enterprise group.

3.1.2 International trade city

The small commodity market is the leading success factor of Yiwu, the cornerstone of the circulation center of small commodities in the whole country and the world. It also took the initiative to build an international trade city and expand "Yiwu Business Circle". In the future, Central Zhejiang CBD and "Yiwu Business Circle" will become the heart of the international trade city, which is the main window for Yiwu to enter the international market and exchange information, capital, technology, and commodities with the world. Therefore, further planning and building of the international trade city market is the key to the construction of the international trade city. Yiwu should seize its historical opportunities, improve the market level, expand the level of internationalization, and strive to become the small commodity distribution center with the lowest commodity transaction cost, the best credit, the best service, the latest means, and become well known in the whole country and even in the world. Yiwu Small Commodity Market has a business area of 5.5 million square meters with its position as the world's largest small commodity circulation center and the exhibition center being even more prominent. In the future, it is necessary to achieve new breakthroughs in the supporting core aspect, namely the information logistics function, to make it really become the "International Trade City" and the core and symbol of "Yiwu Business Circle".

3.2 Strong pillar of the international trade city and "Yiwu Business Circle"—industrial high-end upgrading and regional development

3.2.1 Industrial high-end upgrading

Construction and development of the international trade city and "Yiwu Business Circle" must be based on a solid industrial foundation and strong innovation ability, which is the basis for ensuring the position of Yiwu's international commodity circulation center,

innovation advantages of new products and low cost advantages of production. The support of the local superior industries is indispensable for the Yiwu Small Commodity Market for leading the country's similar markets in the whole country. Without strong industries, there is no prosperous and stable market, and no construction of "Yiwu Business Circle". The prospects of Yiwu Small Commodity Market and "Yiwu Business Circle" not only depend on the number and size of similar domestic and foreign markets, but also depend on whether there is strong industrial support. Informationization and branding are two key elements needed for Yiwu to upgrade the industrial structure. Informationization enables enterprises to grasp the market situation in time and design products with newer models and higher quality. At the same time, the use of information technology to transform the whole industry can improve the efficiency and benefits of the industry from R&D, manufacturing, logistics to sales, and other links. It can be seen that it is the only way for Yiwu to build an international commercial city by using informationization to transform traditional industries and improve the service, radiation, and integration functions of the market. Continuous brand improvement of the small commodity market also benefits many famous brands like Neoglory, Lanswe, Mengna, and NDL, which grow and enter the international market by relying on it; in turn, these well-known brands have promoted the prosperity of the small commodity market and enhanced the reputation of Yiwu. Therefore, it shall fully establish the brand concept of manufacturing enterprises and systematically promote the brand creation project; the market should further strengthen the domestic and foreign famous brands and build the international brand market.

3.2.2 Regional development

Industrial park is an important carrier to promote industrial agglomeration and promotion. We can effectively solve the problem of "low, small, and scattered" small commodity production enterprises, realize resource sharing, reduce production costs, and increase the efficiency of scale by concentrating efforts to run the industrial park.

It is also possible to create conditions for the construction of the international trade city through population gathering with industrial agglomeration and accelerating urbanization. Thus, Yiwu should strengthen the planning and integration of its existing parks and make unremitting efforts in accordance with the medium and long-term plans for the development and construction of the two major industrial belts in the southwest and northeast of Yiwu. It shall adhere to the policy of industrial cluster development, rely on the advantage industry, construct characteristic industrial parks for cultural goods, cosmetics, clothing, zipper, wool spinning, ornaments, printing, and so on, lead scale enterprises to build factories in the park, and guide small and medium-sized enterprises to rent standard factory buildings, completely changing the past industrial situation of "blossom everywhere". In particular, it is necessary to strengthen the planning and construction of 100 square kilometers of the main urban area (which consists of international trade city facilities like commerce, business, convention and exhibition, finance, insurance, R&D, administration, science, education, communication, culture, health, and tourism), and make it the core area of Central Zhejiang CBD.

Chapter **5**

Construction of "Yiwu Business Circle" and Innovative International Trade City

The formation and development process of "Yiwu Business Circle" is filled with innovation, which is the result of a range of independent innovation activities. Taking an overall view of the development course of Yiwu, we can see that it has a pioneering and courageous history of innovation. To further establish and exert the radiating, leading role of "Yiwu Business Circle" in its future development, Yiwu must first enhance its own sustainable development ability. To this end, it is necessary to set the goal of building an innovative international trade city and make efforts to improve the capability of independent innovation based on actual conditions by combining the first-mover advantage with independent innovation activities, thereby promoting the transformation of the investment-driven growth mode that relies on the intensive input of labor, capital, resources, and other elements to the innovation-driven growth mode that relies on independent innovation and provides sustained momentum. This is a concrete response to the call of the Central Government and Zhejiang Provincial Party Committee for building an innovative nation and an innovative province. It is not only a new requirement for implementing the scientific outlook on developing and building a harmonious socialist society, but is also an inevitable trend for Yiwu's continuous creation of new advantages and the promotion of construction, development, and functional upgradation of "Yiwu Business Circle".

I Decisive Significance of Independent Innovation to the Construction of "Yiwu Business Circle"

1. Innovation, independent innovation, and construction of "Yiwu Business Circle"

1.1 Understandings about innovation and independent innovation

The Austrian-born American economist J. Schumpeter comprehensively expounded the theory of innovation for the first time in his book *The Theory of Economic Development* published in 1912, pointing out that innovation is to "create a new production function",[1] which is "a new combination of production factors by entrepreneurs". Schumpeter's definition of innovation covers the following five situations: obtaining a new source of supply for a raw material or semi-finished product,

---

[1] Schumpeter, J. *The Theory of Economic Development*. Beijing: Beijing Commercial Press, 1990, p. 12.

adopting a new production method, implementing a new organizational form, introducing a new product or providing a better quality product, and opening up a new market. The above five situations, in turn, correspond to resource allocation innovation, technological innovation, organizational innovation, product innovation, and market innovation. Schumpeter noted in particular that innovation does not mean invention. An invention can only be regarded as an innovation if it has been applied to economic activity and yielded success; an innovator is not a laboratory scientist but an entrepreneur with courage, risk-taking, and organizational capability. He believes that in a static system, capital, population, technology, and production organization remain unchanged, where the result of competition is the price equal to cost; without the generation of profits, such a society is stagnant. Comparatively, in a dynamic society, entrepreneurs, as innovators, improve efficiency by using new technologies and methods so that the cost becomes lower than the price needed to make profits. In addition, innovation always begins with individuals, yet the profits from innovative activities encourage others to imitate, thereby generating a wave of innovation. At this point, the productivity of the whole society is boosted, which prompts economic development and social progress.

Schumpeter's description of innovative activities is mainly from the perspective of corporate production and operation, and he is more focused on the consideration of micro subjects. In our opinion, from the perspectives of micro–macro integration and the complementary, coordinated development of the economy, technology, and society, by breaking through the micro dimension of enterprises and the dimension of the role of technological innovation in economic development, innovation can be understood as putting forward new theories, establishing new systems, formulating new policies, creating new organizations, forming new mechanisms, inventing new technologies, adopting new methods, providing new products, acquiring new raw materials, opening new markets, fostering new cultures, creating new arts, etc.; it is a creative activity involving all fields of economic and social life, including theoretical innovation, institutional innovation, system innovation, mechanism innovation, technological innovation, cultural innovation, management innovation, and other innovations. Independent innovation, on the other hand, refers to the strengthening of original innovation, integrated innovation, and the introduction, digestion, and absorption of reinnovation based on enhancing the innovation ability. Among them, original innovation refers to the proposal of unprecedented, pioneering theories, views, ideas, or carrying out the corresponding activities and achieving new results; integrated innovation refers to the gathering of integration-related resource factors, mature technologies, innovation achievements under certain conditions, or a combination or linkage of several activities for exerting respective advantages, so as to obtain new creative achievements; finally introduction, digestion, and absorption for reinnovation refers to equipping oneself with an advanced level in the corresponding field by learning, imitating, and using others' achievements and seeking a breakthrough on this basis to put forward new ideas and methods, develop new or more advanced technologies, and adopt new or more efficient modes of management operation.

1.2 Significance of independent innovation to the construction of "Yiwu Business Circle"

The fast and favorable development from extensive management to intensive management, from "manufactured in Yiwu" to "created by Yiwu", from "Yiwu Market" to "Yiwu Business Circle", and from "regional trade city" to "international trade city" all depends on the enhancement and exertion of independent innovation ability. The past, present, and future developments of Yiwu Small Commodity Market, as the core of "Yiwu Business Circle", are all closely related to independent innovation. It not only played a decisive role in the birth of Yiwu Small Commodity Market, which was an institutional innovation in the early 1980s, but also contributed greatly to the expansion of "Yiwu Market" to "Yiwu Business Circle". The business owners and manufacturers associated with the market can change with the times

and constantly innovate the trading philosophy, methods, and means, as well as the operating patterns, management modes, and corporate structure to actively promote the outward expansion of market space; they strive to achieve the transition from imitation processing to the independent development of new products; they alter the design as per market demand to produce new products keeping up with the times; they gradually transform from a simple focus on the introduction of advanced equipment and techniques into the striving for innovation on the basis of digesting and absorbing advanced technologies and management experience around the world and develop products with independent intellectual property rights via the establishment of R&D centers and other means of industry–university–research institute collaboration with the aid of R&D, scientific innovation abilities of research institutes, and higher learning institutions to create their own famous brands. In this process, the government fully respects and carries forward the pioneering spirit of the masses while constantly reforming its own functions, innovative management modes and means, and advancing with the times to put forward a range of innovative development strategies and policy opinions to guide, support, and encourage business owners and manufacturers to carry out innovative activities in the areas of concept, organization, technology, and management. These strategies would thereby greatly enhance the independent innovation ability of business owners and manufacturers associated with the small commodity market, drawing and cultivating a number of innovative talents, establishing a number of corporate R&D (technology) centers and independent brands, fostering a number of high-tech and technology-based enterprises, and forming a range of invention and patent achievements. It is precisely because of Yiwu Small Commodity Market-associated business owners, manufacturers, and the government's full recognition of the importance of independent innovation and active launch and guidance of independent innovation activities that the world's largest public trading platform, Yiwu Small Commodity Market, has emerged. The close link among domestic and foreign traders, manufacturers, and transporters has been promoted to

form a huge cross-regional division of labor and cooperation network, i.e., "Yiwu Business Circle".

2. Original innovation laid the core and foundation of "Yiwu Business Circle"

"Chicken feather for sugar", street market, "Four Permits", "Flourish Business and Build City", fixed taxation, zoned operation, separation of regulation from management, boosting industry with commerce, linking industry to trade, International Trade City, etc.: all of these concepts are the summary of a range of independent innovation activities in the history of Yiwu's development, especially the original innovation activities. They either carry out unprecedented innovative activities, or come up with unprecedented innovative policies, strategies and goals, or adopt unprecedented innovative management models. All of these are in line with the connotation that the original innovation is to put forward unprecedented, pioneering theories, views, and ideas or to carry out those corresponding activities and make new achievements. Therefore, in a broad sense, they are a range of typical original innovation activities.

2.1 Original small commodity market and the "Four Permits"

"Chicken feather for sugar", this original activity enabled Yiwu merchants to gradually form a business tradition. In 1982, the then Yiwu County Party Committee and government boldly made the decision to open up the small commodity market; later, they also creatively put forward the "Four Permits". It abolished the "frame" that peasants could only be "agriculture-based" and must not be involved in the wholesale trade or production of industrial products, which greatly stimulated the masses' creativity and released the tremendous business potential of "chicken feather for sugar" peddlers, thus making the first generation of the small commodity market come into being. This became the key factor for the growth, expansion, and recognition of the small commodity market at home and abroad, which also laid a solid foundation for the future evolution of "Yiwu Small Commodity Market" to "Yiwu Business Circle".

2.2 Groundbreaking "Flourish Business and Build County" strategy

In October 1984, the Yiwu County Party Committee and Government responded promptly to the situation and creatively put forward the development strategy of "Flourish Business and Build County". After upgrading the county into a city in 1988, "Flourish Business and Build County" was adopted as the overall development strategy, thereby establishing the market's dominant position in the development of the regional economy. Over the past 30 years, "Flourish Business and Build County" has always been upheld to assign tasks around the market, build the city around the market, and organize businesses around the market. Meanwhile, compliance with the idea of "seizing the market is grasping the economy" further stimulates the masses' enthusiasm to participate in market management, so that the development of commerce and trade becomes the first impetus for Yiwu's economic development. This is the key for Yiwu's market to become the world's largest small commodity market today. Ensuring the continued prosperity and development of the market laid a solid foundation for Yiwu's gathering of domestic and foreign resources by exploiting market advantages to carry out cross-regional division of labor cooperation, which also created the necessary conditions for the formation of "Yiwu Business Circle".

2.3 Cross-regional division of labor and cooperation network based on mutual promotion and common prosperity

After the flourishing, Yiwu Small Commodity Market was named as "China Small Commodity Mall" by SAIC in 1992 and its functions of gathering various kinds of commodities, information, and production factors and of spreading and radiating across the whole province and country were exerted more fully. Yiwu, relying on its large international market, continues to provide commercial support to the surrounding areas and drive the employment of surplus rural labor, while the surrounding areas develop manufacturing industries relying on the market division of labor to offer industrial support to the market. They complement each other and promote each other. Such an original cross-regional division of labor and cooperation mode allowed Yiwu Small Commodity Market to gain expanding influence and a growing reputation, thereby contributing to the birth of the cross-regional division of labor and cooperation network centering on it, i.e., "Yiwu Business Circle". In terms of management, zoned operation and classified agglomeration were adopted, thus not only achieving the effective integration of market resources to facilitate the purchase of merchants and cut the transaction costs, but also motivating the rational division of labor and sufficient competition between owners to promote the construction of a market-centered cross-regional division of labor and cooperation network. Yiwu Small Commodity Market places equal importance on "bringing in and going out" and proceeds with internal and external radiations simultaneously. After gradually occupying the domestic market, it has also actively explored the international market and achieved the transition from "buying and selling goods nationwide" to "buying and selling goods worldwide". Meanwhile, the Municipal Party Committee and Government creatively put forward the goal of building an International Trade City on the basis of analyzing their actual situation and grasping the development trend of global commerce and trade, thereby further integrating into the international commercial and economic system and extending the influence of the market from the domestic to the international arena. These up-to-date innovative ideas, development strategies, and management modes promoted the domestic-to-international expansion of Yiwu Small Commodity Market, the specialization, aggregation, and standardization of market layout from scattered disorderliness, and the development of cross-regional division of labor and cooperative relations centering on the small commodity market, thus gradually forming "Yiwu Business Circle", radiating nationwide and worldwide.

2.4 System, mechanism and management innovations

All previous municipal (county) party committees and governments fully respected and carried forward the pioneering spirit of the masses, and encouraged and supported the masses, enterprises, and relevant organizations to carry out system, mechanism and technological innovations. In the early 1980s, Yiwu Choucheng Credit Union lent its first loan of 10,000 Yuan to individuals, which set a national precedent for loaning to individuals and the private economy. Moreover, it took the lead in breaking cash payment limitations, accepting cash payments no matter how much money was withdrawn. This initiative won the time and trust needed for Yiwu businessmen to purchase goods in Guangzhou and other places in the then context of "cash on delivery". While other places set limitations and restrictions on the approval of limited liability companies, Yiwu took the lead in loosening up, "as long as the masses need, approval is granted to them."[2] In the early stage of development of Yiwu Small Commodity Market, the taxation administration department adopted "fixed taxation", in order to reduce the burden on operators, so that numerous small commodity dealers could grow rapidly without much burden to become the main force for the future economic development of Yiwu. Yiwu also took the lead in opening a primary market for state-owned land use right in 1992 and launched a public auction of the right to use construction land. In 1995, it took the lead in adopting a "self-financing, self-construction, self-charging, self-repayment, and self-management", "Five Selfs" construction mode, and in 1998, built the first "Five Selfs" reservoir in China, i.e., the Badukeng Reservoir. On these bases, in 2000, it took the lead in trans-regional water rights trading and invested 200 million Yuan to purchase the perpetuity of 50 million cubic meters of high-quality water resources from the Hengjin Reservoir in Dongyang to resolve the water shortage contradiction via the market mechanism. The city then actively

---

[2] A shining pearl in Central Zhejiang urban agglomeration: A close look at one of Yiwu's development experiences. *Jinhua Daily*, 2006-05-11(1).

encouraged the adoption of the "self-loaning, self-construction, self-charging, and self-repayment", "Four Selfs" construction system for highway traffic and guided industrial and commercial capital investment in infrastructure construction, thus creating favorable conditions for the external transportation of commodities traded in the market.

In short, it was precisely a series of original innovations on the system, mechanism, and management that fully respected and exerted the fundamental role of a market in allocating resources, reduced the flow costs of commodities and factors, established a low-cost advantage in the production and marketing of small commodities, and ensured the standout of the small commodity market in the fierce competitive environment and the continued expansion of market scope and functions, thereby laying the foundation for "Yiwu Business Circle", a cross-regional division of labor and cooperation network that links relevant small commodity dealers at home and abroad.

3. Integrated innovation promoted the formation and development of "Yiwu Business Circle"

The birth of Yiwu Small Commodity Market is attributed mainly to the institutional changes promoted by the reform and opening-up, which is the result of original innovations carried out jointly by the masses, enterprises, and government. Meanwhile, its development benefits come from the ongoing integrated innovation activities. Especially during the implementation of the overall development strategy of "Flourish Business and Build County", the Yiwu Municipal Party Committee and Government began to adopt an integrated innovation strategy of "Promoting Industry by Commerce" and "Connecting Trade with Industry" as early as the mid 1990s to vigorously develop the small commodity processing industry and promote the scale expansion and industrial upgrading by guiding the expansion of commercial capital to the industrial circle, so as to integrate the respective advantages and functions of the market and industry. This was done to drive the industry with the market and support the market with the industry for mutual complementation, promotion, and common prosperity, thereby creatively forming a pattern of market–industry interactive development.

The small commodity but large industry pattern in Yiwu became evident, and some of the advantageous industries had a domestic market share of over 50%. Several national industrial bases were also established, which made the feature of the small enterprise but large cluster more prominent, and a pattern in which large-scale enterprises were leading and numerous small and medium-sized enterprises (SMEs) were developing together and growing stepwise was formed gradually. Taking the jewelry industry as an example, led by the Neoglory Jewelry (Holding) Group and other leading enterprises, there were over 4000 jewelry production and management enterprises throughout the city, with output and productivity both accounting for 70% of the national jewelry industry. In addition, the sensitive feedback of market information spawned a number of emerging advantaged industries, such as the seamless underwear industry, the chemical fiber industry, and the cleaning product industry, thus making Yiwu the world's second largest industrial base for seamless underwear. The implementation of a series of decisions such as "Transforming Industry by Commerce", "Connecting Trade with Industry", and "One body, Two wings" industrial belt construction has created a huge group of SMEs and initially formed two major industrial belts in the northeast and southwest of Yiwu. The prosperity and development of the market also effectively promoted the vigorous development of the tertiary industry. The modern service industry system consisting of commerce, trade, logistics, finance, convention and exhibition, shopping, and tourism basically took shape.

Meanwhile, Yiwu has also taken full advantage of its large international market, loose policy environment, and favorable infrastructure to attract domestic and foreign innovative resources to the local area, thereby facilitating the concentration of superior resources such as high-end talents, capital, technologies, and information to make up for its lack of strength and to achieve integrated innovation. In particular, it has set up processing bases in the areas surrounding Central Zhejiang urban agglomeration to develop processing with supplied materials by utilizing the rich, cheap local human and land resources. Such an innovative division of labor collaboration mode that integrates regional superior resources has enabled Yiwu Small Commodity Market to export supplied materials processing business worth over 10 billion Yuan every year, which is driving millions of rural surplus labors in peripheral areas to engage in the processing of small commodities and earning billions of Yuan in processing fees for these areas, thereby promoting the development of the local economy. Moreover, it is also effective in breaking through the bottleneck of resource constraints in Yiwu's development, thereby accelerating the transformative pace of industrial structure and growth patterns and realizing mutual benefits and multi-win scenarios. The development of such a complementary, harmonious, and co-prosperous cross-regional division of labor and cooperative relation further strengthened the core, dominant position of Yiwu Small Commodity Market. It also prompted the spread of its influence to the exterior and international arena, thus eventually forming "Yiwu Business Circle", a cross-regional division of labor and cooperation network linking small commodity R&D institutions, manufacturers, transporters, distributors, and other proprietors at home and abroad.

Although Yiwu's markets mostly deal with small commodities, manufacturers are closely linked to the markets and have a strong ability to collect and feed back market information. They are good at quickly integrating relevant personnel, capital,

technology, and information resources as per market demand and development trends, improving the existing R&D, manufacturing, and technology levels, synthesizing a variety of popular elements and highlights of mature products, and making bold innovations on product variety, color, pattern, and raw materials, so that new varieties and new styles are launched continuously. Therefore, in Yiwu's markets, shoppers can certainly find everything they can think of as long as it is related to people's daily life; they can even find commodities they never imagined. It is precisely because of the widely varied, new style, fast updating, and global trend-following small commodities here that have led to the gathering of domestic and foreign merchants. Numerous foreign merchants have relocated in Yiwu to engage in business activities, and China's Ministry of Foreign Affairs, Ministry of Commerce, the UN Refugee Agency, Carrefour Asia Headquarters, etc., have all set up procurement centers in Yiwu.

4. Introduction, digestion, and absorption for reinnovation further accelerated the internationalization process of "Yiwu Business Circle"

Most enterprises in Yiwu are small-sized. In consideration of their own strength limits and economic benefits, they have generally taken the introduction, digestion, and absorption for reinnovation mode in terms of independent innovation. The process spans roughly three periods:

In the early period (from the 1980s to the mid-1990s), many production operators tended to purchase equipment from developed cities such as Guangzhou and Shenzhen to learn about their manufacturing techniques and imitate their product designs and styles for local production. At that time, the products were basically imitation-based, and were lacking independent brands, or technologies; market space was competed for relying mainly on the price advantage, and the manufacturing capacity and level were subject largely to production equipment limitations. Therefore, it was necessary to constantly eliminate old equipment and purchase advanced new equipment, whereas the industrial upgradation was rather difficult. Nevertheless, this mode played an important role in supporting the development of the small commodity market, which enabled the gradual growth of the market, its increasingly enhanced influence, continuously expanding scope of influence, and closer relations with the surrounding areas to begin exerting the functions of aggregating regional advantageous resources and promoting regional economic development.

In the medium period (from the mid-1990s to the end of the 20th century), some key enterprises had enhanced product design and production capacities after going through the early learning and imitation stages. Moreover, the development and upgrading of the small commodity market had raised higher, multi-level requirements on product quality. At that time, the production equipment and manufacturing techniques of developed cities in China (mainly Guangzhou, Shenzhen, etc.) were no longer able to meet the rapidly changing market demand. Hence, many key enterprises actively sought to introduce advanced equipment and technologies from countries like Japan, R. O. Korea, France, and Italy, closely followed the international trend, and vigorously digested and absorbed the international advanced manufacturing techniques, equipment operating procedures, and design concepts to gradually catch up with Guangzhou, Shenzhen, and other domestic developed cities. Compared to the early period, the improvement of manufacturing capacity and level played a more supportive role in the development of the small commodity market. The continuous launch of internationally popular products, designs, and styles that were up to international standards stimulated the potential market demand and promoted further market prosperity. This established Yiwu Small Commodity Market's position as the center for regional commercial circulation, which transformed gradually to the largest circulation, exhibition, information, and manufacturing center of small commodities in China. Its connection with surrounding areas became closer, the division of labor and cooperative relation developed rapidly, and its ability to gather regional advantageous resources and drive regional economic development was increasingly strengthened. During this period, high-end products remained primarily imitations of international brands, while the medium and low-end products were basically designed and produced independently, with some proprietary brands and technologies. Meanwhile, market space expansion was initiated through product upgrading and by relying on product differentiation, so that the manufacturing capacity and level followed right after the developed countries and regions. During this period, many enterprises were still largely constrained by the production equipment introduced from abroad and needed to constantly purchase more new advanced equipment, thereby plunging into a "vicious cycle" of "introduction— backwardness—more introduction—more backwardness".

In the late period (from the beginning of the 21st century to the present), the further prosperity of Yiwu Small Commodity Market has prompted the city's industry to become more closely linked with the international economy, science, and technology. The international advanced manufacturing technologies, equipment, and the latest popular colors and styles have been applied here at the fastest speed. The small commodity market has become a large international market, with an increasingly enhanced ability to gather internationally advantageous resources and generate a widespread impact on other countries and regions in the world. On the basis of preliminary introduction, digestion, and absorption, some powerful enterprises started to seek breakthroughs from different aspects and angles, and adopted industry–university–research institute collaboration and other means to actively carry out reinnovation activities, develop new raw materials, design new products, manufacture new independent equipment, and create new independent brands while promoting the implementation of integrated innovation and original innovation activities, thereby beginning to enter the world's advanced level. Some weaker SMEs, on the other hand, followed the pace of large enterprises, which was equivalent to closely following the international development trend, to seek distinctiveness and novelty in the product color, style, raw material, combination, and other aspects, thus forming a multi-field, multi-level pattern of independent innovation activities among large, medium, and small enterprises based on respective strengths and advantages. In this period, some well-known enterprises in Yiwu also launched a series of high-end products with proprietary brands and intellectual property rights, which were in a position to lead the domestic trend. Famous brands, reputed trademarks, and patented technologies started to emerge in great numbers, whereas brand strategy, intellectual property strategy, and informatization strategy became the dominant strategies for opening-up market space and expanding market share among many key enterprises. Some science and technology-based enterprises led the R&D, design, and production of small commodities in China based on the independent innovation achievements made by the abovementioned approaches; they also achieved mutual promotion and common prosperity via cooperation and exchanges. Meanwhile, these independent innovation achievements have resulted in a complementary and win–win situation with the products at the advanced international level. Although the product manufacturing capacity and techniques of some enterprises have reached the advanced international level, the production equipment still needs to be imported from abroad in large quantities. Weaker SMEs can still hardly get rid of the restriction of production conditions, where independent development remains difficult. Compared to the early and medium periods, the supportive role of improved manufacturing, R&D and design capabilities, and levels in market development are even more evident during this period. Products which blend the latest international fashion colors and styles are introduced continuously, which have attracted the attention of numerous foreign manufacturers.

Foreign-funded enterprises and institutions have set up business centers and procurement centers in Yiwu in succession, thus allowing Yiwu Small Commodity Market to evolve gradually from China's largest circulation, display, information, and manufacturing center for small commodities to the world's largest such center, with the scope of regional contacts extending from the surrounding counties and cities to the province, country, and abroad.

In summary, it is precisely the reinnovation activities which break through the original level on the basis of introduction, digestion, and absorption that have enabled Yiwu to gradually replace Guangzhou and Shenzhen to become China's circulation, display, information, and manufacturing center for small commodities. Such reinnovation activities have also equipped Yiwu Small Commodity Market with continuously extending influence and an increasingly stronger ability to gather domestic and foreign resources, thereby gradually forming a cross-regional division of labor and cooperation network centering on it, i.e., "Yiwu Business Circle". This suggests that the introduction, digestion, and absorption for reinnovation mode is extraordinarily significant to the development of Yiwu's enterprises, markets, and the city itself. It is the key for SMEs in Yiwu to develop, grow, have their own brands and independent technologies, and go international, which also helped Yiwu get rid of product imitation and embark on the path of independent development, thus promoting the transition of "manufactured in

Yiwu" to "created by Yiwu" and the evolution of "Yiwu Market" to "Yiwu Business Circle" (as shown in Figure 5.1).

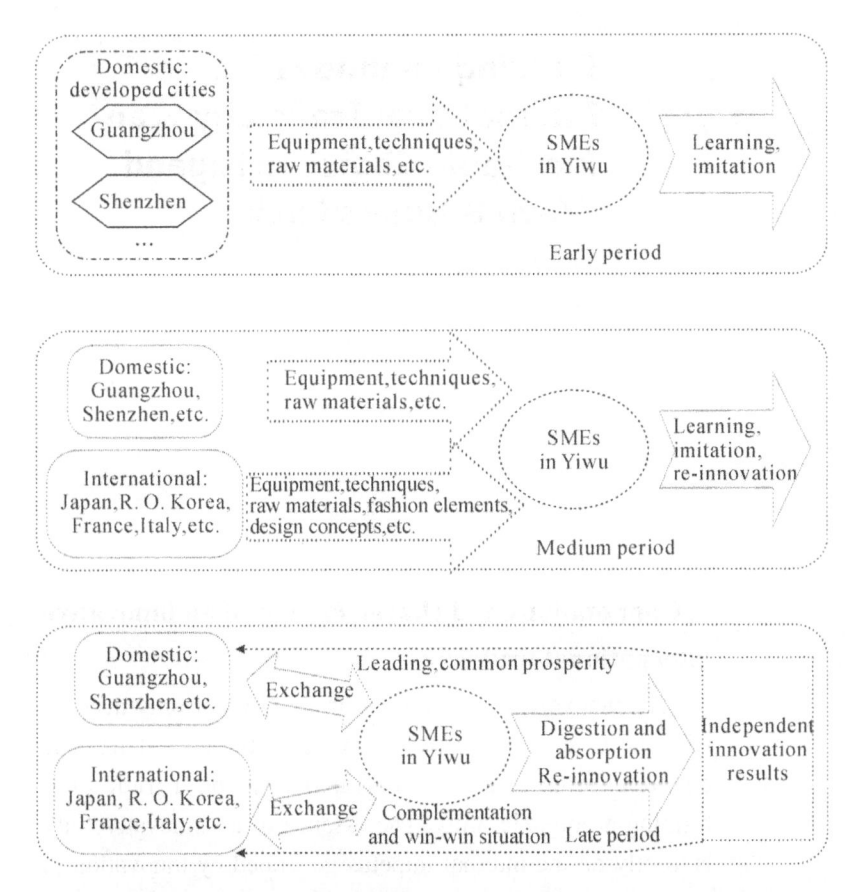

**Figure 5.1:   Introduction, digestion and absorption for reinnovation
course of enterprises in Yiwu**

Building an Innovative International Trade City Is an Inevitable Choice to Expand "Yiwu Business Circle"

II

1. Connotations and characteristics of an innovative international trade city

An innovative international trade city not only accords with the essence of an innovative city, but also shares the characteristics of an international city and a trade city, forming an organic unity. The essence of an innovative city is to rely on the internal impetus generated by innovation to promote all-round, coordinated, and sustainable development of the economy and society, and to change the situation in which rapid economic and social development is sustained through high resource levels, factor inputs, and enormous environmental costs. To build an innovative international trade city, Yiwu must grasp the above essence first. By implementing this dominant strategy, it can inspire the innovative spirit of the whole society, cultivate high-level innovative talents, foster innovative enterprises with international competitiveness, and form system, mechanism, and cultural environments conducive to independent innovation. Meanwhile, the Yiwu Innovative International Trade City also has prominent international characteristics. To be specific, it has the momentum and attitude of opening-up, widening exchanges, and conforming to the international community, and possesses modern urban infrastructure and highly diversified ideologies, value concepts, population composition, and ethnic structure. Here the multinational headquarters, large group companies, and internationally renowned finance, insurance, and research institutions are clustered, with a huge stock of assets, elemental flows, and internal and external trade volumes. Additionally, the Yiwu Innovative International Trade City also shows the unique character of a commercial city, where market space expansion and business pattern upgrading become the direct motives of its industrial development and urban expansion, and thereby forms a cross-regional division of labor and cooperation network centering on Yiwu Small Commodity Market.

The Yiwu Innovative International Trade City has the respective features, traits, and characteristics of an innovative city, an international city and a trade city. There are also mutually supportive, influential, promoting, and co-prospering internal relations among an innovative, an international, and a trade city, which are integrated into an organic whole. The formation of a trade city provides the economic basis and conditions for the development of an international city and for the construction of an innovative city; the development of an international city drives the promotion of a trade city and the construction of an innovative city; and the construction of an innovative city provides the impetus for the promotion of a trade city and for the sustainable development of an international city. The joint action of the three has allowed Yiwu to preliminarily realize the evolution from a trade city to an international trade city. In the next step, it will be transformed into an innovative international trade city (see Figure 5.2).

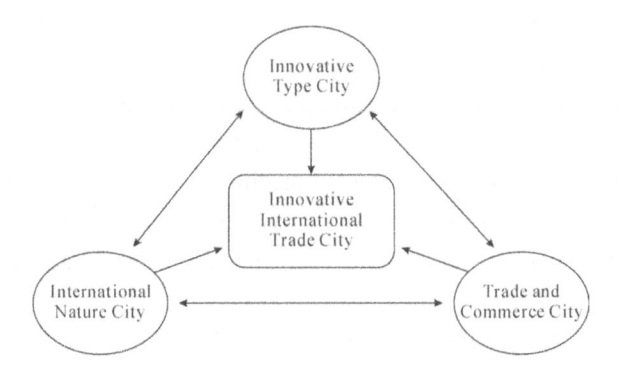

Figure 5.2:   Framework of Yiwu Innovative International Trade City

Currently, Yiwu is moving towards a truly international trade city. The innovative international trade city, as an expansion and upgradation of the international trade city, is an international trade city that integrates the characteristics of an innovative city, which is the future development direction of Yiwu. Building an innovative international trade city means that Yiwu will continue to implement the overall development strategy of "Flourish Business and Build City" in its future construction and will regard independent innovation as the fundamental direction and leading force of practicing the "Flourish Business and Build City" strategy, facilitating industrial upgrading and driving urban development. To this end, it will promote the formation of persistent international competitiveness in commercial circulation by enhancing the independent innovation capability to accelerate the process of urban modernization and internationalization. It will also fully utilize the advantages of internationalization and the commerce industry, and gather innovative resources both at home and abroad to promote the comprehensive, coordinated, and sustainable development of the entire economy and society through continuous independent innovation activities, so as to become an innovative city with worldwide influence, prominently internationalized urban functions, and a highly diversified social structure that plays a greater role in the international commercial circulation, information display, R&D manufacturing, and price formation systems of small commodities.

In summary, the connotation of the innovative international trade city is to regard independent innovation as the fundamental direction and leading force insisting on the overall development strategy of "Flourish Business and Build City", facilitating industrial upgrading and driving urban development under the new historical conditions, to cultivate the independent innovation ability guided by the international expansion of commercial functions and scope, and to realize the comprehensive, coordinated, and sustainable development of the economy and society by relying on and fully utilizing the advantages of the commerce industry and international environment to become an innovative city with a strong innovative ability, great commercial advantages, and a high degree of internationalization.

2. Tremendous significance in building an innovative international trade city to expand "Yiwu Business Circle"

The construction of the Yiwu Innovative International Trade City is a concrete manifestation of the regional innovation system, while a vitally important point in the construction of a regional innovation system is the innovation-related exchanges and cooperation between enterprises. So far, the links between relevant economic entities and regions in "Yiwu Business Circle" are mainly business and commercial exchanges, and what accompanies the inter-enterprise business dealings is the transfer of information. After the CPC Central Committee's proposal of building an innovative country and Zhejiang and other provinces and cities' setting of goals to build innovative provinces and cities, independent innovation has been receiving increasingly broader social attention. Many enterprises have established their own independent innovation strategies one after another, putting more emphasis on the roles of technological, organizational, and management innovations in enterprise development

and in collaboration among industries, universities, and research institutes. The inter-enterprise exchanges and cooperation have also been infused with more innovation-related contents. The construction of Yiwu as an innovative international trade city coincides exactly with and will effectively boost the above development trends. This greatly enhances the independent innovation awareness of business owners and manufacturers associated with Yiwu Small Commodity Market at home and abroad, and promotes their further launch of independent innovation activities in business pattern, organizational form, management mode, technological craft, and other aspects. These activities thereby prompt the transformation of information transfer between enterprises, and between enterprises and business owners from the market supply and demand-dominant business information to more diversified information including market supply and demand, product innovation, technological innovation, and management innovation, so as to enrich the contents and forms of inter-enterprise cooperation. The strengthening of inter-enterprise and inter-regional innovative information transfers and exchanges attributable to the construction of the Yiwu Innovative International Trade City will facilitate the Yiwu Small Commodity Market-centered cross-regional division of labor and cooperation network on innovative relations, which will be supplementary to it when concerning business relations. The former will continue to enrich and expand the connotation and denotation of the latter, while the latter offers important support to the deepening and development of the former. To be specific, on the one hand, the exchanges and cooperation between enterprises, between enterprises and research institutes, between enterprises and tertiary institutions, and between regions carried out based on the needs of independent innovation will continuously intensify the cross-regional business division of labor and cooperation relations formed. These exchanges prompt the Yiwu Small Commodity Market to form a new division of labor and cooperation network respecting independent innovation on the basis of the original contents and forms of division of labor and cooperation such as the transportation and trade of goods, the processing with supplied materials, the export of labor services, the investment in factory establishment, and the introduction of talents. This will surely enrich and expand the connotation and denotation of the original relations between all economic entities and regions related to "Yiwu Business Circle" to great extents. On the other hand, the original business-based division of labor and cooperation relations between the relevant economic entities and regions in "Yiwu Business Circle" ensures long-term contacts and exchanges between enterprises, and between enterprises and business owners, thus laying the foundation for the transfer of innovation-related information and for the innovation-based cooperation and exchanges between them. Since the ultimate purpose of innovation-related communication and cooperation is to gain corresponding economic benefits just the same as the business contacts, the business division of labor and cooperation relations provide important support to the further deepening of the innovative cooperation and exchange relations. To sum up, the construction of an innovative international trade city will promote the independent innovation-related information transfer, cooperation and exchanges among all relevant economic entities and regions that carry out division of labor and cooperation around Yiwu, and facilitate the formation of an innovation-based cross-regional network centering on Yiwu Small Commodity Market, thereby enhancing and expanding the connotation and denotation of "Yiwu Business Circle" immensely.

With the increasing degree of internationalization of "Yiwu Business Circle", the business owners and manufacturers associated with Yiwu Small Commodity Market will face ever-fierce international competition, which requires them to strictly follow the international market norms and to participate in fair competition in accordance with the international trade rules. At present, the number of disputes over international trade is increasing, and the intellectual property rules and protection strategies initiated by western countries and multinational corporations have become the "killer" that restricts the development

of China's industries and enterprises, which have also become an impenetrable obstacle to the participation of Yiwu Small Commodity Market-associated business owners and manufacturers in international competition. Today, with increasingly intensified international competition and ever-deepening exchanges and cooperation at home and abroad, the old way of occupying the international market relying mainly on low-value-added processing, OEM production, and quantity is no longer feasible, and the low price advantage of the small commodity market will face serious international challenges. Therefore, all relevant economic entities and regions in "Yiwu Business Circle" must make all-round innovations in the fields of market, pattern, technology, service, and management with the support of concept, system, and mechanism innovations, which is the only way of enhancing their international competitiveness and ensuring enduring prosperity in the fierce international market competition. To this end, it is not only necessary to develop a large number of competitive products with independent intellectual property rights and brand names in the field of production, but more importantly, one should fully utilize the innovative traditions and advantages in terms of institution, system, and mechanism to make further bold innovations on commercial circulation patterns, organizational forms, and management modes while laying a particular emphasis on enhancing the intensity of intellectual property protection.

Some scholars believe that independent innovation is only suitable for the country, provinces, municipalities, autonomous regions, and some prefecture-level cities with powerful economic and technological strength, while county-level cities should not propose to build innovative cities. In our opinion, a specific analysis is necessary in targeting different situations, rather than simply considering the administrative level as the determining criterion. This is because the essential and fundamental purpose of advocating for independent innovation and establishing the goal of building an innovative country, province, or city is to break through the constraints of resource factors and environmental bottlenecks, and to seek a brand new impetus for maintaining the comprehensive, coordinated, and sustainable development of the economy and society. That is, to sustain rapid economic and social development by relying on the continuous independent innovation activities of science and technology, knowledge, manpower, culture, and the system instead of the intensive inputs of resources and huge environmental costs. In short, they aim at upgrading the industrial level, optimizing the industrial structure, and accelerating the pace of knowledge orientation, marketization, urbanization, industrialization, modernization, and internationalization by enhancing the independent innovation capability to uplift economic and social development to a new level. Hence, there is no fundamental difference between innovative country, innovative province, or innovative city regarding the fundamental objective and essential connotation. They are consistent overall: to make efforts toward such a goal to create a risk-taking, boldly-innovating cultural atmosphere in all of society for forming an open, inclusive, and competitive innovation environment; to cultivate a sense of cooperation for helping each other and working together; to establish an industry–university–research institute collaboration system comprising enterprises, research institutes, and tertiary institutions for stimulating the innovation enthusiasm and potential of enterprises; and to train a group of high-level innovative talents, raise a number of high-level innovative entrepreneurs, foster a batch of innovative enterprises with strong core competency, form a range of internationally influential innovative industries, and create a series of internationally renowned trademarks and brands, thereby enhancing the comprehensive competitiveness of the entire country, province, or city to gain the initiative in open international competition.

Clearly, the innovative country, province, and city are inherently consistent. Whether an independent innovation goal can be established or not depends primarily on the development stages and trends of relevant subjects, rather than on the administrative level. We should see

whether the subjects accord with the objective law of economic and technological development, and whether they confront the urgent need of independent innovation, especially if they have the corresponding basic conditions. As long as they are in conformity with their actual development and in line with the law of objective development, there is an urgent need for promoting comprehensive, coordinated, and sustainable development of the entire economy and society relying on independent innovation. If the corresponding basic conditions are satisfied, it is possible and feasible to establish a goal of building an innovative country, province, or city. Yiwu's construction of an innovative international trade city is in conformity with its actual development, which is not only needed for breaking through the turning point in development and stepping into a new steady, rapid, and sustainable development, but is also needed for further deepening the division of labor and cooperative relations between economic entities and regions in Yiwu Small Commodity Market and for extending the connotation and denotation of "Yiwu Business Circle". Building an innovative city is conducive to guiding the relevant economic entities in "Yiwu Business Circle" to enhance their own competitiveness effectively by strengthening independent innovation ability and to introduce new technologies, adopt new techniques, develop new products, create new brands, and open up new markets. It is also helpful for relevant economic regions of "Yiwu Business Circle" to concretely transform the sustained impetus driving economic and social development into various independent innovation activities to enhance their own core competency and improve their international competitiveness.

In summary, the construction of an innovative international trade city has become the fundamental outlet for a large number of domestic manufacturers associated with Yiwu Small Commodity Market to get rid of being "production workshops" for foreign companies or relying on OEM for their livelihood so that consequently they cause intellectual property issues. It has also become the correct choice to guide the relevant economic entities in "Yiwu Business Circle" to enhance their awareness of independent innovation, increase innovation input, strengthen innovative cooperation among industries, universities, and research institutes, and improve core competencies. Also, it has become an effective way to prompt the relevant economic regions of "Yiwu Business Circle" to transform the growth mode, optimize the industrial structure, and realize sustainable development, which is of great significance to enhancing and expanding the connotation and denotation of division of labor and cooperative relations between the relevant economic entities and regions in "Yiwu Business Circle".

3. Realistic basis for building an innovative international trade city

Yiwu enjoys a powerful international market advantage, well-developed commerce and trade, as well as gratifying achievements in the development of industry and trade led by Yiwu Small Commodity Market, which have been described in the previous chapter and will not be repeated here. Yiwu has been increasingly internationalized, with diverse ideologies, value orientations, and population compositions. It has favorable conditions for gathering innovative resources both at home and abroad, and enjoys international environmental advantages unmatched by many other county-level cities. The majority of goods produced and sold in Yiwu are small commodities. Unlike high-tech products, some hit products have little gap with the world's advanced level, which even reach and surpass the world's level and some are leading the international development trend in some fields. In 2005, the UN Refugee Agency set up an information procurement center in Yiwu, which is the second center in China by the agency after Beijing. In 2005, Yiwu Public Security Bureau became the first county-level public security department in China authorized to handle the visa and residence permit for foreigners, and the Yiwu People's Court became the first grass-roots court in China that had jurisdiction over foreign-related civil and commercial cases. Clearly, Yiwu has already possesses some

characteristics of internationalization, which lays a solid foundation for further construction of an innovative international trade city.

Yiwu has a good culture of innovation and tradition. After four decades of development, the city has gathered a range of innovative resources, fostered a batch of hi-tech and technology-based enterprises, established a number of R&D centers and independent brands, owned a number of inventions and patents, introduced and cultivated a group of innovative talents, formulated a series of policies to encourage independent innovation, and possessed a certain independent innovation capability. In general, an independent innovation pattern dominated by the high-tech industries such as bio-medicine, electronic instrumentation, opto-mechatronics, and new materials, and radiating such traditional advantageous industries as knitwear, hosiery, jewelry, garments, handicrafts, zippers, cosmetics, and stationery has been formed.[3] Meanwhile, Yiwu has vigorously implemented the brand-led strategy, intensified the protection of intellectual property, formed a sound patent management network, enhanced the enterprises' patent awareness and utilization ability, and established the pre-censorship system for patent offices to strengthen patented product supervision in the "Yiwu Fair" and other major exhibitions from the source, thereby creating a good atmosphere of "respecting creation, protecting innovation".

Enterprises in Yiwu continue to strengthen the exchanges and cooperation with the tertiary institutions and research institutes via the platform of R&D centers, thereby improving the sci-tech innovation system with enterprises as the mainstay and with tertiary institutions and research institutes as the supports that combine independent development with the introduction, digestion, and absorption for reinnovation. In 2003–2005, Yiwu organized

---

[3] See: Enterprises become the main body of independent innovation in Yiwu. *Yiwu News Network*, 2005-12-19. http://news.ywol.cn/200501101/ca56891.htm.

two sessions of "Technological Docking Activities between 100 Experts and 1000 Entrepreneurs", as well as over 20 sessions of technological docking activities between the Chinese Academy of Sciences (CAS) and Yiwu, and between Shanghai and Yiwu. The city has also signed more than 200 scientific and technological cooperation projects and reached over 300 cooperative intentions. The R&D centers of Yiwu's enterprises had established close scientific and technological partnerships with more than 120 tertiary institutions and research institutes both at home and abroad through various forms of technological cooperation docking activities. For example, a batch of R&D institutions jointly established by academia and enterprises such as the CAS Yiwu Base for Innovative Research and Social Practice, the Zhejiang University Sci-Tech Cooperation and Exchange Center in Yiwu, the Zhejiang University Power Link Technology R&D Center, the Zhejiang University– Neoglory Material & Chemical R&D Center, the Langsha–Donghua University Hosiery Research Institute, and the Zhejiang Sci-Tech University–Jinhui Chemical Fiber R&D Center had been set up, which greatly improved the technological innovation and new product development capabilities of enterprises.

To promote scientific and technological innovation activities, Yiwu has successively formulated and promulgated a series of important policy opinions such as the Planning for Strengthening the City Through Science and Technology, Measures for Awarding Scientific and Technological Prizes, Measures for the Use and Administration of Special Funds for Developing Sci-tech Industrialization, Several Policy Opinions on Promoting the Construction and Development of Corporate R&D Centers, Several Policy Opinions on Strengthening the Patent System to Promote Technological Innovation, the Decision on Fully Implementing the Modern Talents Project and the Notification of Several Provisions on Introducing Talents at Home and Abroad to create a sound innovative and entrepreneurial environment, thus providing a strong policy support to the scientific and technological development in the entire city and to enhancing its independent innovation capability.

In summary, with a well-developed commerce and trade industry, prominent internationalization features, and a good foundation for innovation, Yiwu has already satisfied the basic conditions for building an innovative international trade city. Under the favorable external atmosphere in which the CPC Central Committee, the State Council, and the Zhejiang Provincial Party Committee and Government strongly advocate independent innovation, Yiwu should seize this rare opportunity for development and make full use of its unique advantages to make bold attempts, dare to innovate, and construct the platform and system for independent innovation from various aspects, such as the systems and mechanisms, policies and regulations, cultural environment, market subjects, technological intermediaries, and personnel training. Yiwu should also take feasible measures to achieve effective integration and optimal allocation of independent innovation resources; it should mobilize the enthusiasm of industrial and trade enterprises, business operators, tertiary institutions, research institutes, and intermediary service agencies to the maximum extent; and it should give full play to its role as the main force of independent innovation. Meanwhile, Yiwu should create a socio-cultural environment that encourages innovation and tolerates failure, and vigorously recruit and train innovative talents, especially a group of innovative leader-type talents with internationally advanced and domestically leading academic, technological levels who are capable of organizing and leading major sci-tech innovation activities, as well as technical leaders with strong organizational innovation capability, and a backbone R&D staff with a strong innovation ability. The city should establish and improve the innovation failure protection mechanism, develop a diversified innovative investment business and a multilayered capital market, improve and perfect the guarantee market and the technological property rights transaction market, effectively transform government functions, further promote the implementation of relevant policies, and amply reward the achievements of independent innovation, so as to offer a comprehensive coordination service to boost the construction of an innovative international trade city.

We believe that the goal of building an innovative international trade city needs to be accomplished by relying on three levels of driving forces: (1) Innovation platform, innovation culture, innovation government, innovation guarantee, and innovation intermediaries are as the primary boosters. They provide the necessary environmental basis, condition support, and social atmosphere for the independent innovation activities of innovation entities, which are important basic conditions for the implementation of an independent innovation strategy. (2) Innovative enterprises, innovative industries, research institutes, and tertiary institutions constitute the secondary driving forces, relying on which the innovation activities are carried out primarily. These entities are the key forces in implementing the independent innovation strategy, which determines the speed of scientific and technological progress, the size of human capital motivation, and the strength of independent innovation capabilities for the city. (3) Innovative talents are the ultimate engine. The formation of independent innovation capabilities in the innovative enterprises, innovative industries, research institutes, and tertiary institutions must all rely on the subjective initiative of innovative talents. The results of all innovative activities are ultimately the fruits of corresponding R&D activities carried out by the innovative talents. Only by relying on the innovative talents can the independent innovation strategy be put into practice. Therefore, the construction of an innovative international trade city ultimately comes down to the motivating role of innovative talents, as shown in Figure 5.3. This will be discussed further in Section III.

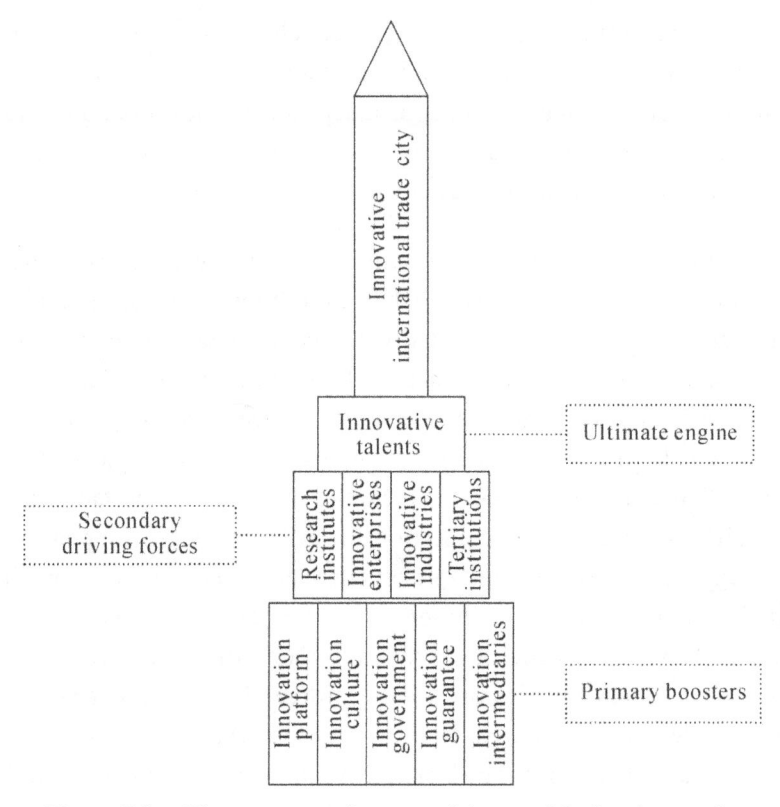

**Figure 5.3:   Three-stage rocket propulsion model of an innovative
international trade city**

III Countermeasures for Building an Innovative International Trade City

1. Consolidating the foundation of innovation, creating an innovative environment

1.1 Building an innovation platform

The independent innovation platform is the network node for gathering innovation elements, activating innovation resources, promoting knowledge flow and technology diffusion, and transforming innovation achievements in an innovation system. It is the "converter" and "distributor" of innovation achievements, and the connector of innovative functions of different innovation entities in the regional innovation network. The construction of an independent innovation platform is of great significance in effectively tapping innovation potential, utilizing the innovation advantage, and cutting the innovation costs for carriers led by Yiwu Small Commodity Market, such as industrial and trade enterprises, research institutes, and tertiary institutions; it is the crucial condition and guarantee for Yiwu in building an innovative international trade city. Hence, it is necessary to vigorously strengthen the establishment of independent innovation platforms such as the public infrastructure platforms, the industry-specific innovation platforms, and the regional innovation platforms.

The first category is the public infrastructure platforms. They make full use of modern technologies like information and networks to strategically reorganize and systematically optimize the basic conditions and resources for innovation, in order to promote the whole society's efficient allocation and comprehensive utilization of innovation resources, and to enhance the capability of independent innovation. Their role is similar to that of energy, transportation, water conservancy, and other infrastructure in the national economy, so they have the attributes of public goods and are inseparable from governmental support and investment. They mainly include: (1) Literature data platforms. Literature retrieval, patent retrieval, and standard search are the necessary tasks at the beginning of innovation. The timely updating of literature data helps the innovation team accurately grasp and keep up with the innovation pace of international peers. (2) Experimental condition platforms. Due to the high specialization degree of many laboratory equipment and instruments and the heavy investment in individual construction, especially for large-scale instruments and equipment, SMEs are even less capable of investing. Therefore, building a public experimental condition platform is highly necessary, which creates a good foundation for the development of industrial generic technologies. (3) Information service platforms, such as the technology market and sci-tech achievement sharing platform, the intellectual property rights public service platform, and the standardized technology service platform. They link information about achievements, funds, and projects together, which are an important medium for innovation activities and achievement transformation that helps accelerate the pace of the innovation and transformation of related achievements.

Further development of "Yiwu Business Circle" will make the sharing of innovation resources easier between the relevant economic zones at home and abroad that are linked together around Yiwu Small Commodity Market. During the construction of public infrastructure platforms, Yiwu should actively promote the exchanges and cooperation in these economic zones concerning the construction of independently innovating public infrastructure platforms to strive to build cross-regional public infrastructure platforms for independent innovation.

The second category is the industrial innovation platforms. They are independent innovation platforms built from the perspectives of industrial generic technologies and key technologies. They include the vertical temporal connection and the horizontal correlative ties, with a scale larger than the platforms composed of several innovation carriers. Their functions also cover financing and the industrialization of innovation achievements. Industrial innovation platforms are more closely linked to enterprises, which are more capable of providing enterprises with more direct independent innovation services. In particular for Yiwu, which is filled with SMEs and lacks large enterprises, the construction of industrial innovation platforms can make up for the weak technological innovation ability of SMEs, integrate the innovation resources, optimize the allocation of innovation resources, fully utilize the efficiency of limited innovative elements, and take the road of intensive independent innovation. At present, the enterprises engaged in independent innovation activities in Yiwu are primarily the industry leading enterprises, while many small businesses can only follow and imitate them due to limited strength. This not only undermines the large enterprises' enthusiasm for independent innovation, but is also adverse to the long-term development of small enterprises. Therefore, the government must play a crucial role in the construction of industry innovation platforms, which should focus their support on the basic fields and the research and development of industrial generic technologies aiming at the innovation needs of vast SMEs.

The third category is the regional innovation platforms. They generally take the leading industries in the region as the main entry point, which are established to strengthen the massive economy and support local economic development. They contain broader elements and resources than the industry innovation platforms. With the rapid economic development in Yiwu, the shortage of production factors such as capital, land, and human resources and the issue of price rises have become increasingly prominent, which have become important constraints to sustainable development. The construction of regional innovation platforms is conducive to "developing Yiwu by jumping out of it", effectively integrating the innovation resources and elements of surrounding counties and cities, "valuing usage over possession", and promoting innovative resources to break through the limits of administrative divisions and flow freely in a rapid and extensive way. Through such exchanges and cooperation, the counties and cities around Yiwu can more effectively develop and utilize their own innovation resources and improve the efficiency of resource utilization while driving local enterprises to enhance their independent innovation capability by building regional innovation platforms, thereby achieving the win–win and multi-win goals. To this end, it is necessary to take full advantage of the cross-regional division of labor and cooperative relations resulting from the development of "Yiwu Business Circle" and to further strengthen the exchanges and cooperation between relevant economic regions concerning the construction of independent innovation platforms to jointly build the regional innovation platforms.

To promote and strengthen the construction of the above independent innovation platforms, Yiwu can start from the following aspects:

Firstly, professional and comprehensive incubators can be established within the economic development zones and hi-tech parks to promote the incubation of high-tech projects that meet the development prospect. A good entrepreneurial environment can be created by concentrating manpower, material resources, and financial resources, so that the high-tech projects satisfying the economic and technological development trends and requirements can be transformed into productive forces promptly to achieve good economic efficiency. Industries like electronic information, new materials, and environmental protection can be developed vigorously within the high-tech parks. They can then become a clustering center for domestic and foreign high-tech enterprises, an R&D design service center for small commodities, and a training center for innovative personnel to attract the entry of domestic and foreign high-tech enterprises, enterprises with independent brands and proprietary technologies, as well as high-tax enterprises, so as to produce agglomeration effect.

Secondly, a number of innovation service platforms, such as the industrial design service centers and virtual research institutes, can be set up. By establishing the industrial design service center and separately setting up the design service centers for industries like hosiery, jewelry, garments, handicrafts, zippers, cosmetics, stationery, and toys, the overall R&D strength of related industries especially the advantaged industries can be enhanced, thereby promoting the creation of independent brands and the development of proprietary technologies. By integrating the scientific research strengths at home and abroad, the virtual academy of sciences can be established in Yiwu in accordance with the principle of "favoring existence over possession, valuing efficiency over appearance". A modern network-based information exchange platform, an exhibition platform, an innovation service center, an on-line diagnosis system, an evaluation and testing system, a virtual laboratory, and a library can also be constructed, so that the advantages in document literature, experiment equipment, talents, and technology of relevant domestic and foreign organizations can be integrated with Yiwu's trade, capital, and international advantages to strengthen enterprises in Yiwu, especially the independent innovation strength of SMEs.

Thirdly, an innovation carrier consortia can be established based on the market-oriented principles. Yiwu can encourage different innovation

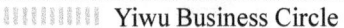

carriers, especially numerous SMEs, to freely create joint innovation platforms or independent innovation alliances based on market-oriented principles and respective shortages and limitations in technological structure and innovation capability on the basis of mutual trust, thereby integrating the superior resources of groups, carrying out research and development of generic technologies, and popularizing the application of generic technologies, so as to enhance the overall sci-tech innovation capability and make up for the deficiencies of individual innovation capability. The city can also give full play to the core and leading role of large enterprises' R&D (technology) centers in the platform construction and establish special academic teams for particular research topics by uniting relevant enterprises, research institutes, and tertiary institutions around the R&D centers. On these bases, cooperation can be deepened gradually to ultimately form smooth, efficient, and long-term collaboration among industries, universities, and research institutes. A special administration office for innovation carrier platforms can be set up in the management sector of scientific research institutions to strengthen the information exchanges between carriers and to provide comprehensive and coordinated services for the construction of joint innovation platforms.

Fourthly, a regional independent innovation platform network can be nurtured and built actively in accordance with the principles of mutual benefit and win–win idea. At present, although Yiwu has conducted various forms of innovative exchanges and cooperation in different ranges, it has not really formed any mechanism for sharing innovative resources in the region, nor has the decentralized use of innovative resources been changed fundamentally, so the utilization efficiency remains low. Therefore, it is urgently necessary to advocate various economic agents related to innovation in the region to make explorations and practices themed by government–industry–university–research institute cooperation under the framework of certain science, technology, and economic policies. Although the construction of independent innovation platforms shortens the bridge between industries, universities, and research institutes to a certain extent and promotes regional innovation with enterprises as the main body, it is also prone to insufficient exchanges and cooperation between different innovation platforms and between different innovation carriers of similar innovation platforms, thus resulting in repeated construction of innovation platforms, unreasonable layout or structural configuration and other drawbacks. Hence, during the construction of independent innovation platforms in Yiwu, the city must explore the establishment of a cross-regional cooperation mechanism for independent innovation platforms, promote the collaboration among various relevant innovation platforms through a certain coordination mechanism, and actively nurture and build a regional network for these platforms. The cross-regional division of labor and cooperative relations already within "Yiwu Business Circle" will provide very convenient conditions for achieving these.

1.2 Promoting the innovation culture

At present, the majority of cities in China focus on sci-tech input, taxation, and financial policies in promoting independent innovation and the innovative city construction, while paying insufficient attention to the overall urban innovation culture and the improvement in the quality of citizens. Nevertheless, the construction of an innovative city is not merely a task of one or a few departments such as science and technology, finance, and taxation, nor can it be achieved by a few departments, several projects, a few high-tech enterprises, or a few high-tech parks alone. It is a systematic project that requires the extensive participation of the entire society, whose realization ultimately depends on the improvement of the broad masses' overall innovative quality. Therefore, Yiwu must vigorously publicize and earnestly implement the sci-tech work guidelines of "independent innovation, focusing on strides, supporting development, and leading the future", as well as the spirit of the national, provincial science and technology conferences, and independent innovation conferences; and it must build a value system that advocates innovation, in order to further

stimulate the whole society's enthusiasm for innovation and creation. By establishing learning organizations and building a learning society, a good atmosphere of learning and innovation can be created throughout society to provide an important environmental basis for independent innovation, so as to bring innovation to the general public and to the grass-roots level, thus allowing the broad masses of the people to become an important factor and a key force of innovation.

In the early period of entrepreneurship, receiving positive encouragement and support can enhance the self-confidence of entrepreneurs. This is an intangible asset and is crucially important for improving the success rate of entrepreneurship and innovation. In this regard, Yiwu should advocate its "Qiaotang Sect" team spirit,[4] deepen the innovation subjects' team awareness, and strive to cultivate entrepreneurship, team spirit, and cooperative consciousness. Independent innovation is a brand new thinking and practical activity, which is full of uncertainties and risks. This requires the brave exploration by innovators and the adequate understanding and support from all sectors of society. Therefore, Yiwu should vigorously advocate an innovative culture of daring to take risks, being brave to innovate, tolerating failure, pursuing success, openness and inclusiveness, upholding competition, being full of passion, and avoiding fickleness; it should internalize innovation into an urban spirit and form industry and trade enterprises, universities, research institutes, and government agencies that are conducive to the leading role of small commodity market in Yiwu to vigorously promote and implement the new-era "Yiwu Spirit" in the independent innovation strategy.

Innovation has a broad extension, which includes not only technologies and products, but also various aspects of economy, society,

---

[4]See Lu Lijun, Bai Xiaohu, Wang Zuqiang: *Market Yiwu: From Chicken Feather for Sugar to International Commerce*. Hangzhou: Zhejiang People's Publishing House, 2003, p. 52.

and culture such as concepts, institutions, systems, mechanisms, management, and development strategies. It can be said that any act which shatters the original framework to gain a new idea or a new product and transforms such into economic and social benefits is an innovation. Therefore, we should advocate viewing things from new, different perspectives. For example, after the overcapacity of middle and low-end yarns and shirts, some wool textile enterprises in Yiwu shifted to the production of special flame-retardant yarns, whereas some shirt enterprises shifted to the production of higher value-added seamless underwear. This is a typical example of successful civilian innovation activities. Yiwu must vigorously carry forward such a flexible work style throughout the process of building an innovative international trade city, encourage innovators to cultivate a mercurial consciousness to seek breakthroughs in various aspects such as decision-making, production arrangement, quality inspection, product transportation, external cooperation and exchanges, personnel systems, and financial systems and to put forward new ideas, new frameworks, and new models to facilitate system innovations in enterprises.

In addition, vigorous research and publicity on building an innovative international trade city are necessary, so as to allow the governments, enterprises, intermediary organizations, and the general public to reach a consensus, and to correctly understand and grasp the connotation, the characteristics, the evaluation criteria, the objective system, the starting point, and the work focus of the innovative international trade city. Particular emphasis should be placed on profoundly understanding the significance of building an innovative international trade city to transform the pattern of economic growth, promoting the industrial upgradation, and expanding "Yiwu Business Circle", so as to create a new situation in which the economic entities and regions associated with "Yiwu Business Circle" work together to jointly promote the construction of Yiwu as an innovative international trade city.

1.3 Building an innovative government

While advancing the construction of the innovative international trade city, the Yiwu Municipal Party Committee and Government must further establish innovation consciousness. First of all, they should vigorously promote the spirit and culture of innovation within the system, reform the means, modes, and ways of management and service, introduce, train, and reserve innovative personnel and give them more room to display their talents, and promote the construction of an innovative government from multiple perspectives to offer innovative governmental services in various fields. Specifically, they must further proceed from the goal of building a service-oriented government, then respect the market economy rules and the innovation activities of masses, and provide a favorable external environment for the city's independent innovative activities. In particular, the science and technology department should transfer the function of sci-tech innovation management gradually from the direct management of projects and funds to the strengthening of sci-tech planning, institutional improvement and environment construction, the enhancement of service and organizational capabilities, and the promotion of platform construction. It must also shift the focus of science and technology funding support from general project support to the major support for the weak links in the innovation chain, to the organization of R&D and promotion of the key generic technologies, and to the construction of various infrastructures for scientific and technological progress. The emphasis should be placed on guiding, encouraging, and pushing rather than direct investment. Through a small amount of governmental funds, enterprises should be encouraged to invest large amounts of funds into the field of innovation, so as to produce the effect of "moving mountains with few resources". All departments should change the idea of contending for or extending power for departmental interests, eliminate the fear of getting their functions weakened, allow the market to give full play to its fundamental role in the allocation of innovative resources, and guide the organic integration of sci-tech innovation elements with other elements of social production. They should also organically combine carrier construction, project research, and personnel training together through funding arrangements, breeding projects relying on bases, and training personnel relying on projects, so that various innovation resource elements can truly concentrate towards highly capable, efficient innovation teams with a strong innovation awareness. It is also necessary to promote the transformation and upgrading of research institutes and encourage the development of private non-enterprise scientific research institutes, to fully exert the guiding role of government procurement and promote independent innovation of enterprises, to try to invite industry professionals (randomly selected rather than from large enterprises only) into the government decision-making advisory committee to fully listen to the industrial sector's views and suggestions concerning independent innovation and innovative international trade city construction, to formulate the research framework plan for sci-tech innovation to coordinate and guide the independent innovation activities as a whole, to evaluate the benefits from innovation investment, and to establish a set of tracking and analysis systems to carry out effectiveness management.

There are many factors that affect the independent innovative capability of a city. So aside from directly affecting innovation itself, the independent innovation policies may also include various indirect influential factors acting on innovation, such as consumer preference, the degree of market competition, and the extent of enterprise agglomeration. To drive the scientific and technological progress and enhance the independent innovative capability of enterprises, Yiwu has formulated and issued a series of policy opinions. Facing the arduous task of building an innovative international trade city, it is necessary for Yiwu to further promulgate more policy opinions on encouraging independent innovation in various fields such as science and technology, economy, education, culture, and urban construction, and to further lower the "registration threshold" and overall operating costs of innovative enterprises. In particular, concerted innovation incentive

policies should be formed in terms of investment and financing, technical standards, foreign trade, government procurement, financial assistance, and consumption; and a policy system that promotes the effective implementation of the independent innovation strategy in an all-round way should be constructed from two aspects: direct effect and indirect influence. Meanwhile, it is necessary to earnestly step up publicity and the implementation of these policy recommendations, so that they can truly be transformed into a powerful impetus for promoting independent innovation by enterprises, industries, and the broad masses of the people.

In addition, the relationship between technology imports and independent development must be handled properly. While continuing to encourage multinational corporations to set up R&D centers in Yiwu, it is more important to adequately digest and absorb the already introduced technologies for reinnovation, to facilitate integrated innovation on more mature, highly correlated technologies, and to strive for original innovation on technologies that are difficult to introduce. It is by no means advisable to launch R&D of any product that has entered a recession period. Yiwu is recommended to combine the attraction of foreign investment with the adjustment and optimization of product mix, and to formulate the appropriate planning and regulatory policies to attract more foreign investment in the high-tech industries and the technological updating of existing enterprises. The city should strengthen the international exchanges and cooperation in science and technology and introduce advanced foreign technologies at a high starting point, especially patented technologies, software, and essential key equipment. It is of particular importance to strengthen the digestion and absorption of some key strategic technologies and the efforts in independent innovation.

1.4 Creating the innovation security system

1.4.1 Perfecting the IPR protection system

Intellectual Property Rights (IPR) is the basis and measure of independent innovation, and an important means of market competition.

Many foreign multinational corporations obtain IPR through independent innovation, and then seize the commanding heights of global competition through a strong IPR protection system, thereby providing a steady stream of motivation for independent innovation. Such a market competition strategy provides a remarkable enlightenment for the construction of Yiwu as an innovative international trade city: to form a virtuous circle of independent innovation, IPR protection is the crucial key. In the course of the development of Yiwu Small Commodity Market, there had been some acts of infringement on IPR and the manufacturing and sale of fake goods. This had disrupted the market order and undermined the enterprises' enthusiasm for independent innovation and the scientific researchers' motivation for innovation. It has undoubtedly seriously damaged the international image of Yiwu as an international city connected with the world, easily triggering appeals from foreign companies. Therefore, efforts must be stepped up in respecting independent innovation achievements, protecting independent innovation products, maintaining independent innovation technologies, and encouraging independent innovation brands.

It is necessary to actively implement the IPR strategy, cultivate the IPR awareness of enterprises and market operators, form an IPR protection system integrating patents, trademarks, copyrights and know-hows, and support the establishment of an international IPR protection and assistance mechanism led by industry associations. Yiwu should, by means of the inherent division of labor and cooperative relations among the economic regions associated with "Yiwu Business Circle", strengthen the exchanges and cooperation in the protection of IPR, jointly enforce the law on IPR protection through cross-regional collaboration, and intensify the efforts for patent protection. It should also actively promote the transformation of patent protection from discrete protection to portfolio protection, the transformation of patent application from the domestic application to the rational distribution of domestic and foreign applications, and the transformation of patent type

from the appearance design and utility model to the patent for invention. Meanwhile, the city should promote the standardization of products, businesses, and industries, guide and support enterprises to actively participate in the formulation of international, national, and industry standards, and form technologies and standards with independent IPR through digestion and absorption for reinnovation. In addition, it should encourage enterprises to establish technical standards alliances, so as to promote the integration of independent IPR with the technical standards to form de facto standards[5] for competitive industries.

1.4.2 Improving the innovation risk protection mechanism

In general, independent innovation activities are characterized by large investment, long duration, great variability, and a high probability of failure. For numerous SMEs in Yiwu, the high risk resulting from such activities is hardly bearable. Therefore, establishment of a sound innovation risk protection mechanism is necessary, so as to enhance the strength of SMEs in carrying out independent innovation activities with the help of external forces to reduce their worries. To this end, Yiwu should encourage the development of diversified venture capital firms and venture capital funds, boldly introduce foreign venture capital institutions, and draw on their mature experience in operation management to encourage and guide the domestic and local private capital to establish venture capital funds in Yiwu; it should adopt a diversified equity structure and management mode, and invest in independent innovation projects that meet the market demand and have great development potential, thereby providing an incubator function for the innovative activities of SMEs. Improvements of the independent innovation loan guarantee system for SMEs is necessary by reducing the proportion of commercial bank guarantees, establishing the loan risk guarantee reserve, increasing the financial discount interest rate, and

---

[5]Refers to the business standard or industry standard that has been successfully accepted by the industrial sector without the approval of any official or quasi-official standard setting body.

encouraging the development of innovation risk investment guarantee organizations, so as to alleviate the capital bottleneck restriction of SMEs in their independent innovation activities. The development of intangible asset evaluation agencies should be supported to give full play to their professional advantages in assisting innovation venture capital funds and venture capital guarantee agencies in acquiring information on investees and the guarantee timely and accurately. This would provide decision support for their operations, so that the innovation funds can be truly used for innovation projects with development potential to effectively improve the utilization efficiency of innovation resources. SMEs should be encouraged and guided to take such measures as the establishment of mutual aid and cooperative funds for independent innovation; meanwhile, the independent innovation projects of enterprises which have a greater impact, a shorter operation cycle, lower risks, and higher expected benefits should be supported. Insurance companies should be encouraged to actively develop and launch independent innovation insurance products, enhance the confidence and enthusiasm of SMEs in carrying out independent innovation activities, and act as an "umbrella" for SMEs by providing a larger buffer zone in case their innovative activities fail. The exchange market of technological innovation property rights should be improved and perfected, so that the innovative achievements can flow rapidly and extensively, and their allocations are optimized to enhance the efficiency of independent innovation. Meanwhile, the tertiary institutions and research institutes should be prompted to industrialize and transform their own independent innovation achievements into actual productivity, thereby further mobilizing their enthusiasm for carrying out independent innovative activities. In addition, Yiwu should intensify financial support, encourage financial institutions to establish an authorized credit granting system, increase credit varieties, and expand credit investment in technological innovation.

Through the above various ways, a multilayered capital market, a guarantee market, and an innovation achievement exchange market can be established and improved to form a capital chain that effectively supports independent innovation activities, thereby enhancing the independent innovation strength of numerous SMEs in Yiwu, reducing their worries, expanding the buffer zone, optimizing the allocation of innovation achievements, and enhancing the efficiency of independent innovation.

1.4.3 Creating a good informational environment

The construction of an innovative international trade city must vigorously implement the informatization strategy and promote the application of information technology around two pillar industries: small commodity trading and small commodity manufacturing. During the transformation of traditional commerce and trade industry into a modern service industry, Yiwu must build an "invisible market" featuring e-commerce gradually relying on the scientific and technological progress and accelerate the development of supplementary modern service industries such as finance, tourism, and logistics. Yiwu should also improve the technology development center, the industrial design center, and the public technology platform, which rely on sci-tech innovation and progress, so they become technological information channels for promoting the economic development of the whole city. Great efforts should be made to strengthen the market information collecting and analyzing services under the prerequisite of meeting market demand aimed at enhancing the core competence of enterprises. According to the status and trends of development, breakthroughs should be achieved emphatically in the application of design automation (DA) and computer aided design (CAD) technologies to promote their development from the research and application of single techniques to the application of complex, comprehensive design techniques and engineering application of products. Great efforts should be made to popularize the manufacturing information support systems such as enterprise resource planning (ERP), product data management (PDM), as well as the advanced manufacturing methods such as consecutive number control (CNC) manufacturing technology, flexible manufacturing technology, and fuzzy control among enterprises. In addition, it is also necessary to improve the automation of manufacturing processes, intellectualization of industrial products, modernization of business management, and the networking degree of business communication in enterprises to promote the large scale development of information industry.

1.4.4 Developing innovation intermediaries

Innovation intermediaries set up a bridge between technology and production by connecting the R&D institutions with the enterprises, which is a vital force that promotes the exchange and cooperation among industries, universities, and research institutes, provides the innovation information, and promotes the transformation of innovation achievements.

In particular, the innovation intermediary service agencies' function of promoting the transformation of innovation achievements is of paramount importance because innovation only makes sense if it is transformed into economic and social benefits. A product or management model, no matter how technically sophisticated or advanced, can only be a waste of limited economic and social resources if they cannot bring economic benefits. Therefore, it is necessary to encourage the development of intermediary innovation service agencies and the expansion of innovation service contents. While expanding the number and scale of intermediary service agencies, special attention should be paid to improving the overall quality of the agencies in order to offer prompt, adequate, and quality intermediary services for innovative activities.

High-tech enterprises, large and medium-sized enterprises, and private sci-tech enterprises in Yiwu have basically established their independent R&D centers and possessed certain independent R&D capabilities. In contrast, large numbers of small businesses still rely on the introduction of technology and simple imitation, which are not only

free of independent R&D institutions, but also lack the ability to digest, absorb, and reinnovate on the basis of technology imports. In response to such a situation of strong impetus for innovation but insufficient innovation capacity among SMEs, it is imperative to establish regional-oriented productivity promotion centers and business service centers selectively, to encourage the development of sci-tech innovation consulting firms, technology incubators, technological property rights, and sci-tech achievement exchange intermediaries and other organizations, to enhance the enterprises' ability to acquire and utilize sci-tech innovation information, and accelerate the transformation and industrialization of sci-tech innovation achievements.

At present, a particular emphasis should be placed on developing the production intermediary service industries targeting SMEs, which offer small and medium-sized manufacturers with services such as financing, guarantees, property rights exchanges, technology transactions, labor and employment agencies, means of production brokerage, and freight forwarding. It is also necessary to actively develop the tourism business' intermediary services that mainly include various commodity trading intermediaries, convention and exhibition service intermediaries, and tourism distribution intermediaries, and to steadily develop knowledge-intensive intermediary services to offer intelligent high-end services (i.e., R&D, design and planning) to the government, enterprises, and individuals. In addition, Yiwu should also encourage the development of economic appraisal and intermediary attestation services to offer professional analysis, appraisal, and assessment services such as accounting, asset appraisal, certification, authentication, testing, and inspection; it should also encourage the development of intermediary legal services mainly including professional services such as the attorney and notary, consultation, investigation, litigation, examination, and legal counsel, and the development of intermediary coordination services consisting mainly of industry associations, chambers of commerce, trade associations, and other self-regulatory organizations. In some areas (such as Shanghai and Hangzhou) influenced by "Yiwu Business Circle", there are already rather advanced systems of intermediary innovation services. Hence, the economic regions associated with "Yiwu Business Circle" can be guided and prompted to realize the remote sharing and system construction of intermediary innovation services with the aid of modern network information technology.

2. Fostering innovative enterprises, strengthening innovative industries

2.1 Fostering a group of innovative enterprises with core competence

In a market economy, enterprises are the main body of economic activities. Independent innovation is, in essence, an economic process. Therefore, only by taking enterprises as the main body, can the independent innovative activities truly stick to the market orientation and reflect the market demand. In this regard, the experience of Shenzhen, the national frontrunner in independent innovation, is worth learning from. In Shenzhen, more than 90% of R&D institutions are located in enterprises, over 90% of R&D personnel are concentrated in enterprises, more than 90% of R&D investment comes from enterprises, and over 90% of invention patents come out of enterprises. Enterprises have become the investors, organizers, beneficiaries, and risk bearers in technological innovation.[6] Yiwu has a good tradition of market economy operation and a high degree of marketization. Therefore, it can learn from the experience of Shenzhen to give full play to the fundamental role as a market mechanism in independent innovation, so as to allow enterprises to become the main body of R&D investment, technological innovation activities, and innovation achievement application. The institutional and mechanical obstacles affecting independent innovation should be further broken to accelerate the establishment of a technological innovation system and an operational mechanism that

---

[6] See: Independent innovation to provide surging impetus to Shenzhen's development. *Economic Daily*, 2006-05-18 (1–2).

integrates science and technology with enterprises as the mainstay. Taking market demands as the guidance and application-oriented technological innovation as the breakthrough point, innovative activities should be organized by concentrating superior resources and then further extended upstream and downstream after the innovative products reach a certain market size to form a virtuous circle of technological innovation and enterprise development. Industry–university–research institute collaboration should be carried out around the market, so that the papers are written about the products, the projects are conducted in the enterprises, and success or failure is determined by the market.

There are numerous SMEs in Yiwu, and the vast majority of business owners and workers were originally farmers or small traders, with an inadequate educational level and a weak sense of innovation. They tend to pursue investment with quick returns, while lacking investment momentum for technological and product innovations that are characterized by high investment with slow returns. In addition, due to their small scale, limited strength, and lack of innovation capacity, the majority of SMEs have not set up innovative R&D institutions, nor do they have much cooperation with tertiary institutions or research institutes. Even for those with cooperative relations, most stay at the primary stage of technical service and technological consultation, so it is difficult to carry out basic research innovation or original innovation through a deeper, closer collaboration. Thus, for SMEs in Yiwu, the integrated innovation mode and the introduction, digestion, and absorption for reinnovation mode are more appropriate.

Integrated innovation can form multiple channels by way of constituting the community of interests via industrial and trade enterprises, research institutes, tertiary institutions, and collaboratively launching independent innovation activities to aggregate social funds for the sci-tech innovation incentive mechanism. Through researching and integrating two major sci-tech innovation resources at home and abroad, international cooperation in sci-tech innovation activities is carried out, thereby broadening the source channels of innovation resource elements. Since integrated innovation emphasizes strategic integration, it is conducive to overcoming institutional obstacles at the macro-management level to establish a scientific and democratic decision-making mechanism, thereby improving the efficiency of investment in innovation resource elements macroscopically. Meanwhile, it requires the establishment of a scientific, reasonable cooperation mechanism among relevant actors of independent innovation activities, thus helping to overcome the inefficient operation of independent innovation investment at the micro level.

Numerous SME owners in Yiwu must recognize that independent innovation does not equal their own innovation, and that innovation in the context of economic globalization should try every means to integrate global innovation resources for self-use. Yiwu SMEs have large internationalized market resources as a support, so they should exploit this unique advantage to vigorously carry out the introduction, digestion, and absorption for reinnovation activities. This approach can greatly save time for self-exploration, shorten the gap between domestic and foreign advanced technologies at a relatively low cost, and achieve new breakthroughs on the basis of advanced technological innovations, which is also the "late-mover advantage" of Yiwu SMEs with a weak innovation capacity. Yiwu SMEs have also taken this mode of innovation in the course of their development. Nevertheless, many companies tended to just introduce advanced production equipment, while failing to introduce, digest, or absorb the corresponding advanced concepts, management modes, technological innovation strategies, etc., thereby getting caught in a vicious cycle of "introduction—backwardness—more introduction—more backwardness". In fact, the introduction of equipment can bring multi-level technologies such as production technology, equipment operation technology, product development technology, product design technology, test and inspection technology, etc., while the effectiveness of imported technologies depends largely on the learning ability and effort level of the importing

parties. The stronger their learning ability is, the stronger their ability to absorb external technologies is, and thus the better the acquisition of independent innovation ability is. Most enterprises in Yiwu have a good grasp of production and operation technologies after introducing advanced equipment. Yet other technologies, especially design technology, have not been grasped sufficiently in terms of digestion and absorption. As for product development technologies, technological equipment exporters generally do not transfer them for strategic consideration of enterprise development, nor do Yiwu enterprises make enough efforts to fight for them. Thus, product upgrades can hardly break through the limitations of equipment, which can only rely on the continuous introduction and upgrading of equipment. Hence, enterprises in Yiwu must be encouraged to make full use of the industry–university–research institute collaboration mechanism after introducing advanced technology and equipment. Preferably, the city must complete the integration of the industrial chain upstream with downstream, the integration of single technology systems, the integration of advanced foreign technologies with domestic technology systems, and the integration of relevant disciplines, in order to effectively digest and absorb the imported advanced technologies to improve their own capability of independent innovation. On this basis, they should be encouraged to boldly make reinnovations to break through and surpass the original level.

The carriers through which enterprises launch independent innovation activities are mainly their own R&D institutions, so it is necessary to further encourage qualified enterprises to establish technological innovation and development agencies, and regard them as important content in policy documents on scientific and technological progress issued by the government. The qualified enterprises are encouraged to establish such agencies by themselves, while the unqualified enterprises can establish them jointly with the support of tertiary institutions and research institutes. Key enterprises such as high-tech enterprises, technology-based enterprises, large and medium-sized enterprises, and leading enterprises in advantaged industries, are required to establish and improve the technology development agencies, support and encourage the sci-tech development projects undertaken by these agencies by giving priority to the approval of such projects, and consider whether to establish a technology development agency as one of the conditions for evaluating high-tech and technology-based enterprises.

It is noteworthy that in the fields of technology diffusion and technical services, the spillover effect of corporate R&D institutions is inevitably constrained by the market strategy of enterprises, and the concealment of technologies and information among enterprises is unavoidable. This kind of constraint is both an incentive and an obstacle to the innovation. Constraints enable pioneering enterprises to enjoy the first-mover advantage in their field and expand market share, thereby stimulating other enterprises to innovate competitively. This is caused by mutual competition among enterprises. However, excessive constraint and concealment lead to the inevitable duplication of investment and R&D among enterprises, which not only wastes human and material resources, but also affects the exchanges of ideas among researchers, so that the opportunity of cross-innovation may be lost. Therefore, during the development of corporate R&D institutions, not only full encouragement and protection of the IPR acquired by innovations are necessary, but the establishment of relevant mechanisms is also required to achieve maximum exchanges and cooperation among enterprises.

During the cultivation of innovative enterprises, the government should vigorously encourage them to create their own brands. Today, many international brands such as Coca Cola, McDonald's, Wal-Mart, IBM, and SONY have entered the Chinese market, thus announcing the advent of the brand era. Some large domestic enterprises including Haier, Changhong, etc., have also picked up the brand weapon and have been using it handily. However, many SMEs are still in their growth stage, and

they remain sluggish in terms of brand awareness and creation. Some business owners even think that brand building is a matter for the future, while the current priority is to accumulate capital and boost sales.

The creation of independent brands for SMEs relies on the needs of their own development. Facts have proved that enterprises that have formulated long-term strategic objectives for their brands, established brand awareness, and implemented a long-term brand management philosophy in the early stages of development tend to have more growth opportunities. The first reason why SMEs create their own brands is to meet the needs of consumer trends. The world has now entered the era of the brand, with an increasing number of consumers beginning to deepen their brand awareness tendency to buy brand products. The second reason is to meet the needs of competition. The ever-intensifying price war leaves increasingly less room for product price reduction, especially for SMEs, who can hardly deal with price wars due to the size and cost constraints. Therefore, they urgently need to pick up the brand weapon and launch competition at the level of independent IPR. The third reason involves the needs for international marketing. Since Yiwu's economy has become increasingly in line with international practice, it must rely on brand recognition and loyalty rather than solely on low prices, so as to further open up the international market. Otherwise, enterprises without a brand or with weak brands not only easily arouse the "anti-dumping" complaints, but also gradually fall prey to the OEM factories of foreign strong brand enterprises, which thus cannot own their own terminal markets, and will surely be defeated in the competitive international market.

For the government, it must create a good environment for numerous SMEs to nurture and develop famous brands. The government should further stimulate the internal motivation for enterprises' creation of famous brands by amply rewarding brand-name enterprises, entrepreneurs, and other means; it should give more support to the brand-name enterprises through financial support, policy leverage, and other means to promote brand-name development in depth; it should organize and coordinate departments and enterprises to jointly establish brand names by intensifying the control, services, coordination, supervision, and guarantees and by providing guidance and relevant information, so as to give full play to the overall advantages and to cooperate with enterprises in facilitating publicity, services, and training; it should crack down on counterfeit, shoddy products, and IPR infringement cases by strengthening famous brands' protection to maintain fair market competition and protect the legitimate rights and interests of famous brands' manufacturers; and it should enable the identification and management of famous brands to be more scientific and orderly by intensifying the management of famous brands, establishing and perfecting famous brand recognition and evaluation system, improving the management measures and evaluation standard system, and creating brand-name products, brand-name trademarks, as well as brand-name enterprise archives and economic indicator databases.

2.2 Forming a number of innovative industries with international influence

2.2.1 Intensifying the transformation of traditional industries using high technology

The traditional industries still have ample room for development, though they will become increasingly smaller if without transformation. Therefore, the transformation of traditional industries using high technology is an important task in carrying out independent innovation and building an innovative international trade city. To this end: (1) Imported technologies can be used to transform traditional industries. For traditional industries such as knitwear, hosiery, accessories, garments, handicrafts, zippers, and cosmetics, it is generally possible to enhance the product structure of enterprises by introducing foreign technologies and equipment. (2) Generic technologies can be used for transformation. For industries like wool textile, electromechanics, food, medicine, building materials, and hardware, the application of some generic technologies, such as computer aided design (CAD), computer aided manufacturing (CAM), computer integrated manufacturing systems (CIMS), virtual manufacturing, industrial automation, high-efficiency energy saving, and new environmental protection technologies, must be promoted actively to enable a favorable transformation of enterprises. (3) Specialized technologies can be used for transformation, such as the anti-shrinking, crease-proof, and other finishing technologies in the wool textile industry, economical NC and industrial electronic control systems in the electromechanical industry, coal saving, energy saving, smoke and dust removal technologies in the building materials industry, and genetic/enzyme engineering in the food and pharmaceutical industries.

2.2.2 Accelerating the development of high-tech industries

Accelerating the development of high-tech industries is an important means of advancing independent innovation and building an innovative international trade city. Therefore, top priority should be given to speeding up the development of high-tech industries to vigorously develop the emerging innovative industries that rely on technological progress and human capital. Firstly, enhancement of existing high-tech and technology-based enterprises is necessary. Enterprises that have been identified as high-tech or technology-based shall be guided in terms of development direction and priorities to enhance their technological innovation capability, so as to develop products and technologies with independent IPRs. The informatization level of the manufacturing industry should be improved by popularizing digital design and manufacturing technologies (CAD, CAM), product data management (PDM) systems, CNC equipment and manufacturing execution systems (MES), computer integrated manufacturing systems (CIMS), enterprise resource planning (ERP) systems, etc. With business informatization as the starting point, emphasis should be placed on building intelligent, international modern business centers, vigorously promoting e-commerce, improving the e-commerce system and modern logistics distribution system of international trade city, developing the digital market of "China Small Commodity City", striving to create a "Digital Yiwu", and speeding up the electronization of service industry. Meanwhile, R&D and the application of automatic control, optoelectronic technology, and embedded software should be strengthened, the opto-mechatronic technology should be promoted, and the advanced equipment manufacturing industry should be developed progressively. Technologies like bio-technology, high-quality efficient cultivation technology, safe food production technology, and agricultural product storage and preservation technologies should be developed vigorously by relying on modern agriculture to promote the biotechnology demonstration projects. The application and research of nanotechnology in magnetic materials, textiles, and other fields should be strengthened to reduce production costs and improve product performance. Secondly, nurturing a number of emerging high-tech industries is necessary. The electronic information industry aims mainly towards the development of software technology that is represented by embedded software, industrial platforms, e-commerce, and information security, microelectronic technology represented by the integrated circuit design and fabrication, digital multimedia technology represented by the digital broadcast equipment and the digital audio–video terminal products, and automotive electronic technology represented by the vehicle network system and automatic control system. The new materials industry focuses on the development and production of nano, reflective, magnetic, biological, special composites, and other new materials; it pays equal attention to the research and development of new materials and the potential tapping and rational use of traditional materials. The environmental protection industry aims mainly to tackle the major environmental protection technologies such as water resources protection and water pollution control technology, safe drinking water indicator systems and production support technology, vehicle exhaust pollution control technology, and solid waste recycling technology; it also aims to develop an environmental monitoring and prevention instrument manufacturing industry. In addition, the active development of supporting modern service industries such as finance, tourism, and logistics is also necessary in order to provide all kinds of support for the independent innovative activities of enterprises.

2.2.3 Making efforts to foster 20–30 innovative pillar industries

To enhance the independent innovation strength, a number of large-scale, powerful, and high-skilled enterprises were selected among the existing superior industries like knitwear, hosiery, accessories, garments, handicrafts, zippers, cosmetics, stationery, and toys to implement the preferential policy, so that they can grow continuously and can guide the gathering of peers, thereby fostering 20–30 innovative pillar industries with stronger regional characteristics and comparative advantages.

2.3 Promoting exchanges and cooperation among industries, universities and research institutes

At present, the research institutes and their potential demand are still small in Yiwu. Despite the intensification of exchanges and cooperation with famous higher education institutions such as the Chinese Academy of Sciences, Zhejiang University, and Donghua University, the majority of industry–university–research institute collaborators are large enterprises, while numerous SMEs have not yet found any mode of cooperation suitable for them and are unable to integrate into the industry–university–research institute collaboration system. Due to the long years of establishment, strong governmental support, and a considerable concentration of high-level talents, the scientific research institutes have a well-structured talent team and good hardware facilities compared to the general corporate R&D institutions, which is an exceptional boost to building an innovative international trade city in Yiwu. Therefore, it is imperative to establish a cooperation mechanism centering on the achievement of sharing through a variety of approaches such as joint research, technical guidance, technical training, transfer of achievements, purchase of patents, joint development, commissioned training, and co-construction of R&D institutions or science and technology entities to form stable, effective support for technological innovation.

The introduction of famous scientific research institutes at home and abroad should be intensified further. Internationally renowned research institutes, in particular, should be introduced vigorously by actively creating favorable conditions, and the establishment of post-doctoral research stations needs to be attempted continuously. Regular organization of exchange activities between domestic and foreign research institutes and Yiwu enterprises is necessary. In particular, the exchanges and cooperation between Yiwu enterprises and numerous famous tertiary institutions and research institutes in the Yangtze River Delta region need to be promoted further to accelerate the establishment of the "Yiwu–Yangtze River Delta Innovation Collaboration System" to promote their long-term stable cooperative relations for innovation and to jointly establish innovation carriers such as the technology R&D centers. Universities and enterprises should be encouraged to jointly apply for innovation projects and set up specialized committees for promoting the industry–university–research institute collaboration. Publicity efforts should be stepped up to encourage relevant policies and opinions on industry–university–research institute collaboration, so that numerous SMEs can broaden and deepen the understanding of these policies to better conduct exchanges and cooperation with scientific research institutes.

It is noteworthy that the enterprises should be at the center of the industry–university–research institute collaborative relationship, and that all innovative activities must be carried out around the market demand faced by enterprises, rather than being content with the traditional practice where the tertiary institutions and research institutes find enterprises for realizing the industrialization of innovation achievements after obtaining them. These "achievements" are mostly projects chosen by the research institutes themselves, which did not go through sufficient market demand surveys at initiation, nor were there any corresponding economic analyses, formulations of specific cost index assessment criteria during the R&D process, or corresponding market forecasts after the obtainment of "achievements". Thus, they easily lead to the "mismatch" among technology R&D, innovation, and

the economy. To this end, such a project–finding–enterprise mode must be gradually transformed into an enterprise–finding–project mode, so that enterprises truly become the center of independent innovation.

3. Gathering innovative talents, stimulating innovation momentum

The key to developing the primary productive forces, i.e., science and technology, lies in grasping the first resource, human resources. Because humans are the ultimate force in promoting economic and social development, the realization of any development goal eventually needs to be promoted by humans as a carrier; besides, the development of history is itself the result of human activities and progress. The practice of economic and technological development both at home and abroad demonstrates that the creation of new knowledge, the invention of new technologies, and the guidance of new disciplines are all inseparable from innovative talents. Employing large numbers of outstanding innovative talents means possessing a wealth of intellectual capital and independent innovation. Therefore, talents, especially innovative talents, are the ultimate engine in building an innovative international trade city, which determines whether Yiwu can realize the innovative development strategies and goals. To this end, it is necessary to actively tap the potential of human capital and vigorously promote the construction of innovative talent teams, so as to provide reliable intellectual support for the construction of an innovative international trade city.

3.1 Characteristics of innovative talents

Innovative talents have the following four characteristics: (1) *Innovative consciousness*: They have the passion and desire to seek novelty, new knowledge, new ways, new means, and new conclusions. They think diligently and can often break the routine and break through the paradigm. They are good at putting forward new ideas, new theories, and solving problems with new methods and thoughts. (2) *Innovation ability*: They have a rich imagination and keen insights, with a rather strong learning ability, a practical operation ability, information collecting and processing capabilities and scientific research capacity. They are good at attaining innovative achievements by putting different things together, making up for the deficiencies in their own knowledge structure and ability by learning from others' strong points, and making new breakthroughs with the help of past achievements and external forces. (3) *Knowledge base*: They have a personalized ideological and cognitive system, are capable of tracking and absorbing the latest knowledge and information to keep up with the world. They have a broad knowledge structure, with a certain understanding of all sectors of the economy and society, and are proficient in a profession or a domain, with professional theoretical knowledge, practical experience, and an in-depth research background. (4) *Innovative personality*: They respect objective laws and actual situations, without blindly obeying authority, relying only on books, or only on teachers. They possess strong individualized, independent thinking, and operational abilities, and a scientific spirit of daring to doubt, criticize, and take risks. They are progressive, self-confident, unafraid of frustration or failure, and do not give up easily, possessing a spirit of persistent pursuit.

3.2 Cultivation and introduction of innovative talents

It is necessary to earnestly establish the concept of "human resources are the first resource", and highlight the strategic thinking and social values of "talent orientation", so as to create a good custom of "valuing knowledge, respecting talents, respecting labor, and valuing creation" in the whole society. In the process of building an innovative international trade city in Yiwu, the core position of human resources in the construction of an urban innovation system must be established, and the supply of human resources must be fully optimized. It is necessary to take cultivating a huge team of innovative talents as an urgent and significant task, and earnestly grasp the training, attracting, and using aspects; it is also urgent to concentrate on expanding the scale of human resources supply, improving the quality of human resources,

and optimizing the competence structure of human resources, and to appreciate, respect, and motivate talents in terms of education and training, competition and career, assessment and hiring, remuneration, social status, etc. In particular, more powerful measures should be taken to actively introduce high-level professionals, especially leading figures, and accelerate the training of highly-skilled personnel to build innovation teams. The outstanding innovative talents in the economic regions involved in the development of "Yiwu Business Circle" should be integrated into the human resources supply channel in constructing the innovative international trade city, so that the cross-regional division of labor and cooperation network plays a greater role in promoting the sharing of innovative human resources. Efforts should be made to build an innovation platform that gives full play to the talents' key role in independent innovation by motivating talents with good conditions, treating talents with a tolerant spirit, and accomplishing talents with an innovative career. Specifically, emphasis should be placed on the following two tasks:

Firstly, profoundly implement the strategy of strengthening the city with qualified personnel, intensify the development of human resources, give play to the core supporting role of innovative talents, and strengthen the construction of independent innovation talent teams. According to the needs of innovation, Yiwu should rationally allocate the investment in development, improve the efficiency of human resource development, and cultivate a group of high-tech innovative talents, highly-skilled personnel, and entrepreneurs with a strong independent innovation conscience, so as to create a talent team with a reasonable structure, excellent quality, and a grand scale. A number of innovative teams and sci-tech leaders should be cultivated relying on major sci-tech projects, key disciplines, and key laboratories. Particular attention should be paid to the training of entrepreneurs, so as to raise the scientific and cultural qualities of large numbers of private entrepreneurs created by the development of Yiwu Small Commodity Market and related industries, and to enhance their innovation awareness, international awareness, brand awareness, and collaboration awareness. Meanwhile, it is necessary to actively attract businessmen from other places to gradually transform them into part of "Yiwu Business Circle" team, so as to infuse new blood into "Yiwu Business Circle" to promote its growth in scale and enhancement in overall quality and innovation awareness, thereby maximizing its core role in the enterprises' independent innovation activities.

Secondly, eliminate various barriers to the inflow and outflow of human resources, improve the talent introduction mode, and explore the functional use mechanism of human resources. By taking advantage of good division of labor and cooperative relations among the relevant economic regions formed by the development of "Yiwu Business Circle", as well as the exchanges of talents and cooperation between economic entities, Yiwu can further promote the construction of the cooperation and exchange system for the sharing of talents across regions; Yiwu should encourage the industrial and trade enterprises, tertiary institutions, research institutes, and public R&D platforms led by Yiwu Small Commodity Market to recruit leading talents for independent innovation with interdisciplinary expertise, cross-industry experience, and broad vision both at home and abroad; and it must introduce innovative R&D personnel and technical workers vigorously. A flexible technician introduction policy should be practiced to attract a wide range of high-level talents at home and abroad to work full time, part time, or short term in Yiwu with various forms of "talent agencies" as the carrier.

3.3 Giving full play to the role of innovative talents

It is advisable to strengthen the incentive mechanism, improve the income distribution system, and establish the performance and capability-based resource allocation and evaluation mechanisms that encourage innovation, competition, and coordinated development. Sci-tech personnel should be allowed to input intellectual expenditure as the technological development expense, the patented invention rights

enjoyed, respectively, by the intellectuals and investors should be clarified through contracts, the involvement of technology factors in the profit distribution should be promoted, and the sci-tech personnel should be motivated through stocks and options, so as to fully mobilize the enthusiasm of both intellectuals and investors for innovation. The practice of providing ample rewards for sci-tech innovation projects and individuals that have made significant contributions should be continued, and supplementary rewards should be given to the sci-tech personnel who have won the state or provincial science and technology awards. For innovative talents who have made outstanding contributions in terms of economic, R&D, financial, cultural, and management innovations, a significant reward should be given. Multiple measures such as providing resettlement subsidies and building employee apartments should be adopted to strive to solve the housing problem of introduced high-level personnel. The "Yiwu Entrepreneur Service Center" should be set up by learning from Shenzhen's experience to provide entrepreneurs with services ranging from production and operation to all aspects of personal and family life. In particular, conveniences should be created in such areas as health care, schooling for children, and social security to create a good working and living environment for high-level personnel, so that Yiwu can become the entrepreneurs' "entrepreneurial paradise".

Conclusion

Expansion of "Yiwu Business Circle", Innovation of "Yiwu Development Experience"

Over the past four decades of the reform and opening-up, Yiwu has worked many noteworthy, thought-provoking "miracles". Yiwu has achieved rapid economic development under the condition of a large population with little land, a lack of state investment, and a deficiency of resource endowments; Yiwu has nurtured the world's largest small commodity market under a lack of location or traffic advantages and built "Yiwu Business Circle" centering on it; it has become an important growth pole of the regional economy on the basis of developing traditional industries; it has become one of the most dynamic regions in the country in the absence of support from national preferential policies; it has achieved rapid progress of urbanization and urban–rural integration under very weak urban infrastructure, and has sustained harmonious development of production, living standards, and ecology in the complex and diverse social environment. The development and changes of Yiwu are surprising, the "Yiwu Phenomenon" is worth pondering, and the successful practice of Yiwu has been referred to as the "Yiwu Development Experience" by the Zhejiang Provincial Party Committee, the Provincial Government, academia, and the press. The author of this book, as an academic team that has been observing, practicing, and studying in Yiwu for many years, intends to concentrate on discussing several points of gains and experience regarding the expansion of "Yiwu Business Circle" and the innovation of "Yiwu Development Experience" in the conclusion.

I Our Firsthand "Yiwu Development Experience"

During the participation in the development of Yiwu Small Commodity Market, economy, and society, we have accumulated some firsthand experiences about "Yiwu Development Experience", which include:

1. Ideas and methods generated by "Yiwu Development Experience": conducting in-depth investigations, making scientific decisions

Leaders' decision-making mistakes are the biggest waste, while all previous Yiwu Municipal (County) Party Committees and Governments had attached great importance to the in-depth investigation of actual situations and made scientific decisions accordingly. For example, the "Four Permits" policy in the early 1980s was a significant historical breakthrough in the development course of Yiwu Small Commodity Market, and the "Flourish Business and

Build City" strategy that contributed to the sustainable prosperity and development of Yiwu was precisely put forward by the Municipal Party Committee and Government after repeated discussions and arguments on the basis of thoroughly investigating the actual situations and understanding the real wishes of the masses. The "Transforming Industry by Commerce", "Connecting Trade with Industry" strategies implemented in the early and mid 1990s and the strategic goal of building an "international trade city" established at the turn of the new century were also promulgated by the Municipal Party Committee and Government after investigating the long-term development needs of Yiwu and fully studying its own advantages.[1] As another example, the complicated market development planning and construction is a very sensitive issue that draws the attention of all parties. In the event of a mistake, not only will huge economic losses be incurred, but social instability is also probable. Over four decades of the reform and opening-up, Yiwu Small Commodity Market has undergone relocations and expansions many times, each of which were a major interest adjustment featuring a domino effect. Not only has there been no major mistakes in decision-making, but the sustained market prosperity has also been maintained. Some theorists have always insisted that the holding of state-owned stocks should be lowered to sharing or even an entire sell-off. It can be said that these thoughts are also reflected in Yiwu. However, the main leaders of the Municipal Party Committee and Government have a clear understanding and a unified viewpoint, and are always firmly seizing the regulatory power over two resources with a quasi-public good nature, i.e., the market resources and the logistics stations, thereby adapting to the needs of industrial development and pattern upgrading, balancing the interests of all parties, and taking the initiative in development. All previous Yiwu Municipal Party Committees and Governments had correctly positioned the relationship

---

[1] See Lu Lijun, Bai Xiaohu, Wang Zuqiang: *Market Yiwu: From Chicken Feather for Sugar to International Commerce*. Hangzhou: Zhejiang People's Publishing House, 2003, pp. 183–187.

between the government and the market, which practiced adequate control and liberalization, so that the market had fulfilled the functions of "Economic Mediation, Market Regulation, Social Management, Public Service" while playing a fundamental role of resource allocation on the rule of law track. In the initial stage of market development, they paid attention to the investigation of actual situations, grasped the objective laws of development, and fully respected the pioneering spirit of the masses. After the gradual maturity of market development, they conducted further investigations, and promptly implemented the "Separation of Regulation from Management", thereby offering market players more room for independent development. In the meantime, nevertheless, the market was not left uncontrolled. Instead, the Municipal Party Committees and Governments had accurately grasped the long-term development direction of the market, firmly seized the initiative in market building, and held the regulatory power over the market booths, freight yards, and other strategic resources concerning the long-term development of Yiwu. An important reason why the municipal leaders can make the above series of "forward-looking" correct decisions is because they insist on theoretical innovation and make decisions on the basis of conducting thorough investigations and listening widely to the views of all sectors of society.

The scientific nature of the Municipal Party Committee and Government's decision-making is enhanced precisely because they attach great importance to the investigation study, fully understand and respect the objective reality, respect the law of market development, and respect the pioneering spirit of the masses. In this regard, Yiwu has taken three major measures according to the author's observations. Firstly, the members of the municipal leadership team, as well as the main leaders of municipal governmental institutions, townships, and streets are explicitly required to write a weighty survey report by combining their own work experience in the second half of each year. The surveys are reported for exchanges in advance, and then compiled into a book for submission and issuance. Being earnest, open, and transparent, the speeches and

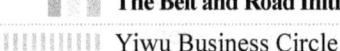

written materials are tantamount to a public examination of the cadres' investigative skills and working ideologies, which are greatly helpful for improving the decision-making level of the leadership team. Secondly, adhere to the principle of democratic centralism, encourage the free airing of views, and draw on collective wisdom. In the event of any major issue concerning the overall situation such as the market relocation or adjustment, major engineering, and the key project, the party-government joint meeting and the enlarged meeting of the municipal standing committee attended by all members of the municipal leadership team and the leaders of relevant departments, townships, and streets are convened often before making decisions by separately organizing the municipal standing committee, secretary working meeting, and municipal government executive meeting to let all participants express their views, or even launch arguments. In the author's impression, meetings were held seven or eight times around some major issues, and sometimes there were heated arguments, and the meetings continued until 11 or 12 o'clock in the night, thus truly achieving open dialogues, upholding the truth, correcting the mistakes, fully promoting democracy, and ensuring scientific decision-making. In addition, a group of renowned experts and scholars both inside and outside the province have long been concerned about and supported the development of Yiwu. They have carried out investigations and studies and put forward opinions and suggestions, which also offer a strong support for the scientific decision-making of the municipal leaders.

2. Key to formation of the "Yiwu Development Experience": sticking to the practical, progressive development strategy

Since the reform and opening-up, the overall strategy of economic and social development in Yiwu has always been "Flourish Business and Build City". The formation and development of this strategy has generally gone through three stages:

The first stage (1978–1983) was the preparation phase of the overall development strategy marked by "Four Permits". After the reform and opening-up, a group of small traders who evolved from the traditional "Qiaotang Sect" were the first to sense that the rural areas, as the weakest link of the planned economy chain, needed "small daily use articles", especially the mountainous peasants, while the state-owned and cooperative trade networks were still blank at this niche. They seized the opportunity timely to evolve the contents of pedlar trading from "chicken feather for sugar" to the sales of small daily use articles, which led to the formation of small vendors that provided convenience for pedlars' local distribution, as well as the prototype of the small commodity market. The then County Party Committee and Government set up the first-generation small commodity market with merely over 700 stalls in September 1982, based on reality in the name of the industrial and commercial department. Meanwhile, the county authorities also adopted five supportive policies of "political encouragement, financial care, technical guidance, preferential tax treatment, and legal protection" for the nascent individual and private business owners. In November of the same year, the County Party Committee and Government promulgated the "Four Permits" decision, which has played a decisive role in the development of the small commodity market ever since.

The second stage (1984–1991) was the formation and perfecting phase of the overall development strategy marked by "Flourish Business and Build County" and "Flourish Business and Build City". In October 1984, the Yiwu County Party Committee and Government put forward the development strategy of "Flourish Business and Build County". As a result of this strategy, the number of stalls in the small commodity market increased to 6,131 by 1988 when the county was upgraded to a city, with a turnover reaching 265 million Yuan. The development of rural industries and urban infrastructure supporting the small commodity market made greater progress, thus laying a solid foundation for the establishment of a city. After the withdrawal of the county for the establishment of a city in 1988, the "Flourish Business and Build City" strategy enjoyed greater popularity among the people, and its denotation was also increasingly expanded.

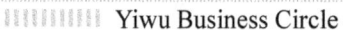
The third stage (1992–present) is the expansion phase of the overall development strategy marked by "Transforming Industry by Commerce", "Connecting Trade with Industry", and the goal of building an "International Trade City". At this stage, encouraged by Deng Xiaoping's Southern Talk, the vast cadres and masses further strengthened their confidence in adhering to the "Flourish Business and Build County" overall development strategy. In response to the flooding of similar markets in China and the whole province and the insufficient industrial support for Yiwu Small Commodity Market, the Municipal Party Committee and Government proposed to guide some traders, who had completed primitive capital accumulation, to shift commercial capital to industry in the early and mid-1990s for the realization of "Connecting Trade with Industry". In the mid to late 1990s, the municipal authorities proposed to take the lead in building a medium-sized modern city in the province, in order to promote the process of marketization, industrialization, and urbanization. From the end of the last century to the beginning of this century, the municipal authorities proposed the construction of a famous modern trade city first, then after a few years of practice, they further unanimously clarified their goal of building an international trade city, and formulated and implemented the first "Outline of Urban–Rural Integration Action" in the province.

In the course of the above four decades of development, Yiwu has always adhered to the overall development strategy of "Flourish Business and Build City" while continuing to deepen and expand the connotation and denotation of the strategy based on the actual conditions of various historical periods. It is precisely such a spirit of seeking truth from facts and keeping pace with the times that has ensured Yiwu's previous leadership teams and vast cadres and masses the ability to constantly innovate in development concepts, management tools, and work contents according to the historical stage in compliance with the objective law of development, and to put forward specific strategies, tactics, and goals that were in line with their reality, thereby rapidly advancing the marketization, industrialization, urbanization, internationalization, and urban–rural integration to embark on a road of harmonious development.

3. New highlight of "Yiwu Development Experience": adhering to the coordinated development, promoting the harmonious society building

While unswervingly adhering to the overall development strategy of "Flourish Business and Build City" centering around the economic construction and driving the development of the manufacturing industry, modern service industry, cultural industry, urban agriculture, and urban construction led by the market, no previous leaderships of Yiwu neglected the development of social undertakings such as education, science and technology, culture, health, and sports. They boosted the prosperity of various social undertakings based on economic strength. The development of social undertakings, in turn, further served and promoted the sustained rapid development of economic construction, thereby realizing the mutual promotion and common prosperity of economic and social undertakings. The city's climate for learning became increasingly enriched, the tertiary network system of lifelong education for citizens was continuously improved, and the practice and experience of building a "learning society" were promoted across the province. The overall strength of science and technology improved significantly, walking in the forefront of the province's county-level cities. The people's cultural life was increasingly enriched, with public cultural facilities amounting to over 90,000 square meters. The city, township, and village (community) tertiary system of public health were basically formed. The city's regular physical exercise population reached about 50%, Internet broadband users totaled 66,000, and the population with junior college or above education reach 430 per 10,000 people, which has already made it enter a comprehensive enhancement period of citizens' overall quality.

At present, Yiwu has already stepped into the era of becoming an urban economy and the period of urban–rural coordinated development, which is steadily pushing forward urbanization and urban–rural integration. By the end of 2005, the city had formed a 100 square kilometers central urban framework, with significant improvements in urban agglomeration, radiation capability, and service functions. The construction of major projects was promoted in an all-round way. Projects such as the Yangguang Avenue Phase I was completed in succession, and the construction of the Zhejiang–Jiangxi Railway relocation, Ningbo–Jinhua Expressway, Sihai Avenue, Wuzhou Avenue, and the new Municipal Party School site were basically completed. Since 2003, China's first "Outline of Urban–Rural Integration Action" has been announced and implemented to solidly advance new rural construction. In 2005, the expenditures on agriculture, rural areas, and farmers accounted for more than one-third of public finances, with newly-built rural houses totaling 5.1 million square meters. Renovation of 18 villages was completed, as well as the "non-hometown well-off" residence first phase construction in five townships and streets, so that more than 12,000 farmers moved into new homes. A total of 40 million Yuan was invested in the full implementation of integrated urban–rural garbage disposal, and the "dressing" project for 58 villages on both sides of the provincial roads and highways was basically completed. A more than 40,000 person rural labor force completed training, and a processing output value of 720 million Yuan was achieved by the "market leading hundred villages" campaign. The hierarchy and hardening of village highways were fully accomplished, and the urban–rural integration of roads, buses, and garbage disposal was basically realized.

Along with steady economic and social development and accelerated urban–rural integration, the whole city firmly established the guiding principle of scientific development and overall planning, which promoted the all-round development of people throughout the entire process of economic and social development, made overall plans for harmonious development of the economy and society as well as man and nature, successfully built a state-level hygiene city, and became one of the province's most suitable city for entrepreneurship and living. While paying attention to the material needs of people, more emphasis was placed on their spiritual pursuit and cultural needs, on improving their quality, and on propagating humanism, thereby enhancing the humanistic connotation of development, promoting the overall coordination of development, facilitating the sustainability of development, and enhancing the overall quality and level of development. Yiwu vigorously builds a harmonious society, accelerates the development of social undertakings, and continuously improves the people's quality of life. The "old Yiwu people" live in harmony with the "new Yiwu people" who are from 43 ethnic groups and people from more than 100 countries have come to Yiwu for doing business or being hired as workers to create a harmonious atmosphere of "seeking common development among Chinese and foreign businessmen, creating common security among Chinese and foreign residents, and enjoying common happiness among Chinese and foreign families", and to create a favorable situation of "coexistence of development space, sharing of living resources, sharing of social responsibilities, co-management of social order, and co-creation of economic prosperity" for jointly building a "Peaceful Yiwu", "Harmonious Yiwu". A socialized rights-safeguard mechanism has been established, and some people who were enthusiastic about resolving difficulties for workers were organized to set up a workers' rights protection center under the guidance of the Municipal Federation of Trade Unions for resolving labor disputes and other issues between workers and business owners. Rights protection content has been innovated, and the migrant workers' rights issues have been regarded as the central issues to be resolved by the trade union and rights protection center. The rights protection system has been innovated; a coordinated effort involving the women's federation, labor and personnel bureau, judiciary, and news media was established and led by the Municipal Party Committee and Government and works around the trade union and the rights protection center.

II Expanding "Yiwu Business Circle", Innovating "Yiwu Development Experience"

1. Changing the development concept, promoting the reinnovation of "Yiwu Mode"

The author once summarized the main characteristics of the "Yiwu Mode" in 1999: starting with "chicken feather for sugar", developing commerce and trade focusing on the circulation of small commodities by utilizing the market's first-mover advantage and agglomeration function, continuously accumulating capital, expanding the scale of operations, prompting the expansion of commercial capital into the fields of manufacturing and urban infrastructure construction, realizing the linkage development between market, industry, and city, and promoting the industrialization, urbanization, and internationalization of a regional economy.[2] It now appears that the "Yiwu Mode", as one of the main manifestations of the "Zhejiang Mode", is facing the problem of changing its development concept and innovating the development mode. Yiwu must continue to carry forward the innovative spirit in the future development, and enrich and upgrade the "Yiwu Mode". Only in this way can the lasting vitality of "Yiwu Business Circle" be maintained, and the sustainable economic and social development of Yiwu be realized, which can play a greater role in the construction of Central Zhejiang's urban agglomeration and the leapfrog development of Central and Western Zhejiang.

In our opinion, the basic points of the "Yiwu Mode" innovation are as follows: continuing to adhere to the overall development strategy of "Flourish Business and Build City" and the ambitious goal of building an "International Trade City", taking enhancing the independent innovation capability and construction of an innovative city as the main orientation and development emphasis, accelerating the process of marketization, industrialization, urbanization, urban–rural integration, and internationalization, expanding the cross-regional division of labor and cooperation, realizing coordinated sustainable economic and social development in urban and rural areas, and promoting the construction of Central Zhejiang urban agglomeration and "Yiwu Business Circle".

The "Yiwu Mode" has created the "Yiwu Development Experience". In the context where Yiwu's development experience is vigorously studied and spread throughout the province, and many cities and counties across China are paying close attention to Yiwu, the city must remain calm and reflect deeply on the existing problems in the "Yiwu Mode". It should be noted that the past rapid economic growth in Yiwu was based largely on intensive inputs of factors such as labor, capital, and resources,

---

[2]See Lu Lijun: "The rise of 'China Small Commodity City' market and the 'Yiwu Mode' in rural market economy development". *Comparative Economic and Social Systems*, 1999, (1):71–79.

 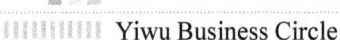
which was generally classified as an investment-driven growth mode, with a competitive advantage derived largely from the low price of resource factors and products. In today's world with increasingly severe constraints on resource factors and the environment, such an extensive mode of growth is hardly sustainable. Clearly, the industrial foundation for the development of the "Yiwu Mode" must be upgraded, so that the low price advantage of resource factors can be transformed into an independent innovation advantage, and the vitality of the mode's long-term development can be promoted relying on continuous innovations in science and technology, intelligence, human resources, mechanisms, culture, and management. Therefore, Yiwu must establish a sense of crisis and take the enhancement of its independent innovation capability and the construction of its innovative city as the main direction and focus of development for implementing the overall strategy of "Flourish Business and Build City" over a long period in the future; it must also consider maintenance of market prosperity as the core and introduction, digestion, and absorption for reinnovation as the main channel; it must regard key areas, major industries, key technologies, key enterprises, and major products as the support, and strengthen the driving roles of technology, entities, mechanisms, and the linkage of the whole society.

2. Building an innovative international trade city guided by independent innovation

Independent innovation is the only way for Yiwu to break through the bottleneck of factors and the constraints on human and technological resources, to take the initiative in the international market competition, to exploit the advantage of an internationalized market, and to promote the construction of an international trade city. Building an innovative international trade city is a strategic goal in line with Yiwu's own characteristics and development trends, which is an inherent requirement for Yiwu's future development unlike the commonly called innovative city. To this end, firstly, Yiwu must persist in institutional innovation and environmental innovation simultaneously. It should practice policies of taxation, finance, and government procurement that support independent innovation guided by institutional innovation based on environmental construction, and make efforts to foster new institutional and environmental advantages that are conducive to enhancing the independent innovation capability, transforming the growth pattern, adjusting the industrial structure, and upgrading the urban functions of the city. Secondly, Yiwu must persist in organizational innovation and management innovation simultaneously. Emphasis should be placed on restructuring and optimizing the organizational structure of SMEs in Yiwu, and on actively cultivating a number of large enterprises with core competence. SMEs should be encouraged to exert their features and advantages of being flexible in mechanism and responsiveness to market changes, to actively learn from international experience, and to carry out management innovation, so as to make up for their shortcomings in technology, capital, and talents. Large enterprises should be encouraged to adopt advanced international management modes, techniques, and tools to tap and manage the productive forces, improve overall operational efficiency and international competitiveness, and evolve into modernized and internationalized large group companies. Numerous commercial and trade enterprises should be encouraged to strengthen their exchanges and cooperation with local and foreign manufacturers and further expand and innovate the forms of cooperation on the basis of existing cooperation methods such as exclusive distribution and general agency to shape the industrial chain and enhance their competitiveness. Thirdly, Yiwu must persist in technological innovation and intellectual innovation simultaneously. Relying on the existing manufacturing base, it should exert its powerful commercial and trade advantages, strengthen its ability to gather global high-end innovative resource elements, and continue to strongly support and encourage enterprises to introduce, digest, and absorb foreign advanced technologies, equipment, and management experience and enhance technological innovation capability. Yiwu should also carry out secondary innovation and integrated innovation in a targeted,

focused manner to form a new mode of production where economic growth is promoted relying on independent innovation. It should also prompt the transformation of the traditional industrial structure into an innovative industrial structure. The education on innovation awareness should be strengthened, the independent innovation ability of young people should be cultivated, and their independent innovation potential should be tapped. It is also necessary to actively cultivate and introduce high-level innovative talents, especially the technologically innovative talents and organizers and leaders of innovative activities, to enhance the accumulation of human capital, to extensively implement intellectual innovation projects, to inspire innovation awareness and enthusiasm of the whole society, and to enhance the innovative quality and ability of all citizens. Fourthly, Yiwu must uphold the government's "visible hand" and the market's "invisible hand" simultaneously. The government's leading role in formulating innovation plans, perfecting an innovation system, improving innovation policies, optimizing the innovation environment, and attracting innovative talents must be fully exerted; the enterprises' principal role in applying high and new technologies, setting up innovation venture capital institutions, and establishing innovation incubators must be fully exerted; and the market's fundamental role in allocating innovation resources must be fully exerted to form a "government-led, enterprise-dominant, and market-operational" independent innovation mechanism, so as to achieve the "integration of three forces" (i.e., the government's leading force, the enterprises' principal force, and the market's fundamental force) to jointly promote the strategic transformation of economic growth mode and the upgrading of industrial structure. Through the above approaches, a solid foundation can be laid for Yiwu's progress toward the goal of building an innovative international trade city.

3. Enhancing the market's driving role, vigorously expanding "Yiwu Business Circle"

With its small commodity market as its core competence, Yiwu offers huge commercial support to the surrounding areas.

The surrounding areas, in turn, develop a manufacturing industry relying on the market division of labor, which becomes an enormous industrial support for Yiwu Small Commodity Market. The two complement and promote each other to realize common prosperity. In the future, Yiwu should pay more attention to reducing business costs, optimizing the economic environment, strengthening regional cooperation, "developing Yiwu by jumping out of it", and opening-up a broader space for development. Yiwu should also give full play to its advantages in commerce and trade, vigorously push forward the new industrialization in itself and the surrounding areas, strive to become Central Zhejiang CBD, better serve the construction of Central Zhejiang urban agglomeration, and serve the economic development of surrounding counties and cities. It is necessary to stick to the goal of developing an international trade city, strengthen the characteristics of business tourism, further enhance the market's driving role, and expand the connotation and denotation of "Yiwu Business Circle". To this end, firstly, Yiwu must vigorously push forward the upgrading of specialized markets and enhance the international competitiveness of the markets. Bold innovations should be made in terms of market organizations, transaction modes, and management patterns to be further geared to the international practice, and to accelerate the internationalization process of the small commodity market. The development trends of modern service industries should be grasped, the accelerated development of MICE, logistics, finance, shopping, tourism, and other modern service industries should be prompted by the market prosperity, and efforts should be made to build Yiwu Small Commodity Market into an international circulation, display, information, manufacturing, and R&D center for small commodities with the lowest transaction costs, the highest credit, the first-line information, the latest means, and the best service. Through the above measures, the growth pole role of Yiwu in Central Zhejiang urban agglomeration can be strengthened, the international development of surrounding counties and cities can be promoted, and the international exchanges and cooperation can be enhanced, so as to bring about a leapfrog development throughout

Central and Western Zhejiang. Secondly, Yiwu must vigorously promote the upgrading of industrial structure to provide strong support for the construction of the international trade city. According to the goal and requirements of building Yiwu into an international circulation, display, information, manufacturing, and R&D center for small commodities, the city must take the informatization-driven new industrialization road with industrial belt construction as the carrier while fostering characteristic industries and large-scale enterprises as the emphasis. Yiwu should also form a lasting impetus for economic and social development by relying on independent innovation activities in science and technology, human resources, systems, and management; it should transform and upgrade the traditional industries with high and new technologies and advanced applicable technologies; it should also actively develop emerging innovative industries, and promote the transformation of industrial structure from the labor and resource-intensive types to the capital, technology, and knowledge-intensive types. The leadership of Yiwu should profoundly understand the great responsibility of Yiwu as a member of the "Central Zhejiang urban agglomeration" to further deepen the complementary division of labor and cooperation with other cities, counties, and districts in the urban agglomeration to improve the overall development quality, level, and competitiveness of the agglomeration. Thirdly, Yiwu must strive to advance urban internationalization and accelerate the pace of urban modernization. It should stringently revise the urban master plan, build an eco-city with high quality, vigorously develop multiculturalism, strive to cultivate an urban civilization, actively build a new immigrant city, and foster "new Yiwu people" who facilitate the international era by learning from the successful practices of world-renowned international cities from the aspects of infrastructure, ecological environment, cultural atmosphere, entrepreneurial environment, science and technology, education, and sports hygiene to gradually build Yiwu into an international trade city in conformity with the demands of the modern information era. Through the construction of the international trade city, Yiwu can attract a concentration of more domestic and foreign advantageous high-end resources, enhance the impetus for the development of Central Zhejiang urban agglomeration, and improve its sustainable development and outward radiation capabilities.

4. Intensifying the concept of "strengthening city with qualified personnel" to make Yiwu a highland gathered with all kinds of mid-to-high end talents

Yiwu's original talent advantage is that it has fostered a large number of folk business professionals during the long-term practice of "chicken feather for sugar" and the business practices after the reform and opening-up. They are quick-witted, well-informed, hard-working, and risk-taking people who have contributed tremendously to a series of pioneering efforts in the 1980s and 1990s. As of today, they or their teams are still the backbone pushing forward Yiwu's economic development. Nevertheless, it should also be noted that with the growing internationalization of the small commodity market and Yiwu's economy as a whole, especially with the increasing status of Yiwu as Central Zhejiang CBD urban agglomeration, not only must the original business talents be expanded, upgraded, and improved, but the quality of existing civil servants must also be improved greatly. Besides, substantial introduction of various mid-to-high-end talents in the areas of science and technology, macroeconomics, public administration, urban and rural planning, humanities and social sciences, and foreign economy and trade are needed, who should be encouraged to settle down, take root in Yiwu, and make efforts toward success. To this end, it is necessary to further establish the concept of "strengthening city with qualified personnel", improve the personnel training and introducing mechanisms, and optimize the entrepreneurial environment. The small commodity market-led industrial and trading enterprises, tertiary institutions, research institutes, and public R&D platforms in Yiwu should be encouraged to innovate the personnel training, introduction, use, evaluation, and incentive mechanisms; they should intensify the participation of technological factors and IPR in the income distribution, and further explore the ways of realizing technology capitalization and capital personalization. Relying on the international market's advantage in bringing together high-end talents both at home and abroad, Yiwu should actively introduce top talents with interdisciplinary knowledge, cross-industry experience, and broad vision, as well as advanced talents with management experience in multinational corporations. A performance-based entrepreneurial environment that encourages innovation, competition, and synergetic cooperation should be created to maximize the development potential of various talents. Great efforts should be made to train and introduce entrepreneurs and to build a contingent of high quality innovative entrepreneurs that adapt to the needs of international competition; the cultivation of leader type entrepreneurs is especially needed. Conditions should be created to help foreign businessmen improve their own quality, so that they can gradually be transformed into a part of the Yiwu merchant team, thereby injecting new blood into the team and facilitating the expansion and overall quality improvement of "Yiwu Business Circle". Importance should be attached to strengthen the re-education and on-the-job training of cadres and workers. It is also necessary to accelerate the adjustment of educational structure, vigorously develop vocational education, improve the quality of re-education, strengthen staff training focusing on the training of senior technicians, raise the overall quality of workers, and strive to foster a large number of excellent technical and managerial personnel. By creating a good atmosphere for learning, vigorously promoting lifelong education, and actively developing a learning society, Yiwu can become a training and gathering center for all kinds of talents and an entrepreneurial highland for high-end professionals.

5. Building "Legal Yiwu", "Secure Yiwu" around the goal of "Harmonious Society"

As a new type of city speeding up toward the goal of becoming an international trade city, Yiwu has higher percentages of alien populations, ethnic minorities, foreigners, religious believers, and susceptible groups, which has lead to the highly diverse ideologies, values, and customs in social development, with complicated social structures and relations. In a manner of speaking, Guangzhou's yesterday is Yiwu's today regarding the influence from Hong Kong and Macao, while Yiwu's today is Guangzhou's tomorrow regarding international influence. Faced with such a complicated social situation, Yiwu must further emphasize the "Two Focuses and Two Respects", i.e., paying attention to the coordinated development of the economy and society, as well as to the reasonable demands of different interest groups, respecting the principal status of laborers and the cultural diversity. It is necessary to standardize the market order and crack down on economic crimes centering on the promotion of market construction and economic development; to further explore new mechanisms for the administration of industrial, commercial, and foreign-related police affairs, and to innovate the service and management mechanisms for non-native constructors. It is also necessary to deepen the concept of rule by law, strengthen the authority of law, and govern the society strictly in accordance with the law rather than other powers to create a "Legal Yiwu", so that the rule of law becomes an important means and path of creating and maintaining a harmonious society. To this end, Yiwu must strengthen its service awareness and never ignore the reasonable demands of the masses, respect the fundamental role of the market in resource allocation and never leave aside the problems of market management, never give up leadership over the major issues concerning the overall economic and social development, and never do anything about the constraints of resource bottleneck. It should promote the development practice with a reformist spirit, solve the emerging problems in its development by reformatory measures, turn the fruits of development into the material basis for social harmony and stability, and guarantee the smooth progress of reform and development with social harmony and stability. It should also actively create the equal competition and common development-based legal, policy, and market environments; meanwhile, it should regard the realization of social justice as an important policy orientation, reasonably adjust the interest structure of all sectors, respect the democratic rights and legal status of citizens, care for vulnerable groups, improve and perfect the social security system, and ensure the realization of social justice in a multi-faceted way.

Bibliography

[1] Arthur W. B. *Increasing Returns and Path Dependence in the Economy*. Ann Arbor: The University of Michigan Press, 1994.

[2] Barnes T. Review of Paul Krugman's development geography and economic theory. *The Canadian Geographer*, 1997, 41(1).

[3] Boschman R., Lambooy J. Evolutionary economics and economic geography. *Evolutionary Economics*, 1999, (9).

[4] Brulhart M. Economic geography, industry location and trade: the evidence. *The World Economy*, 1998, (21).

[5] Bryson J. *et al.* (eds.). *Economic Geography Reader*. Chichester: John Wiley & Sons, Ltd., 1999.

[6] Buchanan J., Yoon Y. (eds.). *The Return to Increasing Returns*. Ann Arbor: The University of Michigan Press, 1994.

[7] Clark G. Stylized facts and close dialogue: methodology in economic geography. *Annals of Association of American Geographers*, 1998, 88(1).

[8] Clark G., Feldman M., Gertler M. *The Oxford Handbook of Economic Geography*. Oxford, New York: Oxford Press, 2000.

[9] Coase R. H. The nature of the firm. *Economica*, 1937, 4(3).

[10] David P. Krugman's economic geography of development: NEGs, POGs and naked models in space. *International Regional Science Review*, 1999, 22(2).

[11] Dixit A. K., Stigliz J. E. monopolistic competition and optimum product diversity. *American Economic Review*, 1977, (67).

[12] Dymski G. A. On Krugman's model of economic geography. *Geoforum*, 1996, 27(4).

[13] Ekinsmyth C. *et al.* Stability and instability: the uncertainty of economic geography. *Area*, 1995, 27(4).

[14] Fujita M. *Urban Economic Theory: Land Use and City Size.* Cambridge, New York: Cambridge University Press, 1990.

[15] Fujita M., Krugman P., Venables A. J. *The Spatial Economy: Cities, Regions, and International Trade.* Cambridge, MASS: MIT Press, 1999.

[16] Gerlter M. Flexibility revisited: districts, nation states, and the forces of production. *Transactions of the Institute of British Geographers,* 1992, (17).

[17] Hanson G. Localization economies, vertical organization, and trade. *American Economic Review*, 1996, (5).

[18] Haynes K. E., Fotheringham A. S. *Gravity and Spatial Interaction Models.* London, New Delhi: SAGE Publications, 1984.

[19] Herod A. *Notes on a Spatialized Labor Politics: Scale and the Political Geography of Dual Unionism in the US Longshore Industry.* London: Arnold, 1997.

[20] Higgins B., Savoie D. J. Regional development theories and their application. *Transaction Publishers*, 1997.

[21] Johnston R. Review of Paul Krugman's geography and trade. *Environment and Planning A,* 1992, (24).

[22] Junius K. *The Economic Geography of Production, Trade and Development.* Mohr Siebeck(printed in Germany), 1999.

[23] Kaldor N. *Further Essays on Economic Theory*. London: Duckworth, 1978.

[24] Kravis I. B., "Availability" and other influences on the commodity composition of trade. *Journal of Political Economy*, 1956, 64(2).

[25] Krugman P. Complex landscape in economic geography. *American Economic Review*, 1994, 84(2).

[26] Krugman P. *Development, Geography and Economic Theory*. Cambridge, MASS: MIT Press, 1995.

[27] Krugman P. First nature, second nature and metropolitan location. *Journal of Regional Science*, 1993, (3).

[28] Krugman P. *Geography and Trade*. Cambridge, MASS: MIT Press, 1991.

[29] Krugman P. Increasing returns, monopolistic competition, and international trade. *International Economics*, 1991, (9).

[30] Krugman P. The current case for industrial policy. In: Salvatore D. (ed.), *Protectionism and World Welfare*. Cambridge: Cambridge University Press, 1993.

[31] Krugman P. *The Self-organizing Economy*. Cambridge, MASS: Blackwell Publishers, 1996.

[32] Krugman P. What's new about the new economic geography? *Oxford Review of Economic Policy*, 1998, 14(2).

[33] Krugman P., Venables A. Integration, specialization and adjustment. *European Economic Review*, 1996, (40).

[34] Lee R., Wills J. *Geographies of Economics*. London: Arnold, 1997.

[35] Leontief W. Interrelation of prices, output, savings, and investment. In: *The Structure of American Economy*. New York: International Arts and Sciences Press, 1937.

[36] Liu Weidong, Lu Dadao. Rethinking the development of economic geography in mainland of China. *Environment and Planning*, 2002, 34(12).

[37] Marden P. Real regulation reconsidered. *Environment and Planning*, 1992, 24(5).

[38] Martin R. Economic theory and human geography. In: Greogry D., Martin R., Smith G. (eds.), *Human Geography: Society, Space, and Social Science*. Minneapolis: University of Minnesota Press, 1994.

[39] Martin R. The new "geographical turn" in economics: some critical reflections. *Journal of Economics*, 1999, (23).

[40] Martin R., Sunley P. Paul Krugman's geographical economics and its implications for regional development theory: a critical assessment. *Economic Geography*, 1996, (72).

[41] Myrdal G. *Economic Theory and Underdeveloped Regions*. London: Duckworth, 1957.

[42] Nolan P. China's post-Mao political economy: a puzzle, contributions to political. *Economy*, 1993, (12).

[43] Pine II. B. J. *Mass Customization: The New Frontier in Business Competition*. Boston: Harvard Business School Press, 1992.

[44] Piore M., Sabel C. *The Second Industrial Divide: Possibilities for Prosperity*. New York: Basic Books, 1984.

[45] Porter M. Competitive advantage, agglomeration economies and regional policy. *International Regional Science Review*, 1996, 19(1-2).

[46] Porter M. *The Competitive Advantage of Nations*. London: Macmillan, 1990.

[47] Romer P. M. Endogenous technological change. *Journal of Political Economy*, 1990, 98(5).

[48] Romer P. M. Growth based on increasing returns due to specialization. *American Economic Review*, 1987, 77(2).

[49] Rothschild M., Stiglitz J. E. Increasing risk: I. A definition. *Journal of Economic Theory*, 1970, 2(3), 225–243.

[50] Schmuztler A. The new economic geography. *Journal of Economic Surveys*, 1999, 13(4).

[51] Scott A. *New Industrial Spaces*. London: Pion, 1988.

[52] Vernon R., International investment and international trade in the product cycle. *Quarterly Journal of Economics*, 1966, 80(2).

[53] Wilson A. G. A statistical theory of spatial distribution models. *Transportation Research*, 1967, (1).

[54] Wilson A. G., Brirkin M. Dynamic models of agricultural location in spatial interaction framework. *Geographical Analysis*, 1987, (19).

[55] Hirschman A. *Economic Development Strategy*. Beijing: Economic Science Press, 1991.

[56] An L., Li F., Zhao S. Comparative study on the business cost of 5 cities in the Yangtze River Delta. *Management World*, 2004, (8).

[57] Bai C. Investigation of Yiwu Small Commodity Market. *Economic Forum*, 2005, (18).

[58] Bai X. Economies of scope and economies of scale of Yiwu specialized market cluster. *Finance & Trade Economics*, 2004, (2).

[59] Bao W., Wang Y. Yiwu mode: a historical study from the town economy to the market economy. *Zhejiang Social Sciences*, 2002, (5).

[65] Krugman P. *The Return of Depression Economics*. Beijing: China Renmin University Press, 1999.

[66] Cai N., Yang X. The internationalization of small business clusters and SMEs. *Business Management Journal New Management*, 2002, (8).

[67] Chen J. An empirical study of China's industrial regional transfer at present stage—analysis of the survey report of 105 enterprises in Zhejiang. *Management World*, 2002, (6).

[68] Chen Y., Wang J. Yiwu Market: the hidden worry behind prosperity. *Economic & Trad*, 2003, (2).

[69] Ricardo D. *On the Principles of Political Economy and Taxation*. Beijing: The Commercial Press, 1983.

[70] Braudel F. *Material Civilization, Economy and Capitalism: 15th-18th Century*. Shanghai: SDX Joint Publishing Company, 1996.

[71] Feng S. Research on the breadth and depth of international operation of Yiwu China Commodity City. *Business Economics and Administration*, 2004, (1).

[72] Jin G. Research on the mechanism and path of professional market expansion—A Case Study of Yiwu Small Commodity market. *Market Modernization*, 2004, (11).

[73] Jin X. Some thoughts on the strategic direction and the institutional support of the internationalization of Yiwu market. *Report of the members of Economic Consulting Committee of Zhejiang Provincial People's Government*, 2005.

[74] Jing X. *Economic Cooperation between the East and the West*. Shanghai: Shanghai Academy of Social Sciences Press, 2002.

[75] Lin Y. *China's Miracle: Development Strategy and Economic Efficiency*. Shanghai: SDX Joint Publishing Company, 1995.

[76] Liu Q. Analysis of the path of China's foreign trade system innovation since the founding of the People's Republic of China. *Xinhua Digest*, 2004, (5).

[77] Liu Y. Thoughts on developing economic and technical cooperation between east and west regions. *China Economic & Trade Herald*, 2001, (4).

[78] Lu T. The stage, measuring method and case study of enterprise internationalization. *The Journal of World Economy*, 2000, (3).

[79] Lu D. *et al.* 1997 *China Regional Development Report*. Beijing: The Commercial Press, 1998.

[80] Lu L., Bai X. The expansion of the cooperative group—a case study of the changes in the system of Yiwu united consignment market. *Economic Research Journal*, 2000, (8).

[81] Lu L., Bai X. From "chicken feather for sugar" to enterprise clusters—further discussion on "Yiwu Mode". *Finance & Trade Economics*, 2000, (11).

[82] Lu L. et al. *Market Yiwu: From Chicken Feather for Sugar to International Commerce*. Hangzhou: Zhejiang People's Publishing House, 2003.

[83] Lu L. et al. *The rise of Central Zhejiang—Theoretical and Practical Innovation Based on Central Zhejiang City Groups and "Yiwu Business Circle"*. Hangzhou: Zhejiang People's Publishing House, 2011.

[84] Lu L., Wang Z., Yang Z. *Yiwu Mode*. Beijing: People's Publishing House, 2008.

[85] Lu L., Wang Z. *Professional Market: The Evolution of Local Markets*. Shanghai: Gezhi Publishing House, Shanghai People's Publishing House, 2008.

[86] Lu L., Yang H. Market expansion, increasing returns and regional division of labor—analysis of "Yiwu Business Circle". *Economic Research Journal*, 2007, (4).

[87] Lu L., Yang Z., Zheng X. Yiwu Pilot. Beijing: People's Publishing House, 2014.

[88] Lu L. Agglomeration development, high-end climbing—a new strategy for Yiwu's industrial development. *Zhejiang Economy*, 2004, (4).

[89] Lu L. A brief discussion on the essence and innovation of "Wenzhou Mode". *Chinese Rural Economy*, 2004, (12).

[90] Lu L. The rise of "China Small Commodity City" market and the "Yiwu Mode" in rural market economy development". *Comparative Economic & Social Systems*, 1999, (1).

[91] Luo X. Empirical research on market business cost—based on questionnaire survey and analysis of Yiwu Small Commodity Market. *Theory Journal*, 2005, (7).

[92] Luo X. The internationalized operation mode of professional wholesale market—a case study of the internationalization development of Yiwu China Commodity City Market. *Journal of the Party School of CPC Ningbo*, 2005, (3).

[93] Stiegler G. J. *Industrial Organization and Government Regulation*. Shanghai: SDX Joint Publishing Company, 1989.

[94] Shanghai University of Finance and Economics Regional Economic Research Center: *China Regional Economic Development Report*. Shanghai: Shanghai University of Finance and Economics Press, 2003.

[95] Sheng S., Yang H. Modularity: a new organizational mode. *Science Research Management*, 2004, (2).

[96] Tan Z. *The Choice of Trade Policy in the Evolution of China's Economic Structure*. Beijing: People's Publishing House, 2008.

[97] Wang D. *The Way Home: the Ideological Track of Economists*. Beijing: China Social Sciences Press, 1998.

[98] Wang Y. *et al. Mining Cooperation—Dynamic Mechanism and Operational Mechanism*. Yinchuan: Ningxia People's Publishing House, 2001.

[99] Wang Y., Li S. China's East-West cooperation in the face of economic globalization. *Economic Geography*, 2003, (2).

[100] Wang Z. Relocation of Yiwu and innovation of "Yiwu Mode". *Zhejiang Economy*, 2004, (2).

[101] Wei H. The theoretical frontier of current regional economic research. *Research On Development*, 1998, (1)

[102] Wu J. *Research on the Coordinated Development of China's Eastern and Western Economy*. Beijing: Reform Press, 1999.

[103] Kojima K. *Foreign Trade Theory*. Tianjin: Nankai University Press, 1987.

[104] Xu J., Duan S. *Regional Development Theory and Research Methods*. Lanzhou: Gansu Science and Technology Press, 1994.

[105] Xu J., Yue W. *Research on the Late Development Effect and Late Development Advantage and Innovation Countermeasures in Western China*. Beijing: China Ocean Press, 2002.

[106] Xu X., Zhou Y., Ning Y. *Urban Geography*. Beijing: Higher Education Press, 1997.

[107] Smith A. *An Inquiry into the Nature and Causes of the Wealth*. Beijing: The Commercial Press, 1981.

[108] Yang L. Mode innovation in the promotion of market economy— a case study of the development of Yiwu Small Commodity Market. *Shanghai Economic Forum*, 2004, (5).

[109] Yang W., Liang J. *Higher Economic Geography*. Beijing: Peking University Press, 1997.

[110] Yang X. *Principles of Economics*. Beijing: China Social Sciences Press, 1998.

[111] Yiwu Municipal Bureau of Statistics: Yiwu Statistical Yearbook on National Economy and Social Development (1999-2005), Yiwu Statistical Information Network.

[112] Yin X. Theoretical analysis of Japan's foreign direct investment and its implications for China. *Northeast Asia Forum*, 1997, (1).

[113] Zhang C. Differences and choices of international market entry ways. *Jiangsu Commercial Forum*, 2003, (9).

[114] Zhang H. *The Dynamic Advantage Change of China's Foreign Trade and the Transformation of Foreign Trade Growth Mode*. Beijing: People's Publishing House, 2010.

[115] Zhang J. *"Double-track" Economics: China's Economic Reform (1978–1992)*. Shanghai: SDX Joint Publishing Company, 1997.

[116] Zhang W. *Enterprise Entrepreneur—Contract Theory*. Shanghai: SDX Joint Publishing Company, 1995.

[117] Zhang W., Zhang J. The influence of economics and geography on the development track of location theory. *Progress in Geography*, 1999, (18).

[118] Zhang W. *Economic Location Theory*. Beijing: Science Press, 2000.

[119] Zhou D. Analysis of the limits of "moderate differences" in China's regional economic development. *Journal of Hunan Business College*, 1999, (2).

[120] Zhou Q. *et al*. *Regional Economics*. Beijing: China Renmin University Press, 1989.

[121] Zhu J. Internationalization of private economy: the path and innovation of Yiwu. *Zhejiang Economy*, 2005, (15).